CENTRAL

AMERICA

juela
• Heredia
• San José
ago •

PANAMA

COLOMBIA

Travels in Central America
1821–1840

Travels in Central America 1821-1840

Franklin D. Parker

UNIVERSITY OF FLORIDA PRESS
Gainesville / 1970

A University of Florida Press Book

The type for the text of this book
is ten-point Times New Roman.
The display is Torino Roman.

COPYRIGHT © 1970 BY THE STATE OF FLORIDA
DEPARTMENT OF GENERAL SERVICES

All Rights Reserved

DESIGNED BY STANLEY D. HARRIS

*Library of Congress
Catalog Card No. 71-99214
ISBN 0-8130-0282-6*

MANUFACTURED FOR THE PUBLISHER BY
THE TJM CORPORATION
BATON ROUGE, LOUISIANA

*To our daughters Ginger and Jeannie
who were our first travel companions
in Central America*

Preface

OLD TRAVEL BOOKS are fun; they are also full of learning. They can make history spring alive. This study is intended to serve as a critical examination of a chosen set of them, less known and less available than more recent accounts, but nonetheless valuable.

Thomas Gage, John Lloyd Stephens, and Karl Scherzer—Gage the renegade priest turned Puritan, Stephens the searcher for lost ruins and governments, Scherzer the indefatigable professor versed in all realms of knowledge—were among those who created our first interest in this project. They had traversed all the Central American lands, as had my wife and myself. We found that their company, though separated in time, could contribute immensely to the enjoyment of an isthmian trip. And we learned that what they wrote is essential for Central American knowledge. They and others like them —British, North American, German, French, Italian, and Dutch authors of forty travel books—we have studied with this object in mind: What does each have to offer modern pleasure-reading and scholarship?

For sheer reading charm, we have turned up many a delight: naturalist Arthur Morelet of France clinging to the crossbeams of a house in the Petén, with an escaped crocodile and a sleeping servant beneath; adventurer Gustav von Tempsky of Mosquitia contemplating similarities between the Izalco volcano and his hostess for the evening, each displaying "alternate movements of gentle playfulness, and of fiery ravening"; prospector William Wells of California conducting wary negotiations with elderly Francisco Zelaya and his family for

Olancho gold rights; envoy Ephraim George Squier of the United States stopping to change mud-encrusted clothes before riding into León with the bishop at his side and the Stars and Stripes flying; Wilhelm Marr of Hamburg, fascinated by languages more than by linguistic compatriots, visiting a European colonization project near Turrialba; sea captain Orlando Roberts of Britain dancing at Sandy Bay in company with the Miskito king, his right-hand men General Blyatt and Admiral Earnee, and their women.

For pertinency to scholarship, we were intrigued with pious Henry Dunn's allusions to Guatemala's organs and wax works, newspapers and books; scholarly Moritz Wagner's account of the destruction of San Salvador by earthquake; bookish Jegór von Sivers' discussion of the flora and fauna of Honduras; filibuster William Walker's biased but dispassionate relation of his own Nicaraguan thrust; novelist Anthony Trollope's frank treatment of Costa Rican mores; and administrator Thomas Young's practical comments on emigration to Mosquitian lands. Young's advice is a species of wisdom; not so, much of the comment from other hands. Many judgments run contrary to twentieth-century attitudes. Yet the observations are there, in every volume, waiting to be employed by the twentieth-century mind.

The purpose of this book is to share with others some of what we have found, and to smooth the path for those who want to make use of this literature. Our prime concentration is upon ten authors, who dealt with Central America in its critical first twenty years of independence from Spain (1821–40), the last period when the isthmus was united. We wish to reveal under one cover the full nature of the writings of these ten, so that the reading of their entire works will be facilitated, for those who can take the time, or so that a real acquaintance may be had by those who deem this all that is desirable or necessary. For background, five other books from the Spanish colonial period (1524–1821) are sampled in the Prologue, along with comment on marginal items from that epoch. Listed and indexed at the end are not only the ten from the first two decades of independence, but also twenty-five more travel works on Central America from the following twenty years (1841–60). The purpose of the indexing is to pave the way for effective use of these books by other scholars.

The presentation of each of the ten books from the period 1821–40 is made insofar as seems practicable in the author's own language. We have selected excerpts, following the author's intent without reproducing all his words, which would reveal not only his style but his interests and passions. The people and places each of these ten authors encountered, amounting to the unfolding of his whole travel plan, are revealed in Chapters 1 and 2. These chapters also include representative comments on politics by those of the ten writers who were interested. The brief introductions to the political events of the respective decades, placed at the beginning of Chapters 1 and 2, are designed only to give proper perspective to names. Chapters 3 through 6 are composed of extracts illustrating separate facets of the Central American scene—the economy of the isthmus, its state of learning, its world of recreation and the arts, and its orientation in religion.

In employing extended excerpts, certain rules were followed. (1) No word was changed, with the exception of obvious *typographical* errors and the modernization of place names. Old spellings, misspellings, bad grammar, awkwardnesses are all allowed to stand. The object is to reveal these books as they are, not to dress them up in smooth language. (2) Deletions, which are of course legion, are all marked. The ellipsis made of dots signifies an omission involving less interruption of thought. A line space means that at least an entire page has been cut out, or that a new chapter has begun, or that a political interlude is being presented in the midst of a travel narrative. Capitalization after ellipses follows that natural for the readers of this book rather than that given in the original. (3) Notes are presented on those items where we felt curiosity might be aroused that would not easily be satisfied. Words are explained if they cannot be found in the standard abridged dictionaries of the English, Spanish, and French tongues. Place names are defined if they cannot be located on modern highway maps of the Central American countries. Significant errors are discussed, and cross-references between accounts provided. (4) Notes in the originals, on the other hand, and reference symbols to them are ignored except as an occasional one is incorporated into the analysts' series. (5) All references to population counts have also been removed. Most of them seem of dubious merit; at the least, they would mislead unless their presuppositions and sources were considered in careful demographic study. (6) Modernization of place names is done wherever differences of spelling are involved for entities other than states or countries. Anglicizations and their equivalents in other languages, however, are allowed to stand.

For following the geography of place names, each reader will be well advised to keep a copy of a modern highway map close at hand. We knew the isthmus from previous travel experiences, and we used various specialized maps in constructing the topical index. The highway map was nevertheless indispensable for us. Two sets are available showing the individual countries separately. One, prepared by the General Drafting Company, can be obtained from Humble Touring Service, 15 West 51st Street, New York, New York 10019. The other, drawn by Rand McNally & Company, is available from Texaco Touring Center, 135 East 42nd Street, New York, New York 10017. A few of the unbracketed place names in the topical index are shown only on older editions of the General Drafting maps.

The topical index which follows Chapter 6 is a key which can unlock for scholars the considerable storehouse of information in the thirty-five books which we deem the most worthwhile travel accounts of Central America over a forty-year period. During that time (1821–60) Central America became independent, then separated, then united again in spirit against interloper William Walker, who was executed in 1860. The divisions of this index, presented in schematic outline at the outset, follow those used in the heart of this book. References to specific people and places were picked up for this purpose even when the comment was quite fleeting, the criterion being whether the author had made contact with each item through first or rather close second hand. References to other categories are used only in those instances where an account has something quite revelatory to offer. For example, nearly every author saw maize growing, but only three are designated as having taken the trouble in some way to gauge its significance in the Central American lands.

Gage, Stephens, and Scherzer, as well as others like them, led to all this. But it is important to mention that we might not have read these travelers without the inspiration of Professor Charles E. Nowell of the University of Illinois, who first encouraged us to take a close look at Central America. Likewise we are indebted to Professor C. Harvey Gardiner of Southern Illinois University, who suggested to us several features of the topical index as well as the entire idea of systematic travel literature analysis.

The project would have been impossible but for the skillful and patient cooperation of the staff of the Walter Clinton Jackson Library of the University of North Carolina at Greensboro, especially in the location of obscure materials; and but for the great financial assistance of the Research Council of the University of North Carolina at Greensboro, the Southern Fellowships Fund, and the Henry L. and Grace Doherty Charitable Foundation. Miss Susan Griswold's help was indispensable for the treatment of the item in Dutch. To these persons and agencies, my wife Jennie (who did masses of detective work) and I (who did the twentieth-century portion of the writing) offer our appreciative thanks.

FRANKLIN D. PARKER

Contents

Prologue / 1
Girolamo Benzoni, 3; Thomas Gage, 4; Raveneau de Lussan, 6; John Cockburn, 8; John Roach, 11

Chapter 1
People, Places, and Politics, 1821–30 / 14
Orlando W. Roberts, 17; James Wilson, 56; George Alexander Thompson, 68; Jacobus Haefkens, 96; Henry Dunn, 98

Chapter 2
People, Places, and Politics, 1831–40 / 121
James Jackson Jarves, 124; George Washington Montgomery, 142; George Byam, 172; Thomas Young, 178; John Lloyd Stephens, 204

Chapter 3
The Economy / 229
Agriculture, 229; Commerce, 237; Other Industry, 243; Transportation, 245; Welfare, 247

Chapter 4
Learning / 249
Education, 249; Natural Science, 254

Chapter 5

Recreation and the Arts / 257

Recreation, 257; Music and Dance, 259; Theater, 264; Other Arts, 273

Chapter 6

Religion / 275

Paganism, 275; Neglect and Apathy, 277; Earnestness and Zeal, 279; The Everyday Church, 283; The Church in Festivity, 292

Topical Index (1821–60) / 307

Bibliography / 321

Index / 329

Prologue

EYEWITNESS reporting of the internal Central American scene begins with events of July 4, 1510: "Our grandfathers Hunyg and Lahuh Noh were reigning then.... On the day 1 Toh the Yaquis, messengers of the king *Modeczumatzin,* king of *Mexicu,* arrived. We saw the Yaquis . . . arrive. These Yaquis, who came many years ago, were very numerous, oh, my sons!"[1]

The year 1510 was a momentous one for Central America. The Spaniards, from overseas, were securing their first tenuous footholds on the American mainland, located a little farther south in Panama and Darién. Their arrival on these shores late in 1509 was quite possibly known to Moctezuma II of Mexico, some of whose subjects lived and traded along the Central American shore as far south as Panama. Concern over Spanish expeditions may indeed have inspired the visit of Moctezuma's messengers to a Guatemalan nation, remembered by a young Cakchiquel prince who years later recorded it for history.

The drive of the Spaniards into Mexico began ten years after the first move into Panama. The Spanish occupation of Central America, which lay between these two beachheads, may be said to have started with an epidemic of European disease in 1520, two reconnoitering expeditions of 1522, or the four separate intrusions of 1524 with the intent of conquest and settlement. The defeat of the chief Indian nations of Nicaragua, Guatemala, and El Salvador was completed by 1527. Those of Honduras held out until the 1530's, and the heartland

1. Francisco Hernández Arana, *The Annals of the Cakchiquels,* pp. 112–13. For complete information regarding references in notes, see Bibliography, pp. 321–27.

of Costa Rica was occupied only in 1561. By that time, great changes had taken place in the way of life of a great part of the Central American isthmus. These transformations, as they affected his own people and person, were chronicled from the viewpoint of the conquered by the same Cakchiquel prince who had seen the messengers arrive in 1510.[2]

Several Spaniards contributed personal accounts of the excitement of these four decades of conquest. First was Gil González de Avila, who commanded a reconnaissance trip to Nicaragua. He left Panama for that purpose on January 21, 1522, and wrote his account two years later.[3] Pedro de Alvarado, *conquistador*, described the rough wars in Guatemala and El Salvador in graphic reports to Hernán Cortés: "Seeing that by fire and sword I might bring these people to the service of His Majesty, I determined to burn the chiefs. . . . We are in the wildest country and people one has ever seen. . . . They shot an arrow at me that passed through my leg and entered my saddle, from which wound . . . one leg remained shorter than the other a good four fingers."[4] Cortés wrote of his own expedition to Honduras, concluding with comment on the distresses of his one-time subordinate among the Indians: "Although Pedro de Alvarado has unceasingly waged war against them, he has so far been unable to reduce them to Your Majesty's service. . . . I believe that, had I been able to go that way, I might with God's help, through kindness and other means, have won them over."[5]

Gonzalo Fernández de Oviedo y Valdés, Spanish chronicler of the conquest of many nations, wrote from his own memory the description of Nicaragua's lakes and volcanoes as the Spaniards first knew them.[6] Bartolomé de las Casas, the Dominican friar who devoted the last part of his life to the protection of the Indians of all Spanish-American countries, committed to manuscript eleven chapters of description of the traditions and customs of those he knew in Nicaragua and Guate-

2. From the plague of 1520 to another of 1560, *ibid.*, pp. 115–42.
3. "Carta del Capitán Gil González de Avila a Su Majestad, dándole cuenta del descubrimiento de Nicaragua," in *Documentos para la historia de Nicaragua*, 1:89–107; written March 6, 1524.
4. *An Account of the Conquest of Guatemala in 1524*, pp. 62, 66, 81. The two letters contained in this account were dated April 11 and July 28, 1524.
5. *Fernando Cortés: His Five Letters of Relation to the Emperor Charles V*, 2:331–32. The fifth letter which includes this comment was dated September 3, 1526.
6. *Historia general y natural de las Indias, islas y tierra-firme del mar océano*, pt. III, bk. IV. Oviedo lived in Nicaragua 1527–29 and wrote his great work 1532–57.

mala.⁷ Bernal Díaz del Castillo, veteran soldier of combat and resident of Guatemala in his old age, reminisced his way through the conquest of Mexico and Cortés' subsequent march to Honduras. Regarding a nonreluctant farewell to the latter province, "I recollect," said Díaz, "we threw stones at the country we left behind us."⁸

Díaz del Castillo and the grandson of Hunyg (who came to call himself Francisco Hernández Arana) were the only ones of the authors so far mentioned who reached the end of their days in Central America. The others may all in some sense be considered travelers in this land and their writings travel accounts. Still they were Spaniards who lived in Central America as it was becoming Spanish. Girolamo Benzoni was the only genuine outsider who left a record of his impressions of the isthmus at the time of the conquest.

Benzoni came from Milan in Italy. He journeyed to the New World with Spaniards in 1541. During the next six years he visited the major islands of the West Indies, colonies on the north coast of South America, and Panama, Costa Rica, Nicaragua, Honduras, and Guatemala. (In Costa Rica he served as member of an unsuccessful conquest band.) After three subsequent years in Peru, he was expelled from that land as a foreigner in 1550. Much of the time until he was able to sail for Europe in 1556 he again lived in Central America. Finally back home, he wrote in Italian of his travels, making them a part of an account of the New World which has never been published in Spanish.⁹

". . . Having read the histories that the Spaniards have written of their enterprises in those countries," remarked Benzoni, "I find that they have eulogized themselves in some respects rather more than they ought to have done. . . ." His comment on his hosts is caustic at times, even when individual Spaniards are chosen for admiration: "When I first arrived at Guattimala, the Licentiate Ceratto was president; . . . with truth I can testify that throughout India there never was a better judge, nor one who practised good precepts more strictly, obeying the royal commands, always endeavouring that the Indians

7. *Apologética historia de las Indias*, Tomo I of *Historiadores de Indias*, Chs. 177, 180, 234–40, 242–43. Las Casas lived in Nicaragua about 1532–36, in Guatemala 1536–39, and finished most of this piece of writing by 1550.

8. *The True History of the Conquest of Mexico*, p. 490. Díaz wrote most of his history in the period 1564–68 but polished the text of one copy until 1580.

9. *La historia del Mondo Nuovo* (Venice, 1565 and 1572) did become available in Latin (1578), French and German (1579), Flemish (1610), and finally English (1857).

should not be ill-treated by any Spaniard; and sometimes through the little respect that was shewn him by his countrymen, in consequence of his considering the welfare of the Indians, he used to pray that God would liberate him from such a bad people. . . ."[10]

In other Benzoni passages, the picturesque quality outweighs the critical. He learned to drink chocolate in Nicaragua: "I was upwards of a year in that country without ever being induced to taste this beverage; and when I passed through a tribe, if an Indian wished occasionally to give me some, he was very much surprised to see me refuse it, and went away laughing. But subsequently, wine failing, and unwilling to drink nothing but water, I did as others did." In Honduras the natives were not always so hospitable to Benzoni and a companion: ". . . Having walked for four days without meeting a single house, the provisions we carried were exhausted; finally we reached a small Indian population, and entreated them to furnish us with something to eat, but there was no means . . . to induce them to give us anything whatever. On the contrary, they cursed us, and spitting on the ground in contempt, desired us to go away."[11]

As Central America settled down for two and a half centuries of life under the Audiencia de Guatemala (1570–1821), the vividness of its documentation became sharply limited. The freshness of viewpoint which an observer like Benzoni could provide was simply not desired in colonial Spanish America. During all this period, Central America was seen by only four book-writing foreigners who traveled far enough inland to be out of contact with coastal vessels. The first was a noted English friar, the second a French buccaneer, and the other two British sailors.

Thomas Gage, the friar whose very controversial book has won him considerable fame, came from a Roman Catholic family of England at a time when the English government proscribed the teaching of Catholicism. He was educated at a Jesuit school in France and a Dominican college in Spain. After taking the Dominican habit, he volunteered for missionary duty in the Philippine Islands in 1625. In Mexico

10. *History of the New World*, pp. 159, 168. The "Licentiate Ceratto" was Alonso López de Cerrato, from 1548 to 1555 president of the Audiencia de los Confines then ruling Central America. "When he arrived, he condemned the Spaniards, he liberated the slaves . . . , he cut the taxes in two, he suspended forced labor and made the Spaniards pay all men, great and small. . . . I myself saw him, oh, my sons!" said Hernández Arana of the same individual, in *Annals of the Cakchiquels*, p. 137.

11. *History of the New World,* pp. 150, 145.

on the way to their field of duty, however, he and three young companions changed their minds and escaped from the party, making their way to Chiapas, Mexico's southernmost state then a part of the Audiencia de Guatemala. From there, in 1627, Gage traveled on to the Guatemalan capital, in whose vicinity he lived, studying and preaching, for the next ten years. Escaping once again from duty in 1637, he traveled overland to Costa Rica and then by sea to Panama, Spain, and England. In 1642 he renounced his Catholic faith and joined the Church of England. By 1648, when his book of travels was published, he had swung on over to Puritanism, England's creed of the following decade. Many passages in the book seem indeed to have been composed in such manner as to prove that Gage was a good Puritan at a time when it was distinctly to his advantage in England to be thought so.[12]

The first three years of Gage's life in Guatemala were spent pleasantly at the Dominican house in the capital, which he described in the following terms: "Within the walls of the cloister there is nothing wanting which may further pleasure and recreation. In the lower cloister there is a spacious garden, in the midst whereof is a fountain casting up the water, and spouting it out of at least a dozen pipes, which fill two ponds full of fishes, and with this their constant running give music to the whole cloister, and encouragement to many water-fowls and ducks to bathe and wash themselves therein. Yet further within the cloister, there are other two gardens for fruits and herbage, and in the one a pond of a quarter of a mile long, all paved at the bottom, and a low stone wall about, where is a boat for the friars' recreation, who often go thither to fish, and do sometimes upon a sudden want or occasion take out from thence as much fish as will give to the whole cloister a dinner."[13]

The remaining seven years in that vicinity were spent, according to Gage's own testimony, in amassing a fortune as he carried on pastoral duties in four Indian villages. After describing his various sources of money (all contributions and fees), he commented drily, "I thought this benefice might be a fitter place for me . . . than in the cloister of

---

12. *The English-American, His Travail by Sea and Land: or, A New Survey of the West-India's* (London, 1648) was republished while Gage yet lived, with the alternate titles transposed (London, 1655). Later it appeared in French (1677), Dutch (1682), German (1693), and Spanish (Paris, 1838). The earliest editions from Spanish-speaking countries were printed in Guatemala (1946) and Mexico (1947).

13. *Thomas Gage's Travels in the New World*, p. 189.

Guatemala, wearying out my brains with points of false grounded divinity. . . ." When he finally prepared to leave for home, ". . . I found I had in Spanish money near nine thousand pieces of eight, which I had got in . . . twelve years. . . . So much money I thought would be too cumbersome for a long journey; whereupon I turned above four thousand crowns into pearls and some precious stones. . . . The rest I laid up, some in bags, some I sewed into my quilt. . . ." One day months later when a Dutch man-of-war stopped the frigate on which he was attempting to leave Costa Rica, ". . . I lost . . . the worth of four thousand . . . pieces of eight in pearls and precious stones, and near three thousand more in money. . . . Other things I had, such as a quilt to lie on, some books, and . . . pictures in brass, and clothes, which I begged of that noble captain. . . . He, considering my orders and calling, gave me them freely, and wished me to be patient, saying that he could not do otherwise than he did with my money and pearls, and using that common proverb at sea,—'Hoy por mi, mañana por ti.' . . ."[14]

A half century after Thomas Gage's lesson in take-and-give, inland Central America's next traveler-writer was engaged in his turn at the wheels of fortune. He was the *sieur* Raveneau de Lussan, come from France to Haiti in 1679 seeking adventure and money. In Haiti he found neither, going into debt instead. After five years, his luck changed when he cast his lot with a band of filibusters (as they were called by the French) or buccaneers. Early in 1685 his group marched across Panama to the Pacific Ocean. For three years, the French and English with whom he sailed marauded the towns of Costa Rica, Nicaragua, and El Salvador as well as others in South America. Finally a party including Raveneau de Lussan fought its way through Honduras and Nicaragua to the Coco River, which it descended to the Caribbean. The one who wrote their story, being a good gambler as well as adventurer, was able to return to Haiti and France with a profit.[15]

Raveneau gives a much closer view of the life of his comrades than of that of the Spaniards whom they so frequently encountered, though he does not ignore the latter entirely. The life of the buccaneers while ashore was most varied, but seldom easy. After a year on the Pacific side, Raveneau complains of ". . . this coast . . . which, charming and agreeable though it may be for the local residents, is not worth

14. *Ibid.,* pp. 259, 297, 315–16.
15. His *Journal du voyage fait a la Mer de Sud* (Paris, 1689 and 1690) was first published in English in 1698.

so much as your little finger to men like ourselves with no vessels, usually without food, and constantly surrounded by enemies without number, where it is necessary to be constantly on the watch and where everything possible is done to keep us from making a living." There was sickness and death too, of course: "We remained only a day . . . to give our wounded a rest, two of whom died here of cramps that paralyzed the entire nervous system. These are so deadly out in this country that when they attack a man who has been wounded, he never recovers." Only occasionally while on shore (as in the instance which follows) does Raveneau speak of anything resembling laughter or a lapse into indolence: "The Spaniards had received warning to save themselves at all costs, but since out in this country the heat is so excessive . . . we were inclined to loiter in the shade or rest our weary feet on a grassy place rather than chase them."[16]

Nevertheless, through fighting and gaming, Raveneau de Lussan according to his own testimony made more of a fortune than had Thomas Gage with his preaching. Like Gage, in the last moments he had to part with a portion. Raveneau's problems began as the freebooters set out to march overland to the Caribbean: ". . . Although my pack was light, it was no less valuable, since I had converted thirty thousand pieces-of-eight into gold, pearls, and jewels. However, as most of this represented winnings at gambling some seventeen or eighteen who were the losers grieved over returning virtually empty-handed and plotted to massacre indiscriminately those who had the most treasure. Happily, I was forewarned by some friends. . . . I decided to distribute what I owned among several . . . comrades with the understanding that . . . the amount agreed on would be returned. . . . True, I paid dearly for this precaution. . . ."[17]

A few other buccaneers wrote of Central America from personal experience, but did not get far from their vessels. Alexandre Olivier Exquemeling, Dutch but in the French service until he joined the company of the sea rovers (as the Netherlanders were wont to call them), in the best known of all buccaneer books included brief descriptions of shore calls on the Caribbean side of Costa Rica and Nicaragua in the year 1671.[18] William Dampier, an Englishman and the most literary of all those who did some freebooting, wrote of the

16. *Raveneau de Lussan: A Translation,* pp. 128–29, 132, 134.
17. *Ibid.,* pp. 256–57.
18. *The Buccaneers of America,* pp. 243–55. The original of this work, *De Americaensche Zee-Roovers* (Amsterdam, 1678), was early translated into German (1679), Spanish (1681), English (1684), and French (1686).

Caribbean side of Nicaragua as he saw it in 1681, the Pacific shore from Costa Rica to El Salvador in 1684, and the Pacific coast from Costa Rica to Guatemala in 1685, the last trip being the same in part as that described by Raveneau de Lussan.[19] Comment by other buccaneers was even more restricted.[20]

In the eighteenth century, sea-roving (whose ablest practitioners were dubbed knights while the more imaginative wrote autobiographies) gradually degenerated into ordinary piracy. Pirates seldom wrote books; but an occasional contrabandist of the same century might do so if caught in unusual circumstances. Such a person was John Cockburn, British sailor who in March, 1731, was taken prisoner by a Spanish coast-guard vessel, in company with some shipmates, and deposited on the north shore of Honduras. Cockburn and four companions made their way, encountering privation and danger through nearly all the distance, from this critical point to El Salvador and thence along the Pacific side of Nicaragua and Costa Rica to Panama, where they were finally able to find passage for Jamaica and England in January, 1732. Cockburn's fascinating account of the vicissitudes of their journey, short at times on comprehension of the milieu in which they traveled, but long on credibility (even where place names remain uncertain) and full of human warmth, was published three years after the adventure was ended.[21]

Not all the British sailors set ashore (Cockburn names ten besides himself) made their way back to England. Wounded as most of them

19. *Dampier's Voyages*, 1:62–68, 137–55, 235–49. These sections are a part of Dampier's first book, *A New Voyage Round the World* (London, 1697), which was published in both Dutch and French in 1698.

20. Basil Ringrose on the Pacific side of Costa Rica, 1681, pp. 418–28 of *The Dangerous Voyage and Bold Attempts of Captain Bartholomew Sharp*; William Ambrosia Cowley at the Gulf of Fonseca, 1684, pp. 42–43 of *Voyages and Adventures of Sir Walter Raleigh: With the Voyage of Captain Cowley*; Lionel Wafer at the Gulf of Fonseca and Coco Island, 1685, pp. 173–76 of *A New Voyage and Description of the Isthmus of America*.

21. *A Journey over Land, from the Gulf of Honduras to the Great South-Sea* (London, 1735) appeared in Dutch in 1740, as well as in two new printings in English, one entitled *The Unfortunate Englishmen*. Further editions under the latter title appeared in London in 1773, 1779, 1794, and 1810, and in Edinburgh in 1831. Cockburn's book is studied in Franz Termer, "El valor histórico, geográfico y etnológico de los apuntes de John Cockburn sobre Centroamérica en el siglo xvIII," in *Los viajes de Cockburn y Lievre por Costa Rica*, pp. 55–93, translated from *Von fremden Völkern und Kulturen* (Düsseldorf, 1955), pp. 255–76. "El viaje de Cockburn: de Nicoya a Chiriquí," in *Los viajes*, pp. 10–54, is a translation into Spanish of the Costa Rican portion from Cockburn's first edition.

were from the sea battle during which they had been taken, they stayed together for a few days. Then ". . . a negro-man coming to discourse with us . . . was greatly moved with our sufferings, and acquainted us that the governor . . . , who was to determine our fate, was a cruel man to the English, and that he would certainly condemn us all to the mines, as he constantly served those of our nation, who were so unhappy as to fall into his hands. This information terrified us to that degree, that Thomas Rounce, Banister, and myself, resolved if possible, to make our escape . . . and try if we could get to some part of the South Seas. We were much troubled . . . to think of leaving our countrymen behind; but hoping the governor would not deal so hardly by them, who were all disabled men; and considering, that if he did, our being partakers with them would be no manner of service, we put our project into execution, unknown to them, and stole out of the town about ten o'clock at night. So far the law of self-preservation will prevail."[22] (Two of those left behind caught up with Cockburn, Rounce, and Banister later.)

Though the stranded sailors often lacked food and clothing as they continued their long trek, they were seldom treated by persons they met as badly as they expected. Even Spanish officials—and their wives —proved to be somewhat less than obdurate to their circumstances: "On the third day of our confinement, we were sent for to the Governor's house, to be examined. . . . After due respects paid to his Excellency, and that we had obtained his leave for so doing, I related our whole story to him in brief . . . and then added, that our wives and children were not only in great sorrow for the loss of us, but must be reduced to extreme poverty by this our . . . long hindrance from returning home to their relief. . . . The Governor ordered that we should be told that he had had strict commands from the King, his master, not to suffer any Englishman to pass through this part of the country; that it was not impossible but our story might be feigned, and that we might be sent hither as spies; but however, we were given to understand that if we would become new Christians, and be baptized, that, and nothing else, would save us from going to the mines. . . . I replied, with some warmth, that, as we were subjects of England, we could not, without violation of the known laws of nations, be detained here as prisoners or captives, at a time of settled peace and good understanding, as I supposed it was, between the two crowns; . . . and that, as for our being sent to the mines, we were not brought hither

22. *The Unfortunate Englishmen*, p. 12.

as criminals to have sentence passed upon us, but came only as strangers and travellers, though poor ones, and might rather claim his pity; but for being baptized afresh, we could not, I said, tell what that meant; for we had already been baptized in the Holy Catholic and Apostolic church, in the faith and communion of which, by God's grace, we hoped to continue to the end of our lives. . . . Upon the close of my discourse, the Governor advised us to consider better of the matter for our own sakes. . . .

"The Governor's lady, who . . . had heard our misfortunes, sent for me to talk with her, desiring to know our case, and whether we had wives and children? When I told her we really had, she took great compassion on us, promising to use her interest with her husband to grant us a pass, and to procure us what other assistance she could, and ordered victuals to be given us in a very courteous manner; . . . two days after, Providence ordered it so, that this good lady obtained the pass she had promised me she would endeavour to procure; upon which we were released from our confinement, and went to return the Governor and his lady thanks on our knees, who each of them gave us a real apiece, with three hats made of cane plaited by the Indians, and wished us well, and safely to return home to our own country."[23]

Through the courtesy of another governor farther along, Cockburn's party were provided boat transportation from the Gulf of Nicoya, with Panama their destination. Cockburn's worst chain of experiences came when, traveling apart from his companions, he further became separated from the Indians who had accompanied him and had to walk for more than a month, alone, along the uninhabited coast: "Amidst all my former fears, toils, and sufferings with my fellow-travellers, who were ready at hand to advise with and assist each other, I may truly say that my spirits never once failed me; but how did I bitterly lament my now most calamitous circumstance! . . . All the provision I had was some plantains. . . . I took care to keep as close to the sea as possible, believing no wild beast would venture to attack me near it. . . . I ate so very sparingly of my plantains, lest I should never come at more food, that I soon grew so weak as scarcely to be able to stand on my legs. . . . Thus I went drooping along, till I came to a place on the beach where grew abundance of cocoa-nuts. . . . I went on, day by day, with little hope of ever seeing the face of mankind more . . . nor was all the courage and resolution I sometimes began to think I had acquired, of the least use to allay my fears, any

23. *Ibid.*, pp. 43–45.

more than the thorough resignation I sometimes presumed to think I had made to the will of God, was of any force to expel my doubts of his mercies yet to come."[24] Cockburn's exit from Central America into Panama came after he spent five nights in a tree, waiting until the sea became smooth enough so that he might swim from rock to rock along the coast to round difficult Point Burica. No one could accuse Cockburn of having looted the isthmus in either the Gage or the Raveneau fashion.

John Roach, who maintained the pace set by Benzoni, Gage, Raveneau, and Cockburn of one travel book on Central America each half century, had experiences in some ways similar to those of Cockburn. Originally from England, Roach had ten years' experience as a sailor when he began to serve on ships which put out from Jamaica. One of these, in April, 1770, placed him ashore, evidently in Nicaragua, to cut firewood along with five Negro companions. Of a sudden, his helpers fled and he alone was taken captive by a group of Indians. For over two years he lived with this tribe, whom he called the Woolaways (doubtless the Woolwas or Ulvas), and with two others in turn, the "Buckeraws" (Cucras?) and "Assenwasses," escaping from each as the occasion presented itself, only to find himself eventually at the mercy of the Spaniards. Nine jails and dungeons in Nicaragua, Honduras, and Guatemala were his residence for the next ten years until he arrived in Havana at a time of war between Great Britain and Spain. There he served as interpreter for the interrogation of prisoners and (though he had been on his way in detention to Spain) was allowed after a time to "escape" on a ship bound for Jamaica. He arrived home in April, 1783. Unable to sail more, Roach wrote a book of his adventures instead.[25] His short account deals more with the Indians, by whom he was treated as an associate, than with the Spaniards who kept him in prison. It nevertheless bears many marks of general authenticity and ought more properly to be taken into account by modern science.[26]

24. *Ibid.*, pp. 90–94.
25. The second edition, printed in Whitehaven, England, 1784, is called *The Surprizing Adventures of John Roach, Mariner of Whitehaven* and contains sixty-four pages. Later printings were at Liverpool, 1785; Dumfries, 1788; and Workington, 1810.
26. Embellishments and perhaps distortions of the theme are found in *The Surprising Adventures and Sufferings of John Rhodes, a Seaman of Workington* (New York, 1798, with 250 pp.; Newark, 1799, with 268 pp.) written in the first person "By a Gentleman perfectly acquainted with the unfortunate sufferer," in which the subject spends eight years with the Indians and five with

If Roach's original timetable can be trusted, he arrived in present-day Guatemala City in 1776, just three years after its foundation in what had been called the Valle de la Ermita. His spelling of the latter name in good English phonetics is but one of many ring-true features of his presentation: "At length we arrived at my destin'd place, the town of Guatamala, or rather of Larmeta: for Guatamala, formerly the capital of the province, and the residence of the Spanish president or governor of the southern provinces of New Spain, had lately been destroyed by an earthquake, and its inhabitants had begun to build themselves habitations at a convenient place, a few miles distant from it, which they called Larmeta. On our arrival here, my guards conducted me to the entrance of a subterraneous dungeon, and there ordered me to dismount my steed. This being done, a ponderous door was opened, which presented to my view a gloomy passage under ground, into which we immediately entered, and the door was firmly secured again. Being now enlightened by candles we walked a few yards forward, by a gradual descent, and came to another door. . . . And in this manner we passed four stupendous doors; after which we arrived upon level ground . . . the dismal habitation of murderers, traitors, robbers, thieves, and other malefactors; along with whom I was now obliged to take up mine abode. . . .

"But happily"—and here Roach returns to a theme of kindness inside calamity, expressed more than once by both himself and Cockburn—"my grievances were in a short time redressed. . . . A short time after mine examination before the obdurate president, a beautiful female was conducted into the dungeon. . . .

"Her sympathetic heart seemed to be greatly affected by my former as well as present sufferings; and now, in her turn, she informed me, that, having descended from English parents, she entertained a great affection for those whom she esteemed her countrymen. . . . Being a lady of high rank, and very opulent circumstances, she soon prevailed

---

the Spaniards. Workington is but five miles from Whitehaven and is mentioned in Roach's 1784 edition. See also *The Powow* (Otsego, 1808), another related item. Thomas W. Field, *An Essay Towards an Indian Bibliography*, p. 330, says of these three books: "There is nothing in this narrative to attest its truth, and the internal evidence is not sufficient to settle the question of its veracity. Without something more definite than we now possess regarding its authenticity, it must remain worthless for historical purposes." Neither Roach nor Rhodes is listed in Eduard Conzemius, *Ethnographical Survey of the Miskito and Sumu Indians of Honduras and Nicaragua*, or in J. H. Steward, ed., *The Circum-Caribbean Tribes*. Bell, 1899, p. 122, speaks of a Tauahca settlement of "Accawass maya" whose name suggests that of Roach's "Assenwasses."

upon the governor to free me from a great part of my fetters; and, during the remainder of my long confinement, supplied me plentifully with candles . . . and likewise sent me, from her own table, a comfortable repast of chocolate twice a-day, together with a sumptuous dinner and supper; so that my fare was now excellent; and I had little to discompose me but the wretched crew with whom I was doomed to inhabit."[27] According to his own original account, Roach stayed three years in this place and waited two and a half more in other prisons before embarking for Havana on his way to Spain. He had first gone to sea at the age of eleven; he had now reached thirty-three; and according to the last book which he seems to have helped write, at the age of fifty-four he was yet ". . . alive, tho' much crippled."[28]

In the nineteenth century before the rule of the Audiencia de Guatemala ended, there was yet another recorded visit to the Central American shore, made by Captain George Henderson of the British army garrison in Belize. Henderson in 1804 visited the Miskito Indians who lived on Caratasca Lagoon; he was also marooned on the largely uninhabited Bay Islands, but had no contact with a small Spanish force on Roatán. Henderson, like the majority of buccaneer-writers long before him, did not stray far from his sailing vessel.[29]

In the first forty years of Central American independence, no less than thirty-four travelers from abroad followed in the footsteps of Benzoni, Gage, Raveneau, Cockburn, and Roach, nearly every one of them making observations far exceeding in detail those of the colonial period. Most of them were free to go wherever they pleased, though danger was often their companion. The unfolding of their accounts, the first ten by textual exposition and all of them through an analytical index, is the object of the pages which follow.

27. *The Surprizing Adventures* (1784), pp. 55–58.
28. *The Powow* (see note 26 above), title page.
29. *An Account of the British Settlement of Honduras* (London, 1809 and 1811). In the second edition, the "Journal of a Voyage to the Mosquito Shore" occupies pp. 163–209; "Sketches of the Manners and Customs of the Mosquito Indians," pp. 211–26; and a short Miskito vocabulary, pp. 227–29.

Chapter 1

People, Places, and Politics, 1821–30

A RECORD of five travel books for inland Central America's first decade of independence contrasts quite strikingly with the colonial rate of one every half century. Each of these five, like others for the decades to follow, will speak for itself in these pages, first of all in relation to the people and places the author met and the politics he encountered. But before the leaves of each ten years are opened, a brief sketch of Central American politics covering the same short period of time will help the reader keep his balance.

The decade of the 1820's, despite the civil war which raged toward its close, held more promise for Central America than any other of its century. First came independence from Spain, on September 15, 1821, without the accompaniment of bloodshed. Then came a resolution of difficulties with Mexico, whose early imperial government (1821–23) hoped to encompass Central America within its territory, but decided finally to desist from action toward that end. Next a constituent assembly brought five states together as one, called the *Provincias Unidas del Centro de América* (July 1, 1823). A succession of triumvirates, ruling from Guatemala City, gave the nation responsible government while a constitution for a *Federación de Centro América* was prepared (1823–24) and put into operation. Manuel José Arce entered the presidency (1825) with considerable bipartisan support and in an atmosphere of peace, though José Cecilio del Valle had done better in the original balloting.[1]

---

1. British diplomat G. A. Thompson spoke highly of both men and at length concerning Valle. See below, pp. 87–91 and 253–54.

Clouds gathered as Arce quarreled with liberals and intervened in the affairs of state governments in Guatemala (1826) and Honduras (1827). Two years of intermittent warfare followed (1827–29), and vice-president Mariano Beltranena took Arce's place (1828–29); but neither was able to contain the rebellion. The victors, under the provisional presidency of senator José Francisco Barrundia (1829–30) and after the presidential election (1830) of the winning general Francisco Morazán, swept away the entire conservative governing structure, exiling lay and clerical supporters of the fallen regime, including Archbishop Ramón Casaus y Torres.[2] Blood had been shed and violence had already become common. But the new regime did represent a real isthmian hope for the ideals of democracy and liberalism.

About half a million of Central America's million and a quarter people lived in the state of Guatemala. The politics of this unit in the first decade devolved chiefly upon jurisdictional disputes with the federal government. The state's constitution was completed at Antigua in 1825 (though the capital was changed to Guatemala City before the end of the year) and liberal Juan Barrundia chosen as first *jefe*. The arrest of Juan Barrundia by Arce in 1826 led to the isthmian civil war already mentioned. Mariano de Aycinena was chosen the new *jefe* of Guatemala (1827–29) in a regime dominated by aristocrats and was on the losing side in the fighting. But wrangling among the winners made immediate reconstitution of the state's affairs difficult.

San Salvador (originally this state had the same name as its capital) held about a quarter of a million people. Its independent spirit was shown in its struggle against control by Mexico (1822–23) and its completion of a constitution (1824) before that of the federal government. From this time until ten years later Salvadoran resentment of Guatemalan dominance in the federation caused problems. A strong effort made by San Salvador to obtain a bishopric separate from that of Guatemala caused a rupture between federal President Arce and his own uncle, José Matías Delgado, who hoped to become the first bishop. Juan Vicente Villacorta, the first *jefe* in San Salvador (1824–26), gave way to *vice-jefe* Mariano Prado (1826–29) at the time when liberals in the state were preparing to take action against Arce. Much of the civil war was fought on Salvadoran territory, with Prado allied with Morazán of Honduras. José María Cornejo, the next *jefe* (1829–32), was less closely associated with the liberal cause.

2. Thompson discusses freedom of religion with Archbishop Casaus, before his exile, on pp. 280–82 below.

Honduras, with 150,000 or more people, finished its constitution in 1825, the capital being set at Comayagua. The choice of Dionisio Herrera as first *jefe* (1824) led to a quarrel as to whether Herrera was serving provisionally or should continue through the first constitutional term. This dispute brought Arce's intervention in 1827 and the end of Herrera's tenure. Consequent battles enabled Francisco Morazán (1827–28) and his friend Diego Vigil (1828–29) to seize control and lead this state's forces in the greater civil war then in progress. But Morazán had to return to end further unrest in Honduras (1829–30) before becoming Central America's president.

A year and a half elapsed after Central America's first declaration of independence before it became clear that the state of Nicaragua (with about 180,000 inhabitants) would follow Guatemala's lead.[3] Nearly constant struggle between Nicaragua's cities, especially León and Granada, made the writing of a constitution difficult in this state even when the two municipalities agreed on independence. Feuding between cities carried over to bitterness between the first *jefe* Manuel Antonio de la Cerda and the first *vice-jefe* Juan Argüello even while the charter was being prepared in 1825–26. The violence continued until Cerda was executed in 1828 and the federal government sent Honduran Dionisio Herrera to mediate. Argüello stepped down in 1829, and Herrera himself was elected *jefe* (1830–34) in the first real peace Nicaragua had known in the decade.

The remoteness of Costa Rica enabled this state (with only about 60,000 people) to carry out its own development during the beginning years without similar troubles and molestations. Prior to declarations concerning final political plans, Costa Rica, in the period 1821–23, stayed aloof from rule by Nicaragua, Guatemala, or Mexico, simply by minding her own affairs. Then subscribing to the plans for a united Central America, Costa Ricans wrote their constitution (finished in 1825) and elected as *jefe* Juan Mora Fernández, with the capital at San José. Mora's nearly nine years in office (1824–33), including two regular terms, gave Costa Rica a tranquil start not enjoyed by the other states of the isthmus. When the federal government's tenuous hold on constitutionality was broken in 1829, Costa Rica seceded from the union; but this action was rescinded in early 1830 as federal affairs were again being regularized.

3. English trader O. W. Roberts was seized and brought to León in 1822 for allegedly aiding the cause of independence. See pp. 33–52 below for his experiences.

Outside the jurisdiction of any of Central America's five states lay Mosquitia, a great stretch of the Caribbean coast, and the Bay Islands which today pertain to Honduras. The Bay Islands were uninhabited by human beings at the beginning of this decade.[4] Mosquitia contained some 10,000 persons under the nominal rule of the king of the Miskitos who received his title and crown from the British.[5]

ORLANDO W. ROBERTS came to Spanish-speaking Central America from Mosquitia after coming to Mosquitia from England. His book published in Edinburgh in 1827 was called *Narrative of Voyages and Excursions on the East Coast and in the Interior of Central America; describing a journey up the River San Juan, and passage across the lake of Nicaragua to the city of León: pointing out the advantages of a direct commercial intercourse with the natives.* (It was republished in facsimile by the University of Florida Press, 1965.) Roberts' book is of a practical sort, written to instruct prospective traders as to what they might expect in these regions. It is also warmly human, Roberts' friendships and animosities being based on the worth of persons as he judged them individually without respect to race or creed. The account of his detention as an alleged spy contains real drama and offers the only outsider's view (albeit a quite limited one) of the Central American isthmus in transition to political independence.

Roberts went to sea early in life, visiting lands as far away from his native England as India and China. As a sea captain, he fought in the war of 1812–14 against the United States. In 1815, when the wars were over and the shipping trade in a temporary slump, he turned to the West Indies for new interests. His next six years can be followed through his own account:[6]

Arriving at Kingston, Jamaica, in the early part of the year 1816, I shortly afterwards obtained the command of a brig of about one hundred and sixty tons burthen, with an assorted cargo of no great value, but suitable to the Indian trade.

We left Port Royal, Jamaica, in the month of July, and, on the fourth

---

4. See pp. 54–55 below for a description of the Bay Islands at that time.
5. A merrymaking attended by Roberts and king George Frederick (1815–24) is portrayed on pp. 23–28 below.
6. Roberts, 1827, pp. 33, 52–54, 58–59, 83, 86, 89–90, 96–104, 112, 121–22, 124–26, 128–36, 145–50, 154–55, 162–65, 168–77, 190–95, 200–206, 211, 214–17, 221–22, 224–25, 228–29, 241–45, 261–63, 264–66, 271–79.

day, we saw the high land at the back of the Bay of Mandingo, between Porto Bello and the Gulf of Darien.[7]

In the year 1817, my voyages to San Blas were interrupted by severe indisposition, which reduced me to a state of great debility. When convalescent, I accepted the offer of a friend, to accompany him on a general trading voyage to . . . different parts of the Mosquito Shore. His object was to lodge supplies of goods, with his agents, at various trading depots; and to bring away from them, such quantities of fustic, tortoise-shell, sarsaparilla, cocoa, &c. as they had collected. . . . Returning from the coast of San Blas, we passed Porto Bello, and proceeded to Chiriquí Lagoon; which, although so far to the southward, is considered part of the Mosquito Shore, under the jurisdiction of the Mosquito King; who, notwithstanding that the Spaniards consider it a part of their province of Veragua, annually sends his admiral to collect tribute from the natives. . . .

On our arrival at Chiriquí Lagoon, I gladly assented to a proposal, made by my friend, to ascend the River Chrico Mola (or perhaps more properly Chrickam Aula), about twenty-five miles, to the principal settlement of the Valiente Indians; a station said to be exceedingly healthy—there to remain for the recovery of my health—become acquainted with the manners and customs of that tribe, and open a trade with the Indians in the interior of the country.[8]

From my first arrival at Chrico Mola, I gradually acquired bodily strength,—and I followed the example of the inhabitants, old and young, by daily bathing in the river, which is here as clear as crystal, and pleasantly cool. Alligators do not ascend higher than the first fall, so that there is no danger of annoyance from them, and to these frequent ablutions I attributed, in a great measure, my rapid recovery to perfect health.

In less than six weeks after my arrival I had procured upwards of five thousand pounds weight of sarsaparilla; and conceiving that a regular supply of this valuable article might be obtained here for supplying the Jamaica market, provided the Indians were properly encouraged to collect it, I came to the determination of remaining at Chrico Mola,

7. In modern Panamanian and Colombian terminology, at the back of the Golfo de San Blas, between Portobelo and the Golfo de Urabá.
8. The river is now called Cricamola; remnants of the Valiente tribe, known as the Mové (of the Guaymí language), still live upstream along its banks.

until next season at least. On the return of the vessel which had left me here, I went down to the Lagoon and communicated my ideas on the subject to her owner, who, forseeing the advantages likely to be derived from the residence of a European among the Valientes, immediately assented to my proposal.

During one of the turtle fishing seasons, I fitted out a large canoe; loaded her with goods to the value of about three hundred pounds, and, taking two stout lads to assist me, I visited several places on the coast of the Province of Veragua....

This short trip was a very profitable one, and only occupied three or four days. As I could have disposed of double the quantity of goods, I was encouraged to undertake similar voyages, in larger canoes, and on a regular plan, along the whole coast of the Mosquito Shore; and, for the purpose of procuring such canoes, I embraced the opportunity of accompanying a trader returning along that coast in a convenient vessel.

Between Matina and Monkey Point,[9] the country, which is thinly inhabited, presents a beautiful appearance of hill and vale, well watered, but destitute of good harbours and headlands. . . . Salt Creek is . . . the principal resort of the contraband traders, when their cargoes cannot be landed at Matina River. . . .[10] The Americans from the United States, have regularly, but secretly, visited this port every season for the last ten years;—one house in New York annually sends three or four fast sailing schooners to their agent, a Mr Smith, at Salt Creek, who disposes of the cargo, and collects the proceeds, during the time schooners are running down the coast, trading with the Indians for tortoise-shell, copal and other gums, sarsaparilla, tassao, &c.[11] This business is extremely lucrative to the Americans; who are enabled to dispose of a considerable quantity of Indian goods at such prices, as prevent the Jamaica traders from effectually competing with them.

Pursuing our voyage from Turtle Bogue, we come to the Rio Colo-

9. Between Punta Mona and Matina in Costa Rica, to follow the direction traveled.
10. Salt Creek seems to have been in the vicinity of the present-day city of Limón.
11. "Tassao" is presumably from the Spanish *tasajo*, for jerked beef, but used on this coast to designate dried meat of other origins; see Squier, 1855W, p. 137.

rado....[12] The next harbour, viz. that of San Juan de Nicaragua, is unquestionably the best for ships of war, or large vessels, on the whole range of coast between the Bocas del Toro, and Cape Gracias a Dios—to which latter it is also superior in not being exposed to southerly winds. There is a sufficient depth of water, and room, at the upper part, for fifteen or twenty sail of vessels of the largest class, besides smaller vessels....

Many of the fishermen, Indians and others, on their return from the southern fishing grounds, call in this neighbourhood, for the purpose of taking manatees, which are very plenty in the river, and in a creek at the upper end of the harbour. Hundreds of these fishermen remain to cure the meat, on the low sandy point, at the entrance of the harbour, without being molested by the Spaniards.... At a short distance from the coast the country here rises considerably; and, from the neighbourhood of San Juan to Bluefields, it is occupied by the Rama Indians, whose principal settlement is at ... Rio de Punta Gorda, a noble stream.... The bay is shallow, but there is good anchorage under the lee side of Monkey Point, ... farther to the northward....[13] The country from San Juan River to this point abounds in vanilla of the finest quality....

The Rama Indians were formerly numerous, but, at present, do not exceed five hundred; they are under subjection to the Mosquito King, to whom they pay an annual tax in tortoise-shell, canoes, hammocks, and cotton lines. The Ramas are considered mild, and inoffensive; they have little intercourse with other Indians; ... they are more expert in the management of canoes and other boats, than the Mosquito men, and will effect a landing in their barks, where the best European boats would meet certain destruction....

Bluefields is the next place of importance on the coast.... For trading vessels of an easy draught of water, the upper lagoon is perhaps superior to any other harbour on the Mosquito Shore, being completely sheltered from all winds....

Colonel Hodgson, the British Superintendant, resided at this place for a number of years, during the time the English held possession of the Mosquito Shore, and he had extensive mahogany works on the banks of the principal river, and a very considerable trade was carried

12. Boca del Tortuguero. "Bogue," meaning *stream* or *creek*, is used in Louisiana French.
13. This Monkey Point is Punta Mico. The Ramas as a separate ethnic group now live chiefly on an islet named for them near Bluefields.

on with the Spaniards and Creoles in the interior. This active and intelligent gentleman, had also extensive grants of land at Black River, and left the Mosquito Shore with much regret, at the time when the extraordinary policy of the British Government compelled their settlers to abandon that country in the year 1786. He spent a great portion of his life on this coast; and the old Indians still speak of their former Governor, with respect, and marks of regret, that no accredited person now resides among them.[14]

Previous to his leaving Bluefields, several of his slaves and people who were established in the interior, refused to leave the place. These people and their descendants, who are Mulattoes and Samboes, are settled at the southernmost extremity of the harbour, about nine miles from its principal entrance, and they have considerably increased in numbers since Colonel Hodgson's time. They live without fear of molestation from the Indians, none of whom reside within many miles of them; and, although it is not acknowledged as such by the British Government, it may be truly considered a British settlement. It is principally under the influence of two intelligent young men, who claim affinity to the late superintendent. The river of Bluefields . . . rises in the country possessed by the Spaniards . . . ; but few of the present people at Bluefields have ascended its course to any great height. The Cookra and Woolwa tribes of Indians, who are settled on its banks, at a considerable distance in the interior, are a quiet peaceable race of people, on good terms with the . . . people at Bluefields Lagoons. . . .

These Indians occasionally descend the river, to the settlements at Bluefields, bringing peccary, warree, iguanas, and other provisions.[15]

. . . Remaining some time at Pearl Kay Lagoon,[16] I proceeded to Rio Grande and Prinzapolca, . . . being the best places for obtaining the large canoes wanted.

Having arranged . . . for three dories, and a small quantity of tortoise-shell, I returned to Great River (Rio Grande), and from

14. A memoir written in 1757 by this Colonel Robert Hodgson was published or republished in Edinburgh, 1822, as *Some Account of the Mosquito Territory*. Black River is Río Negro in Honduras.

15. The Cookra (Cucra) group of Indians have become dispersed since Roberts' time; the Woolwas (Ulvas) still hold out in the back country of Río Grande and Río Escondido (the "river of Bluefields"). The *warree* is a species of peccary which ranges from Paraguay to southern Mexico, white-lipped and more fierce than the collared peccary seen from Patagonia to Texas and Arizona.

16. Laguna de Perlas.

thence, after having agreed at both places to become the purchaser of their next season's collection of tortoise shell, I removed with the craft I had purchased ... to Pearl Kay Lagoon, intending to return from thence, to my residence at Chrico Mola, by one of the trading vessels from Jamaica, expected to call, as usual, ... on her way down the coast. ...

In a few days afterwards the traders with whom I had in some measure connected myself, arrived; ... I could easily perceive by the coolness of their behaviour to me, that the activity of my proceedings had excited their avaricious jealousy, which keeps them at all times on the watch, and ready to crush every person likely to break in upon their trade. As a proof of the extent of this concealed, and strictly secret trade, I may mention, without fear of contradiction, that one trader alone generally has goods, tortoise-shell, and outstanding debts, at the different depôts along the coast, never amounting to less than between five and six thousand pounds sterling in value. By artfully connecting himself with some of the leading natives ... , he contrives not only to receive the whole proceeds of their exertions; but, by some manœuvre or other, keeps the Indians constantly indebted to him, and his party, however great may be their success, in fishing, or otherwise.

It might be tedious and uninteresting to narrate all the occurrences which now induced me to separate myself from their interests:—suffice it to say, that, having successfully used great exertions to forward their views, in the reasonable hope that they would consider me entitled to share in the profits of my own labours, I was very much disappointed to find this was quite contrary to their policy: and, indignant at such treatment, I determined on endeavouring to interest more liberal and enlightened people in the plans which I had conceived for trade and discovery. With this intention I determined, instead of returning to Chrico Mola, to proceed to the northward. ...

In pursuance of my determination to proceed to the northward, I quitted Pearl Kay Lagoon, and, returning, by Rio Grande, to Prinzapolca, I there, according to my expectation, met Admiral Earnee, one of the three principal chiefs of the Mosquito Shore, who had been as far to the southward as Bocas del Toro collecting the King's tribute. He came to Prinzapolca in a large boat or dorie, attended by others of a smaller description. ... He is a complete black, or negro, without the least appearance of Indian blood; but I found him to be, when sober, a sensible, shrewd, and intelligent man, a descendant from some of the

Sambo negroes, who were, many years ago, wrecked on this coast. As he had announced the day when he should arrive here, preparations had been made for him and about twenty-five people his attendants, who were amply supplied with provisions, and feasted at the King's house. The tribute was also in readiness, the principal part in tortoise-shell; a single *back* of shell being demanded from every canoe employed in turtleing during the season. The same value in dories, hammocks, or coarse cotton cloth of the country being exacted from those canoes employed in any other manner.

In reference to the King's houses; it is necessary to observe, that the principal settlements of the Samboes and their immediate allies, form a chain of hamlets, at certain distances, from one end of the Mosquito Shore *proper*, to the other; and, in each of these, a house called the King's, is erected by the joint labour of the community, and appropriated for the reception of the King, or his officers, when they visit the settlement. In it, also, the headman of the settlement, or one of the three principal chiefs who govern the coast, decide controversies, and frame laws and regulations, which are afterwards sanctioned by the King before being carried into effect. Some of these houses are of considerable size, and built with great care and solidity.

So soon as Earnee knew my intention of visiting the King, he offered me every assistance in his power; and, after remaining a few days at Prinzapolca, I accompanied him on his journey to the Cape.[17] We left the settlement at midnight with the land breeze down the river.

At the southermost part of Sandy Bay is the entrance to a small Lagoon, on the borders of which is a principal settlement of the Mosquito Indians, where the King frequently resides. . . . On our arrival, the Admiral was met and welcomed by the principal people: English colours were hoisted, as the signal of festivity; we were informed, that a canoe having arrived from the Cape, with information that the King was on his way to visit the settlement, and having met the Admiral, preparations were making for a grand feast and mishlaw drink.[18] For this purpose the whole population were employed,—most of them being engaged collecting pine apples, plantains, bananas, and cassava, for their favourite liquor. The expressed juice of the pine apple is alone a pleasant and agreeable beverage. The mishlaw from the plantain and banana, is also both pleasant and nutritive; that from the cassava and

17. Cabo Gracias a Dios.
18. "Mishlaw"=mushla.

maize, is more intoxicating; but its preparation, is an operation so disgusting, that, did I not consider it an imperative duty to suppress nothing that tends to elucidate the manners, and habits, of these different tribes, and their still great distance from civilization, I should pass it over, without notice. The method of preparing it, is as follows. The root of the cassava, after being mashed, and peeled, is boiled to the same consistence, as when to be used for food. On its being taken from the fire, the water is poured off, and the roots allowed to cool. The pots were then surrounded by all the women, old and young, who, being provided with large wooden bowls, commenced an attack upon the cassava, which they chewed to a consistance of thick paste, and then put their mouthfuls into the bowls before them, until these vessels were filled; the bowls were then carried to the king's house, and the contents tumbled into a new canoe which had been hauled up from the landing-place, and put there for that purpose, there being no cask in the settlement sufficiently capacious. I observed that some few of the young men also joined in the masticating process, which was continued with much perseverance, until the joint produce of the wooden bowls, from every house in the settlement, had filled the canoe about one third. Other cassava was then taken, and bruised in a kind of large wooden mortar, with a wooden pestle, to a consistence of dough, which was afterwards diluted with cold water, to which was added, a quantity of Indian corn, partly boiled and masticated, in the same manner as the cassava; the whole was then poured into the canoe, which was afterwards filled with water, and frequently stirred with a paddle, until, in a few hours, it was in a high, and abominable state of fermentation. The Admiral affirmed that the saliva imbibed, was the principal cause of the sudden fermentation; that if the whole had been bruised and prepared with water only, the liquor would, before fermentation, become too sour for use; and, that the liquor was more or less esteemed, according to the health, age, and constitution of the masticators; that, therefore, when he himself wished to give a private . . . drink, he took care that none but his own wives, and young girls, should be employed; but, as there had been few old women engaged in its preparation, he thought the liquor before us would be tolerable, and "make drunk come soon." The canoe would contain about three puncheons, and there was nearly the same quantity prepared at two or three houses of the chief men, in the neighbourhood; besides drink of a less beastly description, viz. the simply expressed juice of the pine apple; and, the plantain and banana mishlaw, being the ripe fruit roasted, bruised, and mixed with water.

... Earnee, had invited the head men and old people of ... the neighbouring country and Lagoons, to meet the King, receive an account of the state of the different tributary settlements, which he had been visiting, transact public business, and get drunk.

The King's house, Earnee's, a Samboe chief designated *General Blyatt*, with a few others, were tolerably large ... and tolerably well furnished with benches, tables, plates, glasses, basins, knives and forks, and other articles. A hammock was hung up in the Admiral's house for each of his guests, according to custom; and, after a great deal of conversation about the state of the country, the customs, strength, and trade of the different settlements, and the general policy of the Mosquito-men, I retired to rest, pleased with the attention shown to me, but rather puzzled and alarmed, by the magnitude of the preparations, for the approaching feast.

The Admiral, during our journey up from Prinzapolca had related several anecdotes of the King, and had given me some knowledge of his character. The Admiral seemed to regret the King's want of attention to the real interests of his country; his too great partiality for liquor and women: his extreme levity, and, the facility with which he associated with, and listened to, every visionary scheme submitted to him by the traders; the ease with which the patriot General Aurey had got him entangled in one of his expeditions against the Spaniards at Trujillo;[19] and his general inattention to the safety, and prosperity, of his subjects. He also regretted that there was no British superintendants on the coast, as formerly, in the time of Colonel Hodgson, when the Mosquito Indians could find employment, and a demand for their produce, at Black River, and the other settlements; and the chiefs, throughout the coast, could dress themselves, and live, "right English gentleman fashion." The chiefs, and old men, agreed with him in these observations; and, they also, universally disproved of the arbitrary manner in which the Jamaica traders exerted the influence they had acquired at some of the settlements of the coast, adding, that rather than deal with them, they had actually, this season, sold the greater

---

19. The "patriot General Aurey" was a French seaman, Louis Aury, who carried on privateering activities against the Spaniards in the Gulf of Mexico and the Caribbean Sea from 1816 to 1821, cooperating with Simón Bolívar during the latter's final campaigns (1819–21) in Colombia and Venezuela. Roberts speaks as though Aury appeared at Trujillo more than once. The conversation with Admiral Earnee recorded here took place in 1819. An unsuccessful attack by Aury on Trujillo April 21–23, 1820, in which troops were landed, is probably the one Roberts mentions on p. 41 below.

part of their tortoise-shell to the Americans, who, although they had such a variety of goods, were fairer dealers, and gave a better price.

Early in the morning, I was awakened by the noise of the drum; the natives were in a state of bustle and activity, preparing for the drinking match, and the reception of the King. He arrived, in a large canoe, with ten people, escorted by the same number in two smaller ones. At the landing-place he was met by Admiral Earnee and General Blyatt, with some of the chief men of the neighbouring settlements; the two former dressed in uniforms, with gold epaulettes. There was little form or ceremony used in their reception of the King; a shake of the hand, and "how do you do, King," in English, being the only salutation from all classes. Briefly inquiring my motives for coming to see him, he invited me to go with him to the Cape, and I could then, at leisure, judge how far he could second my views, and how he was situated with his people, amongst whom, four years ago, on his return from Jamaica, where he was educated, he found himself quite a stranger.

He was a young man, about twenty-four years of age, of a bright copper colour, with long curly hair hanging in ringlets down the sides of his face; his hands and feet small, a dark expressive eye, and very white teeth. He was an active and handsome figure, with the appearance of greater agility than strength. In other respects I found him, on further acquaintance, wild as the deer on his native savannahs.

During the day, Indians arrived from various parts of the coast, and interior. At the meeting which took place in the King's house, various matters relative to the government of the neighbouring settlements, disputes, and other public business, was discussed; and I observed, that the King left every thing to the discretion of Earnee, Blyatt, and a few others. In fact, he seemed to take little interest or trouble, further than to sanction the resolutions passed, so that they might be promulgated as "the King's own order." Such is the expression; and that order is invariably obeyed, and carried into effect. During the time the council was sitting, no women were admitted; a few only were afterwards permitted to enter, during the drinking match, to take care of their husbands, when reduced to a state of insensibility by intoxication.

The discussions in the King's house being ended, the feasting began. Two men were stationed by the side of the canoe, who filled the mishlaw drink into calabashes, which were then carried to the company by boys. As the men became exhilarated, they began to dance, in imitation of country dances, and Scotch reels, learned from the former English settlers; but they soon became too much intoxicated to preserve order. Every one, including the King and his select friends at the Admiral's house, gave way, without restraint, to the pleasures of drinking; and, during the evening, the King's uncle Andrew . . . arrived, bringing one of his majesty's favourite wives. This chief was a short stout man, of unmixed Indian blood, very lively and quick in his motions, disguising, under an appearance of levity, much cunning and shrewdness;— he spoke tolerably good English; and soon, by his ridiculous stories regarding the Jamaica traders, and by his satirical and witty remarks upon some of the old Mosquito men present, kept the company in a roar of laughter. The King observed to me, in course of the evening, that I must not be surprised to see him act in the manner he was doing; as it was his wish, by indulging the natives, to induce them to adopt gradually, and by degrees, the English customs, and mode of living; and he requested me to observe how far he had succeeded, pointing out to me, that all present had thrown aside the *pulpera*, the common Indian dress, and wore jackets and trowsers, with good hats. Some of them had coats, with other articles to correspond; and, as I have often repeated, they prided themselves upon being "true English gentleman fashion."

His majesty, as usual, paid more attention to the women than to the chiefs; and, observing to me that the ladies here could dance fully as well as any of those at the former English settlements, proposed that I should join him, the Admiral, and uncle Andrew, in a dance; and he would send for the women to join us. I of course readily assented to this proposal; and the females having arrived, we commenced dancing, to the sound of a drum, our only music.

Blyatt had orders to keep the party in the King's house from interrupting us, but our music being full as noisy as theirs, and the secret of the women's arrival having transpired, our house was soon surrounded by a crowd, who pressed so much, that it became insufferably warm; and we were obliged to stop the dance; at which circumstance, many of the Indians expressed such disappointment, that the King good-naturedly proposed to renew the dance in the open air. The other party joining us, with their music, we were soon all jumbled together, King, Admiral, General, Mosquito men and women, in one mass of confusion and revelry, from which those who were capable of reflecting were soon glad to escape. Before the chiefs became totally intoxicated, they ordered the women home to their houses, to prevent their being unable to take care of their husbands. The drinking was carried on with great perseverance, during the night, by old and young. The drums were beat, and muskets fired, some of them loaded with powder to the very muzzle, until nearly all the assembly were in a state of beastly drunkenness, and taken care of by the women, who were occasionally called upon for that purpose. At intervals, however, as the men recovered, they found their way back to their favourite mishlaw, and renewed the debauch. All the next day was consumed in drinking; and, it was not until the day following, that the liquors were reduced to the very dregs of the cassava and maize, which, even then, was taken from the bottom of the vessels, and being squeezed through the fingers, by handfuls, into the calabashes, was passed to those who were still craving for more of the precious beverage. By the third night, the whole liquors were consumed; and the Indians began to retire to their respective homes, many complaining, with great reason, that "their heads were all spoiled." It is however to their credit, that, during the whole of this debauch, I did not perceive the slightest quarrel.

On my arrival at Cape Gracias a Dios, I was much disappointed to find only a few houses; and those, with the exception of the King's, that of Dalby, one of his chiefs, and an old merchant's of the name of Bogg, of the very worst description, being mere huts, barely sufficient to protect the natives from the weather.

I remained several months with the King; and had every opportunity of knowing him, and his people, intimately. The circumstances which led to his being sent, in his youth, to Jamaica, where he received a very indifferent education, are briefly these. His father, old King George, was of the mixed, or Negro and Indian breed; he was of a cruel, barbarous, and vindictive disposition; . . . and, like all the other Mosquito chiefs, had a great number of wives and women, whom he often treated with such cruelty, that some of them died under his hands. The murder of one of these women, under circumstances of peculiar barbarity, called forth the resentment of her friends, who created a riot, during which the King was fired upon, and killed, by his own people. He left two sons, George Frederick the present King, and his half-brother Robert, then both very young. A trader, from the Bay of Honduras, conceiving that he might derive great advantages from the possession of these children, contrived to get them into his vessel, and persuaded the chiefs that they might derive great benefits by having their future king educated "English fashion," so that he might understand something of the laws, manners and customs, of their friends the English.

The children were allowed to depart; and the chiefs forming a kind of regency, the three principal ones agreed to retain the country for the eldest son, dividing it, in the mean time, into three governments; the first, from Roman River, near Cape Honduras, to Patook, including the tribes of Kharibees or Caribs, Poyers, Mosquito men, and some negroes formerly attached to the British settlements, was confided to *General* Robinson.[20]

The second division, from Caratasca . . . to Sandy Bay, and Dacura, which included all the Mosquito men proper, or mixed breed of Samboes and Indians, was left under the rule, of a chief, the brother of the late King, under the name of *Admiral.*

The third division, from Brancmans, to Great River (Rio Grande) was under the charge of Don Carlos, denominated *the Governor;* and included the tribes of Tongulas, Towcas, Woolwas, Cookras, &c.[21] These three chiefs each appointed headmen, within their respective districts, subordinate to their authority. The small colonies of Samboes, at Pearl Kay Lagoon and Bluefields, were, however, allowed to choose their own governors.

The children were, after some time, sent from Honduras to Jamaica; and his Grace the Duke of Manchester is said to have shown some attention to the eldest, who always spoke of the Duke with sentiments of respect and gratitude.[22] After going through the routine of an indifferent education, he was sent to Belize; at which place, the principal Mosquito chiefs were invited to meet him, and the ceremony of his coronation was performed with considerable pomp; the young chief being escorted to the church by the British superintendant, the regular troops, militia, and principal people of the settlement. The Reverend Mr Armstrong put the crown (a present from the British to one of his ancestors) on his head; and he was formally invested with the sword, rake, and spurs; a royal salute was fired, and he was styled *King of the Mosquito Shore and Nation.*[23]

20. "From Roman River . . . to Patook" may be read "From the Aguán River . . . to the Patuca." "Poyers"=Payas, who survive in a few towns near the head of Río Paulaya.

21. Brancman's or Bragman's Bluff, of which Roberts had spoken earlier, is in the vicinity of modern Puerto Cabezas. The "Tongulas" and "Towcas" are the Tunglas, now extinct, and the Tauahcas, who survive from the Río Patuca to the Río Cucalaya; for the other tribes, see Ch. 1 n. 15.

22. William Montagu, fifth Duke of Manchester, was governor of Jamaica 1808–27.

23. The 1845 Miskito coronation service given textually in Harry Luke, *Caribbean Circuit,* pp. 66–76, mentions sword and crown, but no "rake" or

Medals, and dresses, were presented to the chiefs; and the whole were sent down to the coast in a British sloop of war. They were accidentally landed at General Robinson's residence, between Black River and Brewers Lagoon;[24] and the King unhappily commenced his reign by grossly insulting and quarrelling with the General, his most powerful chief. At Cape Gracias a Dios, the King was received in the most friendly manner by all the members of his family, who principally reside at an extensive pine savannah called the Ridge, about forty miles from the Cape, at a short distance from the bank of the great Cape River.[25]

He frequently assured me, that, on his arrival at Cape Gracias a Dios, and for many months afterwards, he regretted having returned to his country, or that he had ever left it; for he found himself a perfect stranger, ignorant of the interests of his subjects, and unacquainted with the influence, or abilities, of the chiefs who, in other circumstances, might have assisted him in forming something like a government; while, at the same time, he was expected by his friends the British, to fulfil duties, which he honestly confessed he was but in a very slight manner qualified to perform. He seemed perfectly sensible of these deficiencies, but without having energy, or application, to remedy them; or to assume, and maintain, with propriety, the rank and station in which Providence had placed him. These considerations, at times, embittered his life; his good resolutions, and endeavours at amendment, constantly vanished, when they were put in competition with the pleasures of the bottle, and his other vicious propensities, which were encouraged by the manners and customs of his subjects, whom he considered it necessary to conciliate, until they at length became habitual to him; and, when any vessel visited the coast, or whenever he could procure rum, he was generally in a state of intoxication. At such times, his naturally liberal disposition overcame his prudence; and, his countrymen found it their interest to encourage this vice, and hailed the arrival of the traders, as the signal for indulging in their propensities for drinking, which they were always sure the King would, not only gratify to the extent of his abilities, but that, in those misguided moments, he would readily present them with any thing of value in his possession. Under all these circumstances it is not surprising that George Frederick failed to realize the hopes of those who expected better of him.

---

spurs. If "rake" is indeed the word Roberts intended, may it have been a kind of scepter?

24. Laguna de Bruso.   25. The Coco or Segovia or Wanks.

After his first arrival presents of clothing, blankets, cloth, duck, moscheats and other articles, were sent to him, by the British Government, for the purpose of being distributed among his people with a view to conciliate them, and maintain his authority;[26] and, at such times, the Reverend Mr Armstrong never failed to send him letters of advice regarding the regulation of his conduct, and the duties he owed to his people; with a number of religious tracts, which were generally neglected, the King and his Prime Minister observing, that a present of rum would have been far more acceptable, as he found it impossible to instruct his people on points which he did not himself understand, and which they insisted were 'Englishman lies.' He was naturally of a generous disposition, and not destitute of ability; and, it is perhaps to be regretted that he did not receive an European, rather than an extremely loose West Indian education: by the former he would have had a fair chance of acquiring correct habits, and some idea of the importance of order and good government; whereas, by the latter, he became possessed of very little really useful information, and had an opportunity of engrafting, as it were, the bad qualities of the European, and Creole, upon the vicious propensites of the Samboe, and the capricious disposition of the Indian, by which his life was embittered, and his ultimate destruction caused.[27]

During my sojourn with the King, I accompanied him in several excursions along the coast, and into the interior; in particular, to Black River in the Poyais country, since ceded to General MacGregor. . . .[28] Some Englishmen, and an American, acquainted with the value of the land about Black River, and with the former state of the plantations there, had arrived from Barbadoes, with the determination of forming a settlement at that place, and the King was now desirous of visiting, and giving them encouragement. We left the Cape in a large boat, with about a dozen people.

. . . Reaching Black River Lagoon, . . . we proceeded in canoes

26. "Moscheats"=machetes.
27. George Frederick was assassinated in 1824.
28. For "Poyais," read "Paya." "General MacGregor" was Gregor McGregor, a Scotch adventurer who served Francisco Miranda in 1812, Simón Bolívar in 1816, and himself thereafter. In 1817–19 he fought unsuccessfully as a privateer against the Spaniards. In 1820 he received the grant referred to here, from George Frederick, using it solely to defraud hundreds of persons. See Alfred Hasbrouck, "Gregor McGregor and the Colonization of Poyais, between 1820 and 1824."

towards its entrance. It contains several small islands, some of which were occupied for raising provisions, and cattle, when the British held possession of Black River; on its borders are extensive savannahs, and pine ridges, from whence the former settlers used to draw considerable quantities of tar, pitch, and turpentine: The ruins of the old works are still visible; and, from their present appearance, must have been very extensive. We observed immense quantities of pigeons, teal, muscovy ducks, and other birds, which, in the morning, kept flying about in flocks of many hundreds. . . .

Having crossed the course of the main stream of the river, we passed the point on which the British had formerly a small fort, created for the protection of the settlement; the situation appeared very proper for the purpose. The fort had been surrounded by a ditch, and could still, at a trifling expense, be made tenable. We found the new settlement on the banks of a branch of the river, about three miles from its entrance. The situation seemed to be low and ill chosen, a few houses had been put up, on the site of part of the former town, by the new settlers,—who were at this time Colonel Gordon of the independent service, Captain Murray and his wife, Captain Hosmore and his son, with three or four other white people. Colonel Gordon and his party had been settled some time previous to the arrival of the others; they had cleared a considerable quantity of land, and had already raised one crop, of about five hundred bushels of Indian corn, with which Gordon had gone to Trujillo; having formed a contract with the commandant of that place to take all that he could raise. The quality appeared equal, if not superior, to any raised in the Southern States of the Union. Mr Warren, an American, had been left in charge of the Colonel's plantation; good crops, and a ready demand for their produce, seemed to be anticipated by all parties. Young Hosmore, and another Englishman, had been up the river, on a visit to the Poyer Indians. . . . When there, they, by way of ascertaining how far the extensive trade formerly carried on could be revived, despatched an Indian to the Spanish town of Manto . . . ; he was well received, and brought back letters from several *padres*, inviting young Hosmore to proceed to Manto, and sending mules to bring him, and the few goods he had, to that place. He immediately paid them a visit, was kindly received, and made proposals for a supply of dry goods, for which they offered specie, cattle, sarsaparilla, &c. They also tendered him, in the mean time, mules and cattle to assist in the formation of the settlement; declaring that the withdrawing of the

British from Black River had so injured their trade and former prosperity, that they would, willingly, use every exertion to open a communication with any new settlers. Having no means of conveying the mules, &c. down the river, Hosmore was obliged to decline the offer. He made cautious inquiries regarding the mines in this part of the country, and procured some specimens of silver, and gold ore. . . . : The situation of several mines was known to some of the former settlers, and a regular survey was once attempted by a Colonel Despard, but, being at an improper season of the year, it failed. Hosmore told me he had stopped on his way down the river to examine two mineral springs, one hot, the other cold, close to each other, near the junction of two of its branches: they are situated at the base of an extensive ridge of mountains, extending through the country, in a westerly direction; and, without doubt, connecting those which form the barrier between the Spaniards of Nicaragua, and the various unconquered Indians to the northward and eastward. The highest part of these ridges appears by the course of the rivers to be about the upper part of the Poyer country; and, as the eastern side, in possession of the Spaniards, is known to be full of gold and silver ores, there can be no doubt that the Indian side is equally rich, in these minerals. In passing, up and down the river, he had landed at the ruins of some of the former English plantations, where he found sugar-cane, plantains, bananas, pineapples, coffee bushes, &c. vegetating in a state of wild luxuriance. Mr Hosmore's father had transplanted, from thence, several hundred coffee plants; but, owing to their removal from a rich to a poor soil, I doubt the favourable result of his experiment. Peas, beans, cabbage, and other culinary vegetables of England, were however in a state of great forwardness; and the new settlers found no difficulty in procuring provisions, one draught of the seive being sufficient to supply the settlement with fish for several days; and they could always find plenty of game on the river, and in the woods. These, and trading conveniences, induced them to remain at this place, at present, in preference to ascending higher up, to a richer soil. We were shown the remains of the former church, hospital, and ruins of several houses, all built of brick made in the country—several sawpits, and other indications of the industry of the former settlers were also visible.

Shortly after the journey last narrated, I visited Belize; and succeeded in forming arrangements there, under the sanction of the Mosquito King, for securing a share of the Indian trade. During the interval of carrying these arrangements into effect, I continued to make short voyages along the shore, visiting, and residing occasionally, at many of the Indian, and Mosquito settlements.

One of these voyages, had a termination which unexpectedly afforded me an opportunity of visiting the Interior of Central America, as far as the city of León, within a few miles of the South Sea.

In the year 1822,[29] I left Cape Gracias a Dios, in a small smack of about fifteen tons burden, with goods to the value of about five hundred pounds, intending to run along the whole coast as far as the river Coclee;[30] and to stop at every river, creek, and settlement, where tortoise-shell, and other produce, could be procured. The King furnished me with three of his people to accompany me as far as Prinzapolca, where I knew I could engage proper hands for the remainder of the voyage. . . . On my arrival at Prinzapolca, I entered into agreement with an intelligent Indian, named Brown, . . . who, having been brought up in a Creole family at Pearl Kay Lagoon, spoke good English, and three others, to proceed with me; agreeing to pay them in goods, at the rate of five dollars per man, each month, for their services. I could have hired White people, or Creoles, at Pearl Kay Lagoon, on the same terms, but I have always found the Indians more capable of bearing fatigue, easily satisfied, docile and obliging,—consequently better adapted for my purpose.

With these men I left Prinzapolca early in June; and, after trading at Great River, Pearl Kay Lagoon, Bluefields, and the Rama settlement at Point de Gorda, I arrived at the harbour of San Juan de Nicaragua. It was scarcely daylight when I entered the port, and, before discovering two large schooners, I was under their guns. The appearance of these vessels alarmed my Indians, but it was too late to recede; and I had scarcely come to anchor, when I was boarded by a large boat full of people; the officer, in command, ordered my vessel alongside the schooner, to be searched, and assumed as much importance as if he had made a most valuable capture. I was aware that the Spaniards avail themselves of every opportunity to purchase a few dry goods, from the Indian traders as they pass along the coast; and, that the commanders of Port San Juan, and the Castle of San Carlos, not only wink at this contraband trade, but, indirectly, buy

---

29. The original reads *1802* at this point, an obvious typographical error. The correct year is given by Roberts on his page 31.

30. Coclé del Norte, in central Panama.

goods on their own accounts to a considerable extent, payment being made in gold dust, doubloons, and dollars. I was nevertheless afraid for the result; having a quantity of gunpowder, and cutlass blades, for the Indian trade, knowing these articles to be strictly contraband.

The Commandant of the fort, or battery, having satisfied himself respecting the object of my voyage, told me, contrary to my expectation, that I was at liberty to depart whenever I thought proper.

The schooners were the *Flor-del-mer*, mounting ten, and the *Estrella* eight guns—six pounders; with each a long eighteen pounder on a pivot: they had originally been American privateers, the smallest of them exceeding two hundred and fifty tons, with a crew of fifty men each. The captain of the first mentioned vessel, desirous of information, insisted on my breakfasting with him; and, during the time I enjoyed his hospitality, the man who was kept on the lookout, from the masthead, descried a sail to windward, coming down in the same direction from whence I had arrived. In a moment all was hurry, bustle, and confusion; and, I was annoyed by innumerable questions about the vessel in sight: it was in vain that I assured them I knew nothing about them; and suggested, that she might be one of the Jamaica traders. My assertions were received with distrust, or entirely disbelieved:—a few minutes however put them out of suspense; it became evident that she was a brig of war; and, immediately, preparations were made for action.

As most of my little property was now at stake, I went to the Commandant of the fort, and requested that my small vessel should be taken over the bar, into the river for safety; offering in return, the services of the Indians, to assist in working the guns at the fort; and tendering my own to the Captain of the Estrella. The Commandant coolly observed that his officers strongly suspected I was a spy for the vessel now in sight; but that if I assisted in repulsing her, I would, in some measure, invalid that impression, leaving it however entirely at my own option to act as I judged proper.

By this time the schooners, having springs on their cables, were moored with their broadsides completely commanding the entrance to the harbour. Their commanders ordered the red flag to be hoisted, which was immediately answered by a similar defiance from the vessel in the offing: she took in top-gallant sails, reefed topsails, and in rounding the point within gunshot, hoisted Buenos Ayrean colours, and I then knew her to be the Patriot vessel Centinela, commanded by Bradford, a brave and intrepid officer, formerly attached to the

Mexican squadron under Sir Gregor MacGregor, and General Aurey.[31] The Spaniards immediately began to fire from the battery and both schooners, whilst the brig advanced silently and steadily, towards them, with the evident intention of boarding; and, had she been able to do so, I fully anticipated their capture, as it was with much difficulty that the officers of the schooners, could keep the men to their guns. Fortunately for the Spaniards the breeze died away, almost to a calm, at the moment when the Patriot vessel came in contact with the current setting out of the river; consequently she was under the necessity of letting go an anchor, within musket-shot of the fort and schooners. At this disadvantage, she proceeded to get a spring on her cable; and, before firing a gun, brought her broadside to bear on the schooners, which were moored so close together that the jib-boom end of one was nearly over the taf-rail of the other. In this position, the Centinela continued the action nearly four hours, against twenty-eight pieces of cannon, the random and ill-directed fire of the Spaniards alone preventing them from sinking her at her anchors.

Being by this time much damaged in her hull and rigging, she cut her cable; and, assisted by the current from the river, and a light breeze which sprung up, drifted out of the reach of grape and cannister shot, evidently prepared to repel any attack, if her enemies had dared to become the assailants. The Spanish officers, indeed, called out to their men "aborda! aborda!" but not one of these gentlemen offered to set the example, by jumping into the boats;—she reached the Corn Islands next day in a sinking state; but, few men were killed on either side.

While still employed at the gun which I assisted in working, the officers of the Flor-del-Mer came on board to congratulate us, on what they should have rather considered an escape than a victory.

31. The city of Buenos Aires, in Argentina, had removed its ruling Spanish viceroy in May, 1810, and had joined in an Argentine declaration of independence on July 9, 1816, maintaining thenceforward her independent or "patriot" position while Bolívar yet struggled for the same in Colombia and Venezuela. Roberts' impression that "the Spaniards" still held San Juan and Nicaragua stems from the unwillingness of the authorities in León (expressed September 28, 1821) to go along with the independence proclamation of Guatemala, followed by León's determination (expressed October 12, 1821) for union with imperialist Mexico, which at first hoped for rule by a Bourbon prince and even under the rule of Agustín de Iturbide (May, 1822–February, 1823) followed a course quite different from that of Buenos Aires and Bolívar. The "Mexican squadron" of McGregor and Aury is apparently a reference to ships commanded by those two men in privateering attacks against the Spaniards, 1817–19. See Ch. 1 nn. 19, 28.

One of them came, up to me, and looking steadfastly in my face, swore he knew me, and called to the officers on the quarter-deck to desire I might be secured, as I was a prize-master belonging to the Centinela, who had lately taken his vessel, and plundered his person, under the worst circumstances of aggravation and insult. Such a charge as this, after I had, during so many hours, risked my life in defence of their vessels, completely confounded me; and this confusion was, by all present, taken as evidence of my guilt. The rumour of a spy from the insurgent brig being discovered on board the Estrella, soon spread, and when I was carried on board the other schooner, to be put in irons, her crew were desired to see if any of them could recognise me. A hard featured villanous looking fellow stept forward, and accused me of being the sail-maker of the brig in question; that he would swear that when he was boarded and captured, on his last voyage from the Havannah to Trujillo, I had, in my insatiable thirst for plunder, cut his trowsers, in which he had a number of doubloons, with my boarding-knife, and nearly murdered him.[32]

This was considered sufficient evidence; it was in vain I protested my innocence; I was immediately ironed, and sent under a guard to the fort. My Indians were exceedingly surprised at seeing me brought ashore in this manner; and, before I could fully explain the cause to Brown, I was hurried to the guardhouse.

Next morning, about nine o'clock, I was conducted before the commandant and a number of officers assembled; and, as they appeared to be fully satisfied that I was, or had been, an officer of the Centinela, a paper was presented for signature, which was said to contain the charges made out against me; and the depositions of the two Spaniards now made upon oath.

I resolutely refused, however, to sign this paper, on the ground of my imperfect knowledge of the Spanish language, and having no interpreter on whom I could depend: that I was perfectly innocent, and might, by signing it, criminate myself. They remanded me back to prison; and the commandant of the fort . . . sent me some refreshment. In the evening I overheard one of my guards assuring his comrade that the officers were perfectly satisfied of my being a spy; and had, therefore, come to the resolution of executing me without delay. Early in the morning I was again brought before these judges, and desired to sign the paper, but still refused. After a short delibera-

---

32. "Boarding-knife"=blubber knife.

tion, a sergeant and six men, conducted me to the back of the fort; two others were employed to support me as I could not walk without assistance, both legs being in irons; another person carried an empty cask; and a fourth a chair for the commandant. Arrived at the back of the fort the cask was put down, and I was ordered to sit upon it, the commandant placed his chair close beside me, and informed me by means of an interpreter, that I had been regularly tried, and that it was the opinion of all present, that sufficient evidence had been adduced to prove that I was an officer belonging to the Patriot service, and that, having entered the harbour as a spy, they were justified in putting me to death in a summary manner;— he therefore exhorted me to address myself to Almighty God, as in the course of another half-hour I should cease to live. He then ordered the soldiers to load their pieces and draw up in line about twelve yards distant. When the sergeant came forward to blindfold me with a handkerchief, I refused to submit to it; and on turning my head from side to side to prevent it, and as a sign of my innocence—my eye fell upon my poor Indians, who had been brought out to witness the execution. The agitation of my mind at this crisis cannot be expressed: these men being much attached to me, raised that loud and melancholy howl or lamentation, which I had, often, heard them chant at the death of one of their own tribe. Despair fell so heavily on my mind that all hope utterly left me; but on acquiring new courage, I instantly turned to the commandant, who, by this time, had risen from his chair, and observed, in broken Spanish, and English, that, if he was determined to murder an innocent man, a subject of Great Britain, I could die without being blindfolded. Every tongue was now hushed; save those of my poor Indians, expecting the fatal word or signal, which was to expedite me from a world of strife. I was in the act of recommending my soul to God, when suddenly I heard the splashing of oars; and, a large boat, hitherto concealed by the bushes and bamboos, appeared close to us!

A feeling now darted into my mind, that I should escape the pending catastrophe; and, in consequence, I now and afterwards acted with more boldness than was, perhaps, warranted by my critical situation. The commandant suspended the execution, and I was conducted to the guardhouse.

The boat proved to be a government express, down the river from the castle of San Carlos, with a reinforcement of men, under the command of an officer, who was to supersede the present commander.

I was shortly ordered before the new commandant, to whom I explained my reasons for having called at the harbour, the time I had been living on the coast, and, the nature of my trade with the Indians. I referred him to papers, found in my vessel, corroborative of my statement; but, unfortunately, he could find no one to read them.

I was afterwards ordered to hold myself in readiness to be sent up the river San Juan; and desired to communicate the same order to the Indians, who were now allowed to visit me. Brown seemed to have his horrid ideas of the Spaniards fully confirmed; and, at that moment, swore vengeance against them, if chance should ever place man, woman, or child, of their country, at his disposal; I told him to keep up the spirits of his companions; that I should never desert them, even if I lost all; and, that I equally relied on their attachment.

I was again brought before the new commandant, who desired me to sign an inventory of the articles found in my vessel: but, I saw, that it contained not one eighth part of them; that my trunks, and cases, had been broken open, and plundered of nearly all their contents; the soldiers had taken even my apparel and were wearing it before my face, but, I was obliged to be satisfied with an assurance, that all justice would be done to me, at San Carlos. The provisions which I had in my vessel were ordered to be sent ashore for the support of myself and Indians. I have been the more particular on the preceding occurrences, because they show one of the hair-breadth escapes of an eventful life; and, at the same time, explain the cause of my journey into the interior of a country, which, the jealousy of the Spanish government, had hitherto shut up from the inspection of Englishmen.

In the evening three large craft, by the Spaniards called bongos, came from the schooners to the fort, loaded with dry goods, and demijohns, or large jars of brandy and Dutch gin. Into one of these boats, I was put, with two of the Indians; the other two being sent to a separate bongo, all ironed.

. . . We descried the castle of San Carlos, the Gibraltar of the Lake of Nicaragua. . . . Turning a bend in the river we came . . . in view of the lower part of the fort and village now within one mile distant. . . . Our people took in their sails, and plied their oars so vigorously, that we were soon opposite the castle, from the walls of which we were hailed, by an officer, using a speaking trumpet, with as much formality as if hostility had been anticipated. We lay on our oars in the mean time, the bongos continuing to drop astern with the current, until the requisite answers had been given, and permission to approach obtained. Having pulled through the strong current setting out of the lake, we landed in front of the castle, where we were met by the commandant, with a guard, and half the population of the place apparently attracted by curiosity to see *the spy of the Independents, and his "Indios Bravos;"*—their looks gave evidence that they considered my situation desperate.

We entered the fort by a drawbridge of great strength and magnitude, suspended by enormous iron chains; and, through two immense gates, into a long arched passage, having on each side several cells, those to the right appearing to extend round the whole side of the building. Every door had a strong iron grating, about two feet square, to admit light and air; and there appeared to be prisoners within most of them. Into one of these places I was commanded to enter, and was left to my own cogitations. I gave way for some time to the most melancholy reflections, from which I was agreeably roused by the entrance of a lieutenant and two people, bringing me a supper from the Governor Don Juan Blanco's table, with a bottle of wine and some agua-ardiente. The lady of this lieutenant kindly sent me a pillow and blanket; and he informed me that the Governor would see, and interrogate me in the morning. . . . Next morning the Commandant informed me that he had been looking over my papers, amongst which were some religious tracts, and ten or twelve New Testaments, which he seemed to consider likely to be of a political nature; but that, as he could not find any of his people to explain them properly, he had determined to send them to Granada.[33] He gave me liberty, in the mean time, to walk about the place, of which I immediately availed myself; and I was shortly joined by the friendly lieutenant, who invited me to his quarters, where we were visited by several other officers, one of whom I fortunately recognised to be a person who I had once seen on board a Jamaica trader. He also recollected me, and immediately reported the circumstance to the Governor, who ordered me to attend him next day at his house, which is situated on rising ground near the castle, commanding an extensive view of the lake, and the village of San Carlos. The village contains

---

33. Roberts explains elsewhere (his page 194) that these tracts and Testaments "had been received from the Rev. Mr. Armstrong . . . , to be distributed among the British settlers on the Mosquito Shore, and such Spanish or other traders, as might . . . be desirous of having them."

about one hundred and fifty houses, the walls are of clay or mud, of considerable thickness, neatly white-washed, which gives them the appearance of cleanliness and solidity....

On the afternoon of the day following that last mentioned, I waited on the Governor, who had now determined to send me across the lake, along with my books and papers, to Granada; and said that, in consequence of the information communicated, by one of his officers, he was inclined to believe I was merely an agent of the contraband traders on the coast. He assured me that my Indians should be taken care of during my absence, and, inviting me to spend the evening with his family, treated me with the greatest hospitality, endeavouring however to draw information from me on subjects of a political nature; and regarding occurrences which, for fear of implicating myself, I found it necessary to appear not to understand. Occasionally sheltering myself from his questions by answering, "no intiende Senor,"—expressions of suspicion and disappointment repeatedly escaped from him. He stated that, when Trujillo in the Bay of Honduras was attacked by the insurgent General Aurey, he was commandant of the place; and, that Aurey, who had landed his troops about three miles from the town, had been defeated by the Charib troops alone,—the Spaniards never having come out of their shelter. I happened to know more of the affair, and of the nature of the expedition, than he was aware of; and, although I found it necessary to be prudent, I parried many of his inquiries on other subjects by questions regarding Trujillo, and the attack upon it, which he did not feel disposed to answer.[34] I was accommodated with a hammock in the piazza of his house; and being to depart for Granada next morning, his good lady and her daughter presented me with a quantity of chocolate, bread, cheese, eggs, wine, and cane spirits (agua-ardiente del cania.) My critical situation called forth the most tender expressions of their pity, and the kindest demonstrations of benevolence.

... We came in view of the city of Granada, standing on a gently rising ground, at a small distance from the lake. In the evening we landed at the Playa....

On landing we were received by some black soldiers, stationed as guards at some warehouses built here for the reception of goods. One of these men informed me, in good English, that he had run away

34. See Ch. 1 n. 19.

from his master, a Honduras merchant; and, travelling from Omoa to Guatémala, had there entered the Spanish service,—had been sent to Realejo,—then to the city of León,—and, finally, to Granada. He expressed an inclination to do me any service in his power, and I perceived that the whole of the company, to which he belonged, was made up of such runaway slaves, chiefly from the Island of St. Domingo;—they were all well armed and clothed. The Playa, or landing-place, is a mere open beach without any wharf or other conveniency for shipping goods, which have to be carried to and from the Bongos in small canoes, or on the backs of men or mules, a good cable's length into the water, which is here very shallow, with a bottom of fine sand. The approach to the city is by a good road; and about half a mile from the lake we passed a large monastery and, two churches in the *Calle de Playa,* before entering the market place. I was conducted directly to the Governor's house, before which is a handsome gateway; and, while waiting in the porch until called for, I noticed over the inner-door, a poorly painted portrait, bearing the modest inscription, *"Viva Ferdinando Septimo, el libertador adorable de Europa!!"*

I was shortly ushered into a large hall, where I found the acting Governor, several military officers, a priest, and an interpreter, through whom a great many questions were put to me; but, so far as I could understand Spanish, the interpreter gave replies essentially different to those elicited from me. Being ordered to withdraw in charge of a sergeant and two soldiers, I was conducted to the barracks, and thrust into a cell similar to that which I had first occupied at San Carlos. The black soldier, who had spoken to me at the landing-place, told me, through the grating, that it was the conviction of the Governor and his friends, that I actually was a spy of the Revolutionists; as was more particularly evident by the pamphlets in my possession. Suspecting this man was sent to obtain information to be carried to the Governor, I related particularly how I received these books, and the object of my voyage; observing to him that the answers I had given had not been fairly interpreted: and, I entreated him to make this known to the Governor, from whom he returned about ten o'clock with a supper, some agua-ardiente, and a bottle of wine; with an intimation that I should undergo another examination in the morning.

On sounding this fellow I found him shrewd and intelligent: he hinted that, were I to request it, he himself might be permitted to act as interpreter; he owned that he wished, from motives of self-interest, that he might be ordered to attend me to the city of León, an idea which I encouraged, that I might secure his confidence, being desirous, now that I gave up my small property as lost, to see the country.

My cell was intolerably hot, but having undergone much fatigue during the day, I soon forgot my sorrows, and slept until aroused by the beating of the *reveille*, and the noise of the soldiers hurrying to the parade at daybreak next morning. In a few minutes the bustle was over; a passing soldier threw me a bundle of cigars, and kindly brought me some fire to light one: he expressed much compassion for my situation; and, giving a cautious glance to each side, told me, "los patriotes" were "muy bueno;" and vented some execrations against the present government. About eight o'clock the soldiers returned, and my door was crowded by people whose curiosity was excited by the report that an Englishman, employed at San Juan by the Patriots, as an agent and spy, had arrived. Many of them evinced a kindly feeling in my favour, who evidently dared not express themselves in other language than that of pity and regret for my present situation. Others there were who cursed me as an insurgent, a spy, a pirate, and a heretic,—but these were few in number compared with others who never retired from the grating, without throwing something into the cell, so that in the course of the morning the floor was covered over with cakes, gingerbread, cheese, chocolate, cigars, and not a few quartos, medios, reals, dollars and other coins. In this whimsical situation I found myself placed like a wild beast in a cage, unable, if ever so much inclined, to withdraw for one moment, from observation. I had this consolation, however, that nearly all my visitors seemed to consider themselves bound to pay something for the sight, or contribute towards my support. Many of them, who were evidently afraid of being observed by those attached to the existing government, hastily threw money into the cell and withdrew; almost every one who peeped in, had a cigar in his mouth, and the smoke and heat became so intolerable, that I found myself in danger of suffocation, which obliged me to beg a few minutes respite, that fresh air might be admitted. When the smoke began to disperse, I set myself to collect the various articles which had been thrown into my cell; and was agreeably surprised to find that the contributions in cash amounted to twenty-seven dollars, besides sweetmeats, chocolate, cheese, gingerbread, cigars, &c. sufficient for several week's consumption. About eleven o'clock my negro friend brought me a substantial breakfast, and a bottle of wine; and what rather surprised me—the chocolate was in a silver pot, on a tray covered by a clean white napkin. I mentioned the donations I had received in the morning, to show that I could now reward him if he acted faithfully, giving him a dollar *as earnest*, and impressing upon him the certainty that I should be able to provide amply for every expense if we were sent to León:—He retired, assuring me I might depend upon him, and carrying my thanks to the good lady, the Governor's mother, who had sent me breakfast. I was again visited by several persons desirous of seeing the pirate, patriot, or heretic; for, in the opinion of all, I must be one of these, and consequently an extraordinary character. A heretic, they agreed, I must be, at all events, as I neither prayed, crossed myself, nor pulled off my hat, on passing the churches. In the evening, after the acting governor had taken his *siesta*, I was conducted to his house, and examined by the same assemblage as on the preceding night, and by two additional *padres*; the negro was there, and the former interpreter, who having shamefully misinterpreted my reply to a question regarding the introduction of British goods at Matina, and persisted in eluding my meaning, I requested the negro to make known, to his Excellency, the ignorance and wilful prevarication. This at once called forth the malignity of the man, an old Spaniard, who could not read one word of English:—he denounced me immediately as an insurgent and spy, alluded to the books, and observed to the padres, who had put many questions on the subject, that he had no doubt I had distributed pamphlets in the Spanish tongue; and that I ought to be sent to León, where it would soon be ascertained what, and who I was. As I persisted in declaring my innocence, and expressed my willingness to proceed to León, the Governor informed me I should depart next day, assuring me, through my negro interpreter, that I should want for nothing,—that his duty compelled him to act, at present, with rigour against those who were known to be disturbers of the government, but that if it eventually turned out that my representations were correct, Don Miguel Seravia, the governor of the district of León, who was the proper person to decide on my case, would treat me with the greatest justice.[35] I was conducted back to the barracks, ordered a better apartment than the cell I had last occupied, and had liberty to walk about in the square. Next day I again attended the deputy-governor, who informed me that every thing had been prepared for my departure to León, and that a sergeant, my negro

---

35. Miguel González Saravia, the last governing intendant of Nicaragua by Spanish appointment, held office from 1818 until April, 1823.

friend, and three other black soldiers, well armed and mounted on mules, would form my escort. A good horse, a pair of boots, and enormous iron spurs, had been provided for me; and in about twenty minutes after setting off, we found ourselves clear of the city, on a good road, sufficiently broad to admit of our riding abreast.

We entered Managua . . . , and rode directly to the house of the alcalde, from whom the sergeant demanded provisions for his party. After giving the negro soldier money to buy wine, &c. for the entertainment of the escort, I endeavoured to rest myself in an open apartment, but was soon annoyed by finding the house beset by people anxious to get a sight of the *Independente*. I had no remedy but patience, and I endeavoured to bear their scrutiny without manifesting discontent; many of them laid down money before their departure, and I was at last relieved from their troublesome attentions by the *cura* of the place, who kindly procured the sergeant's permission to take me to his own house where I was free from intrusion. After an excellent dinner, followed by coffee, my worthy host . . . retired, according to the universal custom in these countries, to enjoy his *siesta*; and, a hammock being slung for me, I was requested to do the same; the room was darkened, and in a few minutes the house was as quiet, as if it had been midnight. In the evening I was questioned regarding my connection with the Patriots, and the progress of the revolution in Mexico and South America; but I was necessarily obliged to give general and very cautious replies.

My good host seemed so pleased with me, that he wrote to his friend the Governer of León in my favour; and requesting that, if I should be declared innocent of the charges against me, I might be permitted to remain with him a few days on my return; and during the remainder of the evening treated me with the greatest kindness and hospitality.

. . . The road was very good, and lay through a level well wooded country abounding in game. Deer were frequently seen on the road, and stopped to gaze on us, attracted apparently by the soldiers red jackets, until they were within a very short distance. We passed several cultivated farms; and in some of the court yards, we saw deer mixed with the cattle, as if domesticated. Several large waggons and mules were on the road, and every appearance indicated our approach to a populous city. About seven in the morning we emerged from the woods into what may properly be designated the plain of León, covered by immense fields of Indian corn, and large grass plains extending as far as the eye could reach, covered with numerous herds of cattle, and horses; many of the latter would have been considered beautiful even in Europe. . . .

Before we entered the city, we passed the cathedral, a building of considerable magnitude in the form of a cross, surrounded by the houses and gardens of the clergy. . . . By an easy ascent, we then came to the suburbs, the houses one story high, built of hardened clay white washed. Having passed two or three mean looking streets, we entered the city, and the sergeant proceeded immediately to the Government House with his despatches. I did not wait long until I was ordered, by an officer, to follow him; and, being ushered into an apartment, Don Miguel Seravia in a few minutes made his appearance. He addressed me with the mildness and urbanity of a gentleman, inquiring, in good English, what unfortunate circumstance had induced me to enter the harbour of San Juan? Encouraged by his manner, I briefly related every thing that had happened to me then, and subsequently. The packet of papers, and the pamphlets that had created so much distrust, were in his hands; he read and examined part of the latter, and referred to my papers, among which were some invoices of goods intrusted to me, and some letters from my family in England. I directed his Excellency's attention to the dates of these papers, which clearly proved that I could not have been present at the capture of the vessels, or guilty of the crimes charged against me. He seemed convinced in a moment of my innocence, and expressed some dissatisfaction at the stupidity of the Commandants who had ordered me forward, telling me that I should forthwith return by the same route.

In the meantime I was ordered to one of the apartments of the Cuartel, usually appropriated for the accommodation of officers; but charged not to quit these barracks, or to have free communication with the inhabitants of the city.

Early next morning after my arrival, I was ordered to wait on the Governor, with whom I found the Archbishop and "Don Allemagne," as the Spaniards called him, a merchant of Bremen or Hamburgh, who had been some years resident here. The Governor had now the *finesse* to conceal his knowledge of the English language, and the German acted as interpreter. I was particularly questioned regarding the force and intentions of the Patriot cruisers, &c. in the

Charibbeian Sea; but, pleading ignorance on that subject, I was examined regarding the intercourse between the Indians and English, and whether I knew of any communication by water from the Lake of Nicaragua to the Atlantic, otherwise than by the River San Juan. The Governor having, as he thought, elicited all the information on these subjects in my power to give him, told me I should leave León in three days, that in the meantime I might walk about the city; but he refused the request of the German who wished me to remove to his house, and also my request to remain a few days longer, observing, that if my health was bad, I would be better in the country than in town, and that I might remain with my friend the Cura of Managua a month if I wished it; that four reals a day would be allowed for my travelling expenses, and that Don Juan Blanco, should have orders to return as much of my property as could be discovered on my arrival at San Carlos; but that my small vessel would be condemned. His Excellency expressed regret that I had experienced so much annoyance, observing, that, under all circumstances, the Commandant at the harbour of San Juan would have been perfectly justified, by the appearances against me, if he had put me to death.

On gaining the street, I expressed my thanks to the German for his kindness, and promised to visit him;—he observed, that I might consider myself fortunate in being so soon allowed to leave the country, that a resolution was hourly expected to take place, which, added to my having assisted in defence of the vessels at San Juan, was the sole cause of my having received permission to depart.[36]

... In the evening the German accompanied me in a walk through the city. It covers a good deal of ground, and is, on the whole, handsome;—many of the streets are broad, and intersect each other at right angles. The houses are large, but none exceed two stories;—the fronts in general white washed, and the lower windows secured by bars of wrought iron, or ornamented gratings, which, with the shutters and lattices—the upper ones painted a light green—have a cool and pleasant appearance. Most of the houses are entered by a large gate leading into the court-yard or quadra, round which are

36. The resolution of Nicaraguan affairs "hourly expected to take place" did not come until a half year after these incidents, when González Saravia lost his position. The shifting tides of Mexican imperialism were enough to cause the intendant to feel insecure, however, at the time at which Roberts was detained.

the warehouses or store-rooms of the merchants, the apartments of the domestics, the stables, and other offices. Usually a piazza or portico runs round the court, affording a complete shelter from the sun and rain. The centre is enlivened with a few trees, shrubs and flowers, or, in some instances, there is a fountain or reservoir of water. The roofs are in general flat and overhang the footpaths, which are clean, and paved with large pebbles. The city and suburbs, according to the estimate of my friend, contain about three thousand houses. . . . I observed eight churches, exclusive of the Cathedral, and several monasteries and nunneries. The markets are abundantly supplied with beef, pork, fish and fowls; and all the varieties of fruit and vegetables produced in a tropical climate, or even in the more temperate regions. . . . The general mode of living is luxurious. My allowance from the Government was four reales, or half a dollar per day, which was a great deal more than sufficient to enable me to live, in every respect, like the officers in the Cuartel, whose daily provision was as follows:—Shortly after daybreak half a pint of excellent chocolate or strong coffee, with a slice or two of bread; about nine o'clock a breakfast of fish, flesh, or fowl, and sometimes all these; to which was added an omelet, tortillas, and excellent wheaten bread, with claret or agua-ardiente:—about noon a soup composed of boiled beef and vegetables, and a saucer of sweetmeats, for those who chose them, ushered in a dinner consisting of the same materials as the breakfast, after which a cup of strong coffee prepares them for their siesta or afternoon's sleep, to which all then retired, the city, from that period until about four in the evening, being as quiet as at midnight. About nine supper was served,—thus ending the day, the principal business of which seemed to be eating, drinking, smoking and sleeping. The meanest persons smoke tobacco, although it is the dearest article in the place. . . .

On the fourth morning from my arrival, I again received orders to attend the Governor, who desired me to prepare to depart for Granada the following day, under the same escort; but, that I was not now to consider myself a prisoner, and might take my own time in travelling.

. . . At Managua . . . my good friend the cura was from home, but his family received me with the greatest kindness and attention; refreshments were set before me, and when he arrived, he embraced and welcomed me with all the warmth of an old friend, expressing himself much satisfied with the manner in which I had been received in León.

At supper we had much conversation regarding the political state of the country; and although the cura expressed himself cautiously, it was evident he contemplated with pleasure, the change progressively taking place. Some of his friends having called to inquire for him, readily joined in our conversation; and, over a bowl of punch, a liquor I taught him to compound, reserve was soon banished from his convivial board; he observed, that he hoped the day was not far distant when Managua, and the Interior of Central America, would be better known to my countrymen, and every one seemed to speak freely of the state of the country, deplored the commercial and other restrictions under which they laboured; and it was evident that the worthy cura, who is a native Creole, and his friends, wished well to the cause of independence, and anticipated a great, and certain change in the political government of Central America. I ventured to explain, that although for some time I had confined my exertions entirely to commercial pursuits, I once commanded a vessel in the service of the Independents, and wished well to their cause. Some of the gentlemen present expressed their hopes, that the trade would soon be more open; that British goods of almost every description were much wanted; that the towns in the vicinity of the Lakes of Nicaragua and León could consume and pay for a very large quantity; and that, by perseverance, I might then avail myself of the knowledge I had acquired, to recover more than I had at present lost.

There seems no doubt that my detention in Granada was to give the schooners Flor del Mer, and Estrella, time to receive their cargoes and proceed to sea, before I should be able to leave the coast, or be in a situation to communicate with any of the Independent cruizers. The cargoes consisted of the choicest productions of the country, collected and sent down in bongos, and these schooners, with their cargoes, would have made the fortune of any cruiser who might have captured them. Contrary to the Governor's promise, I was not allowed to proceed in the bongo which sailed on the first day of the month;—that boat was accompanied by others, having on board goods to complete the cargoes above named. About eight days afterwards I had a final interview with the Governor, who furnished me with the means of laying in provisions; and, I obtained a passage in one of these bongos, belonging to traders or sutlers, who cross the lake to San Carlos with groceries, liquors, tobacco, &c. at the time the soldiers there, and on the river San Juan, are receiving their pay. These people open a temporary store for the sale of their commodities, and generally realize a profit upon cocoa, coffee, &c. of one hundred to one hundred and fifty per cent. . . .

I left Granada in the boat mentioned, with two men and a woman, the joint owners, a padrone, and a crew of twelve Indians. . . .

On the evening of the sixth day we landed at San Carlos. Immediately I waited on the Governor, who now received me politely, and mentioned that he had recovered some of the goods which had been plundered from my little vessel; that these would be returned to me, and that my Indians were well, but that he had been obliged to keep four of them confined, to prevent their escaping, but that one was allowed to be at liberty, in succession, to provide additional comforts for his companions. Brown came to me overjoyed at my safety; but loudly complained that the Governor . . . had used every means to induce them to criminate me as a spy for the Patriots, offering to give them clothes, send them safe home with presents, &c., but all to no purpose. Finding these efforts of no avail, they were then confined to the castle, as already mentioned, and compelled to perform menial services for the officers. They were allowed only half rations, and the remainder of their subsistence was procured by the labour, or solicitations, of the one at liberty in the village—a line of conduct, than which none could have been better adapted to keep up their enmity to the Spanish name. Some of the Spaniards may have since suffered for it,—they were now allowed their liberty, with half a real a day for subsistence. I gave them money, supplied Brown with a good suit of clothes, and each of the others with a new shirt and trowsers; bargaining with the woman who crossed the lake with me, for their provisions. This conduct seemed to surprise the Spaniards, who were not at all aware of the genuine worth of these men. . . .

I received, from the Governor, about three dozen of moscheats which he had recovered; with a small quantity of dry goods; and I was permitted to dispose of them in the village. The moscheats cost me about forty-five shillings per dozen, and I sold them at from two to three dollars each; the other goods produced me about one hundred dollars. On finishing this business I began to prepare for my departure, by providing a sufficient stock of provisions, chocolate, rum, &c. for myself and my Indians; two bongos with supplies of provisions, and a reinforcement of men for the defence of the river, being ordered shortly to proceed.

On the afternoon of the third day we arrived at the fort. I do not think we were more than thirty-six hours in motion, descending the river, and I am convinced that the Indians could ascend to the lake in one of their common dories, with great ease in three days; and, would come down in less than half of that time. The commandant at the battery received me politely, regretted that I had been so long detained at Granada and San Carlos, which had been requested by those interested in the two schooners, who were still suspicious I might be in communication with the Independent cruisers:—that for fear of being again attacked in the harbour, the garrison had been augmented; but that the vessels had sailed some time ago, and were now either in port, or in the hands of their enemies.

The day after we returned to the harbour, some Mosquito men arrived. . . . They had heard of our seizure, and, in common with all the other Mosquito men, had orders from the admiral to furnish me, on my reappearance, with all things necessary to enable me to reach the Cape without delay, there being "a King's order," to supply provisions, men, horses, dories, &c.; and so eager were they to comply with this order, and hear our adventures, that they immediately proceeded for the Rama settlement, without waiting to kill manati, according to their first intention. Accordingly, after taking another view of the place where I had so narrowly escaped death, and having again viewed the entrances to the river in as careful a manner as prudence would admit, I embarked with these Indians, and, at the Rama settlement, was received by Pedro, the chief man, with great kindness and attention. He furnished a large canoe to convey us to Bluefields, and from thence to Pearl Kay Lagoon, where we were welcomed with great rejoicing, it having been reported that I had been put to death, and the Indians sold as slaves. At this place I parted with the Ramas, and . . . on the following day, we reached Prinzapolca the native place of my Indians. By some means or other our approach had been made known, and before we had well entered the savannah leading to the settlement, we were met by a great many of the people, who showed the most lively joy at the safe return of their friends, thus, as it were, restored from death. . . . Para the headman, with other elders, who . . . had, for some weeks past, contemplated an expedition against some of the Spanish settlements nearest to them, with the view of seizing as many Spaniards as possible, to be held as hostages for the safety of Brown and his companions—made many inquiries regarding the strength of the Spanish posts, and a mishla drink being prepared, we spent the evening of our return in mirth and rejoicing.

During the few days I remained at Prinzapolca settlements, the headman earnestly entreated that I would determine on settling entirely amongst them, assured me that if I did so and became identified as one of their tribe, they would not only defend me to the last man, but that I might command such a trade, through their means, both on the coast and in the interior, as would in a few years make me wealthy. Although my connection at the moment prevented me from listening to their proposals, I had no doubt of their feasibility. I stated to Brown and his companions, that, by the loss of my goods, vessel, &c., I was deprived of the means of remunerating them at present for the time they had lost, and the distress they had suffered; but I divided the remainder of my money among them, reserving barely as much as would pay my expenses to the Bay of Honduras. At first they not only refused remuneration entirely, but, to my surprise, their friends told me that they had reserved a part of the tortoise-shell intended for me before they heard of my seizure, that it was now entirely at my service, and that I might pay for it hereafter when I had recovered my losses. Moreover, although Brown and his Indians had, through my misfortunes, lost an entire fishing season, they generously insisted, upon paying over to their countrymen, the money they had just received from me, on account of this shell—a trait of character I might have in vain looked for among the Mosquito-men: But it must be kept in mind that these Prinzapolca Indians are of the genuine unmixed breed, and that, in all my visits to them, and in every transaction, I had found them just, upright, and honourable in their dealings. . . .

I arrived at Cape Gracias a Dios in the latter end of October, and was received by the King with every mark of attention. He expressed much satisfaction at my safe return; explained the measures he had taken to assist me, and seemed pleased that his letters had been so far attended to. I agreed, at my departure, to take charge of two very large dories, which he was desirous of sending to the British settlement in the Bay of Honduras, to convince the merchants there of the extraordinary size, and excellent quality of the timber which could be procured in his country.

The large dories . . . being put in order for the passage to Belize, and a crew of ten expert Indians appointed to each, with a plentiful supply of provisions, I took charge of the one made of cedar; and the other, of mahogany, was intrusted to Racon, a Mosquito man, acquainted with the navigation of the coast, and with the different kays and shoals in the bay,—we were accompanied by other Mosquito-men in canoes with various articles for sale at Belize, upon the value of which I was to have a commission.

We . . . considered it prudent to run over the bar at Black River, to endeavour to procure a compass from some of the new settlers. We found these people in good spirits, and in hopes of being soon joined by emigrants daily expected from England.—I here met with two chiefs of the neighbouring Kharibs, one named Big, the other Little Louis, the former of whom had, with some of his people, been assisting the settlers to erect houses, and clear ground, and enable them to secure a good crop of early provisions. I promised to meet these men at their principal settlement; and Mr Warren, and Colonel Gordon, having furnished me with what I wanted, we took advantage of the landbreeze in the evening, and again recrossed the bar. . . .

These Kharibees, or Caribs as they are usually called in Europe, were originally natives of the Leeward Islands, but having become troublesome to the Government of St Vincents, were, sometime ago, banished from that Island, and conveyed to Roatán or Rattan, an island in the Gulf of Honduras, and means afforded them for forming a settlement there. . . . Being visited by the Spaniards, from Trujillo, many of them went to that place, and built a village to the westward of the town. As their liberty had been guaranteed, many of them entered the Spanish service, under subalterns appointed from their own tribe; and, at present, they are the most numerous part of the population of Trujillo.

Some of them, however, who were at first discontented with their situation, emigrated from thence, and from Roatán, to the Mosquito Shore. . . . The Mosquito King having given them all the encouragement in his power, they extended a chain of small settlements as far as Patook. But by the oppressive conduct of the late chief, Robinson, and his successor Barras, they have for the most part retired, and concentrated themselves to the northward of Black River, where they are rapidly increasing in numbers, and now bid defiance to their enemies. Their houses are built more neatly than those of the Mosquito-men, and have an air of greater comfort and independence. Each house has its small plantation attached to it, kept in very neat order; they had assisted the few settlers at Black River in erecting houses and clearing ground; but these settlers were not possessed of sufficient capital to turn the labours of these men to farther account. Louis, one of their headmen, informed me, that they never interfered with the Indians, by intermarriages or otherwise; and, whatever their ancestors of St Vincents may have been, they are now honest and industrious. . . .

They are in general of a dark red colour approaching to, and often not easily distinguishable from black; they have the short curly hair of the Negro; but are remarkably clean skinned, well made, active, and vigorous. . . .

We left the Kharibees in the evening, and . . . stood over for Bonacca or Guanaja, a small island discovered in 1502 by Columbus on his fourth voyage, when he had his first interview with the natives of the continent. We reached this island early on the following morning, and landed opposite a watering place in an excellent harbour on the south side; the beach, above high watermark, was thickly covered by cocoa nuts; and near the watering place, innumerable tracks of the wild hog. . . . From the east end of Bonacca to the small island of Barbareta, there is an unconnected chain of reefs and patches of rock. . . . We landed on Barbareta, which is thickly overgrown with prickly plants and thick underwood, on the borders of which I found three or four sorts of wild grapes. Our fishers procured a large green turtle, and caught some very fine fish; in the evening we pursued our voyage, running along the remaining part of Barbareta . . . towards the island of Roatán.

Roatán is about thirty miles long, and eight or nine in breadth; the land is moderately high, covered with wood, except at the west end, where there are some savannahs on which mules and other cattle used to be raised. This beautiful island has an excellent harbour, easily defended; it was once in possession of the English, who erected batteries completely commanding this harbour, and marked out a space at its end for the erection of a town. The woods abound in deer, wild hogs, gibeonites, pigeons, with millions of parrots and other birds, many of them excellent food, and the whole coast swarms with fish and turtle, both green and hawksbill.[37] The English withdrew their troops from it at the time they abandoned the Mosquito Shore, and owing to their

---

37. "Gibeonites" are the more common of two species of pacas, known from central Mexico to southern Brazil, to judge by the description given in Squier, 1855W, pp. 213–14.

liability to attacks from the Indians and others in those troublesome times, none of these fine islands are now inhabited.

From Roatán the Island of Utila is visible; and after a short run we landed at a low beach at the west end, where the water was perfectly smooth. . . . Innumerable flocks of parrots and pigeons were flying about; and cocoa nuts were so very plentiful, that whole cargoes could be procured with very little trouble. . . .

We found, on one of the Kays, . . . a party of fishermen curing fish and turtle for the Belize market; and . . . I had an opportunity of obtaining a passage to Belize in a trading vessel from Omoa, the crew of which had stopped to gather cocoa-nuts for sale there. The Mosquito men being desirous of remaining for the same purpose, and to procure fish for sale at the British settlement, I left *the fleet* under charge of Racon, and they in a few days joined me at Belize. . . .

The suspicion and even hostility with which some officials (left over from the colonial regime) received Orlando Roberts in 1822 were not encountered three years later by the first literary-minded travelers to reach the new state of Guatemala. Three of them arrived at Guatemala City, then the capital of all Central America, within a period of ten days in May, 1825. One was interested in mining, one in merchandising, and one in diplomacy; none had to worry about politically inspired detentions.

The first of these three was "Francisco" Lavagnino, who reached the port of Omoa, Honduras, on April 26, 1825, went from there to Izabal on the lake of the same name (where he stayed April 30–May 2), and from Izabal traveled a path to be traced several times in these pages, reaching the capital on May 14. In December, 1825, two years before the appearance of the first book describing the same route, *The New Monthly Magazine and Literary Journal* of London published an article which included five pages of extracts from Lavagnino's journal. Other information in the same report came from the writings of José del Valle and the verbal communications of a "Senor Herrera, Ex-Deputy of the Constituent Assembly of Guatemala."[38] Próspero Herrera served in 1824 as a representative from Tegucigalpa, Honduras, in the Central American constituent assembly. It is obvious that the team from whose efforts the article was drawn is the same as one identified by George Alexander Thompson, the diplomat who arrived in Guatemala City just a few days after Lavagnino. Thompson, speak-

38. "Guatemala," *The New Monthly Magazine and Literary Journal,* 1825.

ing of the mining business, said: "Another company was forming, whilst I was in the capital, under Mr. Viré: his partners afterwards came to London; one of them Don Francisco Lavagnino and the other Don Prospero de Herrera, a cousin of Don José de Valle. The views of this company were chiefly directed towards working the mines in the province of Honduras. . . ."[39] In his journal, Lavagnino (whose nationality is not revealed in these sources) spoke briefly of mining prospects in the department of Chiquimula, Guatemala, close to his route, but dwelt more on the primitiveness of the country through which he traveled. Roberts used Lavagnino's rather uncareful and exaggerated language (such as his mention of "the roarings of lions and tigers" in a "scene of horror and affright around") to show the difficulties of travel by either Omoa or Izabal and the consequent advantage, for arriving at either the Pacific or the "interior" of Central America, of using Roberts' Nicaraguan route.[40]

JAMES WILSON traversed the way from Izabal to Guatemala City May 8–23, 1825, only six to nine days later than Lavagnino. He returned by way of Omoa in August, but died in Belize before he could re-attain his native Scotland. A close friend who admired his life and dedication to religion published in London in 1829 *A Brief Memoir of the Life of James Wilson, (late of Edinburgh,) with extracts from his journal and correspondence, written, chiefly, during a residence in Guatemala, the capital of Central America*. Most of this book, after the introductory pages, is from Wilson's own pen. His employment, that of preparing the way for a London commercial house to do business in Central America, enters little into Wilson's rather laconic diary. His religious differences with the Guatemalans were, on the other hand, a theme nearly always on his mind. Though a young man (he died at the age of twenty-seven) Wilson was so unbending in his puritanical scruples that certain facets of Central American life seemed abhorrent to him. But whether he is dealing with religious polemics or the cost or the manner of living in a strange land, his notes reflect faithfully the reactions of a Scotchman of a humble class to the circumstances he found.

The *Memoir* begins with comment from Wilson's unnamed friend on Wilson's earlier years in Scotland:[41]

39. Thompson, 1829, p. 215.
40. Roberts, 1827, pp. 287–91.
41. Wilson, 1829, pp. 1–3.

The amiable and interesting subject of this Memoir was born in Leith. His father was a sailor on board one of His Majesty's ships, and was lost . . . during a tremendous hurricane. His mother was left destitute, with the care and responsibility of several young orphan children; but, when James became of the proper age, she was so fortunate as to procure his admission into that valuable institution, the *Orphan Hospital,* of Edinburgh. . . .

Young Wilson . . . made fair progress in his education; and his general conduct was so marked by sobriety, steadiness, and order, that, when the period arrived for his leaving the Hospital, the respectable and respected gratuitous treasurer of the institution, the late William M'Lean, Esq., took him into his own warehouse as an apprentice, to learn the business of a woollen draper.

During the period of his apprenticeship, he resided with his mother, in Leith; and he conducted himself so as to secure the approbation and friendship of his master. . . . After the expiration of his apprenticeship he continued in the employ of Mr. M'Lean, but for greater convenience he had removed his residence to lodgings in Edinburgh. . . .

The first occasion on which he began to speak feelingly, and with an apparently deep personal interest in the revelation which God had given concerning his Son Jesus of Nazareth, was in May, 1818. He had been to Mr. Haldane's meeting-house as usual on the Lord's day: and on that Lord's day Mr. James Thomson, so well known as the interesting Agent of the British and Foreign Bible, and British and Foreign School Society in South America, and now in Mexico, was by the church solemnly commended to God, and to the word of his grace, being on the eve of his departure for Buenos Ayres. Mr. Wilson felt a deep interest in the services of the day, . . . and on the following morning he opened his mind to a friend, who was also present, expressing the pleasure and joy he had experienced.

Wilson did not become a missionary for the faith which he adopted, though the missionary motive lingered in his mind. The narrative goes on to explain how he began to read of the emigrations to the United States of America; how he decided to seek his fortune in the new land, sailing there in 1820; and how he quickly came to the conclusion that frontier life was not for him and returned to Scotland. When Mr. M'Lean retired in early 1824, Wilson entered the service of another company of drapers. At this time a friend working for still another firm suggested that Wilson accompany him on a trip to Guatemala. Both new employment and the possibility of engaging in religious activity made the idea attractive. As matters worked out, Wilson made the trip but the friend stayed at home (the friend seems to be the person who is doing the editing). When he left London in November, Wilson sailed for Belize in British Honduras, where he was to meet a gentleman representing the same employers.[42] The narrative continues from the book, soon resolving itself into Wilson's quoted jottings:[43]

After Mr. Wilson's arrival at Honduras, on March 11, 1825, he was busily employed in the commercial business of the house on whose account he had gone abroad.

The gentleman ... under whose direction and auspices he was to act ... arrived at Belize a few weeks after Mr. Wilson, and by the 4th of May of the same year, their arrangements were completed for proceeding into the interior to the city of
GUATEMALA.

" *May 4th*, 1825.—Left Belize in the schooner Mayflower, bound for Izabal, having a convoy from his Majesty's sloop of war, Beaver, consisting of ten men and two officers, in one of the vessel's cutters.

"There have been some reports of pirates having been seen on the coast, which, together with the cargo on board being very valuable, is the reason we are thus protected....

" *May 6th*.—Early in the morning, we anchored outside of the Bar of the river Dulce. About four A. M., run the length of the outer bar, and stuck fast. Descried a schooner at a distance standing in the direction in which we were; as she neared us, made her out to be the George Angas. Boarded her in the man of war's boat. . . . After a good deal of labour, they succeeded in dragging the Mayflower over the outer bar, but she again grounded on what is called the Oyster Bank. From the state of the wind and tide, it was concluded to be useless to make any farther attempt till late in the evening. Our convoy from the Beaver, thinking us safe from any piratical attempt, left us about eight P. M....

42. The gentleman was R. J. Andrew, Esq., partner of the house of Angas and Co. (the Messrs. Angas including G. F. Angas, Esq.), according to Crowe, 1850, pp. 326–29. Andrew and Wilson attended the Baptist mission work in Belize.

43. Wilson, 1829, pp. 60–61, 65–67, 75, 91–92, 99, 114–15, 132, 139, 141–53, 157, 160–61.

"*May 7th.*—About two o'clock this morning, operations were commenced to try and drag the vessel over the bar, but it was daylight ere they were successful. The wind being very light, we were under the necessity of again coming to anchor at the mouth of the river. Got under weigh at eleven A. M., and, after much hard work by warping, reached the middle of the small Lagoon about nine P. M., where we anchored for the evening.

"*May 8.*—Three P. M. arrived at Izabal. This place is composed of about thirty huts, pigsties included—a miserable hole—no sign of cultivation.

"*May 9.*—Detained in Izabal, waiting for mules.

"*May 10.*—Left Izabal at half-past eight A. M. Our train consisted of Mr._____, self, and servant, and five baggage mules. We are accompanied by two American gentlemen, who, besides the mules for themselves and servant, have eight for their baggage. We are all regularly armed, *à la militaire*, with swords and pistols.

"The weather was favourable for encountering the horrors of the much dreaded mountain of Izabal.[44] I had heard much of the badness of the road in this part of our route; but though the account given of it was almost sufficient to deter any from engaging in such a journey, yet it came short of the reality. It is impossible for a person to form any thing like a correct idea of it, unless from actual observation: in the rainy season it must be dreadful.

"*May 23d.*— . . . Arrived at Guatemala about twelve o'clock at noon. The day was very unfavourable for getting a view of the city; but the sight, before descending from the hills into the beautiful and extensive plain in which it is situated, was very imposing. It rained rather heavily all day, which afforded us a specimen, although a faint one, of what the roads must be in the wet season. We are lodged in the spacious mansion of Don ———.

"*June 10.*—The authorities of Belize have been petitioning the Guatemalian government to repeal, or at least to modify, one of their laws which seems to threaten the existence of Belize, namely, the law which declares every slave who enters the central provinces a freeman. After being warmly debated in the House of Representatives, a majority decided in favour of the petition. This decision, however, was

44. The Montaña del Mico, between Izabal and the Río Motagua, was the subject of much commentary in later accounts.

negatived in the senate. The mode of procedure of these two bodies, in which is vested the government of the Republic, is as follows:—In the House of Representatives, a majority of one may decide the fate of any question which comes before them. It is then sent to the senate for its approval. If the senate gives a decision different from the House of Representatives, the case is remitted back to that body to be reconsidered, and then, unless two-thirds decide in favour of their first opinion, the decision of the senate is binding.

" The petition from Belize met with its just doom in the Senate; there not being the required majority, it was negatived. May all such petitions, in whatever part of the world, meet a similar fate![45]

"*June 19th.*— ... We were much importuned to accompany the family to the theatre this evening. Our peremptory refusal seemed to fill them with astonishment. I turned up a Spanish Bible, and requested them to read at Exod. xx. 8, 9, 10, 11, which was complied with. The answer was, 'It is all very good.' They attended mass in the morning, and they thought there could be no harm in recreating themselves a little on the Sunday evening; and, by way of meeting my quotation from Scripture, they adduced the example of two Englishmen, who were frequently present at these dramatic exhibitions on the Sabbath evening. I gave them to understand that, though all England were to set the example, we should not follow it.[46]

"*July 4th.*— ... I have been in the House of Congress to-day, for the first time, which is neat and commodious, and superior to that in which the British Parliament assembles. When we went in, the auditory assembled to listen to the discussion of subjects involving the weal of the state was composed of *two* of the "Ciudadanos;" one of them without stockings or shoes. During the time we remained (about an hour) the audience increased to ten, and before we left decreased to *one!!* So much for the interest felt in the discussions of Congress. The part of the house allotted for members is elevated about four or five feet above that destined for the public, and is separated by a railing. Up both sides is a row of seats for the members; the floor is covered with a sort of

45. As might be expected, British diplomat G. A. Thompson did not share Wilson's outlook on the runaway slaves. His account of the matter, which reads quite differently, is found on pp. 85–87 below.

46. Thompson's amusements included the Sunday theater, which he attended one week after this incident (see below, pp. 269–71). On Wednesday, June 29, Wilson attended a presentation of "The Inquisition Unmasked," which he describes on pp. 271–72 below.

fine matting in general use here, made of party-coloured straw, and somewhat resembling oil cloth. At the top of the hall, in the centre, is the chair of the speaker or president of the house, placed under a canopy of crimson velvet, behind which is the arms of the republic. The members present, other functionaries inclusive, were about thirty:— with a few exceptions, they had the appearance of tradesmen in their Sunday clothes. There seemed to be a number of clergy among them.

" *July* 16.—It is our intention, in returning to Belize, to go by the way of the Motagua, both to diversify the scene, and to avoid crossing the mountain of Izabal, which at this season is almost impassable on account of the rains.

" ... *August* 1*st*.—Left Guatemala this morning, at half past seven A. M.

" *Zacapa, August* 4*th*.— ... Arrived in Zacapa at half-past one o'clock P. M.: we are lodged in the school house. The heat, during to-day's ride, has been most oppressive; we had several times to lay down under the shade of trees; and I felt so debilitated that I frequently thought I should be under the necessity of spending the night in the woods. Mr. ——— was still worse; he dropped behind us; but, having two servants attending him, we felt the less anxious on his account,— as for myself, I required a nurse in place of acting as one. Mr. ——— was several hours later than we in reaching Zacapa: he had to lay down in an Indian rancha (hut), and despatch one of the servants to this place for wine; and it was not till thus supplied with fresh stimulus that he was able to proceed. When here last, the inhabitants were engaged in prayer for rain; this afternoon they have been similarly employed— had a plentiful supply in the evening. The schoolmaster ... states the number of scholars to be fifty.

" *August* 5*th*.—It is agreed to remain here a day, in order to allow our baggage to come up with us. One of the muleteers has just arrived, from whom we learn that our cargo mules are ahead of us at San Pablo, four leagues distant, they missed us, in consequence of having taken a different route. Have despatched the man who brought the intelligence, to bring back Mr. ———'s catere and portmanteau, and my hammock, as there is some intention of remaining here over Saturday. Heat suffocating.[47]

47. The "Indian" village of San Pablo, though it has ceased to exist, was

"*August 6th.*—Have passed a miserable night on the floor; almost dissolved with perspiration, and tormented with insects. Part of our luggage has arrived from San Pablo, by which means I have had the luxury of a change of linen. Our Spanish friends have concluded to spend another day in this place; and Mr. —— also remains to oblige them, but indeed he needs this interval of rest, as he is very much weakened by the fatigue of the part of the journey already accomplished. The heat has been so great that I could scarcely stir or think from exhaustion—have wished for a sleeping draught, to cause me to forget myself for twenty-four hours—my body is covered with the prickly heat—I feel very uncomfortable—this is a trying climate, and a trying journey—I really think it is as much as a man's life is worth to undertake it. Valle's remark, in regard to this country, is certainly a just one, namely, 'fever and death guard its entrance, and salubrity reigns within its bosom.' My dress is a shirt and pair of drill trowsers, and, even with these slight habiliments, the perspiration runs through me like water, upon the slightest exertion. Our companions are rather too fond of frolick. To-night they procured two musicians,—one with a mirimba, and the other with a guitar; they also brought in some Spanish damsels, of what character I know not, though I suspect none of the best; they commenced shouting like madmen;—the consequence was, we got all the *rifraf* of the place around us. Seeing, however, that we neither joined in their amusements, nor showed any sign of relishing them, they adjourned to the street, and commenced serenading throughout the town. Rain late in the evening. Therm. 88° in the forepart of the day, but must have been much higher in the afterpart. I felt as shut up in an oven.

"*August 7th.*—To-day, at quarter from four P.M., the Consul from England to this government arrived at Zacapa, on his way to Guatemala.[48] Therm. at one o'clock A.M. 84°, and middle of the day 85°, in the shade.

"*Gualán, August 8th.*—Left Zacapa at four o'clock. . . . At eleven o'clock, halted at a hut two leagues from Gualán, where we remained

---

mentioned by every traveler who described this route in the 1820's and 1830's. J. J. Jarves, who passed through in 1838, gives an explanation for its decline at that time (see below, p. 138). Wilson's "catere" or "caterie" is a *catre* or portable cot.

48. Wilson's editor explains in a note that this was Mr. (John) O'Reilly, who was murdered by his own servant in Guatemala City in 1828. Thompson had said goodbye to O'Reilly in Izabal on July 24 (see below, pp. 95–96), two weeks before O'Reilly arrived in Zacapa.

during the heat of the day. Previously to reaching this place, I was pitched over the ears of my mule, in consequence of its stumbling with me; providentially, at the place where this happened, the ground was soft, and, though a little stunned, yet I received no particular injury. Started from said hut, and arrived in Gualán at a quarter after five P.M. Road between the two last places comparatively good: fine shade. Thunder, lightning, and rain in the evening.

"*August 9th.*—A good sized decked boat, or as it is called here '*pipante*,' is engaged, and we expect to commence the aquatic part of our journey on Saturday first.[49] Much rain, thunder, and lightning—the thunder appalling. Therm. 89° in the shade.

"*August 10th.*—Our Spanish friends, along with some of the Dons of the place, were engaged most of last night at gambling. There has been much rain to-day, which, with the rain yesterday, has tended to cool the air greatly. Therm. 85°.

"*August 11th.*—The Spaniards and their cronies have again been at cards, till half-past four this morning. This sort of work is a great annoyance to us, but, in present circumstances, we have scarcely a choice. There are four of us, besides three servants and our luggage, huddled into one apartment: this is a specimen of the accommodation to be had in Gualán. . . .

"*Gualán, August 13th.*—The charge by the owner of the *Pipante* for each seron and package of luggage is four dollars;[50] passage money, for each individual, twenty dollars; and he insures the effects to Omoa. Bread in this place is about three times the price that it is in Scotland; a roll, which in the latter place would cost one penny sterling, costs here five pence currency.—Therm. at eight o'clock morning 79°; noon 85°.

"*August 14th.*—This place seems to be a complete nest of gamblers. I am sick of it, and long to quit it. One of our fellow-travellers was out till half-past three o'clock this morning, engaged in gambling; and I understand he lost a good deal of money. They have had their cochineal shipped to-day, and we expect to be off to-morrow morning. Therm. 89°.

"*Rio Motagua, August 15th.*—Left Gualán at eight o'clock A. M. in the Pipante 'Esmaralda,' Porto Rico, Master; number of mariners, including captain, sixteen; passengers eight. . . . Stopped for the night

49. The first Saturday was August 13. The aquatic journey commenced two days later.
50. A "seron" or *serón* is a large basket or pannier.

at half-past two P.M. A canopy is erected upon the beach with the branches of the mahon tree, in order to screen the cateries from the rain. Under this shed our servant killed a poisonous snake, about a yard long, of the species called *Tomy goff*; the bite of this reptile is said to prove deadly in a very few hours.[51] Tormented with mosquitos.

" *August* 16*th*.—It rained very heavily during the most of last night. Started this morning twenty minutes before six; a few minutes after leaving, struck a rock, which caused the boat to leak. Stopped at eight o'clock for breakfast—off again twenty minutes from nine. Saw an alligator basking on a sand bank. The water increasing in the hold, at ten minutes from nine stopped to examine the leak; when it was ascertained that one of the planks was broken in two places. It was found necessary, in consequence, to unload the whole of the cargo, consisting of eighty-two serons cochineal, besides luggage, &c. Quarter past one P. M.—They have taken the boat to a more convenient place, higher up the river, to repair the damage. We are left in the bush; tigers, crocodiles, snakes, and every kind of noxious reptiles and tormenting insects are our companions. Where we are, the banks are steep; to reach the sleeping canopy which they have erected, have to pull ourselves up by the roots of the trees. Señor ——— killed a snake alongside of Mr. ———'s caterie. Very heavy rain in the afternoon. Quarter after six P. M.—The boat has returned. Yesterday we saw huts all along the river; to-day have observed none.

" *August* 18*th*.—Those who had cateries passed the night under the usual canopy of branches; we, who had none, lay squatted along the deck under an awning of the same. Rained all night. Left this morning at twenty minutes before six. . . . At eight stopped for breakfast; off again a quarter before nine: ten minutes after one, stopped for dinner. At this place the boatmen landed their provisions, which were placed in the bush, under a covering of branches, till their return; this, I suppose, was to make room in the hold for what of our luggage was upon deck, to prevent it getting wet in crossing the bar, as well as to lighten the boat. Under weigh again twenty-five minutes after three; moored for the night ten minutes before five: Have seen no houses to-day.

" *August* 19*th*.—A good deal of rain last night—myriads of mosquitos—my bed a coil of ropes. Started a quarter after five A. M. Met a piragua with two men, on their way to Gualán. Passed two canoes

---

51. The "mahon tree" is presumably the *mahoe* or *majagua*, specifically *Hibiscus tiliaceus*. *Tomy goff* is *tamagás* or the fer-de-lance, a pit viper which is seen from Guatemala to Peru and northern Brazil.

moored on the bank of the river; understood the crew were employed in collecting sarsaparilla. Brought to, to cook breakfast, at half-past seven; off ten minutes after eight. Another piragua ascending the river. Five minutes after ten, stopped to take on board the masts and water barrel. They seem to take this method of concealing among the thickets, in convenient places on the banks of the river, what will not be required till they reach these particular places again. Detained only ten minutes. Got sight of La boca del Rio twenty minutes after ten—moored half-past ten—have dropped a little farther down, close upon the bar. The surge upon it, notwithstanding there is scarcely any wind, resembles the sea when agitated by a gale. The captain defers crossing till to-morrow morning, when we shall be favoured by the land breeze, and have the day before us to proceed to Omoa. This is the first time one of our Spanish friends has made a sally from the interior; he begins to lose heart at the sight of the billows, and deafening noise of the surge. In the event of being upset (a circumstance which not unfrequently happens), he has offered 1000 dollars to any one who will place him safely on shore. . . . The mosquitos and sand-flies are most tormenting; we have to keep our handkerchiefs in continual motion to drive them off. My hands, face, and lower parts of my legs, are so stung by these insects that I appear like one that had the measles or small pox. . . . No appearance of houses in this day's sail: indeed the banks of the part of the river traversed for the last three days, but particularly to-day, are low and apparently swampy, and consequently unfavourable for settlements. . . .

" *Omoa, Sabado, August* 20*th.*—Unmoored at ten minutes before five o'clock A. M., and at five were safely across the bar, which is really a dangerous passage. It was almost calm, yet the surge broke over the vessel as if it had been blowing a gale of wind. As we were approaching the agitated spot, the fears of our Spanish friend seemed to increase two-fold, at least he doubled the premium for saving him, in case of any accident happening to the vessel, say from 1 to 2000 dollars. The wind was very light; the oars were plied almost the whole of the distance to Omoa, abreast of which place we anchored about a quarter after ten o'clock A.M. We have thus been five days from Gualán to the mouth of the river, out of which, from the foregoing memoranda, it would appear, that there has only been twenty-five hours and fifteen minutes sailing. . . . The sail from the mouth of the river to Omoa occupied five hours and twenty-five minutes. . . .

" *August* 21*st.*—Have learnt that the schooner was here twenty-five days ago. The person who engaged the schooner expects her arrival in Omoa daily. Visited El Castillo. It is a most respectable fortification—mounts about twenty-seven pieces of cannon of various calibre—miserably garrisoned, the troops resemble the 'ragged rogues' that Falstaff refused to march through Coventry with. . . .[52]

" *August 22nd.* This place seems composed of between 200 and 300 houses, some of which are rather decent-looking places. It is situated on a level space of ground, at the bottom of lofty hills. It is about half a mile from the beach, and the particular spot where it stands seems dry; but the space between it and the beach is swampy; and, besides, there is a large track of similar land to the north, immediately contiguous. The sea breeze passing over this place must be contaminated, which is the cause, I should think, of its being so unhealthy: the hills, too, behind the town confine the air. In Belize, though we are in the midst of a complete swamp, yet there is nothing to obstruct the circulation of air; and, the town being close on the water's edge, we get the sea breeze uncontaminated. This I believe to be the reason of its comparative healthiness. Omoa, however, possesses two advantages over Belize, viz. freedom from mosquitos, and good water. There are great numbers of run-away slaves here, who belonged to individuals in Belize. It is disgusting to see the airs and the insolence of the coloured people here, of whom the population is chiefly composed. Therm. 84°.

" *On board the Swift, August 24th.*—Got under weigh a quarter after eight A.M., but the wind was light and baffling; a breeze, however, is now springing up, and we begin to make progress. . . .

" *August 25th.*— . . . Anchored abreast of the settlement at half-past nine P.M. Have concluded to stay on board all night, as the folks on shore may not have beds ready for us.

" Belize! Oh sweet Belize! I smell thy swamps once more.

" *August 26th.*—Landed at half-past eight this morning. There have been several deaths among the white inhabitants since we left— was not particularly acquainted with any of them. . . . I was sorry to find that a Christian friend, Mr. ———, had left the settlement."

On Mr. Wilson's return to Belize, he found it necessary to remain there for some time, in order to assist in the business of the house in whose service he had gone abroad. Mr. W. was not partial to Belize, and it never was his intention to remain permanently in that place; but, seeing that his assistance was required at the time, he felt it to be his duty to remain. He was always ready to run all hazards when in the dis-

---

52. Shakespeare, *King Henry IV*, part I, act IV, scene 2.

charge of what he considered present duty, and this principle constrained him to remain longer in that inhospitable climate than he ever contemplated....

In September, 1826, Mr. Wilson addressed the following letter to the wife of one of his oldest and most intimate friends: ...

"Belize, Honduras, Sep. 6, 1826.

" My dear Madam,
 " By the arrival of the brig John (August 27) I was put in possession of your much-esteemed letter....

" You state that my friends in Scotland wonder that they hear so seldom from me. . . . I . . . confess myself to be a very careless correspondent. . . . But I must conclude: this is what is termed with us a 'fly-day;' the wind is from the land, and, in consequence, we have myriads of tormenting insects from the swamps. I can scarcely write a sentence without waving my handkerchief around me, in order, in some measure, to preserve myself from their tormenting stings; even, notwithstanding, my forehead is completely blistered by them. . . .
 " Wishing you every spiritual blessing, and every needful comfort,
 " I remain, with the sincerest brotherly affection,
  " Yours very truly,
   " JAMES WILSON."

He again wrote to a friend, under date October 5th, 1826. This was the last letter he wrote to England, and is chiefly on the subject of his anticipated return.

His wish to return home was known to the house in London, arrangements had been made to relieve him, by sending out two young gentlemen, who sailed from London in January, 1827; and it was intended that Mr. W. should return by the same vessel.

A few days after the sailing of this ship, his friend in London was advised of the death of his widowed mother in Leith; and while he was considering with himself whether he should convey the melancholy tidings to meet him just as he was expected to depart from that climate, where distressing news has a more than usually injurious effect upon the health and spirits, or delay the painful communication till his return, the doleful tidings of his own death arrived. . . . He had been taken ill on the 19th of November, and on the 24th of the same month he left this world of sorrow and trial. . . .

On May 10, 1825, when travelers Lavagnino and Wilson were on the trail from Izabal to Guatemala City (Wilson about a week behind Lavagnino), GEORGE ALEXANDER THOMPSON arrived at Acajutla, in the state of San Salvador, en route to the same destination. A week later, while Wilson was yet on the way, Thompson arrived in the capital. On August 1, when Wilson left Guatemala City on the return trip that was never completed, Thompson was already in Belize on a more successful voyage back to England. There (in London, 1829) was published his *Narrative of an Official Visit to Guatemala from Mexico*, one of the few Central American travel accounts which have been translated in their entirety into Spanish.[53] The purpose of Thompson's trip was to gather information about the new isthmian republic for the British government. His book makes it plain that his sojourn was an active one in regard to both business and pleasure and that he returned home optimistic for Central America's prospects.

After the dedication of his book to King George IV, Thompson briefly explains his own qualifications and the manner in which his lone mission to the isthmus had its beginning:[54]

TO THE
KING'S MOST EXCELLENT MAJESTY.

SIRE,

HAVING been the first of YOUR MAJESTY's subjects who was deputed by the Government to visit Guatemala—a country most interesting in every political and commercial point of view,—I experience unbounded gratification in being allowed to submit to YOUR MAJESTY this humble exposition of my inquiries and observations respecting it.

YOUR MAJESTY's exalted and revered name, thus identified with a subject certainly deserving of Your Royal consideration, sheds upon my short Narrative a dignity and consequence which I feel it too much wants, and, I fear, it too little deserves.

53. See Thompson, 1926–27, and Thompson, 1927.
54. Thompson, 1829, pp. v–vi, "Introductory Observations" i–vi, 1–3, 58–59, 62–65, 72–80, 86, 114–16, 127–35, 136–39, 151–54, 156–60, 176–84, 185–87, 220–24, 232–36, 321–25, 326–29, 353, 372–76, 392–99.

Under the deepest and most indelible impression of the distinguished honour conferred upon my humble endeavours,

I AM,

SIRE,

YOUR MAJESTY'S MOST FAITHFUL, OBLIGED,

AND DEVOTED SUBJECT,

GEORGE ALEXANDER THOMPSON.

Another Journal on South America, and that, too, at a moment when the very mention of those countries is apt to excite emotions of distrust, seems to make necessary some apology for its appearance....[55] It may not be unknown to some of my readers that I translated Alçedo's Dictionary of America and the West Indies;[56] that my work was published in 1814, in five volumes quarto, and that it embraced, in addition to the translation, all the authentic information then extant, or which, through the most respectable patronage, could be obtained up to that period:[57] I may be permitted to add, that I went out as Secretary to His Britannic Majesty's Mexican Commission, of which Mr. Lionel Hervey was chief, in 1823. . . . I had also the satisfaction of being there under Mr. Morier, when that gentleman . . . compiled and wrote his report on the state of Mexico . . . ; and . . . was, finally, with the Commission until the despatch of the Treaty which he and Mr. Ward, as Plenipotentiaries of His Britannic Majesty, had been directed to negotiate....[58]

Having been ordered to leave Mexico, after the signing of the Treaty, for the purpose of proceeding to Guatemala, to report to the British Government on the state of that Republic, I spared no pains

55. Thompson's "Introductory Observations," of which this is the first sentence, are not dated. If they were written in late 1828 or 1829, British "emotions of distrust" of the time might have included disappointment over the prevention by force of the accession of Manuel Gómez Pedraza to the presidency of Mexico (December, 1828); over the near assassination of Simón Bolívar (September, 1828) and signs that his ambitions were unlikely to materialize; or over the execution of Manuel Dorrego, governor of Buenos Aires (December, 1828).

56. Antonio de Alcedo y Bexarano, *Diccionario geográfico-histórico de las Indias Occidentales o América*.

57. *The Geographical and Historical Dictionary of America and the West Indies*, 5 vols. (London, 1812–15).

58. Lionel Hervey was replaced as British commissioner in Mexico by James Justinian Morier in 1824. In January, 1825, the British government instructed Morier and Henry George Ward to draw up a commercial treaty with Mexico. The treaty was concluded in early April, 1825, and Ward became the British chargé d'affaires in Mexico City; but this treaty was rejected by London and a new one accepted only in 1827.

in endeavouring to obtain the most authentic information respecting CENTRAL AMERICA; especially, as no correct or adequate account of it had hitherto been received in Europe....[59]

In publishing the following NARRATIVE, I am doing that which I had never the remotest idea of doing till the present moment. It is true, I had taken short notes of the more particular incidents which had occurred to me, chiefly for my own gratification: I have been induced to publish them because they will throw some light and information on a portion of those countries which has been of all of them the least known or visited by Europeans. I have endeavoured to put down my observations with the genuine sensation, I should rather say simplicity of feeling, with which I first noted them in my journal; being aware that the candid recital of incidents, trifling as they may abstractedly appear, often affords the best insight into the manners and feelings of a country....

The HISTORICAL and STATISTICAL account of Guatemala which is included in a supplementary form, contains, I have no difficulty in asserting, much original, and I trust useful, information.

21st April, 1825. The Mexican treaty having been negotiated ..., I set off for the new republic of Guatemala, for the purpose of reporting on the state of affairs in that country. The Mexican government, which had hitherto shewn so much jealousy towards Guatemala, had now come to an amicable understanding with her.... Accordingly, I was informed by Mr. Alaman, on asking for my passport, that an embassy was about to depart in a few weeks from his government.[60] He suggested to me whether it would not be better for me to wait a little longer, to enable me to accompany it. Having heard that the Tartar frigate, Captain Brown, was at Acapulco, I resolved not to follow Mr. Alaman's advice. Captain Brown having been applied to with a request that he would take me to some port in Guatemala, he returned for answer that he was going up to San Blas, and should, in about the middle of April, put into Acapulco, from whence he would convey me, in case I should happen to be there, but that the nature of his instructions would not allow him to detain the vessel

---

59. When Thompson visited Central America in 1825, the latest account was that of Domingo Juarros, *Compendio de la historia de la ciudad de Guatemala* (Guatemala, 1808–18), an abridged version of which was published in English in London the year Thompson left for Mexico (see Juarros, 1823).

60. Lucas Alamán was the Mexican minister for foreign affairs from January to September, 1825.

in that harbour. After some consultation, it was agreed that another letter should be sent by express, pointing out to Captain Brown the urgency of the case, and thus, without waiting for his reply, I prepared to make all the arrangements for my immediate departure. . . .

My equipage consisted of ten baggage mules, besides two for my servants; one sumpter mule for myself, and three horses, with an escort of ten soldiers.

About midday on the 9th, we came to anchor off the port, or rather open roadstead, of Acajutla. At eight o'clock the next morning, Lieut. Morgan went ashore with part of my baggage. There happened to be, at the time, a great concourse of people assembled there from the capital, to celebrate the festival of the Holy Cross. I forgot to mention that the frigate, on coming to anchor, fired a salute which was answered by the fort of two guns, to the number fired by the frigate. This had drawn the attention of the whole population, whether natives or visitors. The morning was very fine, and we could perceive, by our glasses, that the beach was thronged with holiday-dressed company, who, with their shawls, bonnets, and parasols, had a very European-like appearance: indeed, a painter might have transferred the group, with propriety, to his representation of the coasts of Ramsgate or Brighton.

Don Miguel Espinosa de los Monteros is administrator of the customs at this port: he is a civil and intelligent man: he took me about the place. . . .

Don Miguel's was of course an open house, on occasion of the festivities which were going on at the port; accordingly, his great parlour was filled with groups of company of all descriptions. On the window-seat, smoking cigars, sat his pretty little daughter with three other Sonsonate misses, as brown as berries and as merry as grigs. From their ears hung suspended large flat hoop ear-rings of pure gold: some of them wore a profusion of gold chains round their neck, and some of them strings of pearls . . . in their unwrought state. . . . Don Miguel's wife had got possession, ex officio, of one of the hammocks, and the other was vacated for my acceptance, by a Guatemalian dandy. Although of the Mexican genus, he is a variety of the species: he wears the Mexican poncho or cloak, and sometimes the stamped leather leggings, but his dress is altogether plainer: it is seldom ornamented with gold or silver embroidery: his jacket is usually plain cotton, and when he wears woollen, it is more generally an English-cut frock-coat: his hat is also English, except when travelling, when it gives place to a large slouched one of straw or other light material, better calculated to keep off the sun's rays.—Dishes in succession were placed on different parts of the long massy table which occupied the greater part of the hall;—to every one in their turn was brought a dish of frixoles, and as there was no want of attention on the part of the host's servants to the demands of the guests, I naturally concluded that the numerous parties which were thus accommodated would pay for their respective entertainment. Some guitars now struck up before the door; and about a dozen couple began to waltz. I felt a little inclined to join them, but could not screw my courage to the sticking point. . . . I found that, with regard to propriety, I should not have been wrong if I had done so, for the party was highly respectable, and consisted of young persons of the best families of the provincial town of Sonsonate. Most of them were about to keep up the festivities for two or three days longer at Acajutla; but as three of the English merchants were about to return that evening, and kindly offered me their advice and assistance on the journey, I set off with them, about five o'clock in the evening.

There is a carriage-road the whole way from the port to the town, principally over a fine green sod, and through avenues intersecting a thick wood, which, in the summer time, is so umbrageous as hardly to leave the route, where the road should be, distinguishable.

The town of Sonsonate is large and straggling; but it contains many good houses, all built in the usual Spanish fashion. They are only one story high, forming three or four sides of a square, with a court-yard in the centre. The most respectable families think it no degradation to be engaged in trade: as there is no bank and no interest for money, this is the only way in which they can employ their capitals. Most of the richer classes of inhabitants derive their incomes from the cattle bred upon their estates and their crops of indigo, cochineal, and tobacco, which they barter with the European merchants for dry goods; retailing the latter for the consumption of the natives.

The chief kind of manufacture peculiar to this town is that of fancy shell-work, of which they make large quantities, imitating with shells of the most diminutive size, which they stick together in a sort of mosaic, the most beautiful flowers. By this article, and some little fancy birds and beasts, wrought, with equal ingenuity, in silk and velvet, they carry on an export trade to Cartagena, Peru, and other parts of the Western coast, to the amount of £10,000 sterling per annum. There is one large church, which, of course, occupies, as in all Spanish towns, one side of the grand Plaza or square. It is a large antique building, and has no architectural beauty to recommend it: the internal ornaments are uncouth and mean; but it is sufficiently spacious and commodious for the population, which consists almost entirely of Indians.

There are no families, altogether Spanish, residing here: some few remain who have intermarried, or are connected, with the Creolians. Of the latter there are also very few: they form, in this province, not one fiftieth part, perhaps, of the population. It is, therefore, very unusual to see any but dark coloured inhabitants. Some of the finest of them, in personal appearance, are a mixture of Africans and Indians; though many of the latter, especially the young people, are interesting and handsome. The state of nudity in which they are accustomed to appear in public seems outrageous and highly indelicate to a European beholder. Neither the men nor the women have any other clothing than a short apron round their middle. The mode of tying this apron distinguishes the married from the unmarried female.

Having passed a very restless night, from the intensity of the heat, greater, I think, than any I had experienced in these countries, I had risen early to refresh myself with a walk in the morning air. In proceeding through the town, I met groups of Indians, men, women, and girls, bearing on their shoulders fruits and vegetables for the market. They were all heavily burthened, but being disincumbered, as I before mentioned, from all unnecessary, or as we should rather think, necessary, clothing, they glided along with a sort of quick ambling pace at the rate of from four to five miles an hour. Each member of the different families carried a burthen in proportion to its sex and age: little children of five or six years old, obliged to be on the run to keep up with their parents, were thus training to the duties which they were bound to fulfil, without change or intermission, during the whole course of their lives, even to the age, should they be fortunate enough to reach it, of their hoary grandsires who were tottering by their side. I found that they all, without exception, on reaching the Plaza, after having deposited their burthens, went to pay their devotions in the church. Many of them took their bundles in with them, and I was pleased to see the simple but humble offering which some of them would make by sprinkling the floor of the church, for there was no pavement, with leaves and flowers, or as the Poet would call it, "the early incense of the spring." They prayed without books, for their devotion was the language of the heart, and their rustic offering seemed like the humble tribute of the children of nature to nature's God.—In the evening, I took a ride with the English gentlemen to witness an Indian fête, at a hamlet called the Barrio del Angel, about half a league from the town.

The Indians of whom I have above spoken, are not properly residents in the town or in the suburbs, but country or provincial people. The class of inhabitants which met my observation this evening, appeared to be somewhat more civilized; many of them wore shoes and stockings, the men trowsers, and the women petticoats to their ankles. The latter were deeply flounced at the bottom with a bordering different from the petticoat itself, which was a bright scarlet or some other gorgeous colour. There was, however, a neatness and cleanliness about their dress and general appearance superior to what I had observed in the same classes in Mexico.

The fair was carried on at a rising ground, at the extremity of a wood of bananas and other tropical plants. It was surrounded by the cocoa-nut tree, which spread its fan-shaped branches, as it were, to protect and shelter this pleasing sequestered spot. In one part of it was a blacksmith's forge, and in another a most indifferent sugar-mill: they seemed to testify that the arts and conveniencies of life, though not unknown, were known only upon a moderate and humble scale. The lanes, which led in different directions to this spot, were narrow and now so overgrown by the rank vegetation, that two persons could not ride abreast along them; and the little children, as you could perceive them in their white *mantas*, flitting amongst the bushes, put you in mind of rabbits, in the moonlight, sporting amidst the furze....

I . . . now introduce my readers to Don Simon B———o, a dependiente or managing man of the establishment of the family to which I was consigned at Guatemala. He was about five feet six in height, dark complexion, black eyes and hair, with hollow cheeks and of slender stature. His employment was to make sales of the indigo and other articles produced on the family estate, also to purchase wearing apparel and other European goods at the capital; disposing of them either wholesale at the warehouse at Sonsonate, or retailing them, in his journeys which he occasionally made through the provinces, on account of the firm. . . . His journey to the metropolis was fixed for the 16th; and I was anxious to set out as soon as possible. As he was the very character I wished to fall in with, being, as he was, so well fitted to acquaint me with the practical detail of the manner and habits of the trade of these countries, I endeavoured to induce him to depart with me on an earlier day: he was a kind, good natured, man, but had a dash of pomp about him, which shewed a just estimation of the importance of his own functions, and gave me a lesson as to the respect and consideration due to them. . . . The strictness of his arrangements would not allow of their being put aside: and as the business upon which I was travelling was of very different importance, I, of course, accommodated myself to the plans of my proposed companion.

The preparations for my journey to the capital having been made by Don Simon, to his entire satisfaction, and consequently to my own, we left Sonsonate about seven o'clock in the morning of the 14th. . . .

We . . . entered some lanes, with gates, here and there, so disposed as to impound or keep out cattle, and giving one the idea of those leading into an English village. That at which we arrived contained about 1,000 souls.[61] As every Spanish town and settlement is formed on the same model, which varies only as to elegance and size, this village had, of course, its grand Plaza, in the middle of which was a tree, and which, for it was, certainly, one of the largest I had seen in these parts, completely shadowed with its branches the whole area of the place. . . . Of course, our mules and horses wanted no other stabling, and there was plenty of accommodation left for the retinue of a large party of ladies and gentlemen who arrived shortly after us, on their way from the capital to the interior. They were all mounted on mules; some of them with single and others with double saddles: the lady's single saddle consists of a small dickey, or three-sided cushioned seat, with a step for the feet; in short it is a lady's Brighton donkey-saddle. When they ride double, the gentleman sits on the mule's haunches, with a saddle properly shaped for

61. Thompson usually names any settlement he describes, but not this one. Jalpatagua, in Guatemala, seems the likely place, though the first traveler to mention it by name says it "would in most parts of the world be called a miserable little village" (Dunlop, 1847, p. 71).

the purpose, having a flat square surface in front, on which his fair companion is seated, with her legs on the off side or rather shoulders of the animal: in this case, she has no step or stirrup to support her feet, but generally sits cross-legged, trusting, for her equilibrium, to the good offices of the gentleman, whose left arm thus, naturally, surrounds her waist: his bridle is held in the right hand, which, as all my readers know, is the wrong one, but the other being engaged, he has no opportunity of helping himself, or even of lighting his cigar; so that this business devolves, as a matter of course, upon his companion; and thus the journey is accompanied, as might be expected, with a general interchange of mutual good offices. I never passed a party of these travellers but I remarked that those, who were riding in this fashion, seemed to be the most cheerful and contented amongst them, and the least tired with the journey;—a circumstance very difficult to account for, since the position of each is thus rendered very cramped and uncomfortable.

We were now on our last stage to the capital of Guatemala; and as I approached it, I felt, at every step, fresh spirit and invigoration. The object of ambition which I had dwelt upon in all the moments left me for reflection, whilst at Mexico, was on the point of being realised: I was about to enter the capital of a country not only unknown to Europeans, but one with which even the South Americans themselves were little acquainted. . . . I had the gratifying prospect of, perhaps, being able to do justice to the importance of my commission, and of being the humble instrument of opening the same connexion between that country and Great Britain, which had been just established between the latter power and the republic of Mexico. When the heart is cheerful, there are few objects from which it will not draw some source of enjoyment:—for expectation carries in it the leaven which crowns the excitement of the moment. . . .

We travelled on . . . , and arrived at a small village. . . . The name of the place is Fraijanes; and I remember nothing more about it than that we lunched and took our *siesta* under a tree before the hut, and that there were a great quantity of dirty children and a few little pigs.

The country began, from this place, to take the appearance of some considerable degree of civilization. Gates and inclosures manifested the division and estimation of property. As we approached still nearer to the city, we passed some small country villas and gardens, with tracts cultivated with cochineal, and surrounded by small dikes or mud walls. It was about four in the evening, the air was fresh and balmy, the climate resembling a bright English day in the beginning of June. The tract over which we passed was varied with hill and dale: the turf, green and tender, seemed sprouting under our feet as we advanced. In the front, lay the city, with its white domes and spires glittering in the sun, and appearing larger than it really was by the interspersion of the shade and foliage of the fine trees with which it was, on all sides, intersected and environed. . . . The sight was so beautiful and replete with interest, that I . . . stopped behind to enjoy the contemplation of it alone, and at leisure. . . .

I dashed my spurs into the sides of my little horse, who never wanted that encouragement, and was up with my companions, in a twinkling. He continued fretful and gaysome till we had passed the theatre for bull-fights, about a mile out of the town; but, as we entered it, his spirit, most unaccountably, began to flag, his strength and energy seemed, in a moment, to have left him . . . ; he staggered down the long street which led to the abode whither we were going, and, as I alighted in the court yard, had hardly strength to resist the effort of my dismounting. . . .

The late Mr. Secretary Canning,[62] in his letter of the 3d of January 1825 to Mr. Morier, instructed me, after the signing of the Mexican treaty, to proceed to Guatemala, there to ascertain "The present state of its political government, and the disposition of the people, its resources, financial, military, commercial, and territorial, the amount of its population, the number and wealth of its towns, its principal means of communication with itself and with the exterior;"—and "that I should draw up a report upon those heads and upon any other points, on which I might be able to obtain information, respecting Guatemala, of interest to his Majesty's Government."—I revolved in my mind the importance of these subjects, at the breakfast which I took with the hospitable family, whose house I had entered, and of whom I shall have occasion to speak more hereafter. I had made inquiries about a house; but, finding that I could not obtain a respectable one, without taking it for a fixed period, and, even then, paying 6,000 dollars as a *traspaso*, (a good will repayable by the next tenant,) in advance, I renounced the idea, and became domiciliated with the family in question. The consul from

62. George Canning, British minister for foreign affairs from 1822 to 1827, died in the latter year.

the United States of North America, who had arrived two months before me, was not so fortunate as myself: there was not an inn or hotel in the town; he was sitting in the grand Plaza with his baggage, when he was invited to partake of the hospitality of a native merchant . . . who saw him in that situation. . . .[63]

The . . . 18th May, I called on Don Marcial Zebadua, who, I understood, was minister for foreign affairs. . . . On calling upon him . . . , I found that he had shortly before resigned in favour of Don José de Sosa, to whom he introduced me.[64] We, afterwards, all went together to the president. Whatever I might have anticipated in regard to the attention and favourable consideration of his Excellency, the manner in which he received me was far beyond my most sanguine expectations. My official character was not strictly defineable; I had no credentials; and, although a Commissioner of inquiry, I had not about me, like the other commissioners to Mexico, the ministerial appointment which they were, individually, to assume when the case required, to support me in my official pretensions: I had no other introduction to the president than that, which I had been able to obtain by my conduct at Mexico. I explained to his Excellency the object and motives of my journey, and the interest I had taken in the affairs of the Central Republic; the information respecting it, which I had, from time to time, transmitted to his Majesty's Government, and the gratification I should feel in being able to report favourably on the present state of its political regeneration. This candour was fully requited on the part of his Excellency. He told me that my zeal in the cause of their independence was as well known at Guatemala as at Mexico; that he had anticipated the probability of my commission for many months before it was made public in that capital; and, after many other observations of a kind and complimentary nature, observed that, in my future intercourses with him at Guatemala, I should consider him in a double capacity; as president of the republic, and, to use his own expression, "as Juan d'Arze, your friend."[65] I was introduced, the same day, by Mr. Bayley, the agent

63. The North American consul was Charles Savage, whose credentials were recognized on March 1, 1825. Savage was on his way to Omoa on May 9, when his party met that of Lavagnino near Zacapa.
64. Juan Francisco Sosa succeeded Marcial Zebadúa in this position in May, 1825.
65. The "Juan" for Manuel" or "José" should not seem surprising in view

of the house of Messrs. Barclay and Co., to the Marquess of Ayzenena and some other families of influence and distinction; and, on the following day, went down to the congress, which was sitting.[66] The greater part of the members, were in succession, introduced to me, and Mr. Bayley, who had been a long resident here, had the goodness to point out those who were considered as the most enlightened and competent to afford me assistance in collecting the various points of information to which my official inquiries were directed. I could not help remarking the Englishman-like, well dressed, appearance which many of the members exhibited. One of them, a young man with a broad cloth pelisse particularly well furred and frogged, seemed much engaged in contemplating my habiliments: they were far from correct. I had on a blue frock dress coat, with canary silk linings, which, I need not add, is, by no means, a morning dress; but I happened to have no other, as all my baggage was swamped and spoilt in landing at Sonsonate.

Saturday, 21st. The family with whom I had taken up my abode, consisted of Doña Vicente Cuellar y Rascon, and her daughter Maria Jesus, the eldest of a large family, and probably about twenty-five years of age.[67] Don José de Padillo . . . was living with them. The house was large but not very commodious, and very indifferently furnished; it was hired for the Guatemalian season.

Amongst the little festivities with which the time abounded, was one which was going on at a retired and beautiful hamlet about twenty miles from the city, on the road towards the south sea. All the fashion-

---

of the "José" for "Juan" above (see Ch. 1 n. 64). The correct names, Manuel José Arce and Juan Sosa, are both used by Thompson in a letter to London of this same date; see Charles Kingsley Webster, ed., *Britain and the Independence of Latin America, 1812–1830*, 1:330–31.

66. John Baily was the translator of Juarros' *Compendio* (Juarros, 1823; see Ch. 1 n. 59). Much later, he wrote a book of his own describing Central America (Baily, 1850). Barclay, Herring, Richardson, and Company, bankers of London, lent money to the Central American government in late 1824. Vicente, the second *marqués* of Aycinena, who died in 1814, was the older half-brother of Mariano de Aycinena, *jefe* of Guatemala 1827–29. Vicente's son, Juan José Aycinena, a priest, as a member of Central America's provisional government worked for annexation to Mexico in 1821–22. He is the "Marquess of Ayzenena" referred to here, though all titles of distinction were abolished in Central America on July 23, 1823.

67. Earlier (his page 69) Thompson gave this family name as Rascon y Cuellar.

ables were setting off thither to partake of this rural recreation; and, being invited to join the party of my kind hostess, I mounted my little horse . . . and off we set with the rest of the community. The young lady of our party was mounted on a pony, accompanied by a gentleman on horseback, who was very attentive to her; for, in addition to her personal attractions, she had a large fortune, and had had many offers, which she had hitherto refused: her mother was conveyed in a hammock swung upon a stout pole, borne by four Indians, and four others as relays: another conveyance of the same nature was appropriated to the use of Don José Padillo. Then there were three or four female domestics, mounted either on ponies or mules; and sundry mules loaded with beds, kitchen furniture, boxes with wardrobes, eatables and other necessaries. As many other parties, equally well furnished and provided, were issuing out of the town, at the same time, the appearance was very novel and grotesque. The beautiful and bright serenity of the climate, the loveliness of the surrounding prospects, the agreeable variety of the route through which we passed, rendered the journey to me highly interesting and amusing.

About eleven o'clock we had reached a hamlet called Villa Nueva, a very poor spot: the chief house was used as a general place of refreshment: it consisted, as usual, of only two rooms, which were both occupied, almost to suffocation. The yard, also, was so crowded, with the mules and baggage of the various parties who had stopped to refresh themselves, that many of the travellers had left it to congregate, more at their ease, under the hedges and trees in the lane in which the inn stood. We strolled up the village and made a call at a large farm-house, looking into the church-yard. . . . Having taken our lunch, (a very good one by the bye,) in the viranda, in front of the house, it was necessary to lie down and take our *siestas*. Doña Vicente and Don José preferred their hammocks, which were slung in the viranda, and, as there were two beds in the further room, they were occupied by the young lady and myself.

As we approached the village of Amatitlán, the country became more and more interesting.

We entered the village about six o'clock in the evening, and took possession of a house which had been left, I cannot say, prepared, for our reception. It consisted, of course, but of two rooms; one of which was about twenty feet long, nearly three fourths of the length of the building, and the other, running in a right angle at the end, about fifteen feet long and eight wide. The latter apartment communicated with the large one by an open door-way, and formed the left wing or extremity of the house. Behind it were four or five cottages, thickly inhabited with men, women, and children. I wondered, as their huts consisted of only one room and a kitchen, where they could all sleep; but the way in which we managed, quickly solved that difficulty. Eating, drinking, and sleeping, they say, are amongst the nonnaturals of life: but they were here performed in the most simple, and, therefore, the most natural, way that I could possibly have contemplated. Five gentlemen's beds were made up in the room in which I slept, besides three ladies' beds in the room adjoining, not to mention the female attendants, who slept on the floor of the latter apartment.

The dinner table was furnished with a profusion of luxuries: great sobriety was observed by the gentlemen: two or three glasses of wine was all they drank; but before the cloth was removed, they applied themselves to the comfort of the cigar: a glutton might have said, like the apostrophiser in the old play, "All our joys end in smoke," but with my companions it was in the words of the poet, "Never ending, still beginning;" and we had not finished our recreation, before we were summoned, by a special invitation, to a ball. I was a little startled at the proposal, for I had no dress fit for the purpose, and had nothing on but a Cashmire shawl jacket, worked with frogs and lace, according to the Mexican costume, and white waistcoat and trowsers: and I doubted whether my Chinese, who was a great enemy to redundancy in apparel, had put me up, what the tailors term, a "dress frock coat." But my speculations were defeated, upon the first expression of my doubts, as to the propriety of my apparel: I was assured that it was a party, sans ceremonie, and, without ordering the carriage, for the distance was not a hundred yards from the house, we all set off, on foot, to the place of entertainment. The music had drawn to the door of the house in which the ball was held all the idle stragglers and holiday company of the place: we had much difficulty in obtaining an entrance: there were three rows of benches placed round the walls of the three sides of the apartment, and at the end were tables of refreshment, consisting of fruit, cakes, wine, and eau de vie.

If I was struck with the homeliness of the place in which these revels were going on, I was much more so with the bevy of beautiful women with which the apartment was tenanted. I had seen the richest and most superb assemblies which Mexico could boast, but, here, appeared before me, at one view, as it were, selections of all the handsomest I had before seen in that metropolis. It is true, I had previously heard from the Mexican ladies of the beauty of the Guatemalians; but, whilst I was endeavouring to account, philosophically, for the superiority of the latter, suggesting to my imagination the effects of a moister atmosphere, and a table land six thousand feet lower than that of the valley of Mexico, and some such other propositions as an old author says ought "duly to be inquired into for the forming of a well proportioned, *righte*, judgement thereupon;"—I was asked if I should like to dance.[68]

Every evening, during these holidays, there were balls, monte-tables, (a sort of game of odd and even,) and other pastimes to make life slide lightly away: the festivities finished with the evening of Tuesday: the place was all in bustle, making ready for departure: here, some unsold goods were ticketed, as tempting bargains, and, there, were others forced upon the market, by petty auctions. The young people seemed inclined, also, to make the most of their time: their gaiety and good humour were still abundant, and more than they had time to dispose of. However, by six o'clock the next morning, they were all on their return to the capital. As the roads, from without ten miles of it, are, in most places, perfectly impassable for carriages, the whole party were on mules or on horseback, and, as they were accompanied with their retinues of servants of every description, with all their requisite utensils and articles of furniture, even to their beds, they formed, as winding up the wild passes of the mountain, or scattered over the verdant plains, a spectacle highly picturesque and amusing. All the families were, of course, acquainted with each other: every one seemed to know every thing about every body's affairs. According to the custom of the Spaniards, they addressed one another by their Christian names: the servants of one family were riding by the side of, and were in converse with, the gentry of another; whilst the servants of the latter were admitted to the same familiarity with the representatives of the former:—when Jacob had embraced his brother Laban, and veered off to the land of his fathers, he was not accompanied by a

---

68. Thompson says twice later in his work (his pages 239, 467–68) that Guatemala City lies at an altitude of 1,800 feet. The actual altitude is over 4,800 feet, leaving 3,000 feet less working space for his cogitations concerning the differences between women.

more patriarchal-like community than that which was now journeying towards the plains of San Juan.[69]

We had come to a narrow defile in the mountain, where there was room for only one passenger to pass, abreast: the sides of it were composed of high walls of clay which the rain had made smooth and slippery: I was bringing up the rear of the caravan, when my progress was arrested, in the middle of this awkward spot: a mule had slipped down, and would not, or at least the damsel, whom it had carried, could not prevail upon him to, get up. She had slid off his back, uninjured, but her *Benjamin* which was of very fine cloth, and richly embroidered with lace, had not fared so well:[70] it was shockingly besmeared with dirt, and her little black riding hat, which had come in contact with the bank, as, in endeavouring to gain her footing, she had slipped up against it, was very much disfigured, being, now, fawn-coloured on one side and black on the other, having a very harlequinade shape and appearance. However little disposed a man may be for acts of gallantry, there are some cases in which he cannot help himself; this was clearly one of them. I dismounted, twisted the mule's tail, vociferated a word which I do not approve, (I do not mean to say it was swearing,) but which I had observed the muleteers used on such occasions, with infallible effect, and up the creature jumped, in an instant. The damsel was re-seated, and we proceeded after the rest of the travellers, who had, now, got far a-head of us.

My companion was a slight, delicately formed, girl, something of a creole, but showing more of Indian cast than any other; about eighteen years of age: she was very chatty, and communicated many anecdotes of the different families who had been present at the revels: she told me of all the matches which were on the tapis, and hinted at some little pieces of scandal which it would be ungenerous and unnecessary for me to put down: she reminded me, as we jogged along, of a pretty, ambling paragraph of "The Morning Post," which nobody would like to be seen looking at, but which everybody would like to see.[71] What she was I knew not, but found that, although not a lady, she was a lady's maid,—a personage who is generally, and as it proved to be

69. For "San Juan" one presumably should read "Santiago," the name by which Thompson sometimes refers to Guatemala City. It comes from Santiago de los Caballeros de Guatemala, the full name of the capital of the Audiencia de Guatemala until 1776, the city now called Antigua.

70. A "benjamin" is usually a man's close-fitting overcoat, but apparently not this one.

71. The *Morning Post* was a London newspaper, published 1772–1937.

in this case, a *finer* lady than her mistress; she was servant to the amiable little daughter of Doña Vicente, the lady of whose hospitality I was partaking. The girl had now, it seemed, a lawful right to my protection; and I, therefore, hastened on to join the family; but as we quickened our pace, I heard a scream; and, looking round, saw the poor creature in a most alarming situation: the girths of her saddle had given way, being so predisposed to do, perhaps, by the late effects of the fall, which had snapped, but not entirely broken, them asunder: such, however, was now the fact, and the saddle, being deprived, as a counsel would say, of its special retainers, was going upon a circuit very prejudicial to the interest and safety of the plaintiff in the case. . . . I slackened my pace as quickly as I could; just in time to save her from falling: she fell, however, upon my off shoulder; and, in this position, with her arms about my neck, we continued our fearful course for some minutes. I might, perhaps, have checked my horse, but her mule had taken a fancy to gallop, as if determined to make up for the time we had lost. What to determine upon, myself, I did not know: to stop was dangerous,—to leave her was impossible: what was a man to do? —She was now relying upon me rather than her saddle; and it was fortunate that she did so, for this gave way, whilst I, constitutionally, kept my post, like an Envoy Extraordinary, with a troublesome attachée. With my right arm, I supported the poor girl who had swooned with fright, though I switched and jerked with my left. . . . After a precipitous run, for some seconds, my horse, fortunately, became so entangled with the underwood of the forest, that he could proceed no farther: I loosened my hold of my troublesome charge, dismounted, fastened the bridle to a branch of one of the trees, and began to consider what was best to be done: to call for assistance was useless, for no one was within sight or hearing. Recollecting, however, that I generally travelled with a small flasket of brandy in the pocket of my *armas de agua*,[72] I searched for it, and, luckily, found a small portion left in the bottle, which I immediately applied to the temples and also to the mouth of my patient, and soon succeeded in restoring her to a perfect state of sensibility: after some difficulty, she was remounted in the saddle before me, and, having regained the road, we came up, at length, with our party; who were stopping to take their lunch and *siesta* in a substantial-looking building, which stood in a solitary situation, in the midst of a large plain.

72. G. W. Montgomery describes the *armas de agua* of the Guatemalan horseman, below, p. 152.

As it was a convenient resting-place, a sort of half-way house, every portion of it was occupied by the travellers: it consisted of two small rooms, one a kitchen, the other a bed-room, with a viranda running the whole length of the front, and edged with a wall of about two feet in height, on which some of the party were sitting. I thought they seemed to stare at us, as we came up, for they stopped smoking, and knocked the ashes from their cigars: others were smoking *ad libitum* as they lay stretched along their temporary couches on the floor, or were eating or drinking, or sleeping or lounging....

Friday, 27th May. Having arrived, the day previous, at the capital, without further accident or inconvenience, I, this morning, called upon Don José de Valle, a person of great consideration on account of his learning and talents. The election to the presidency had lain between him and the actual president, Don Manuel Arze. The election is carried by a majority of popular votes, which must amount to forty-two, collected by electoral colleges, each representing 15,000 souls. As was natural to suppose, in a business of this nature, much interest and some manœuvring had been exerted. Valle was supposed to be the popular favourite, and, in fact, when the election took place, he counted forty-one votes, wanting only one to establish the actual majority required: Arze could count only thirty-four votes: as neither of them had the majority established by the Congress, the election fell upon that body, and the result was that the oligarchical preference was given to Arze, who was elected by seventeen votes against six.

The two candidates were both known to possess the highest degree of patriotic feeling, and they have both suffered extreme hardships and privations in the cause of their country. Valle is, by profession, a civilian, is passionately addicted to literature, and is a great patron of science: Arze is a soldier, having been one of the chief promoters of the Independence, as far back as the year 1811.... He is of a mild, calculating nature, of a clear, penetrating genius, and is esteemed and respected even by those who differ from him in politics. These two exalted characters were, now, living on a friendly footing: in one point, they were intimately connected; they seemed anxious to outstrip each other in promoting the interests of their country: they were equally assiduous in furnishing me with every information which I was seeking to collect.

... I called on the vice president, Don Mariano Beltranena....

He was living in a large house, in the centre of the town: two of the rooms were filled with the archives of the old government: there was great research making for a certain treaty, which was at length found: it was that dated Versailles, 3d of September 1786, entered into between Great Britain and Spain relative to the settlement of Honduras and the liberty of cutting logwood.[73]

The question concerning this treaty arose out of a subject of much difficulty which, now, agitated the congress: it was as follows:—some slaves belonging to the merchants of Belize, had run away and taken shelter in the territory of Guatemala; conceiving they were protected by a decree of the congress of 17th April 1824, in which, after liberating all the slaves within their own territory, and abolishing future servitude, they set forth that "the schedules and orders of the Spanish government are hereby ratified as far as relates to the emancipation of the slaves who may pass over to our states from foreign nations. . . ."[74] The slaves in question had taken advantage of the above decree, in the latter end of 1824, and beginning of 1825.

In order to reclaim them, General Codd sent to Guatemala a gentleman of the name of Westby, with despatches for the government, in which the necessity of returning them was pointed out. The supreme executive power, then consisting of Valle, Cerda, and O'Horan, were in favour of giving up the deserters, and, referring the matter to the congress, recommended their restoration.[75] The measure, being opposed, was passed over to a committee, which, in its report to the congress, supported the opinion of the executive; and the congress, having agreed to deliver them up, the party who were of the contrary opinion, required that, as the decision had the effect of altering an article of the constitution, it should be passed to the senate to obtain their sanction, as it would not otherwise be operative. After being referred accordingly first to the executive, and then reconsidered in the congress, the question was lost, by wanting only four votes of the two thirds prescribed in such a case.[76]

73. The Treaty of Versailles between Great Britain and Spain was dated September 3, 1783; the Convention of London related to it was signed in 1786.

74. ". . . in order to regain their liberty . . ." continues this translation from Article 4 of the decree passed by the Asamblea Nacional Constituyente.

75. Major General Edward Codd was superintendent of the British settlement in Belize in 1823–30. José del Valle, José Manuel de la Cerda, and Tomás Antonio O'Horan were the executive triumvirate for Central America from October 20, 1824, to April 26, 1825.

76. J. Wilson, whose sympathies lay with the runaway slaves, explained

It must be confessed that the business was decided with great party spirit, and contrary to the wishes of the executive; and, in justice to the authorities, it is necessary to state that, the causes, which led to so unsatisfactory a termination of the affair, originated in some incidental points of gratuitous and pernicious interference on the part of an English gentleman resident there, and who, when the matter was referred to the assembly, advised one or more of the members, in set and plausible terms, not to accede to the restoration sought for by the intendant of Belize. Mr. Hines, the gentleman alluded to, had not any improper intention; but every Englishman, whatever might be his rank or situation in life, felt himself warranted and called upon to dabble in politics; not knowing the mischief they might do; and he could not resist the temptation;—but, when he saw the turn the business had taken, he expressed himself much surprised and very sorry for the difficulties he had unwittingly occasioned. On his return to England, the poor man, who, I perceived, on my leaving Guatemala, was very unhappy, died at Belize.[77]

Saturday, 11th June. One of the Messrs. Ayzenenas being about to depart for England, I addressed a letter to General Codd, informing him that I should be at Izabal on the 20th July, and requesting him to send me his schooner to convey me thence to Belize, in order that I might be in time to return in one of the passage ships of the season, with convoy;—a precaution I understood to be most necessary, owing to the horrible piracies which were daily being committed throughout the Gulf of Florida and the neighbouring islands.

Sunday, 19th. I this day, had the honour of dining with the president, at the Palace.... We were, altogether, only six in number. Dinner was served at two o'clock. There were seldom more than two or three dishes at a time on the table, each of which the President himself helped, by putting some portions of it on a separate plate which was successively offered to the company. As I felt aware it might appear deficiency in good breeding not to take, at least, a small portion of every dish presented to me, I of course helped myself to each in routine: they succeeded one another by such numbers of removes, that my

---

one step of this legislative process more clearly than Thompson; see pp. 59–60 above.

77. One will note some parallel between the experiences of Mr. Hines and J. Wilson. John Hines was the representative in Guatemala City of a London firm interested in lending (to the government) and mining; see Thompson, 1829, pp. 208–9, 215.

fortitude began to falter; fortunately, however, it did not quite yield, as I should have been sorry to have given offence where such marked kindness and attention were evidently meant to be shewn. During the dessert, the President, after a short speech on the rapid progress of their independence and the stability it had acquired, drank a *brinda* or toast to those who had assisted in promoting or otherwise befriending it; and concluded by drinking the health of his Britannic Majesty and the English people. In returning thanks, I wished that Guatemala might continue to enjoy the happiness and tranquillity she experienced;—that, as she was the last to obtain her independence, so she might be the last to lose it; and that, though the youngest of the new states, she might, like Joseph, who surpassed his brethren, eventually exceed in honour and importance all the rest of her rivalling confederates.

The conversation now turned on the central position of the Republic, its consequent facilities for commerce and intercourse not only with Jamaica, and the British islands, but also, through her medium, with Peru and Chile. The proposed navigation by the lake of Nicaragua was also discussed, by which the British intercourse with China and the East Indies would be so much facilitated,—together with other subjects of equal political and commercial importance as well to the Republic as to the empire of Great Britain. I had the pleasure of being told by the President, on this occasion, that he had been informed by Don Juan de Mayorga, their minister at Mexico, of the interest I had taken in favour of their Republic. He had heard, he said, that I had, on many occasions, spoken in support of its new organization, in answer to parties at Mexico who had wished Guatemala to be still dependent upon that Republic; and he concluded by drinking my health, and hoping that I might return and *radicate* (that was his expression) myself in the country. Flattering as these sentiments were, I did not feel that I merited them:—nothing would give me greater pleasure than to return to live amongst them; but as my whole life had hitherto been devoted, however humbly, to the service of my country, at home, I could not expect to be able to return without some official employment, which it was equally uncertain if I should ever have the good fortune to obtain.—The conversation afterwards took a lighter turn, perhaps much more interesting to my readers if I should repeat it, but which, I beg leave to tell them I cannot; they will agree with me that moments passed in friendship and conviviality should always be esteemed sacred, even in the company of our equals; but that to reveal the confidence of superiors, when they honour us with it, betrays, something like a weakness of understanding with a badness of heart.—Tea and coffee were introduced, without the removal of the cloth. We then passed into an adjoining room, where there was a table laid out with liqueurs and cigars, where we spent another hour very socially; and about six o'clock in the evening, we took our leave.

Saturday, 9th July. Being anxious to procure a chart of the divisions of the Five States as newly established, I called on Valle, he being the most likely person to assist my views; in this, however, I was not a little disappointed: it is true that the demarcation had been determined by legislative enactment, but no map had yet been formed to illustrate the new arrangement....[78]

Sunday, 10th. Took leave of the archbishop, who kindly gave me a general letter of recommendation to the hospitality and good services of the curates through whose settlements I might pass. I shall never forget the kindness shewn me by this worthy prelate. Although I had been nearly obliged, so warm was his invitation, to take up my abode with him, I regret to say that I had only seen him three times during my stay in the capital.[79] On taking my leave of him, he good naturedly wished me a prosperous journey to England, and a speedy safe one back again to Guatemala.

I then adjourned to the palace to take formal leave of the president. I could see that he was anxious to discover what was my general impression, that is, whether favourable or not, with regard to the state of the republic. The only subject on which it was reasonable to entertain any doubts upon this point, was that relating to San Salvador, in which State some difficulties had arisen with regard to the appointment of a bishop. The people of San Salvador, conceiving it necessary to establish a bishoprick, had appointed, without the archbishop's consent, the Father Delgado to that function: the archbishop having denied his sanction, and having, in fact, refused to ordain him, the matter was referred to the ecclesiastical Cabildo, who reported that the appointment was not lawful. The matter being then discussed by the Congress, it was agreed that it should await the decision of the Papal See. Such was the state of the business when I left the country; nor should I have attached to it any importance had I not understood that the difficulty in question in some measure affected the president, inasmuch as he had

78. See below, pp. 253–54, for an earlier visit to Valle.
79. See below, pp. 280–82, for Thompson's first visit with Archbishop Casaus.

been thought to have sided with the Delgado party against that of the ecclesiastics in general.

Be this as it might, the disturbances which have since agitated the country are chiefly ascribable to the facts alluded to; and I have mentioned them, on this occasion, because they appeared to me, upon my leaving the capital, to be the only subject on which a difference of opinion might be said to exist.[80] The jealousy of the president's power and of his adherents, which included the majority of the most ancient and respectable families, was publicly admitted, but then the leaders of the opposite party talked so much about liberality and love of country, and in fact had ventured, up to that period, to make so little show of their hostility, that no bad result could fairly be anticipated from it; besides which, the alliance which the government fondly expected it was about to make seemed to secure its protection against any dangerous attack from internal enemies, who had not yet dared openly to declare themselves.[81]

The president took some pains to satisfy me that the differences respecting the ecclesiastics of San Salvador and the Cabildo of the capital were not likely to produce any consequences destructive to the public harmony: he had, on a previous occasion, condescended to ask my opinion on the propriety of sending a minister to Great Britain, and now seemed resolved to come to a final determination with regard to this subject, on the present occasion: negotiations of so important a nature, I felt aware, it was not in my province to enter upon, and the friendly overtures were, accordingly, suppressed. . . . Valle had been offered the appointment, but had declined it, upon the principle, as he told me, "that he could be more useful to his country at home." This observation, I must do him the justice to say, was elicited in answer to one which I quoted from his own writings, extolling "the *abandonment of self* for devotion to the *public good*," and insisting that he ought, therefore, to accept the appointment. He remained at home, and future historians will have to discriminate how far, by so doing, he has been useful to his country. I believe him to be sincerely devoted to its inter-

80. Alejandro Marure, historian-observer of that time, believed that the crisis over the bishopric had little bearing upon the outbreak of civil war in 1827. The matter was decided by Pope Leo XII (denying Delgado's aspirations) in letters dated Dec. 1, 1826, and published in Guatemala a half year later. See Marure, *Bosquejo histórico de las revoluciones de Centro-América desde 1811 hasta 1834*, 1:114–15, 192–97.

81. It was a sore point with Thompson (though he took care not to assess the blame involved) that no treaty arrangement had been made between Great Britain and Central America after his mission; see his pages 315–18.

ests upon that principle of *self abandonment* on which he has acted, and have only to hope that, for the sake of the *public good*, he will not in future refuse any situation which may be offered him, even should it be the president's chair.

The gefe politico of the new town of Guatemala, . . . this day, returned the visit I had made him. . . . The next, for I determined to set off for the coast on the following, was spent in preparations for my departure: in the midst of these, it had never occurred to me before, that I was about to make an arduous journey and perhaps difficult voyage without a single attendant; and in justice to the nature of my employment, began to look out seriously for some respectable person to accompany me, who might take care of my despatches in case of any unforeseen accident or casualty occurring.

There had been domesticated in the family for the last fortnight a young man about nineteen years of age, by name Don Eugenio: he was the youngest son of Doña Vicente, my very kind and hospitable friend: he had just returned from San Blas, where he had been on a visit, of commercial enterprise on his mother's account, to his eldest brother, the director of the customs under the Mexican government. . . . Having ascertained that the youth was intended for a mercantile life, it occurred to me that, by taking him to England, I might benefit him as well as myself by his companionship in my travels; for he had twice passed the port of Izabal, and was in every respect an intelligent, active, youth.

The proposition to take him with me was received with great gratitude by his mother and the rest of the family . . . ;—and my offer being accepted, it was found necessary for me to delay another day in order that the necessary preparations for the youth's departure might be made: these were easily effected, for in every house of any degree of respectability there are seamstresses almost constantly employed. They are usually seated in a row on the floor of the inner colonnade of the building: three or four extra hands had been for some days engaged in order to make me specimens of some of the more curious embroideries and artificial ornamental works peculiar to the country; amongst the latter of which were little birds, monkeys, and other animals beautifully and naturally imitated in silk. In order to get ready the supply of clothing thought necessary for my companion, about half a dozen more hands were added to this list of native spinsters, and the whole group presented a very novel and curious appearance: added to this, all the other domestics, with many who had been called in to help them, were diligently employed in preparations for the journey: some were making wholesale supplies of chocolate, others dulces or sweetmeats, or cooking provisions, such as fowls, tongues, and hams: these were stowed away in two large baskets; the interstices of which were filled up with new rolls, a whole batch of which had been baked for the occasion. In the inner yard, the male servants were busied in preparing the saddles and mule furniture: the latter lay in a large heap, appearing of itself to be a sufficient load for all the poor animals, without the addition of the cumbrous weights which they were doomed also to bear. In looking over my packages which had now been assorted into mule-loads, it was discovered that at least six more mules would be necessary for their conveyance.

... Two leagues from Guastatoya,[82] ... we met a Spaniard travelling from the coast, ... informing us that a British ship of war was arrived at Belize, bringing a consul from his majesty's government, and also three commissioners and a secretary. The information was to me of a very startling nature....

At four leagues from Zacapa, we stopped to sleep at a miserable little village called San Pablo, consisting of 300 Indians, living in cane huts: the inhabitants are particularly stupid, ill formed, and very diminutive.[83] I went into some of these hovels, and sat down to chat with the inmates, but could make nothing out of them: they knew little of the capital of Guatemala, and had never heard of their present rulers: they knew how to make *tortillas,* cakes of Indian corn, and drink aguadiente; not that the habit of drunkenness was common amongst them, but that in the preparation of these two necessaries seemed to consist all their enjoyment of life. The accommodation which we received at this place was of course very wretched: as we were starting, a drunken woman begged very importunately for a half rial to buy some brandy: so unreasonable a request was of course not complied with; and we had the pleasure of being well on our road by six o'clock....

We continued our journey through a country richly wooded and highly picturesque, and, after travelling eleven leagues in the course of the day, stopped at Gualán, putting up at the house of Doña Santa

82. Guastatoya is now El Progreso.
83. See Ch. 1 n. 47.

Maria Zafra: it was here found expedient to renovate our provisions: the bread, having been packed whilst it was hot, had fermented and become sour as well as hard: we had hitherto managed with it pretty well, but as we seldom met with any thing but *tortillas,* and were still less likely to meet with bread during the remainder of our journey, some care was taken by the good young lady above named in providing us not only with that, but such other necessaries as we might require.

Annexed to the Gran Sala was a room in which were four or five females, who were employed as seamstresses and in other light occupations, such as making *puros* and paper cigars. I pleased them much by purchasing largely of these commodities; and by my manner of payment for them, they were induced, I apprehend, to think rather highly of the generosity of the English character, which was the impression I wished them to feel. They congratulated me upon having so large a freight of *tintas,* or indigo, and inquired if I was going to take it with me to my own country. On telling them that my trunks contained no merchandize whatever, they seemed much surprised and very anxious to know the nature of my baggage. The daughter of the establishment, Doña Francisca, a placid, good natured, domestic girl, came and sat by us whilst at supper, gave up her bed in the chief apartment, and seemed to have as much pleasure, as other girls might have found trouble, in waiting upon us. In the mean while, we discovered that she had a very extensive acquaintance in the town; and that, by some curious coincidence, they all appeared unanimously disposed to visit her, at the same time: ladies young and old came to see the little quiet Doña Francisca: she, at first, appeared surprised at so many unexpected calls; but, however, bore their intrusion with great patience, having discovered that their visits were prompted rather by a curiosity of seeing the *lion* than the *lamb.*

Her curiosity was equally excited the next morning by the few ordinary articles of my dressing case, which were now reduced to those only of indispensable utility; for, in the course of my journeys, I had found little difficulty in inducing the admirers of such paraphernalia to accept of them: nevertheless I gave her a small-tooth comb which she appeared particularly to fancy, and I was honoured by her commission to bring her, on my return to the country, one of the finest pair of scissors that England could produce:—I hope she will not be disappointed.

It took us eight hours of hard labour to pass the mountain: about half the time was occupied in the ascent and the other half in the descent; for there were sufficient variations in this route to break any general uniformity in our progress either up or down.[84] The few plains which occurred were deep glens in which the animals found no footing, but plunged along, for the most part in beds of mud. In the slopes they sometimes got fixed in with their baggage in the narrow defiles of the rocks, or foundered, with all four legs so deeply stuck into the cavities as to render them incapable of all exertion: in such cases, the muleteers disburthen the animal, and with their united efforts extricate it from its thraldom. Every step is a labour: each leg is pulled out of one hole, even in the harder plots, and placed on the edge of another into which it slips down by aid of the lubricating mud upon the surface; and in many instances the poor animal rests upon its chest or its belly, the hole being too deep for its legs to fathom. In these cases, I had some difficulty in riding my horse, for he would always endeavor to keep his feet out of the holes, whilst the nature of the road rendered it impossible for him to do so; at first he was violently enraged and threatened to dash himself to pieces; but by degrees, as I pulled him down each step into the holes, he began to walk, much against his inclination: he was the only horse in the whole party; and I was strongly advised to ride a mule; but I knew the value of being well mounted, and had reason to congratulate myself in sticking to my resolution, on the present as well as every other occasion.

We were now within two leagues of the coast, and I ventured on alone some distance through the forest with the joyful expectation of seeing the waters which embraced in their span the coast I was about to leave and that to which I was going. The arduous parts of the journey had been passed, and the tropical foliage evinced the low regions of the port of Izabal. By the rapidity with which I had proceeded I thought that I ought to have arrived there, if I had gone the right way: by the position of the sun it appeared that I could not be mistaken, but as there were still three hours of daylight and the spot was romantically beautiful, I dismounted and refreshed my horse with a drink from a pure stream which crossed our path. Whilst I was remounting, an Indian passed by, who informed me that I was not far from the direct route, and that the muleteers would pass within a small distance of me, or perhaps might come by that very spot. . . . In the course of half an hour, my companion looking through the forest, said, "Alli estan," (there they are,) but I could see nothing. "Las mulas,

84. See Ch. 1 n. 44.

Señor" (the mules, Sir). It was two or three minutes before I could distinguish them, passing, in the distance, through the wild recesses of the forest. In the course of another hour, we entered Izabal: after leaving the woods, the last mile or two lay through wide lanes covered with green sward, and might be passable enough when not so swampy as they now were. . . .

The town consists of thirty houses indifferently built, with a very hut-like appearance, and in a straggling manner, within a quarter of a mile square; some of them being within thirty yards of the water's edge, which is affected by a slight tide. . . .

The only house with any tolerable convenience or comfort is that of Mr. Benson, and thither we were directed to guide our steps. Having entered the outer yard of this abode I met poor Mr. O'Reilley:[85] I shall never forget the delight which he manifested in seeing me: he had suffered much in his passage up the gulf, and entertained many apprehensions at the nature of the journey he had to encounter to the capital: indeed my appearance warranted him in the conclusion that it was not one of an ordinary nature; for my white cotton jacket, as well as my face, had become so splashed and covered with mud as completely to disguise their natural appearance: my leather boots or leggings were one mass of half dried clay, and my English leather breeches (I generally rode in these, without buttons at the knees) had nearly adopted the same extraneous colouring. We had of course much to say to each other, and, being left to ourselves, began to talk over particulars: I now discovered that the Commission which had arrived at Belize was the Commission of Inquiry into the State of the Laws of the West Indies, and had nothing to do with any of the Commissions to the New Republics; Mr. O'Reilley told me that his appointment as consul was not to interfere in any way with the duties I was sent to fulfil, but on the contrary he was ordered to look to me for any advice or assistance which, as a new comer unacquainted with the politics and manners of the country, he might require: and, what in my present situation was not a little consolatory, he also assured me that there was a strong impression at home that I was likely to give satisfaction with regard to the Commission with which I had been intrusted: on the other hand, he learned from me the exact state of affairs in the republic to which he had been sent: I gave him my horse and accoutrements, which were valuable to him, as he was unprovided with a saddle or the leggings of which I have spoken: he had also the benefit

85. See Ch. 1 n. 48.

of such other articles of my travelling apparatus as might be deemed convenient for him to retain;—including the Chinese: he gave me a filtering stone, with other small conveniences for a voyage, and, after this interchange of good offices, we parted on the following evening, Sunday, 24th July, at seven o'clock, when I embarked on board the schooner which had brought him from Belize.

In September, 1826, more than a year after George Alexander Thompson departed these shores, JACOBUS HAEFKENS arrived as the second consul-general to Central America from the Netherlands. Haefkens stayed on the isthmus more than three years, his keen mind and probing curiosity leading him to collect information enough for a major contribution to Central American knowledge. Before he returned to Europe, there appeared in The Hague (1827-28) two volumes from his pen called *Reize naar Guatemala*, the second being subtitled *Behelzende eene Reize door de Provincie San Salvador*. In 1832, as Haefkens began a long period of service in his home country as mayor of the municipality of Leerdam, he put before the public a lengthy account of Central America's first decade of independence, accompanied by a geographical and statistical survey which far surpassed Thompson's.[86] For five years beginning in 1851 Haefkens acted as Dutch consul-general in Athens, Greece; in 1858 he died, in retirement.[87]

Haefkens explains in his *Reize* how he approached Central America from Surinam, touching first at Trujillo on the north coast of Honduras. Trujillo had been sacked by Dutch sea rovers in 1643. Concerning the place and the incident, Haefkens observed:

Hoe geheel vreemd dit oord ook voor ons mogt wezen, was het echter een streelend denkbeeld, dat hetzelve almede eenmaal aan den roem onzer voorvaderen ten tooneele had verstrekt; en wat het streelende van dit denkbeeld nog verhoogde, was, dat den tegenwoordigen inwoners de gebeurtenissen van 1643 niet onbekend waren, zijnde het de militaire kommandant zelf, die mij het eerst van de-

---

86. Haefkens, 1832.
87. Personal data on Haefkens is contained in a communication to Miss Susan Griswold from A. E. M. Ribberink, Netherlands archivist (Aug. 26, 1966) and a report by the Secretary of Leerdam (Aug. 18, 1966). Some of it is also available in Abraham Jacob van der Aa, *Biographisch Woordenboek der Nederlanden*, 8:41–42.

zelve sprak. Deze heer, die den rang van luitenant-kolonel had, overlaadde ons met beleefdheden....⁸⁸

From Trujillo the ship sailed on to Omoa, where Haefkens rented a small vessel to take his party of five (including his wife and daughter) to Izabal. From there they had to climb the Montaña del Mico:

Den 29 September, des morgens te half acht, bestegen wij onze muiltjes, om den beruchten berg te gaan beklimmen, wiens naam alleen den reiziger schrik aanjaagt. Het weder begunstigde ons in eenen hoogen graad, en daar het de laatste dagen, of liever nachten, in het geheel vrij droog was geweest, verklaarden de muilezeldrijvers, dat de weg zeer fraai was. Wat ons betreft, wij zeiden herhaalde malen tegen elkander: « Indien deze weg fraai moet heeten, hoe is het dan mogelijk, over denzelven te komen, wanneer hiji slecht is. » ⁸⁹

A canoe was then used to ascend the Motagua to Gualán:

... Behalve een dorpje op den linker oever, ziet mon hier en daar een hutje met een maïs- of bananenveld, en op ongeveer eene mijl afstands van Encuentro woonden eenige van de engelsche kolonie Belize weggeloopene negers, die alhier in vrijheid, op hunnen eigenen grond, hoofdzakelijk suiker bouwden.⁹⁰

A stay in Gualán gave Haefkens opportunity to study the scene

88. "However completely strange this region might seem to us, it was still a gratifying idea that it once provided the scene as well for the glory of our forefathers; and what heightened the appeal of this idea was that the present inhabitants were not unaware of the happenings of 1643; the military commander himself was the first who spoke to me of this. This gentleman, who held the rank of Lieutenant Colonel, overloaded us with politeness. . . ." Haefkens, 1827–28, 1:26.

89. "On the 29th of September at 8 o'clock in the morning, we mounted our little mules to go climb the notorious mountain whose name alone strikes fear into the heart of the traveler. We were again favored in great measure—since in the last days, or better, nights, it had been fairly dry, as the muleteers explained—that the road was very fine. As far as we were concerned, we said many times to each other: 'If this road must be called "fine," how is it possible to pass over it when it is bad?' " *Ibid.*, 1:42–43.

90. "Besides a small village on the left bank, one sees here and there a little shack with a corn or banana field, and about a mile distant from Encuentro were living a few of the Negroes who had fled from the English colony Belize, and who were raising mainly sugar here—in freedom, on their own land." *Ibid.*, 1:54. Encuentro or Los Encuentros was a hamlet across the mountain from Izabal.

about him; his account is indeed marked by more than casual observation all along the line. He arrived in Guatemala City; his credentials were accepted on October 30, 1826. When his first manuscript was completed in February, 1827, it included visits to nearby Antigua and Amatitlán.

The second trip began in March, 1827. As far as Sonsonate, the route was the reverse of that traveled two years earlier by Thompson. Continuing, Haefkens gives description of the land to the east through the cities of San Salvador, San Vicente, and San Miguel as far as Conchagua, touching Usulután and Santa Ana on the return. The account is simple and unadorned; but since more than ten years elapsed before other book-writing itinerants came this way, Haefkens has something unique to offer. The inaccessibility of all Haefkens' volumes, due to both their rarity and the difficulty of their language, lends much importance to the work of their translation currently in progress.[91]

A personal acquaintance of Jacobus Haefkens was HENRY DUNN, who arrived in Guatemala in May, 1827. Dunn learned some of what he knew about Central America from Haefkens. But Dunn later proved that he understood some features of the isthmian landscape (especially the small world of books and the arts) not touched by his government-appointed contemporaries. Dunn spent a year in and about Guatemala City. His account of that region, *Guatimala, or, the United Provinces of Central America, in 1827–8; Being sketches and memorandums made during a twelve months' residence in that republic,* was the first to be published in English (New York, 1828, a year before those of Wilson and Thompson). A slightly enlarged edition (*Guatimala, or, the Republic of Central America, in 1827–8*) was printed in London in 1829. After this, his first literary effort, Dunn (born in 1800) had a long career as the author of books and pamphlets dealing in dissenting Protestant polemics. When he died in 1878, most of his printed works died with him; but his Central American volume, which along with religious argument contains a broad strain of urbanity, has recently, like that of Thompson, been republished in Spanish.[92]

91. Haefkens, 1832, was used extensively by Mary Wilhelmine Williams in "The Ecclesiastical Policy of Francisco Morazán and the Other Central American Liberals." All three of Haefkens' books have been put into Spanish typescript by Miss Thea van Lottum of the Netherlands embassy in Guatemala, and Haefkens, 1832, into English typescript by Miss Susan Griswold of the University of North Carolina at Greensboro.

92. See Dunn, 1960.

Dunn was an Englishman in Guatemala by invitation. Haefkens says that Dunn had been hired to serve as an adviser in setting up a school system, but that his project was completely frustrated.[93] Dunn does not speak of this reason for his visit. He does not in fact lend the pages of his book to a great quantity of personal comment; he hardly mentions any personal names. He was apparently troubled (at least in some matters) by a constantly nagging conscience, to the point even of apologizing in his first manuscript to those who would "complain of his work not being more exclusively religious." To them, however, he replied that "piety was intended to sanctify, not to exclude the business of the world."[94] A year later, as seen below, it seems to have been to his surprise to have heard from a class of readers who were annoyed more by his overpiety than his deficiency in that respect. But Dunn stood firmly, on very independent ground, and in doing so made his book a worthy one:[95]

The Republic of Central America, formerly the kingdom of Guatimala, is probably less known in Europe than any other part of the civilized world. Its position may perhaps have contributed to keep it in obscurity. With Columbia on one side and Mexico on the other, it has been lost between two more important powers, or, if remembered, has been only considered as an appendage to the latter. The merchant has observed the name affixed to Indigo in the Price Current, but has seldom recognised it as denoting an independent state. Scarcely a single map points out its geographical situation with even tolerable correctness; and, with the exception of a translation of Juarros's Statistical History, no information has been offered to the public respecting its interior condition. A condensed and very well-written sketch, prefixed to one of the volumes of the Modern Traveller, might also be excepted; but as it does not refer to the present state of the country, the deficiency is not supplied.[96] Yet on the shores of this very territory an English settlement has flourished for above twenty years, and sixteen thousand tons of British shipping are annually employed

93. Haefkens, 1832, pp. 232–33.
94. Dunn, 1828, p. vii.
95. Dunn, 1829, pp. 1–2, 4, 28, 30, 34–35, 36–38, 45–48, 51, 55–56, 59–60, 65–67, 71–74, 75–84, 90–96, 103–4, 287–90, 301, 314–15, 320–23, 324, 326–28.
96. Respecting the translation of Juarros, see Ch. 1 n.59. *The Modern Traveller* (see Conder, 1825) offered half a small volume from which Dunn seems to have drawn his spelling of *Guatimala*. Its information is largely from Juarros, 1823, however, and hardly gives a hint that Central America has achieved independence.

in carrying on its commerce.[97] This fact alone justifies the attempt to diffuse a more enlarged acquaintance with its political circumstances and the manners of its inhabitants.

In preparing the volume the author has sedulously avoided what may be termed *painting,* and in every instance has sacrificed effect to a simple narration of the truth. He is aware that some will complain of his work not being more exclusively religious, while others will object to the introduction of any theological sentiments whatever. To the first he can only reply, that *piety* was intended to sanctify, not to exclude, the business of the world; and in his opinion, in order to do good in any country, it is necessary to *know* it, not merely in a moral and religious point of view, but politically and statistically. To the second, his only answer can be, that he is not ashamed of the Gospel of Christ, and is convinced, that, far from degrading any other topic, its tendency is to dignify and to elevate.

After spending two months very agreeably in Belize, we left it on Friday the 4th of May, on board a schooner bound for the port of Izabal.

... We ... came in sight of the *Rio Dulce.* The entrance to this beautiful river, viewed from a distance, is enchanting, and takes a powerful hold upon the imagination. On either side are high mountains covered with the richest verdure, and apparently leaning over, as if to meet each other; while the peculiar bend which the river takes very near the entrance, throws forward the woods which skirt the side of the hills; and the whole forms an archway of consummate beauty.

Slowly ascending the river, ... we arrived at the mouth of a second lake, where the Spaniards have erected a fort, called by them *Castillo del Golfo,* or the Castle of the Gulf.[98] The appearance of its huts from the river is picturesque. The fort, however, consists only of a ruinous wall defended by about twenty Carib soldiers, who live there surrounded by their families.

97. The reference is certainly to Belize, whose existence went back much farther than twenty years, but which may be said to have "flourished" in a new way after the last visit of Spanish commissioners in 1796. See Ralph Lee Woodward, Jr., "Economic and Social Origins of the Guatemalan Political Parties (1773–1823)."
98. San Felipe.

We landed, to shew our passports, and were led to the commandant's house through rows of plantain trees, on the fruit of which he and his troops subsist. It was a miserable hut, with a clay floor not even levelled. A hammock was slung across the room, in which an old woman was reclining; a few coarse prints of the Virgin, and a brass crucifix, ornamented its mud walls; and two or three common wooden stools constituted the whole of its furniture. But, as if to make the contrast more striking, on one of these stools were placed several beautifully cut-glass decanters, cream jugs, and tumblers, with three or four clay jars of excellent water.

The females here seemed to have lost all sense of modesty and propriety; wore considerably less clothing than the men; and appeared, if possible, more depraved. They perform all the manual labour, and are treated as a degraded sex. Numbers of them were bathing round the vessel, and some of them asked permission to come on board.

Our passports being backed by the commandant's secretary, who seemed to have some difficulty in inscribing his name, we crossed the lake to the little town of Izabal, which stands on its shore. Here we anchored for the night, and landed early in the morning.

In landing, we were conducted to the commandant's house, and before him our boxes were opened; but immediately closed, on an assurance that they contained nothing contraband, . . . and no further notice taken of them.

This port consists of about fifty or sixty huts raised at the foot of one of the mountains, and is, in fact, only a depôt for goods passing from Belize to Guatimala. In one of the largest of these habitations we took up our temporary residence, boarding with the owner, and sleeping at a neighbouring hut. The provision was by no means despicable; consisting generally of soup, eggs, a hashed fowl, and wine (somewhat resembling claret) mixed with water, for dinner; and coffee in the morning and evening. This hut, by far the best in the place, was spacious, well built of wild cane, and covered with the leaf of the bay tree. Considerable quantities of goods were remaining in it, waiting for mules to be forwarded over the mountains. Besides the requisite articles of furniture, it contained a thermometer, a French writing-desk, and about thirty volumes of books neatly bound, chiefly translations from the French. . . .

About six o'clock every evening the drum beats to call out the military force of Izabal, which is composed of about twenty men, not only out of uniform, but almost without dress; one wanting a hat, a second a coat, and all without shoes or stockings. These, armed with rusty muskets and old swords, and totally without discipline, are its only defence. The people are excessively indolent; sleeping the greater part of the day on mats stretched upon the floor; and lying on the ground at their house doors, talking with each other, during the night. . . .

Our mules having at length arrived, we prepared to set out over the mountain of Mico the following morning at day-break. The bustle of preparation, saddling and loading of cargo, being over, we started, in good spirits and good temper, one following another merrily, and forming a line of considerable length. Our party consisted of a lady and four gentlemen.[99] Three servants followed with provisions; and the *arriero*, or muleteer, with fifty mules loaded with goods, brought up the rear. Each Spaniard was armed with a brace of pistols in holsters and a large knife fixed in his belt, and the servants with swords.

Immediately after leaving Izabal we began gradually to ascend the mountain, winding in a serpentine direction towards its summit, through narrow passes lined on each side with trees. In consequence of this circuitous rout, without which it would be utterly impassable, the ascent is in many parts very gradual. After riding onward, however, for about an hour, the road became very steep, some of the ascents appearing almost perpendicular from their base. Over these the mules carried us with amazing care and sagacity; invariably placing their feet on the same ledge of rock, or treading on the same crag, over which their predecessors had passed. Many of these are worn with their footsteps, and they are never willing to change them.

Gualán, although a town of inconsiderable size, is the only one of importance between Izabal and Guatimala. . . .[100] The entrance is by the principal street, at the end of which is the *plaza*, or market-place, and a neat church. The houses are all of them low, generally one story only, with white plastered walls, red-tiled roofs, and very heavy antique windows; and have balustrades before them, mostly of wood.

99. Regarding the lady, Dunn says of a stop at a hamlet (1829, p. 53): "The whole of the inhabitants soon appeared at the house where we had stopped; the news of the arrival of an *Ingles* and his *Señora* having rapidly spread throughout the neighborhood. Though exceedingly inquisitive, examining the dress of the lady with the greatest attention, they were very respectful and polite." See also pp. 115–16 below.

100. Dunn explains that Zacapa did not lie on his route.

In Gualán ... there is no inn, or house set apart for the reception of travellers; we therefore accompanied our Spanish friends to the house of their agent, at which place the *alcalde* soon arrived to examine our packages....

The interior of the houses generally consists of only two rooms, separated from one another by a slight wooden partition. In the one which it was our lot to occupy, the whole of us, including the family of our host, dined, and the greater part of us slept; five small beds being placed around it for that purpose. A large wooden table (a fixture), and some common wooden chairs, composed the rest of its furniture. Two hammocks swung constantly from one end of the room to the other; and three or four swords, with several muskets, ornamented its walls. Soon after our arrival, several of the neighbours entered the house, which seemed always open to every visiter. One stretched himself in a hammock; others seated themselves on the table, or on beds; and all began at once to inquire the news, and to discuss politics with the greatest vehemence, smoking the while, and spitting on the floor most profusely.

Nothing can exceed the indolence, licentiousness, and ignorance of these people. Their only idea of freedom is the absence of all restraint, and, consequently, in manners and morals they have levelled themselves with the brute creation. The men, when dressed *a la Inglesa*, of which they are very fond, exactly resemble, in manners and appearance, English ploughmen at a country fair. A few of the women have some degree of softness and polish in their manners, but generally speaking they are disgusting. The mistress of our house, a young woman of about twenty, was a complete specimen of filth and vulgar finery. Terribly afflicted with a *güegüecho*, or swelling of the glands of the neck, she still had sufficient vanity to suppose herself handsome; and, dressed in a dashing printed gown made very low in the body, with pink shoes and silk stockings, and two gold chains hanging about her neck, she paraded the room like a sultana of the East. A more pitiable object could scarcely be seen. Her husband, an old man of about sixty, exceeded her, if possible, in grossness. The servants, as is invariably the case, imitate their masters, and are lazy and insolent. It is said they have considerably deteriorated since the Revolution.

Immediately after rising in the morning, coffee was prepared; and about nine we breakfasted on stewed meat, eggs, *frijollis* (or black beans), bread, and coffee. Dinner generally consisted of four courses, two dishes to each, and included beef cut up and hashed, fowls, turkeys, and sausages—but all roasted to pieces, soaked in bad butter, and thickly strewed over with onions—beans, eggs, and a milk pudding followed, and wine-and-water to drink. In the afternoon chocolate was prepared; and in the evening, about nine o'clock, a supper similar to the dinner, but with less variety of viands. For these accomodations each individual paid a dollar per day. The whole of these messes were prepared under a shed, in a large dirty yard, which served as a kitchen, and was full of filth of all kinds. The knowledge of this, with the sight of the servants, had no tendency to quicken our appetites. The spoons, cups, and knives and forks, were of silver, and, with two lamps hanging from the roof, cased in silver but quite neglected, betokened a country that had once been rich in metals.

After being detained at Gualán for nine days, we at length heard of the arrival of our mules, and joyfully prepared to leave a place which possessed too few attractions to render a longer residence grateful.

. . . After being oppressed with heat, we found ourselves . . . chilly; and when we arrived at Guastatoya, . . .[101] wet with the rain, which had for some time been falling in torrents, we should have rejoiced at the opportunity of surrounding a blazing fire.

This village is one of the most interesting in the whole journey. Its elevated situation and beautiful scenery, rendered still more agreeable by the refreshing rains that had so lately fallen, pleased us exceedingly, and we could willingly have remained here some days, had our time permitted it. The house we inhabited was one of the best in the place, and was at that time tenanted by an old widow lady and her two daughters. The chairs, doors, and two old-fashioned couches, were all of mahogany, antiquely carved; three niches, in the wall of the largest room, contained images of saints, and a large crucifix; while in an inner apartment an old four-post mahogany bedstead, with a few better articles of furniture, indicated some degree of superiority in the owner. It had probably been the residence of a priest in former days, having every appearance of a decayed parsonage. The yard was well stocked with fowls, turkeys, and good milch cows; and under a shed was a loom, on which one of the women was weaving coarse cotton.

. . . As we approach nearer the city, the eye opens on an extensive

101. El Progreso.

plain studded with trees, and ornamented by numerous hedge-rows, enclosing the lands near the capital. In the midst of the plain stands the city of New Guatimala.

Its appearance from this spot, about a league distant, is singularly picturesque. Its numerous turrets and cupolas glistening in the sun, and its low white houses regularly arranged at right angles, with orange trees thickly interspersed among the buildings, form a middle ground; while the mountains encircling it, and especially the beautiful *Volcano de Agua,* as it is termed, generally crowned by clouds, complete a picture, which, for interest and beauty, will bear comparison with any prospect in the world.

The descent from this elevated situation into the valley is by a road cut out of the rock, and winding down it. On one side are deep precipices, and on the other high and perpendicular rocks, each clothed with hanging woods and the richest verdure. At the end of this pass stands the eastern gate, where our passports were required. Between it and the outer street of the city are orchards and meadows for about two miles; and after these a few straggling houses, till we gradually enter the more populated districts. When we arrived, the place appeared almost deserted: the streets were as silent as if the plague had ravaged them, and most of the houses were closed. This we found afterwards to be partly owing to our having entered at the hour of *siesta,* and partly to the civil war, then at its height. The opposing party had a short time before assaulted the city, and the inhabitants were still in a state of confusion.[102] After riding through ten or a dozen streets, all equally silent, and some of them covered with grass, we arrived safely at the place of our destination.

In walking through it, the first thought that strikes a stranger is, that Guatimala is one of the dullest places he has ever entered. This melancholy appearance is chiefly occasioned by the way in which the houses are built. Consisting of only one story, and occupying a great deal of ground, they present to the street only a series of whitewashed walls and red-tiled roofs, with here and there a window, carefully guarded by large bars of iron, and a pair of massive folding doors, studded on the outside with heavy nails; thus giving to it,

---

102. An army led by President Arce attacked the city of San Salvador without success on May 18, 1827, thereafter retreating to Cuilapa. This disastrous campaign, rather than an assault on Guatemala City, must have caused the confusion here mentioned.

at the best of times, more the appearance of a deserted than an inhabited city. . . . It contains about sixty *manzanas,* or squares of houses, formed by the intersection of streets at right angles, which vary in extent from a hundred and fifty to three hundred and fifty yards in front, and these are arranged so as to form one large square. On each side of the city, as the suburbs have increased, other houses have been erected, without much regard to uniformity.

The streets in general are broad, but wretchedly paved, with a considerable declivity from each side, which forms a gutter in the middle; so that while, after a heavy shower of rain, they are almost impassable from the sudden stream of water, at other times the sharp-pointed and ill-arranged pebbles extort groans from the unhappy sufferer who in light shoes is doomed to undergo the miserable penance of passing over them.

The *plaza,* or market-place, is a square of about one hundred and fifty yards each way, with a fountain in the middle; and, besides the daily market, is occupied by numerous temporary shops or stalls, and surrounded by buildings, offices, and shops. Projecting piazzas form a covered walk on three sides, under which trifling articles are exposed for sale. The public buildings are numerous, and consist of an university, five convents, four nunneries, a cathedral, four parish churches, and fifteen other churches or chapels of minor importance; besides a treasury, mint, and other government offices. Most of these are in a good style of architecture, and some of them judiciously decorated.

The houses of the respectable citizens are well built, and commodiously arranged. A description of one will give an idea of the rest. Let us enter, then, at that great folding-door, looking like an inn gate, with blank walls on each side. We open it, and immediately find ourselves in a large square court-yard, in the middle of which is an orange-tree in full bloom. All around it is a covered walk, or piazza, raised about a foot from the ground, the roof supported by wooden pillars. Under this piazza are seven or eight doors, leading into different apartments; each one having an interior communication with the rest, and all, of course, on the ground floor—stairs being almost unknown in Guatimala. The first room will probably be a common chamber. The next, a *sala,* or drawing-room, furnished with ten or a dozen antique chairs; an old-fashioned settee, with a slip of mat before it for a carpet; and two small dressing-tables, placed at an immense distance from one another, each bearing the image of a saint carefully enclosed in glass. Three or four pictures adorn the clean white-washed walls; and two lamps, cased in silver, hang from a roof in which all the naked beams are to be seen, with here and there a straggling cobweb. The floor, like that of all the rest of the rooms, will be paved with red tiles; its cleanliness depending upon the civilization of its owner. From hence we pass into a third apartment; probably the chief bed-chamber; serving also for a daily sitting-room, in which to receive visitors. It contains a handsome bed, a large mahogany wardrobe, a few chairs, and a cupboard with glass doors, in which may be seen carefully arranged all the stock of china, from the blue wash-hand basin down to the diminutive coffee-cup, till lately a more valuable property than a similar service of silver. By the side of the bed hangs an image of the Saviour on the cross, under a little scarlet canopy; and on a small table, in another corner, is placed St. Joseph, or the Virgin. The next two rooms will have little furniture, besides a bed, a chair, and an image: we shall therefore pass on to the *comedor*, or dining-room, which contains only one large oak table (a fixture), and seven or eight common wooden chairs. Next to this will be the kitchen: in one corner a large baking oven, of an oval shape; and in the middle of the room a mass of solid brickwork, three or four feet high, containing six or seven cavities for small charcoal fires, and conveniences for preparing the thousand different stews which are compounded in a Spanish *cocina*. To the right of this will be an inner yard, with its *pila*, or cistern of water; and further on the stables, with a second *pila* for the use of the cattle. The remaining apartments will be occupied according to the property or family of the owner. And this is a fair description of a respectable house, letting for a rent equal to about eighty pounds sterling, in the city of New Guatimala.

Among the various occupations which employ the time and attention of a traveller in a foreign land, few are more amusing, and, if properly exercised, more capable of being made instructive, than observation of the variety of customs which general usage, that imperious tyrant, has imposed upon its inhabitants. We are generally too apt to exult in the thought of our own superior civilization; and while we smile, sometimes contemptuously, at what we deem the absurdities of other nations, forget that we ourselves are no less under similar bondage, and act oftentimes in a way equally at variance with unsophisticated nature. Still, there are fashions in Guatimala which it would require more than common charity to speak of with respect; and among these stands foremost the immoderate use of tobacco, by both sexes. In private or in public, alone or in society, the Guatimalian must have his cigar, and the lady her *cigarrito*. His proudest accomplishment is skilfully to strike a light with his pocket match, which is always at hand, neatly cased in silver, and politely present his lighted cigar to the lady; who, in return, permits him to spit in every corner of her room without molestation. A gentleman consumes daily from fifteen to twenty *puros*; and a lady, of moderate pretensions to celebrity, fifty *cigarritos*.[103] Here, far from being "destructive of society's chief joys," the "pernicious weed" gives a zest to every conversation, and supplies all those vacuums which in English society are filled up by gazing on the carpet. No business can be transacted, no bargain made, without exchanging the cigar; and both in the streets and public places of amusement the ladies are to be seen smoking, with as much composure as in their own houses.

A history of the occupations of a domestic man during one day, will lay open, in great measure, the habits of the more respectable families.—At six he rises; and, if it be one of their numerous feast-days, accompanies his wife to Mass—at which rich and poor, masters and servants, indiscriminately kneel, without distinction of rank or place. Returning about seven, they take chocolate; which answers to our breakfast, with this exception, that it is not made a social meal: each one enters the dining-room (*comedor*) at the hour most agreeable to himself, and is then supplied with his cup of chocolate, made very thick and sweet; which, with a small loaf of bread, an egg, a little fried meat, and a glass of clear spring water, serves him till dinner. At this hour, during the warmer months, the habit of bathing, for which the houses afford so many conveniences, is very general; but in any other way the inhabitants appear to have the greatest aversion to the application of water. For weeks together the most respectable citizens never wash their hands, faces, or teeth; and the slightest sickness serves as a pretext for delaying the operation, as well as that of shaving, frequently for months: so that you have only to look at a gentleman's beard, to know how long he has had a cold; or to a lady's face, to discover when she last fancied herself indisposed.

From ten to twelve are the usual hours for morning calls and receiving visits. These possess, in general, the same characteristics as

103. Dunn explains that ten *cigarritos* are esteemed equal in tobacco content to one *puro*.

in other parts of the world. Friends meet as lovingly, talk as scandalously, hate each other as cordially, and lie as gracefully here, as in the most polished cities of civilized Europe. The only points of difference are, that the ladies shout out their observations in the highest note of the gamut, becloud each other's beauties with the fumes of tobacco, and part with an embrace as cordial as the majority of modern English kisses. These parties generally meet in the lady's bed-room; the gentlemen dressed *a la Inglesa*, with coats cut any thing but anatomically; and the ladies in black silk, with lace veils (*mantilla*) over their heads, splendidly worked silk-stockings, and shoes almost diminutive enough for the Empress of China. Modesty and prudery are here understood to be synonymous, and subjects are freely discussed in mixed parties to which common delicacy would seem to forbid the slightest allusion.

At one they dine, on soup, rice, vegetables, and meat of various kinds, cooked in as many different ways; with *dulces*, or sweetmeats, for a dessert, of which about two hundred different sorts are prepared. Fish frequently appears towards the close of the meal, and fruit is introduced before the cloth is drawn. Scarcely any wine is drunk: in many of the most respectable families it does not even make its appearance on the table. The whole concludes with a recitation, miscalled a thanksgiving. Well-bred people in Guatimala, like well-bred people in England, naturally feel that any thing like serious thanks to their Maker would subject them to the charge of fanaticism, and therefore arrange matters so that this service is merely understood to say that dinner is concluded.

From the *comedor* each individual adjourns to his bed-room, to take the *siesta* and digest his dinner. So universal is this practice, that from two to three the streets are deserted: old and young, masters and servants, are alike reclining on beds and sofas. The very domestic animals at this hour are to be seen stretching themselves in the sun, and, partaking of the infection, "join the general troop of sleep." Between three and four, things begin to revive; and first one, and then another, yawning, rubs his eyes, and strolls to the clock, to see how time has passed during his slumbers. Towards four the kitchen becomes again frequented, for chocolate; after which the occupations of the day are once more resumed.

Let us then take a walk into the streets, and see what is passing there. The shops, although generally well supplied with goods, possess no attractions: all are without windows, and nothing is displayed;

the open door-way being half covered with cloth, to keep out the sun. The daily market is now about over, and contains only a few stragglers buying at a cheaper rate the refuse of the day's sales; ten or a dozen half-naked Indians are basking in the sun; three or four soldiers are reclining against the pillars of the piazzas, humming a revolutionary air; and a little further on are two or three devoted Catholics most devoutly kneeling before the image of a saint, and apparently in a state of the most perfect abstraction. In a little while the tinkling of a bell is heard, notifying the approach of the viaticum. Instantly, high and low, poor and rich, are on their knees; till, as its feeble sound dies in the distance, one by one they rise and pursue their way.

The costume of the street varies somewhat from that of the house. The ladies, who in a morning are to be seen only in black, now parade the streets in dashing silk gowns, and without any covering for the head; while the fashionable beaux lounge by their sides in printed cotton jackets and Spanish cloaks, with one end of the latter carelessly thrown over the right shoulder.

Returning to our temporary home as the evening sets in, we find the gentlemen just come back from an excursion to the suburbs on their pacing mules or horses; each rider seated on a saddle rising three or four inches before and behind, and armed with an enormous pair of silver spurs. Before the saddle is a large skin of some shaggy-coated animal, hanging down to the heavy Spanish box-stirrup, or still heavier and indescribable one of iron; over which lies the long taper end of the bridle, made of narrow slips of hide twisted into a cord, and so long as to serve the purposes of a whip. To this is affixed an enormous bit, under which the poor beast writhes, and is effectually subdued.

By about seven o'clock the last gleam of twilight has disappeared, and the servants enter with the lights, reciting most devoutly the "*Bendito*," which may be thus translated, "Blessed and praised be the holy sacrament of the altar for ever and ever." In another hour the *sala* has assumed its evening character: cloaks and swords occupy the corners of the room; a small table at one end is surrounded by a party busily employed at *monte* (a game of cards) amidst clouds of smoke; and at the other end some lady, regardless of the noisy tongues of the gamblers, is playing a popular air upon a wretched marimba, or still worse piano, accompanying it with her voice. The miserable light yielded by two thin, long-wicked tallow-candles, in massy silver candlesticks, throws a gloom over the apartment, strangely in contrast with the light-hearted gaiety of its occupants. Formal parties are rare: friends drop in towards the evening without ceremony, amuse themselves for an hour or two, and retire generally without taking any kind of refreshment.

About ten o'clock the different members of the family sit down to a supper differing little from the dinner; eat heartily of its various dishes; and with stomachs loaded to a degree that would make most people tremble for fear of apoplexy, retire to bed, and in half an hour are all soundly asleep. In the more religious families, recitations of about a quarter of an hour in length, and mostly to the Virgin, are practised on those evenings when there are no visitors.

In some respects a strong parallel might be drawn between the domestic manners of the old families here, and those of country towns in England about a century ago. The uncarpeted floor—the heavy, clumsy furniture—the well-supplied wardrobe—the stock of china, carefully exhibited—are all characteristic of those days; while the rigid habits of economy—the unbounded hospitality to strangers, unaccompanied by any thing like splendid or showy entertainments—and especially the great degree of familiarity which subsists between mistress and servants—all concur in exhibiting that less refined and simpler state of society which existed in such places at the period referred to.

In some respects, however, they have made sufficient advancement, especially in the art of gambling. Their favourite game, *monte*, appears to have little attraction beside the facilities it affords for the indulgence of this detestable vice. In families the farthest removed from what is termed, by them, high players, I have seen ten or twelve pounds sterling lost and gained by individuals in a few hours.

In insincerity, also, they are by no means behind their European brethren, since there is not, probably, a country in the world where words and feelings have less connection. Mortal enemies, even where their enmity is notorious to all the world, will meet and embrace, after the customs of the country, with every external appearance of intimate friendship. By this procedure nobody is deceived. It seems to be an understood regulation, that, whatever may be the workings within, nothing shall disturb the serenity of the surface: so that even in time of civil war, when factions and party spirit are at their height, and the deepest hatreds are cherished, the external quiet of society remains unmolested. Were this *all*, it might be tolerated; but the moral effects of systematic deception are too melancholy to make one wish to see tranquillity purchased at so high a price.

... The Europeans, proud of their Castilian blood, look with the most ineffable contempt upon the natives, whom they consider their inferiors in knowledge, industry, and the exercise of the domestic virtues. The Americans, frankly acknowledging themselves deficient in information, and especially in knowledge of the world, bitterly accuse the Spanish nation as the cause of their misfortunes, and console themselves with the imaginary possession of a *viveza*, or aptitude, which, properly cultivated, would have produced master-spirits, capable of wielding with credit the rod of empire in the new world. The Europeans, chiefly composed of men who in their younger days have left the mother country, and by dint of honourable exertion have arrived at the possession of wealth, are distinguished by habits of economy, caution, and prudence in their engagements. The leading Americans, descendants of the Spaniards who at an earlier period acquired extensive fortunes by the monopolies they enjoyed and the despotism they exercised, have been brought up in those habits of indolence which seem inseparable from the climate, are dilatory and negligent in business, and too frequently dissipate their mental ennui at the gaming-table. Under the influence of these degrading habits, they frequently descend to little acts of meanness from which national pride defends the Spanish merchant; are doomed to see obscure Europeans acquiring wealth as rapidly as they are losing it; and find themselves in the possession of power and influence, without that steadiness of character, or those habits of business, which might in some measure have supplied the deficiency of education and native talent.[104]

But here it should be remarked, that the Americans themselves are divided into two parties, differing widely both in feeling and sentiment. The *liberals*, composed of the few individuals who have carefully gathered up some of the scattered rays of knowledge which, in

---

104. Dunn seems to have been the only writer in English of his generation who used either the noun or the adjective "American" as a designation in speaking of this region. In the case at hand, most writers would have said "Creoles" instead, as Dunn, 1829, himself on his page 90. On page 289 Dunn says, "Let those enjoy the pleasure of being whirled along in a close carriage, at the rate of fourteen miles an hour, who . . . consider it the height of enjoyment; but give me the romantic interest which belongs to an American party traversing mountainous districts on pacing mules."

spite of the vigilance of Spain, have for some years penetrated into the heart of the new continent, are possessed of a higher degree of intellect, and a greater energy, than the moderate party; but, unhappily, in casting off the slavish yoke of Rome, and effecting their mental independence, they have imbibed the worst doctrines of the French revolutionary school, and strikingly exhibit in the fury of their hatred the evil principles which prevailed at that melancholy period of European history. The *serviles*—consisting of the most influential families, who before the Revolution arrogated to themselves the title of *noblesse*, and ruled the country with a despotic hand, through the medium of the viceroys, whom they caressed and flattered—now fill the different offices of government; act upon Spanish principles; are hated and despised by all parties; yet maintain their posts, through the influence of the church and the resident Spaniards, who support their measures from fear of the excesses of the liberals. These, with the Europeans, from a dislike to every change and a feverish dread of innovation, steadily oppose whatever tends to lessen the influence of the Romish church, or to introduce a liberal system of commercial policy. The liberals, on the other hand, abruptly freed from a thraldom which they had borne for ages, and in some of the provinces suddenly advanced to power and place, seize on every new thing with avidity; plunge into schemes of which they understand nothing; and, in their zeal to overthrow all existing institutions, forget to separate the good from the bad, the wheat from the tares. The latter are as incautious as the former are fearful. The one holds wretched theories, but lessens the evil by mild and moderate practice: the other disgraces better principles by a miserable exemplification of them. In politics, the one is ultra republican; the other, ultra aristocratical. In religion, the former inclines to superstition; the latter, to scepticism. To foreigners, both parties are courteous and obliging, and never suffer local prejudices to interfere with the rites of hospitality.

Into these two classes the White population may be nearly equally divided. Difference of sentiment and of character, both mental and moral, unite in making them determined enemies; and their clashing opinions, feelings, and interests have, as might naturally have been expected, involved the country in all the horrors of a civil war.

This confusion of elements gives to Guatimala a character of its own, differing considerably from that of the sister republics. Liberated from the yoke of Spain not less by uncontroulable circumstances than by the force of moral feeling, it achieved its independence without an effort, and silently exchanged the rule of a despotic monarch for the factious struggles of opposing parties. Each has appealed to arms, excited the passions, and called out the energies of a dangerous ally in the Coloured population. Happy will it be for the disputants on either side, if these dissensions shall have subsided before this third party, powerful enough to extirpate both, wash out their differences in mingled blood!

Nor are such apprehensions altogether without foundation. The Mulatto, or mixed race, form, in fact, the physical force of the nation.[105] To a considerable degree of cunning they unite an energy to which the simple Indian is altogether a stranger, are less subject to the restraints of a superstitious creed, and more abandoned to the grosser vices of drunkenness and revenge. That such a population, armed and disciplined, inflated with new ideas of liberty and citizenship, and at the same time shut out, both by colour and character, from the councils and society of the Whites, must be dangerous to the state, it does not require great penetration to foresee. Perhaps the greatest security from such a contingency may be found in the hatred borne to them by the fourth class of inhabitants, the aboriginal Indians. Still, *these* are negative rather than positive friends. Their indolence, and perhaps their interest, would lead them, in such a crisis, rather to conceal themselves in the woods and mountains, than to act as partisans.

Such is the existing state both of the city and republic of Guatimala. Composed of these combustible materials, its physical and political situation may be regarded as similar. Containing within its bosom an active internal fire, under the influence of which it trembles and is convulsed, it is hourly in danger of eruptions more calculated to desolate than to enlighten, to destroy than to improve.

This prospect, gloomy to the lovers of true freedom, becomes still darker to the eye of the philanthropist and the Christian, when viewed in connection with the state of public morals. If any state, and especially a republic, be strong in proportion to the mass of virtue concentrated in its population; and if it be in vain to look for political integrity in the absence of private honour, then is the situation of

---

105. Dunn explains (1829, p. 90): "The offspring of Negroes and Indians, of Whites and Indians, as well as the descendants of African Negroes, are included under the term Mulattoes, by which they are generally known; sometimes, however, they are called *Mestizoes*, or *Ladinos*."

Guatimala truly lamentable. With a lazzaroni in rags and filth, a Coloured population drunken and revengeful, her females licentious, and her males shameless, she ranks as a true child of that accursed city which still remains, as a living monument of the fulfilment of prophecy and the forbearance of God, "the hold of every foul spirit, the cage of every unclean and hateful bird."[106]

... The ... source of a great part of the wretchedness, and consequent degradation, of the lower classes, is to be found in their prevailing habits of intoxication, and in the multitude of spirit-shops, which on every hand offer temptations too powerful to be resisted by a people untrained to any habits of self-government. The liquor commonly taken is prepared from what are termed *panelas*: these are small loaves of unrefined sugar, drawn from the cane ... ; they are excessively sweet and cloying to the taste. As this liquor can be made cheaply enough to come within the reach of the poorest Indian, immense quantities are disposed of, under the name of *chicha*; and these wretched creatures may be seen rolling about the streets and suburbs, in a state sometimes approaching to madness, and sometimes to insensibility, under its overpowering influence. In this way they spend the little money they acquire by their labour, and never rise higher in the scale of civilization than the low grade in which their progenitors have lived and died.

Having remained in the capital till we had made ourselves in some measure familiar with the manners of the people, and procured such information as could best be obtained at the seat of government, we proposed to undertake a journey to the Pacific. Among the acquaintance we had formed, was the proprietor of an extensive farm about six leagues from the city, on the route we intended to take; of whose invitation we gladly availed ourselves to spend two or three weeks at his hacienda; and a party of his friends was formed to accompany us thus far. On the evening previous to the day fixed for our departure, twelve extra horses had arrived from the farm, and before daylight the note of preparation sounded in our ears. After much delay we started; and a more motley group can scarcely be imagined: Chaucer's pilgrims to Canterbury could hardly have displayed a more whimsical variety either of dress or character. First led the way, a friar of the order of La Merced, dressed in the long white flannel

---

106. The reference is to Rome; the quotation from Revelation 18:2.

gown and little straw hat of his order. Then trotted forward a secular priest, with black gown and clerical saddle-cloth. A Spanish gentleman, dressed in the Mexican fashion, and three others in cotton printed jackets, with high saddles, pistols, and swords, and large shaggy skins hanging down before their knees, followed; immediately preceding a Spanish lady, seated on a saddle similar to an old English pillion, and an English lady and gentleman, in the costume of their own country.[107] Three female servants, with black beaver hats, under which streamed before the wind their long hair carefully plaited with pink ribbons, succeeded; and Indians, with cargo, brought up the rear of this heterogeneous company.

Nor did the characters of the individuals differ less widely than their dresses. The friar, who had a small case hung round his neck by a black ribbon, declared it contained holy oil, the tears of San Ambrosio, and other precious relics; while the lady, who appeared somewhat sceptical, as positively asserted that he would never take the trouble of carrying any thing but brandy: denials were useless; and with a loud laugh, in which his clerical brother heartily joined, he acknowledged the pious deception, nor seemed ashamed of his impudent imposture. . . .

Leaving on the right the small village of Pinula,[108] we began to ascend the ridge of mountains. . . . From their summit the road becomes elevated, and commands a fine view of the adjacent country. . . . A few miles further brought us in sight of the gate leading to lands belonging to the estate, and in a short time we had arrived at the house.

Leaving our party at the farm, two of us set out for the shores of the Pacific. . . .[109] Passing through a long lane, chiefly of wild fruit-trees, and ending in beautiful meadows, we began to descend by a steep and rocky path into the valley of Petapa.

From Sapoti to . . . Raudal, a distance of about two and a half leagues, the road is level, but obstructed by immense quantities of bushes and low shrubs.[110] The latter place, only a fisherman's hut, is situated about a league from the mouth of the Michatoya, across the stream of which, a short distance from the ocean, is formed the

107. Regarding the English lady, see Ch. 1 n. 98.
108. Santa Catarina Pinula.
109. J. Haefkens was the companion; see Dunn, 1829, p. 5.
110. These hamlets lay between El Obero and Iztapa.

celebrated Bar of Iztapa.[111] There is no other mode of going thither except in miserable canoes, which are paddled along the *esteros,* or inlets of the ocean, the banks of which are lined with mangroves. Near the mouth of the river there are a couple of huts, inhabited by fishermen, who pack and salt fish for the capital, of which large quantities are dried and sent up. The population of these places consists chiefly of Mulattoes and Negroes, with a few Indians: they have a small church, but, as the climate is not considered good, no priest will live amongst them. . . . The number of insects is immense: some of the men were horribly disfigured by the bites they had received.

From Almolonga we came to La Antigua, where we spent a few days, one of which was devoted to the ascent of the Volcan de Agua (Water Volcano). . . .

Leaving the Old City a little before day-light, we soon arrived at the convent of San Juan Obispo, which stands at the foot of the mountain, surrounded by a few huts, and almost buried in bushes and flowers. From this point the ascent begins; and from hence to the small town of Santa María it is gradual, and can be accomplished on a mule. . . .

Santa María . . . is an Indian village, which contains a population . . . who chiefly find employment in the old city. In the colder months, many of them are occupied in carrying snow from the mountain, for the supply both of La Antigua and the capital. Here we procured guides, and set forward on foot. The ascent we found steep and painful; the path, which was slippery with the dew, affording us a very uncertain footing.

From the village, to the height of about nine thousand feet, only a few scattered pines, two or three cherry-trees, and some wild apples, diversify the scene. Soon after this we enter the middle region, of forests, consisting almost entirely of American oaks. The soil here was composed of an exceedingly rich black loam. The wild cane we found rising to an amazing height and thickness; the hand plant (*arbol de las manitas*), or *cheirostemon platanoides,* growing to a height of forty feet, with its corolla glistening in scarlet and gold;[112] and many

111. In present-day terminology, the Michatoya (outlet for Lake Amatitlán) is a tributary of the María Linda which reaches the ocean at Iztapa.
112. The hand plant or hand tree, so called because its spreading stamens look like an open hand, is now designated as *Chiranthodendron pentadactylon.*

others were flourishing luxuriantly. A little beyond these, the keen cold air sweeps over the sides of the mountain, unshielded by forests. As we gradually ascend in the scale of vegetation, pines again present themselves, almost devoid of foliage, and highly resinous. These continue till we reach the summit, and spread themselves on the margin of the crater, among the rocks and stones which are scattered around them.

By about two o'clock we had arrived at the top, very much exhausted. The clouds, which had gathered during the ascent, now formed a thick veil around the mountain far below us, through which it was impossible to pierce; and we were thus in great measure disappointed of the view we had expected to enjoy of the surrounding country. The spacious crater is completely concave, and produces a powerful echo. Great numbers of huge stones, covered with moss and grass, are scattered over its surface, which is sterile and unproductive. The thermometer at two o'clock P. M. stood at 42°; the difference between the base and the summit, at the same hour, being about thirty degrees.

About three o'clock we commenced the descent, which, although more rapid, was not much less painful than the ascent: the steep slippery path kept us almost continually on a run, except when interrupted by falls; from which our guides, although possessing the advantage of bare feet, were not exempt. . . . By five o'clock we had again arrived at La Antigua, completely worn out by fatigue, and, although gratified by the excursion, feeling no anxiety to make a second trip.

The following day we bent our course homeward, and arrived safely at the capital.

As there appeared to be no immediate prospect of a permanent cessation of hostilities between the two contending states of Salvador and Guatimala, we resolved to avail ourselves of the first favourable opportunity, which the retirement of the armies from the immediate neighbourhood of Guatimala might present, for repairing with all practicable expedition to the coast, and embarking for England.[113]

Our route back was much the same as that we had taken in our approach to the city. . . . At every stage the inquiry was put, "What news

113. Dunn's subtitle would indicate that he left Central America in May or June, 1828. The federal army made its third invasion of the state of San Salvador in late February, 1828, and remained until defeated in September and October.

from the army?" and each individual had some story to tell of atrocities committed by the guerilla parties. Most of these, however, we soon found to be fictitious tales, invented purely to gratify the natural propensity of man for the marvellous, or the yet baser purpose of exciting our fears. . . .

We reached Izabal in a very exhausted state. The passage of the mountain was truly frightful. The acclivities, which in dry weather we had climbed securely, were now so slippery, and afforded such uncertain footing for the mules, that not unfrequently, in spite of all our care and their sagacity, both beast and rider were precipitated into the dirt. At other times, the deep morasses, which had been formed during the wet season, completely impeded our progress, and rendered it doubtful whether we should not be obliged to sleep on the mountain. At length, however, we reached the eastern base, and, covered with mud and exhausted with fatigue, threw ourselves on some piles of goods which were stored in one of the huts, where we slept till morning, thankful that such a bed (however hard) was ours.

We found the village quite full of emigrants, anxious to leave the republic; several of whom lay ill of fever in the hut where we had passed the night.

The next morning, on inquiry, we learned that no vessel was likely to leave Izabal for some time, excepting a small Colombian sloop of about twelve tons burden, which was in a very shattered condition. But any thing appeared better than remaining at this miserable place, with the risk of falling victims to disease. Accordingly, twenty of us agreed to charter the sloop for Omoa, and to embark on the following day.

Our voyage was a miserable one, and enabled us to form some faint idea of the horrors of a slaver's middle passage. It rained incessantly. No where could we find shelter, excepting in a kind of hole under the deck, about six feet square; and into this we crowded ourselves. The winds roared, and the waves dashed over us; but the same God who had so frequently appeared for us, mercifully preserved our health and maintained our spirits. We consoled ourselves by the hope that it could not last many days; and, at length, experienced the delight of seeing at a distance the mast-heads of several vessels lying at anchor near Omoa.

Omoa, although much larger than Izabal, is but a paltry town, consisting of about fifty houses, generally of wood, and defended by a very respectable fort or castle, which must have cost a considerable sum in its erection. The harbour is safe: there is good anchorage; and when we were there seven or eight vessels were taking in cargoes; but most of their crews were sick, owing to the unhealthiness of the place.

From Omoa we returned to Belize, and, after remaining some time in that settlement, secured a passage in a schooner bound for the port of New York.

Chapter 2

People, Places, and Politics, 1831–40

CENTRAL AMERICA'S second decade of independence, and her last of federation, brought five more book-writing travelers to the isthmus. All five came late in the decade, the first of them arriving ten years and eight months after Henry Dunn found his way to these shores. This means that the era of Francisco Morazán and contemporary liberals in state and federal governments went unreported by foreigners except to a limited extent by Haefkens in his third, nonpersonal volume. The Morazán regime was already hard pressed for its life when the new group of visitors began to appear on the scene.

Morazán's first term in office (1830–35) was marred by two interventions in the affairs of San Salvador (1832 and 1834). The first came in connection with a disturbance in Honduras and an invasion led from Mexican territory by Arce, designed to overthrow the Morazán government. The second happened when federal authorities were moving their capital from Guatemala to San Salvador. The greatest step taken by the federal government during this time was a constitutional amendment (in force in 1833) declaring freedom of religion; but the Morazán regime set the tone for the state assemblies which passed a variety of reform legislation. José del Valle won the federal presidency in elections of 1834, only to die before the votes were counted. Morazán was then elected for another term (1835–39).

Serious revolt broke out again in 1837 in the wake of a cholera epidemic. Leader of the insurrection was Rafael Carrera whose followers were largely Indian. Carrera seized Guatemala City briefly in February, 1838, and from this time on constituted a power with which

Morazán had to reckon. In April, 1838, Nicaragua seceded from the union, and on May 30 the federal Congress virtually invited a dissolution of the federation by resolving that each state legislature might secede or not as it pleased. Honduras and Costa Rica withdrew in November. In January, 1839, Honduras and Nicaragua united in opposition to Morazán. In such circumstances, no federal elections were possible before the expiration of Morazán's term on February 1, 1839. Morazán nevertheless carried on the struggle while vice-president Diego Vigil held together a small remnant of federal officials. Carrera took Guatemala City in April, 1839, and the state of Guatemala seceded. Morazán made a last great attempt in March, 1840, to strike Carrera down, but with the odds against him from every quarter was forced to evacuate Salvadoran territory in April, taking Vigil and a number of friends along.[1]

The most noted of the liberal governments of this decade was that of the state of Guatemala, served by *jefe* Mariano Gálvez from 1831 to 1838. In addition to a number of anticlerical laws designed to separate this state completely from the church, Gálvez' legislature designed an elaborate new system of education (1832), arranged contracts for British colonization of a planned new gateway for Guatemala's Caribbean commerce (1834), and adopted basic codes of law inspired by those of Louisiana (a decision of 1835 implemented in 1837). This state was the one where the cholera epidemic began as well as the insurrection of Carrera. When Carrera seized Guatemala City in February, 1838, Gálvez gave way to his *vice-jefe*, and a new liberal state of Los Altos was proclaimed in Quezaltenango. (Marcelo Molina was its *jefe*, 1838–40.) Mariano Rivera Paz, under aristocratic influence, became the acting *jefe* of Guatemala in July, 1838, was barred from his office by Morazán in January, 1839, and returned three months later under Carrera's auspices to serve out the rest of the decade (with the title of president after November, 1839).[2] In January, 1840, Carrera ended the state of Los Altos by military action. By the end of that year, virtually all of Guatemala's liberal legislation of the decade had been repealed.

1. United States diplomats G. W. Montgomery and J. L. Stephens recorded personal impressions of Morazán, Carrera, and Vigil in the years 1838–40, presented below as follows: Montgomery–Morazán, 1838, pp. 163–65; Stephens–Carrera, 1839, pp. 208–10; Stephens–Vigil, 1840, pp. 214–16, 219–22; Stephens–Morazán, 1840, pp. 222–24; and Stephens–Carrera, 1840, pp. 224–26.
2. Stephens visits Rivera Paz, pp. 206–7, and comments on the lack of dignity in his position, pp. 224–25, both below.

Politics in the neighboring state of San Salvador were meanwhile almost completely dominated by the federal government. *Jefe* José María Cornejo was eliminated from office (1832) for his apparent sympathy with the invasion attempt by Arce. Renovation of the authorities through elections was followed by a new uprising in 1833, bringing Joaquín San Martín to power until he was deposed by Morazán in 1834.[3] A succession of persons amenable to the federal government then followed, with Diego Vigil (1836–38) and Timoteo Menéndez (1838–39) the more long-lasting of the lot. Though various reforms had been adopted, there was little time to put them into effect before the federation ended. Morazán himself acted as *jefe* of San Salvador for seven months in 1839–40. In May of the latter year, after he was gone, appeared Francisco Malespín, chosen by Carrera as San Salvador's *comandante de armas,* who soon showed his ability to rule without being chief of state.

Honduras followed the liberal line of development, though less drastically than Guatemala, from 1831 to 1838, and thereafter became the scene of conflict. The disturbances of 1832 were accompanied by the death by fever of *jefe* José Antonio Márquez (1831–32). Joaquín Rivera, the liberal next in this position, served out his full term (1833–36). Justo José Herrera (1837–38) was not so fortunate, as forces opposed to the federation became dominant. Honduras' secession from the union was followed by the adoption of a new constitution in January, 1839. Francisco Zelaya acted as chief executive (1839–41) until selection of the first president.

Nicaragua in this decade more than the preceding one followed a rational course, though with occasional fierce outbreaks of violence. Dionisio Herrera resigned in the face of one incident in 1833, but was persuaded to finish out his term. His successor José Núñez (1834–35) served only until a new *jefe* could be chosen in delayed elections. José Zepeda (1835–37) was murdered while in office, after which Núñez held the position again (1837–38). Nicaragua's early decision to abandon the union was followed by the preparation of her second constitution, completed in November, 1838. Under its provisions, "supreme directors" were to rule as chiefs of state for two-year terms, but in the disturbed months of 1838–40 none came near serving even half that length of time.

Costa Rica continued its isolated life through the period of the fed-

3. Montgomery visits the horse ranch of San Martín four years after his deposition, pp. 232–33 below.

eration, only to become involved in conflict at its end. José Rafael de Gallegos, *jefe* 1833–35, made arrangements for the capital to ambulate among four cities, but resigned when much fault was found with his regime. Braulio Carrillo, in the anticlerical tradition, was elected to serve out the term (1835–37) and settled the capital again at San José. Manuel Aguilar, his successor (1837–38), was overthrown (in Costa Rica's first disturbance of the constitutional order) by Carrillo, who now ruled (1838–42) by his own determination. Carrillo was unfriendly to the union (hence Costa Rica's secession) and unfriendly enough to Morazán that he would not allow him to seek refuge in Costa Rica when he fled from San Salvador.[4]

Mosquitia was even farther removed from the scene of isthmian events, but not so far that a visitor would not hear of them. The British influence grew in this area as the power of the federation subsided, until English-speaking residents were common along this coast and on the formerly uninhabited Bay Islands.[5]

JAMES JACKSON JARVES, only seventeen years of age, arrived at Acajutla, on the other side of the isthmus from the Bay Islands and Mosquitia, January 24, 1838, on his way from Hawaii to his home in Boston, Massachusetts. His rapid February trip across the isthmus, through territory held by rival forces, has the aspect of real drama. It forms the last chapter of a book published in Boston, 1843, entitled *Scenes and Scenery in the Sandwich Islands, and a Trip Through Central America: Being observations from my note-book during the years 1837–1842*. As one may note by a comparison of dates, the return trip described in the last chapter did not conclude the experiences of the author in the Sandwich Islands. He in fact distinguished himself there, after the Central American venture, as the editor of Hawaii's only newspaper and in 1843 (before the issuance of his book of travels) as the author of a history of the islands. Later in life, Jarves acquired fame as a connoisseur of Pre-Raphaelite Italian art, which he collected for sale in the United States well before most persons in his home country had developed a taste for it.[6] His death came in 1888.

Most of Jarves' trip across Central America was a grand effort to

---

4. Stephens makes brief mention of Aguilar in exile in San Salvador, p. 214, and tells of an interview with Carrillo, pp. 217–19 below.

5. British Mosquitian resident T. Young visits some persons on the Bay Islands, pp. 200–203 below.

6. See Francis Steegmuller, *The Two Lives of James Jackson Jarves*.

avoid meeting people, especially all sorts of officials. His account is thus not one to consult for interviews with prominent personages. Neither should the reader expect from Jarves an understanding of this land which would begin to compare with his great comprehension of life in Hawaii. For a very believable description of fiesta in the face of disaster, however, and of quietness in the midst of havoc, this is an enticing narrative:[7]

It has always been, and seems likely ever to be, a problem of considerable importance to the sojourner at the Hawaiian Islands, when his thoughts and desires are homeward turned, how he shall reach that home. Be he of the United States, or England, or France, the question is one of equal interest to each of them, and whatever may have been their differences of opinions while residing on the sea-girt group, a unison of sentiment is sure, on such an occasion, to manifest itself. All are equally desirous of reaching home the safest, speediest, and most agreeable way, and of a multiplicity of bad and dangerous routes it is no easy matter to fix the choice upon any one.

It was in the fall of 1837, that I found myself at Honolulu, one day, in company with a half a dozen others, all of whom were speculating as to how they should reach the United States. The arguments, pro and con, the several ways that presented themselves, it is now useless to repeat. Panama was to be the first port we should make, and the Isthmus of Darien the crossing-place, thus combining as little land and water in our jaunt as it were possible. A diminutive brigantine was found, the . . . Clementine, . . . the agent of which engaged to land us at the port we sought. A little scouring and furbishing prepared her for our reception. . . .

On the 5th of December, under a succession of cheers from the crowd assembled to witness our departure, and a couple of guns from a friendly brig, hands were shaken, anchor weighed, top-sail sheeted home, and in ten minutes the Clementine had cleared the last point of the reef. . . . In eighteen days, the coast of California was descried, along whose rocky and barren shore we sailed, keeping within a few miles. . . .

We . . . floated along, seldom exceeding seventy-five miles per day, until day-break of the morning of the 10th of January, 1838, when finding ourselves becalmed off the port of Acapulco, the Captain de-

7. Jarves, 1843, pp. 283–86, 290–95, 298–302, 306–9, 314–15, 319–33, 334, 337–39.

termined upon sending a boat ashore to procure supplies of fresh provisions. . . .

On the 20th of January, so slow had been our progress, from twenty-five to forty miles per day, we had only come in sight of the famous volcanoes of Agua and Fuego. From their great altitude . . . they remained in view for several days. At early dawn their summits were remarkably distinct and bold, presenting a giant outline, springing, as it were, from out the very horizon. But at sunset, nothing could exceed the beautiful hues with which their tops were enshrouded. Long after the sun had sank beneath the ocean to the west, his rays hovered and played about their snowy heights, reflecting a flood of light of various colors, sometimes dazzling, then mellow, and gradually disappearing, until the blackness of night shrouded the whole landscape.[8]

On the 24th we dropped anchor in the roadstead of Acajutla. It was our intention merely to replenish our stores, and then make all despatch for Panama, which was still six hundred miles distant.

So prevalent had been the calms, that for the past fortnight we had made but four hundred miles. After so long a confinement on board our small craft, the shore looked more than ordinarily tempting; it was verdant to the beach, which was lined with a formidable row of breakers. It was late in the evening before the brigantine was made snug and riding at her anchor, the first time it had been dropped for sixty days. At night several volcanoes were visible, emitting either smoke or flames. That of Izalco, which was nearest us, glowed like a Brobdignag lighthouse; showing a steady and immense ball of fire. Some of our party fancied, before the light had wholly gone, they felt the shock of an earthquake. It was not improbable, though it must have been very faint, for, novices as we were to such freaks of nature, we could not agree upon a unanimous verdict as to its genuineness or not.

The roadstead of Acajutla is open and exposed to the surges of the Pacific at its greatest width. Consequently, landing through its surf is not altogether fun, as some of our number soon learned, to their cost. The first boat sent ashore was knocked end over end, and thrown

---

8. Dunn, 1829, p. 321, speaks of snow being carried from Agua; Haefkens, 1832, p. 351, says that Fuego's crown is usually covered with white snow; and Dunlop, 1847, pp. 91–92, mentions Agua's ice and heavy hoarfrost. Jarves, however, seems to be alone in his picturing of "snowy heights" for Agua and Fuego as seen from a distance.

high upon the beach, broken and useless for the future. Several of the crew were injured, though fortunately, not seriously. The launch was then tried, and it met with a similar somerset, though owing to its stronger materials it was not stove. The passengers who had ventured in her were rolled up the beach, choking with salt and sand, and most thoroughly soused. After these mishaps, we used the country launches or bungos. An English man-of-war brig, but a few days previous to our arrival, lost two men in the surf, and her boat was detained ashore for one week. . . .

A battery of heavy guns surmounts a steep hill, fronting the landing-place. Ascending the hill by a stone causeway, we reached the custom-house and a range of extensive warehouses, which at a distance made a very imposing appearance, but upon nearer inspection were found to be mostly in ruins. They were formerly occupied as store-houses for merchandise, under the Spanish regime, when trade and industry were in a more prosperous condition than at present. A captain of the port, a few soldiers, and a few other characters, who were neither too lazy nor too proud to bestir themselves, provided they were well paid, constituted the military force. All were very civil and obliging, and gave us not the slightest trouble in bringing our baggage ashore. With all the signs of decay about us, the spot was a cheerful looking one. In the rear of the custom-house was the town. It consisted of about two dozen cane huts, through the interstices of whose sides the weather had free access. Their style of building argued much for the salubrity of the place, and evenness of its temperature. Grass hammocks, a wooden stool or two, a few shelves, and some nondescript articles of earthen-ware, constituted the sum total of their household effects. The climate required but little clothing, and as for the inhabitants, they were of all hues, the copper color greatly predominating. Their occupations seemed to be limited; those we saw were either idly swinging in their hammocks, washing clothes, or else dancing most vigorously to the notes of an instrument resembling the guitar.

Leaving them to the full enjoyment of their pursuits, I wandered again with two of my fellow passengers towards the custom-house. Upon reaching it, a lady, whose personal appearance and the deference paid her showed her to be of a higher rank than the other females whom we had met, accosted us in a courteous manner, and invited us to enter her dwelling. She ushered us into a large room, which formed a wing of the custom-house. The walls, which were several feet thick, were black with age and dirt. The floor was of rough stone. One unglazed window, secured by iron bars and massive shutters, let light into the apartment. The furniture consisted of several trunks made of ox-hide, a bench, a table, a chair, and a stool, all of the rudest construction; the latter of which were allotted to us, while the good lady, *par necessitate*, seated herself on the bed, a diminutive species of couch, decorated with lace curtains, ornamented with silver clasps. Our hostess evidently was young, but appeared to be afflicted with some painful disorder. She soon informed us of its nature, and to verify her assertions, brought forward vials of horrid looking mixtures, the very sight of which was sufficient to make a well man feel qualmish. She seemed to feel all the interest in their several virtues, that a fond mother does in her children.

An invitation to dine had been extended to us, and hungry as our ramble had made us, we were quite curious, with the glance we had already had of her domestic arrangement, to discover how so important a ceremony was to be accomplished. A few weeks more experience in the country, and we looked back upon our entertainment of this day, in much the same light that the Israelites of yore did to the flesh-pots of Egypt. However, it was evident that the lady's hospitality somewhat exceeded her resources, but she knew well that if we left her roof our chance for going dinnerless that day was by no means problematical. There was no going on shipboard, and as for a meal in Acajutla sufficient for three ravenous yankees, you might as well look for an orange-grove in Greenland. It was no fault of hers that we did not fare sumptuously. Two servant women, on whom it would have been difficult to have decided whether filth or rags predominated, made their appearance, and from one of the aforementioned trunks dislodged two perfect knives and forks, two imperfect ditto, and a few plates. These materials, with a couple of tumblers, completed the table gear. Several stews liberally saturated with garlics, and some capital white bread, to which we did abundant justice, I fear to the serious detriment of her store, furnished us a much better repast than we had anticipated. It was our first dinner in Central America, eaten with the more zest from being provided in the spirit of genuine hospitality. The lady's kindness extended even to loaning her pet-horse, a beautiful animal. Her rank was not inconsiderable. She was a niece of General Morazan, then President of the Republic, with whose romantic career, and melancholy end, the public have since been made acquainted. God grant, that his kind niece, if she survived her medicines, did not share his misfortunes.

Such discouraging accounts were told us of the calms between this port and Panama, and the long delay that we should probably be subjected to, in endeavoring to reach that place, that we held a grand council, and came to the unanimous decision to leave the brigantine here, and make the best of our way over land, to the port of Izabal on the Gulf of Dulce,[9] a jaunt which we were informed would occupy us eight days.

Sonsonate lies fifteen miles inland. The road thither is through a forest, dotted at intervals with small Indian hamlets. Upon our arrival there, our first care was a lodging-place. A posâda was first tried, but the gambling, fighting, and carousing, after one night's experience within its precincts, drove us to seek fresh quarters. Fortunately, these were found in a private family, whose attention and kindness to us were unremitted. Upon taking possession of our new quarters, we learned news that was by no means agreeable. Without being made acquainted with the particulars, we heard that a civil war was raging in the interior, on the very line of our intended route, and that the inhabitants were particularly exasperated against foreigners.

Sonsonate is situated amid an exceedingly rich country, and is one of the chief towns of the State of San Salvador. . . . A considerable stream, called the Rio Grande, crossed by a very good stone bridge, runs by one extremity of the town. Its banks are exceedingly picturesque; at one place its waters are diverted into a narrow canal, of about two feet in depth. Passing along its borders, I noticed some twenty negro women, entirely naked, seated in the stream, with the water flowing by them to their waists, while they were unconcernedly laving the remainder of their bodies. As spectators did not at all disturb them, I conceived it to be a custom as common as it was refreshing, and from what I then saw, judged that not unfrequently, hours were occupied in this natural bath. At any rate, they were in most excellent spirits, and passing their jokes from one to another, they shook their fat sides with laughter. Numbers of their sex and color were filling water-jars beside them.

The vicinity of the town is hilly. Near it are a number of valuable plantations, belonging to foreigners, of which the principal, a sugar and indigo hacienda, is owned by Dr. Drivin, a French gentleman. The vats used for the indigo, on his estate, are the same that were built of brick and stuccoed, by the Jesuits, more than two centuries ago; they then owned extensive landed possessions in this neighborhood.

9. The Gulf of Dulce is of course Lake Izabal.

Dr. Drivin discovered them quite accidentally on his lands, and after they were cleaned out, found them quite as serviceable as if new.[10]

Sonsonate was once a city of considerable magnitude and importance. Ruins of houses and other buildings, are to be discovered at the extremities of several of the streets. Farther on, the foundations only of others, and the pavements of the city are to be traced even beyond. Vegetation, which here is so rapid and destructive in its growth, has nearly covered these remains from the eye. . . .

Sonsonate . . . is regularly laid out; the streets are wide and clean, though much overgrown with grass, and well paved. Many of the houses are even elegant. They are mostly of one story, built of stone, with thick and massive walls, and erected around a hollow square. The interior forms a pretty courtyard. Externally, they are whitewashed, and have large unglazed windows, ornamented with green lattice-work. A rural and quiet air pervades the whole place. . . .

The carnival season came on before our departure, and what the town lacked in enterprise for business, it made up in zeal for fun and deviltry. Our hostess underwent a visitation from numerous country cousins, who came in to witness the show. All were hospitably received, and, with her former boarders, made a large household. Now we lived in clover. Cakes and confectionary were showered upon us by the good people, who seemed determined that if our religious sympathies refused to participate in the general jollification, there should be nothing to complain of, on the part of our alimentive.

The town which but a day before was as quiet as a Sabbath in New England, now became a scene of joyful confusion.

Scarcely had the town subsided to its usual degree of quiet, when news from Guatimala threw it into a complete ferment, and proved to us that if we would cross the country we must do it quickly. In peaceful times it was no pleasant matter, and now a sanguinary civil war was raging the prospect was any thing but cheering. Carrera, at the head of three thousand ferocious Indians, after some severe fighting, had just captured the city of Guatimala, killed the Vice President of the Republic, and committed many excesses.[11] His ill-will was particularly directed against foreigners, as they were supposed to favor

---

10. Stephens (see below, p. 213) and Dunlop, 1847, p. 68, both identify this gentleman as Dr. Drivon from the island of St. Lucia.

11. Carrera's seizure of Guatemala City and the death of vice-president José Gregorio Salazar occurred on February 1, 1838.

the administration of Morazan. Indeed, it was by stirring up the dormant prejudices of the lowest and most ignorant classes, that he had been able to attach to himself so large a party. Hatred and revenge mingled with his ambitious views, for his young and beautiful wife had been ravished by some troops of Galvas, the Governor of the State of Guatimala. The religious sentiments of the mass had been enlisted in his cause, and the bigoted portion of the priesthood won, by the assurances of reëstablishing the convents and monasteries, which had been broken up by the liberal party. All heretics were to be banished. Added to this fanaticism, was an infatuation which promised to be more deadly still. The Asiatic cholera, the year before, had swept over the country, destroying thousands, and in some instances proving fatal to almost entire districts of Indians. Their filthy habits aggravated its destructive tendencies. But Carrera or his partisans, for he was then scarcely more than a wild, ignorant, and savage Indian, artfully spread abroad the calumny, that the epidemic was caused by foreigners, who had poisoned the springs, with the intention of exterminating the native population. This tale, notwithstanding its improbability, was greedily swallowed by the blinded multitude, who are ever more desirous of seeking the causes of their misfortunes in the faults of others than in themselves. Many of the foreign residents were wealthy men; a crime in the eyes of the envious brigands, which could only be expiated by their property passing into their hands. Duped by their leaders, the Indians had already begun to commit acts of violence. . . .

A traveller . . . was . . . waylaid, robbed, and obliged to drink at one draught a bottle of milk, which hung at his saddle-bow. A small quantity of arsenic, which he had about him to prepare bird-skins with, fortunately escaped their observation. Had the Indians detected it, they would have sent it in pursuit of the milk. In fact, foreigners of any nation had little to expect, besides robbery and a cruel death, from the roving bands of either party, should they fall in with them. Morazan, at the head of a strong force, was then encamped at Santa Ana, a town eighteen miles from Sonsonate. The roads were infested with ladrones, and travelling was considered unsafe in any quarter. We held a council of war, as to what course it was advisable to pursue. Upon the whole, taking into consideration the revolutionary spirit which had already begun to manifest itself in Sonsonate, we came to the conclusion that we should not add to our dangers, by being on the road, and concluded to start forthwith. It was necessary to be as quiet as possible in our preparations, for fear some of the marauders who were on the watch should learn our plans and destination and intercept us. A valuable auxiliary presented himself at this time in the person of a Mexicanized Englishman, who, thoroughly acquainted with the language and manners of the people, was intending to cross the continent to embark for England. Through his friends, he obtained a letter to the chief of Chiquimula, a large town which had just declared in favor of Carrera. Our road lay directly through it; and, in case of trouble, the letter might be serviceable. The government officers residing at Sonsonate, gave us passports which would be equally useful, in case we met with any of the troops of Morazan, though it was a question whether they would not have proved a passport to greater ill-treatment, were they found upon us by the revolutionists. A trusty muleteer and two arrieros were engaged as far as Gualán, a town on the borders of the State of Honduras.[12]

Three weeks had been passed quite pleasantly in Sonsonate. Our worthy landlady, kind to the last, loaded our *alforcas* with bread and fowls, knowing that we should meet with none half so good after leaving her threshold. The smallness of her bill was a matter of universal surprise, expecting, as we did, that in that particular we should experience the usual fate of travellers. Light as were the charges, I hope, for her sake, that they were double the usual fares; her bill would not have been disputed had we known them to be so. The reception we experienced on entering the country was so different from the treatment we received before we were able to bid it farewell, that it left a strong impression on our minds. We had been cautioned against taking medicines with us, or any thing, the nature of whose composition we should have any decided objections to making a forced meal upon. Accordingly, our baggage was ransacked for all suspicious articles; pills and powders, salves and ointments, lotions, and a host of quackery, were brought from their lurking-places, and speedily consigned to destruction. Some hungry fowls seized upon some pills which I threw away, and devoured them. Not being without some doubts as

12. There is little real evidence, from Jarves' own account or other sources, that Gualán lay in any strict sense on a boundary line. Jarves' statements here and below to that general effect do suggest that at the time of his trip the lower Motagua valley was indeed counted a part of Honduras, whose regime at that point had not yet deserted the federation. Maps printed in the 1830's, republished in *Cartografía de la América Central* (Guatemala, 1929), do not agree on the border line; but neither they nor other travel accounts nor even Jarves' own description of his experiences in Gualán place that settlement in physical touch with Honduras.

to their salutary effect upon chicken-nature, I was glad when the word was given to be off.

We left the main track, and struck into a bye-path to avoid the town of Santa Ana, where Morazan, with his troops, lay watching the movements of Carrera. Towards night we reached an Indian village, six miles from that place, and there prepared to pass the night. Our unexpected arrival created quite a stir among the dingy population. The women, however, bestirred themselves, and provided a supper of stewed beans and tortillas. The men gazed stupidly at us.

. . . We . . . were . . . on the road which was the common track to Chiquimula, the capital of the department of the same name, and at this time the strong-hold of the insurrectionists. . . . Our ride was an excessively wearisome one, and it was late before we arrived at the village of St. Helena, which we found in considerable commotion in consequence of a levy made by the governor of Chiquimula upon its young men, for soldiers.[13] We here got something to eat, and heard bad news. Chiquimula was but three leagues distant. If the plague had been raging within its walls, we should not have been more desirous of avoiding it. The officer to whom we had letters had left but the day before, with five hundred troops, for Guatimala, so that all hopes of friendly interference in that quarter were destroyed. The city was in great confusion; the people of the hamlet eyed us with scowling looks, and appeared to think not all right. We were in the interior of the country; to retreat was impracticable; to advance was unpleasant, to say the least. From existing symptoms it would be unsafe to remain, even that night, where we were. A council was held in the house of the two Indians, young men, to which our muleteers had brought us. They had been pressed to serve in the army, and were anxious to avoid the service. They appeared to be clever, honest fellows; our muleteer was willing to trust them, and we concluded to do the same. They agreed to conduct us to the boundaries of the State of Honduras, for which we were to pay them handsomely. The zeal which they manifested in our cause struck us as favorable. Our mules were unloaded and turned out to feed, while we slung our hammocks and prepared for a night's slumber. These preparations, however,

13. The *municipio* of Chiquimula today includes an *aldea* called Santa Elena, which may or may not be Jarves' village of St. Helena.

were only to lull the suspicions of the watchful inhabitants. As soon as they had retired, and the darkness favored our operations, the mules were noiselessly saddled, our arms carefully examined, and we stole quietly out of the village. By the time the moon had risen we were far on our way to Chiquimula. Journeying on in silence, the white towers of the city soon became visible.

Until this time, we had supposed some by-road would enable us to pass the city unseen. But the guides declared there was none, and our only alternative was to push quickly through before an alarm could be spread. Our spirits rose with the danger, and the romance of the adventure had sufficient charms to blind us to what might be its fatal realities. It was now past midnight, and the moon shone bright and unclouded. We were confident, that the intelligence of our design had not preceded us; still, no little anxiety was felt, as one by one we ascended the steep ravine which led to the town, and found ourselves treading its narrow streets.

Silence and expedition were the watchwords. The mules were hurried on, by dint of spurring and blows, to an unaccustomed rapidity. Poor brutes! they had been both dinnerless and supperless that day, and panting and almost exhausted by the extra labor they were obliged to endure, their empty stomachs, as they trotted on, began to give out sundry distressing sounds, much like the ringing of an empty cask. The slightest noise seemed to our excited nerves louder than a chime of bells. A man stops our guide. He informs him that we are country merchants, leaving for home. 'A very early hour to start,' quoth he, and passes on. The centre of the town was reached, and all remains quiet. Suddenly the guides stop, and consult. One leaves us. Can he prove treacherous? No; he went but to reconnoitre, and has returned. The delay gave time for the patrol to turn their backs upon us, as they passed down a neighboring street. One minute sooner, and we should have been challenged by them. Lights were in many of the houses, and as we proceeded a dog barked, and the bark echoed from street to street, until every yelping cur in the town had a voice in the chorus. The citizens rushed to their doors, in astonishment at such an outcry, and in stupefied wonder beheld the curious procession pass by them. Two men with muskets intercepted our course; we spurred on. The muskets proved to be clubs. Even the mules seemed now to renew their energies, and bore us so rapidly to the extremity of the town, that we had fairly passed the outer fortifications, before the watchmen's whistle had spread the alarm throughout the city; and, before its . . . inhabitants had any clear idea of its cause, we had gained the woods. Luckily, as we afterwards were told, all the horses had been sent off the day previous with the expedition against Guatimala, which alone saved us from an immediate pursuit.

Our situation was now far from enviable. The fear of surprise alone kept us awake. Hungry, and exhausted with fatigue, we looked about for a lurking-place, and finally ensconced ourselves in the rocky bed of a dry river. The mules were unloaded and turned out to rest; the scant herbage they could . . . glean could scarcely be called food. A little water was found for them. As for ourselves, we remained through the succeeding day without shelter; for the forest was entirely leafless, exposed to the fierce rays of the sun, heated to twofold intensity by reflection from the volcanic rocks, which formed our only bed. Sleep was altogether out of the question. The heat was intense, for it was the hottest day that we had experienced in the country, and not a breath of wind to mitigate it. We dared not stir from our hiding-place, for fear of discovery; and could converse only in whispers. Our guides, to whom the country was familiar, went out reconnoitring, and returned with the information, that strict search was being made for us. Several of our number immediately protected their most valuable papers, and concealing them about their persons prepared for a speedy flight on foot, in case of discovery. A hopeless chance, but one they preferred, to encountering the tender mercies of Carrera's banditti. A few cold tortillas, the last of our provisions, were equally divided; but we were too tired to eat; and as for water, none, except the smallest quantity gathered from the hollow of a heated rock, was to be had. Never was night more heartily welcomed, though bringing fresh dangers in its train. The mules were again saddled, and with the utmost secrecy we recommenced our flight. The friendly State of Honduras was now distant but forty miles, and our object was to distance pursuit by getting within its territory.

Another populous town, Zacapa, lay between us and Gualán, the boundary town of the province. The whole country was now upon the alert, for expresses had been sent in every direction to apprehend us; but, this place once in our rear, we felt assured of safety. Much time was consumed in ascending a steep mountain. It was so dark that objects only at a short distance were visible. This was favorable to us. When half-way up, a man on foot, travelling much faster than we, passed our party. He was a courier, bearing an order to Zacapa for our arrest, as we soon after learned. Upon reaching the summit, the lights of Chiquimula could be plainly seen. Numerous watch-fires were also observed on the surrounding heights. Despite our alarm and fatigue, we could not refrain from a hearty laugh, when picturing to ourselves the astonishment and chagrin of its inhabitants at our audacious exploit. If our entrée had been noiseless and humble, our egress had stirred them up considerably. The descent of Morazan and his troops into their plain would scarcely have created more excitement. . . . The descent from the mountain was even more arduous than the ascent. It was too dark to discover even the path, and we trusted entirely to our mules. They stumbled frequently over the loose stones with which the road was strewed, and after several hours' severe exertion carried us safely to the dusty plain beneath. We hurried them on. The soil was a dry chalk, which, rising in clouds, soon gave our company the appearance of a band of millers; it also penetrated our nostrils and mouths, and irritated the already burning thirst with which a fast of twenty-four hours had consumed both man and beast. It soon became insupportable; my tongue seemed like a piece of shrunken leather, and rattled strangely around my mouth. Not a drop of moisture could I conjure up to wet my shrivelled lips; my eyeballs were heated and distended. At every footstep the fine white dust rose in clouds, and settled over us. Suddenly a joyful sound was heard. It was the purling noise of running water. Never did a famishing caravan in the wilderness of Arabia hail the appearance of an oasis with more ardor than we the sight of Zacapa river.[14] Down its banks we rushed. Attached to my saddle was a water-proof basket, such as is made in California. It had served thus far for a wash-basin; now it answered for a drinking-vessel. Filling it to the brim, I drank from it the longest, sweetest draught that ever a thirsty traveller knew. Again filling it, I plunged my face into the cool liquid, bathed it, and bathed it again; men and beasts about me were following my example. . . . I filled my basket for the third time, and spurring my mule from the spot, for he seemed equally fascinated with its refreshing powers, rode on with it before me, drinking and dipping into it, until by an unlucky jolt it was all spilled.

The moon had arisen, and by its light we were soon able to see the white-washed houses of Zacapa glistening directly in front. With the utmost caution, and in single file, we pushed through its outskirts, sometimes passing within a few feet of houses where all appeared buried in slumber. The very dogs kept quiet; if some solitary cur at in-

14. Río Grande de Zacapa.

tervals opened his noisy throat, the cry was unreturned. It was a most lovely night; and, with the exception of ourselves, everything was as still as the grave. Avoiding the town all that it was possible to do, we wound around the numerous hills in its vicinity, eyeing its streets with suspicion, anon stopping to reconnoitre some doubtful point, then hurrying breathlessly onward. Unfortunately we became perplexed and entangled amid a labyrinth of cultivated and enclosed grounds. A hurried consultation ensued, while the guides sought an outlet. One was at length discovered; it was, however, one that a prudent regard for our necks would have counselled us to avoid, but which the urgency of the case compelled us to take. A steep gulley led to the river's bank, a hundred feet or so beneath, and at its head stood a cottage. A fence was taken down, and replaced. Passing so near the house as to brush against its eaves, we forced our mules to the brink of the slippery precipice. With their characteristic instinct, they drew all four feet together, and sitting on their haunches slid rapidly and safely to the bottom, while we kept our seats by clinging to their necks. Fording the river, and rising the opposite hill, we reached a level plain, with two paths in view. By diverging so frequently to avoid the thickly-inhabited parts of the town our guides had lost the run of the true course. One of them retraced his steps, entered the town, and came back by the correct road. He reported all quiet, and we moved on. It was now three o'clock, A. M., and the distance to Honduras was short, and the road plain. Our guides were dismissed with an ample recompense, and they bade us good by, with many wishes for our safe retreat. Another mountain, or more properly a long and rough hill, was before us. Sleep, to which we had been strangers for the last forty-eight hours, began insidiously to steal over us, and overpowered the sense of hunger, which for some time had been rather pressing in its calls. But this drowsiness, unlike the thirst we had encountered, was an agreeable enemy. It crept over one so gently, and with such pleasing sensations, that we knew not of its approach until it had fastened itself securely upon us. Several times I fell asleep on my mule, and was only awakened by a rude shock which destroyed my balance. Finding it impossible to preserve my seat, I rubbed open my eyes, pinched myself, and got off and walked. But this was of no use. I soon again sank into a state of unconsciousness, from which it was misery to be aroused. In this way we walked on, alive only to our situation for a few minutes, by stumbling against some protruding stone; then giving a glance at the road ahead, the eyes would again close, in spite of every exertion to keep them open, until a fresh stumble recalled the slumbering senses. The mere pain of attempting to keep awake was intolerable; the hardest rock would have been a welcome bed. Even the poor brutes began to give evidence of the same unconquerable weariness. At times they would come to a dead halt, and settle down, refusing to proceed farther until coaxed and driven by the muleteers.

In this manner we reached the Indian village of San Pablo, now mostly deserted, the cholera having the previous year carried off the greater proportion of the inhabitants.[15] Passing through it, we noticed a ruined church and calaboose. At the foot of the hill on which they stood, we crossed a small stream. Gualán was now but a few leagues distant. It was our intention to have crossed the boundary line of the contending States that morning. Daylight had already broken, and both we and our beasts were too thoroughly exhausted to proceed farther. Rest we must have, be the consequences what they might. A couple of hours would enable us to proceed. The loads were tipped off the jaded mules, and they and their masters, in less time than I have taken to write it, were stretched out on the grass, wrapped in sound slumbers.

How long we lay thus, I know not; but a hoarse voice, calling us to surrender, first aroused our lethargic faculties; and the sight of several brace of pistols pointed at our heads soon recalled us to consciousness of passing events. The sun was shining brightly and hotly upon us, and a large body of soldiers stood stupidly gazing at our prostrate selves, seemingly as much amazed at the scene as we were. They were evidently forced recruits, a puny, ragged set of fellows, of all colors, looking as if they would gladly exchange their muskets and knapsacks for hoes and a field of maize. But their leaders were fine-looking men, well-dressed and armed, and mounted on good horses. Their uniforms looked too new and shining to be many days old, and their first service in the campaign was our capture. Of course we surrendered peaceably and with all grace; for there they were above us, with their pistols prepared to enforce their summons.

The sense of the ludicrous would have overcome my gravity, had not the scowling looks and fierce glances of our captors reminded me that we were in the hands of those with whom power was law. Here were upwards of seventy men employed to capture seven half-starved travellers, who, if their will to resist had been good, had not the means. Our equipments, indeed, excited their risibles, as they read the decree

15. See Ch. 1 n. 47.

for our arrest, given at Chiquimula. It described us as a well-armed party of foreigners, conveying treasure clandestinely out of the country, and who, in defiance of their established regulations, had passed through their territories. In conclusion it enjoined all patriotic inhabitants to aid in seizing and bringing us to punishment. The paper was sufficiently formidable to have annihilated us. But its warlike phraseology proved a sad stumbling-block to the courage of the gallant alcalde of San Pablo, who was deputized to see it carried into effect. His village could not boast a sufficient number of volunteers, who were willing to risk their persons in contact with a party of 'well-armed foreigners;' and had he not accidentally fallen in with these troops, who were convoying arms to Chiquimula, we should, for all him, have made our escape. This he afterwards confessed to us, when we became better friends. As it was, with his silver-headed cane, the insignium of his office, pointed at us, in one hand, and holding the order for our arrest in the other, he ensconced himself behind his military companions. From this position, so judiciously chosen, he ordered us to prison. But as that order implied the necessity of reascending the steep hill which we had so recently passed over, we flatly refused, intimating that if we went at all, he must find the means of carrying us.

The captain of the soldiers attracted attention from the beauty of his figure and person; he was indeed a remarkably good-looking man. It so happened, that while we were cogitating some plan for escaping from the clutches of these fellows, our office-seeking friend, the spirit of his profession no doubt suddenly inspiring him, remarked that this captain looked like a gentleman.[16] To our astonishment, he immediately spoke to us courteously in English, and from his altered demeanor seemed desirous of retaining that opinion. That chance expression turned the scale of our destiny; and instead of the horrors of a Chiquimula calaboose, thoughts of home took possession of us. Explanations soon satisfied him that we were strangers in the country, as desirous of leaving it as the most fanatical of his party were for having us expelled; and instead of treasure, they themselves were not more deficient in the article than we. But what especially mollified him, next to the personal compliment, was to find us citizens of the United States; for his party was particularly inimical to Englishmen. He immediately claimed us as compatriots, and said, although he was by

16. The "office-seeking friend" was apparently Jarves' first host in Hawaii and his companion on this trip, Peter Allan Brinsmade, who was expecting an appointment by the government of the United States.

birth an Italian, he considered himself a citizen of the great republic, having resided there seven years. The production of our letters to the commandant of Chiquimula wonderfully advanced us in his favor, although at the recapitulation of our midnight march he shook his head, and intimated that it would have fared ill with us, had we been apprehended. While we yankees were thus insinuating ourselves into the good graces of our adopted countrymen, our Anglo-Mexican auxiliary was no less dexterous and successful with the full-blooded Central Americans. He was accustomed to revolutions, having lived for many years in one of the most inflammable states of Mexico. He assured them that their cause was one of the most glorious on record; that history, and above all, Mexico, their rival republic, where he had lived so long, could produce nothing equal to it. In short, he made them think so well of themselves that they could not do otherwise, from mere sympathy, than think well of us, so that in a half-hour from our capture we had become the best friends possible, and they were really sorry they had disturbed the slumbers of so many gentlemen for so trivial a cause as a paltry alcalde. They undertook to procure from the powers that were, a release from any farther attentions on his part, and a safe conduct for the remainder of our journey. The Italian rode on to Chiquimula himself, to see that the necessary papers were sent. We had made a strong interest in the right quarter; still their superiors might desire a personal interview, and the very idea made us nervous. Guards were placed over us; these claimed a liberal fee for their kind protection. Before night, the alcalde, who would not leave us, claimed a similar donative. . . .

Our papers arrived the next morning. Once more at liberty, we rode gayly on, now straggling from each other and the road, admiring the varied prospect, shouting and singing more like boys escaped from the durance-vile of school-hours than sober travellers. The road was through a mountainous but delightful country; vegetation was luxuriant, and the country bright with flowers. In the distance rose the mountains of Vera-Paz . . . , bounding the horizon like a mighty wall. Close to us the Motagua river flowed swiftly along; birds, crocodiles, and Indian girls, were bathing in its waters.

Late in the afternoon we arrived at Gualán, and reached the alcalde's just as he was issuing an order for our arrest. Our passports set him right, and we put him into good humor, by promising to hire mules of him for our next day's journey. Gualán is a small town situated on the banks of the Motagua river, which empties into the Gulf of Mexico at Omoa. Between the two places there is some trade, by means of large boats. The few shops were well supplied with American and English goods. Few names, I suspect, circulate more extensively than A. and A. Lawrence. I had seen them before in Chili and Peru, in the cotton linings to a Hawaiian habitation, and here they were in the interior of one of the wildest and least known of the countries of the globe.[17] We joined the inhabitants in an evening bath in the river. Our Italian friend had recommended us for quarters to a lady of his acquaintance, who lived in a very large but very dirty house. Next door was a much superior mansion; a fair young girl was at the window. This house belonged to the Italian, and the girl was his—housekeeper, perhaps. Our landlady was old and crabbed.

Izabal is a flourishing town, of recent growth, though in a most unhealthy location. It is bordered by low, wet land, covered with the dankest vegetation. Rains are very abundant, and the heat of the sun overpowering. Indeed, it is considered no better than a grave, for a foreign constitution. The inhabitants are thin and sallow. Despite its climate, and the execrable Mico mountain, it has become the principal port of entry for the eastern coast of Central America. . . . There were a few wooden houses, covered with mould, but which looked as if they had been imported from the United States. Vessels drawing above eight feet of water cannot cross the bar at the mouth of the gulf. A fine Spanish schooner, bound in a few weeks for Havana, lay off the town. It was not pleasant to be obliged to wait so long to leave so detestable a place. Luckily in a few days an English steamer arrived; she was to leave again in a short time for the bar. The authorities obliged us to pay five dollars each for the privilege of leaving their soil. We bade them adios with a right good will, and embarked in the steamer. . . .

The steamer went no further than the bar. The coast was low, and covered with giant trees, under the shade of which negro wood-cutters had built their huts. A long ground-swell came lazily tumbling in. We boarded a New York brig, that was lying here, taking in a cargo of mahogany. Some of our party concluded to remain on board until her departure for the United States. Three of us chartered a boat, with a couple of negro boys, to take us to the English settlement at Belize.

---

17. A. & A. Lawrence were distributors of cotton and wool textiles manufactured in both Great Britain and (after 1816) the United States.

James Jackson Jarves arrived in New York on March 24, 1838; his two careers, in Hawaii and in Italy, were yet ahead of him. Eleven days later, GEORGE WASHINGTON MONTGOMERY, citizen of the United States but long-time resident of Spain and England, left New York with Guatemala City as his destination. Montgomery's trip, undertaken like that of Jarves in the midst of civil war perils, was of a quarter year's duration. It was described in *Narrative of a Journey to Guatemala, in Central America, in 1838*, published in New York, 1839, only two years before the author's death at the age of thirty-seven.

Montgomery had the real advantage, as an observer of Central American life, of a boyhood spent in Spain (where his father was a merchant) and a consequent familiarity with Spanish customs and language.[18] After being educated in England, he returned to Spain to work in the United States legation. There he formed a personal friendship with the author Washington Irving, a part of whose *Sketch Book* as well as all of the *Chronicle of the Conquest of Granada* Montgomery translated into Spanish. In 1835 he received an appointment as United States consul in San Juan, Puerto Rico; three years later, he was entrusted with a special mission to Guatemala. Apparently, his task was concerned with the United States government's desire to renew the expiring commerce and navigation clauses of its treaty of 1826 with the Central American federation.[19]

Montgomery scarcely mentions his mission in the account of his travels and unfortunately fails to provide a picture of isthmian public affairs rating anywhere near those of diplomat Thompson and consul-general Haefkens. The linguistic and literary qualities of Montgomery show through, however, as he good-humoredly discusses everyday occurrences in out-of-the-way places, going to and from the city where he delivered his dispatches:[20]

> Having been honoured by the Government of the United States with a commission which required my proceeding to Guatemala, in Central America, I have been induced, since my return, to prepare the following little work, from an impression that a plain, unaffected narrative of

18. *Dictionary of American Biography*, 13:96–97.
19. Charles G. DeWitt, United States chargé d'affaires, received dispatches from Montgomery on June 9, 1838, authorizing DeWitt to negotiate a renewal of the treaty. See William R. Manning, ed., *Diplomatic Correspondence of the United States: Inter-American Affairs, 1831–1860*, 3:149–50.
20. Montgomery, 1839, pp. 9–10, 23–29, 33, 39, 49–54, 55–57, 66–67, 77–80, 83–84, 89, 98–99, 102–3, 103–4, 112, 114, 120, 124–25, 157–60, 162–63, 163–65, 168–69, 177–81, 190, 192–93.

a journey through a country rarely visited by travellers, and but little known, may not be uninteresting to an inquiring and enlightened public. I shall endeavour to discharge the task I have undertaken with fidelity, though I cannot flatter myself with being able to do justice to the wild and magnificent scenery through which I passed, or to impart to the reader those emotions experienced in traversing regions where the pathless forest and almost inaccessible mountain are rendered still more awful and savage by the evil passions of man; where the traveller is less impeded by the yawning precipice and raging torrent, than by the lurking bandit or the rebel guerilla; and where the eruptions of the volcano and the earthquake spread less affright and desolation, than the political convulsions which have shaken the whole frame of society into ruins.

It was on the 4th of April, 1838, that I embarked at New York on board of a packet bound for Havana.

I had waited . . . four days in Havana for an opportunity to proceed to some port in Central America, when I was informed that an American vessel was on the point of sailing for Trujillo, in the Bay of Honduras, from whence, it was believed, I should find no difficulty in proceeding by land to Guatemala, the capital of the country. I accordingly embarked at once. . . .

On the 25th of April, the fourth day after our departure from Havana, we came in sight of the Island of Bonacca, situated immediately opposite to Trujillo; and in the afternoon of the same day, we cast anchor in the harbor of that port.

The town of Trujillo stands close by the sea, at the foot of a lofty mountain crowned with trees, and clothed with a rich vegetation reaching to the very edge of the water. It is an isolated solitary place, of antiquated appearance, with few houses, and those in a ruinous condition. The objects most prominent at first view, are a fort mounted by a few guns, an old dismantled building, which I was told had been the mansion of the Governors in better times, and a church with only half a roof. A little apart from the town, there is a cluster of huts, twenty or thirty in number, inhabited by a little colony of negroes, called *Caribes*, a denomination for which I could find no reason, since they certainly have nothing in common with the Indians of the Caribbee Islands.[21]

21. Montgomery might have found the reason in Roberts, 1827, quoted above, pp. 53–54, and thereby have saved himself an error.

We were not long in receiving the visit of the Custom-house officer, who came off to us in a little canoe paddled by a couple of blacks. When this officer was leaving us, after having accomplished the objects of his visit, I handed him my passport, and requested him to obtain leave for my landing on the following day, if not contrary to the regulations of the place. The next morning, early—for we had scarcely finished breakfast—the same person came again, and delivered me a message from the Commandant of Trujillo, stating that I could go on shore as soon as might be agreeable to me, and that that officer, in the expectation of my landing at once, was then waiting on the beach to receive me. This mark of attention left me no choice, and I hastily changed my dress, while my friend, the Captain, ordered the boat to be manned with four oars, her awning to be rigged, and a flag to be spread on the stern-sheets.

On reaching the shore, I was met by the Commandant, who gave me his hand, and welcomed me with all the gravity and courteousness of an old Castilian. He was accompanied by the *Ministro de Hacienda*, or Collector of the Customs, and by some other persons, to whom he introduced me. In addressing him, I used the style of *Señoria*, instead of *usted*, which, however, he modestly declined admitting.

The Commandant was about 37 years of age; rather tall, and muscular, though of slender form. He had an expressive countenance, with features strongly marked, dark eyes, black hair, and thick eye-brows. He was somewhat sun-burnt, and had a scar near a corner of his mouth; but, altogether, he was a fine, soldierly looking man. His dress was a blue frock coat with military buttons, gold epaulettes a little tarnished, a sword, and a cocked hat, with a plume of blue and white feathers, the national colours of Central America.

We now all proceeded together to the house of the Commandant. As the heat of the sun was oppressive, he insisted on my taking his umbrella, and, on my accepting it, turned, and without any ceremony, took another for himself from the hands of one of his suite. On coming into the house, he said he expected I would make it my home during my residence in Trujillo; but with many thanks for his kind offer, I declined accepting it, saying that while the vessel that had brought me was in port, I proposed retaining my quarters there. He then requested I would at least dine with him that day; and as the sincerity of this invitation was quite apparent, I accepted it with pleasure. The hour appointed being three o'clock—a very fashionable one in Trujillo, and, as I afterwards learnt, some two hours later than the usual dinner hour of my host—I took my leave, and returned on board to pass the time, as the heat, even at that early hour of the morning, was too great to permit my walking about on shore.

The house of my new friend was a good sized building of solid masonry. It consisted of one large room, formed by the four walls, without any division into apartments; and above, instead of ceiling, were the rafters of the roof. On one side was the street door, with two windows grated with iron bars; on the other side, another, but smaller door, opening into the esplanade of the fort, where a swarthy sentinel was pacing to and fro with a straw hat, no jacket, and a rusty firelock on his shoulder. The floor was paved with flat tiles, and covered here and there with little straw mats of a kind peculiar to the country. This room constituted the whole of the establishment, with the exception of the kitchen. It served for parlour, bed-chamber, dining-room, and office. And well it might; for there was the sofa for the reception of visitors, a substantial cedar table for dining, a bed to sleep in, and a desk, with writing apparatus, for the transaction of business. The bedstead was a very neat one, of wrought iron, provided with a handsome mosquito net, and was placed on a platform which raised it about two feet from the floor. A military saddle in one corner of the room, a cavalry sabre in another, and a pair of pistols hanging from the wall, gave a military and picturesque character to this primitive *menage,* which had very much the appearance of a guard-house.

At the appointed hour I returned to the house to dine, where I found the Ministro, and another person, who had also been invited. Where the dishes were prepared I cannot conjecture. I can only say, that they were brought in from the street. The first placed on the table was a good soup, which was followed by the inevitable *olla* of the Spaniards, consisting of beef, mutton, and pork, with an abundant accompaniment of vegetables, served up together. Then came a dish of rice, cooked *à la Valenciana,* and tolerably saturated with oil, which, however, did not prevent my finding it very good. Some beef *à la mode* was then served up, that smacked a little of garlic, but which I had no objection to on that account. The next dish contained a good sized fowl and a small chicken, both together, and side by side, like mother and daughter. A quantity of vegetables—plantains, pumpkins, and sweet potatoes—all in the same plate, were then placed on the table; and, finally, came a pudding, which terminated the dinner.

My appetite, which was unusually good, from my having suffered a little from sea-sickness, allowed of my eating more or less of every dish that was presented. The Commandant was much pleased by my observing, that he ought not to be surprised at my eating so much, when so good a dinner was set before me. And good it really was, though not in the most refined style of cooking. The only thing I was unable to relish was the pudding. This unfortunate dish had no doubt been got up expressly for the occasion, and as something peculiarly adapted to my taste; and on my renouncing it, the disappointment of mine host was distressingly apparent. The desert consisted of fruit and sweetmeats, and then were brought in segars and coffee.

We were attended at table by soldiers in no small number, who performed the part of waiters, and I verily believe that half of the little garrison of Trujillo was that day in requisition for our service.

The conversation during dinner turned on topics chiefly relating to the United States; a country that seemed to have excited the curiosity of the Commandant, but of which he possessed only a slight degree of knowledge. I replied to many of his questions on this subject; but when I stated to him distinctly the population, commerce, and resources of our Republic, the progress of the arts, and the facilities of communication by land and water, he would smile, shake his head, and cast a meaning look at the Ministro, as much to say that he was not to be imposed on. This, though I was relating nothing but the truth, embarrassed me, and made me feel as if I had been detected in using the privilege of a traveller. I thought to extricate myself from this awkward position, by reducing my subsequent statements to the standard of his belief. Accordingly, I relieved the ship Pennsylvania of no inconsiderable weight, by reducing her hundred and forty-eight guns to one hundred. The rate of travelling in rail cars I stated to be from fifteen to twenty miles, instead of from twenty to thirty. I even curtailed the amount of the national revenue, and actually purloined the United States of ten or a dozen millions.

This was not the only occasion on which, in relation to the same subject, I had to combat the incredulity of the natives: it was a difficulty of frequent occurrence in the sequel.

Having taken leave of the Commandant for that day, I rambled about the town, which I was the more curious to view, as being the first I had arrived at in the country. The principal street—and strictly speaking, the only one, for the others scarcely deserve the name—extends from one end of the town to the other, and is paved. The houses for the most part are but one story high, and their sombre, dilapidated appearance, together with the grass-grown pavement, impart to the place a melancholy air of abandonment. It has at the same time something romantic in its situation, being enclosed by mountains, and embosomed in an exuberant vegetation, which the efforts of man seem to have been unable to check. There is scarcely any open ground in the vicinity, except here and there a cultivated spot, where the plantain, the yucca, and a little corn, are raised for individual consumption. As the woods afford a rich pasture, the cattle are good, and milk is abundant; and as the soil, by its fertility, liberally repays the little labour bestowed on it, the very moderate wants of the inhabitants are easily supplied.

In walking the streets I was stared at by both sexes, who would whisper, and point at me, as I passed. The arrival of a stranger seemed to be an event, a little epoch in the annals of Trujillo. I observed some pretty faces and graceful figures among the females, but I am not sure that I saw a real white complexion; for such as were not Indians, or mulattoes, were so tanned by the sun, as to make it difficult to distinguish them from the others. Both sexes wore nothing but linen or cotton, and could not be more lightly clad, especially the women, who, from a sense of propriety, would throw a kerchief round their necks as I approached.

On my way back to the beach, I called at the house of a merchant for whom I had brought a letter of introduction. In the course of my visit, my eye was struck with some fine leopard skins, in his magazine; which I examined attentively, expressing my admiration of their size and beauty. The merchant said nothing, but soon after we had parted, and just as I was stepping into the boat, I was overtaken by one of his servants, bringing one of the finest of the skins. "This," said he, "is a *corta fineza* (a small present,) which my master desires you to accept."

In Spanish America, as in Old Spain, it is considered a matter of course, according to the code of politeness, to offer a person any thing for which he expresses an admiration; it is equally a matter of course to decline such offers. In the present instance, however, the manner in which the present was sent after me, showed that it was made in earnest, and to decline it would have been considered a slight. I accepted it, therefore, without hesitation, and recorded it in my memory to the credit of the courtesy and hospitality of the good people of Trujillo.

From the information I obtained, on my arrival at Trujillo, I found that I had taken a wrong step in coming thither. The journey from that place to Guatemala could not be performed in less than thirty days;

whereas, had I gone to Izabal, a port at the head of the Bay of Honduras, nine or ten days would have been sufficient. There was no alternative, therefore, but to proceed to Izabal; and to get there, it would be necessary first to go to Belize, an English settlement in that neighbourhood. An opportunity for the latter place offered itself after a detention of five or six days in Trujillo. I embraced it, of course, though the size and appearance of the vessel—a little schooner scarcely thirty feet long—might have deterred any one from venturing in her on a sea of such dangerous navigation as the Bay of Honduras.

The rumours I had heard of the distracted state of Central America were confirmed at Trujillo. An insurrection, I was told, had taken place among the Indians, who, under the directions of a man called Carrera, were ravaging the country, and committing all manner of excesses. Along the coast, and in some of the Departments, tranquillity had not been disturbed; but in the interior, there was no safety for the traveller, and every avenue to the capital was beset by parties of brigands, who showed no mercy to their victims, especially if they were foreigners.

This intelligence was discouraging, but there was no alternative: the journey must be performed.

On the third day after my arrival at Belize I was informed that a steamboat belonging to an English company was on the point of sailing from that port for Izabal. A vessel of this description in that remote part of the world was a novelty wholly unexpected by me. Unwilling to lose time by any detention not absolutely necessary, I determined to take my passage in her. From this, however, a Spanish merchant, Don Francisco * * *, with whom I had become acquainted in Belize, tried to dissuade me, by representing to me in the most serious manner the imprudence of trusting to those new fangled inventions of the English, and the probability of being blown up or scalded to death. The remonstrances of Don Francisco, who evidently was no friend to steamboats, or to any thing English, were lost on me, and I went on board.

We anchored before Izabal on the 10th of May. It was not without some misgivings as to the state of things on shore that we proceeded to land. We were by no means sure that the place was not in possession of the insurgent Indians, and the risk of falling into their hands the moment we touched the beach, was far from being agreeable; but happily, these apprehensions were soon dispelled. I had fortunately been provided by my Spanish friend in Belize, Don Francisco, with a letter of introduction to his correspondent in this place. This letter I presented as soon as I landed to Don Valentin * * *, the person to whom it was addressed. He received me with marks of unaffected hospitality; and, as dinner was in the process of being served up, made me take a seat at the table, where four or five strangers, besides Mr. M. and myself, partook of the abundant cheer that was spread before us. . . .

During dinner an animated conversation was kept up, which, however, did not in the least interfere with the eating; for most of the guests talked incessantly, without losing a mouthful. As soon as this repast was disposed of, I retired from the table, and seeing two or three hammocks hanging from the roof, took possession of one; and with an old newspaper in one hand, and a segar in the other, I smoked and read, and swung myself, with the cool breeze of the lake breathing on me, till I fairly fell asleep.

Don Valentin is a sort of patroon, a little great man in the place, and is looked up to with respect even by the Commandant. His dwelling is a goodly house of wood, the frame of which was brought from the United States, but is constructed rather in the Spanish taste, the *sala,* or parlour, being almost the whole house. It is the resting-place of strangers of respectability, and the resort of the better class of the natives. He has, however, a powerful rival in another merchant, called Don Candido * * *, who is perhaps more wealthy, and is, in like manner, liberal in the entertainment of his friends. The houses occupied by these two persons are the only ones deserving the name; the others being little better than mud cabins, thatched with leaves.

In the course of a walk in the afternoon, I took a passing view of the town; but seeing nothing in it to interest me, I turned my steps to the mountain that commands it, and ascended to a spot where the roots of an old tree afforded a pleasant resting-place. Here a fine view is obtained of the lake and of the surrounding country. Before me were scattered the thatched roofs of Izabal, and on each side, as far as the eye could reach, might be seen a series of mountains, towering over each other, and piled up like Pelion upon Ossa. How deeply I regretted not being an adept at drawing, to have made a sketch of the scene before me! Yet it was not without defects. No vessels were to be seen on the lake, with the solitary exception of the steamboat; no signs of cultivation, not a hamlet nor a house were visible on the land, save the little town beneath me.

When I considered the natural advantages of this country, I could not but lament that so little had been done by human industry to improve them. The idea, however, suggested itself, that some day this lake, now little better than a watery desert, might be traversed in every direction by steamboats and sailing vessels engaged in profitable trade; when the country around, instead of being encumbered with a wild and useless vegetation, might smile with fields of corn, and the neat cottage of the peasant, the thriving hamlet, and even the flourishing town, enliven the quietude of these solitary shores. . . .

It is proper, however, to remark, in justice to the natives, that the natural advantages . . . are in some degree counteracted by circumstances over which they have no control. The unhealthiness of the climate in the neighbourhood of the lake, is a powerful check to the increase of population in Izabal. Another great obstacle to the prosperity of the place exists in the mountainous and rugged nature of the country, which renders the construction of roads exceedingly difficult and expensive. That leading to the capital is a mere mule path. It is, therefore, on mule-back that they transport their goods from the coast to the interior, or from the latter to the former. The expense and labour attending this mode of conveyance will easily be conceived. The time required for the performance of a journey, is another consideration; the distance travelled by a loaded mule during a whole day, being scarcely that which a rail-car would advance in half an hour.

My first inquiries on arriving at Izabal were in reference to the political state of the country, and the chances of reaching the capital without being molested. On this subject I obtained but little information, except, indeed, that the insurrection had not reached that part of the country. The tranquillity of the neighbourhood had not been disturbed, but of the occurrences in the interior no late intelligence had been received.

After duly considering the circumstances of the case, Mr. M., the English gentleman with whom during our passage in the steamboat I had formed an intimacy, and myself, resolved to undertake the journey. A Spanish gentleman and merchant, Don José * * *, whom we met with at Don Valentin's, was induced to join the party. He had a quantity of goods with him sufficient to load a dozen mules, and was desirous, in the furtherance of his commercial pursuits, of proceeding to Guatemala.

The first step was to procure the necessary number of mules. This, after a couple of days, was accomplished; and all other preparations being now made, we were ready to commence our journey.

Previously to leaving Izabal, I felt it in some sort a duty to visit a spot calculated to inspire the most melancholy reflections. It was the grave of Mr. Shannon, formerly Chargé d'Affaires of the United States to Guatemala, and his niece. This gentleman had arrived at Izabal, with his wife and the young lady just mentioned, on his way to the capital. They had scarcely set foot on shore, when a sad instance occurred of the mortiferous nature of the climate here, not inferior, in this respect, to that of Belize. The niece, a young and blooming girl, full of health, was attacked by the fever peculiar to the country, and in forty-eight hours after was a lifeless corpse. The suddenness of this catastrophe produced such an effect on Mr. Shannon, as to disturb his mental faculties. He became delirious, was seized with the fever, and, in like manner, fell a victim two days after he was attacked. I will leave the reader to conceive the distress, the grief, the despair of Mrs. Shannon, when she found herself, in the short space of three or four days, bereaved of the two objects dearest to her in life. I will leave him to form an idea of her situation, alone in a foreign country, without any knowledge of the language, without a friend to console her, or even the means of performing in a proper manner the last duties that we owe to departed friends; the circumstances of the place precluding the possibility of a funeral solemnity.

The interment of these two unfortunate persons was attended to by Don Candido in the night-time, and by torch-light, with the assistance of a few of his friends. The bodies were deposited in a spot which he had set apart as a burial-place for his own family. The graves are only distinguishable by a slight elevation of the earth, and a few trees that have been planted there, but there is no stone or monumental record whatever to point them out to a stranger.[22]

We rose early on the 12th of May, to enter upon the long and difficult journey that lay before us. My preparations, and those of Mr. M., were soon brought to a conclusion. Such was not the case with our Spanish friend and companion, Don José. The caparisons of his mule alone, consisted of such a variety of articles, that no little time and ingenuity were required for their arrangement. After putting into the animal's mouth three or four pounds of iron in the shape of a bit, a sheep's skin of fine long wool, dyed blue, was thrown over a ponderous Mexican

22. The story of Mr. James Shannon, who died in June, 1832, is but one of a long, sad series in the attempt of the United States government to establish diplomatic representation in Central America. See Joseph B. Lockey, "Diplomatic Futility."

saddle, and the whole fastened on by sundry girths and straps. This saddle was secured, in front, by a *poitrel*,[23] or broad strap, rudely embroidered with silk of various colours, and behind by a crupper of the same description. The saddle-bow was graced with a pair of heavy horse-pistols, and on each side was suspended a goat's skin with the hair on, reaching from the shoulders of the mule to her knees. These skins were called *armas de agua*, and their object is to protect the legs of the rider from the rain.

The equipment of Don José himself was a riding-dress of serge, a broad-brimmed Panama hat, a pair of heavy plated spurs, and a sort of gaiters called *rodilleras*, consisting of two pieces of fine calf-skin wrapped round the lower part of the legs, and secured under the knees by a piece of coloured tape.

In fine, Don José looked so well and so grand, that Mr. M. and myself almost felt ashamed of the plainness of our appearance. Even my mule seemed uneasy at the simplicity of her furniture; and, in fact, as she had nothing on but a common, though new, English saddle and bridle, there was something strange and ludicrous about her that did not fail to excite the risibility of the natives.

The baggage mules, and those that carried the goods of Don José, being now laden and ready, we took leave of Don Valentin, and departed on our journey, preceded by our guide, a tall, swarthy fellow, well mounted, with dagger in belt, no shoes or stockings, and an awful pair of spurs on his naked heels. Our road lay across the mountain which overlooks the town, and over a rough and rocky ground, the difficulties of which are increased by the abruptness of the acclivity. Before commencing the ascent, we had to follow for some time the channel of a mountain torrent, where, though there was not much water at the time, there was such an abundance of loose stones, that the mules scarcely knew where to set their feet. We then proceeded up the side of the mountain by a narrow winding path, which the trunks of fallen trees rendered almost impassable in some places, while, in others, it was so steep, that our beasts were in danger of rolling down the mountain: an accident which was very near happening, for one of the mules actually lost her footing, and fell back with her load to the ground and her feet in the air. Fortunately she was saved from further harm by an intervening tree, and prevented from carrying the hinder animals along with her in her fall. Sometimes the path would diverge into various ramifications, when the voice and the lash of the muleteer

23. Evidently from the French *poitrail*.

were exerted to prevent the convoy from going astray. Now and then, on coming to a rocky place, it would assume the appearance of broken stairs. The agility of the mules in clambering up these rugged places was remarkable, while the care with which they picked out their way, avoiding the holes and loose stones, and never moving a foot till they had secured a firm stepping for it, was a proof of their patience and sagacity that struck me with surprise.

On these occasions, the rider, if he is wise, will be careful not to meddle with his mule, but will tie the reins of her neck and abandon himself to her discretion. For my part, I had enough to do, in another way, without attending to the mule, since I was kept a great part of the time drawing up my legs to avoid the projecting rocks, and bobbing my head to save it from the branches.

We were within half a mile of Gualán, when we heard the report of a gun from the town, and a moment after, several more shots were fired in succession. The effect upon the whole party was paralysing; it brought us all suddenly to a halt. Were the factious Indians in possession of the town? Would it be safe to advance? Would it not be more prudent to retreat? Such were the hasty reflections of the moment. Happily, our apprehensions were removed by a woman who was coming from the town, and found us in the midst of consultation. "What is the meaning of the firing we hear in the town?" was the question addressed to her. "*Es una fiesta,*" (it is a festival,) said she, and proceeded on her way. There was no reason for distrusting this woman, for she was not an Indian, and we resumed our march. As we entered the town, guns were popping off in every direction. I turned to a lad near me, as he was on the point of cocking his gun, and asked him what festival they were celebrating. "*Es un bautismo,*" (it is a christening,) said he, and the reply was followed by the discharge of his gun, which blazed within half a yard of my face.

Our companion, Don José, now conducted us to one of the best looking houses in the place. It was the dwelling of a friend of his, Don Juan * * *, who received us with great kindness and attention. This gentleman united in his own person the two professions of farmer and merchant. His house was full of people. A party of musicians was playing there, under the directions of a *maestro de capilla*. On a table at one end of the room, was an inviting display of cakes, sweetmeats, and bottles of red wine. On another table lay scattered the remains of an abundant breakfast; but the partakers had not yet left the table. I recollected the wedding of Camacho, and thought the inimitable description of that scene by Cervantes was here on the point of being realized.[24]

Don Juan informed us that he had that day christened his first-born, and had invited a few friends to celebrate the event. He had also furnished the boys of the town with powder and crackers, according to the custom of the country. We now took seats at the table, and such of the dishes as had not been touched were set before us; the other guests retained their seats to keep us company. All this time the music was playing in a strain more remarkable for loudness than harmony; the boys were blazing away in the street, and the newly made Christian was squalling at the top of its voice; so that altogether a din was produced which, but for the sound state of our nerves, would have been insufferable.

Having been furnished by Don Juan with an introduction to a friend of his in Zacapa, Don Mariano * * *, we alighted at the house of this gentleman, and met with a favourable reception. . . .

Soon after our arrival at Zacapa, we became satisfied by the statements of Don Mariano, that to proceed any further on that road would be the worst of follies. He assured us that, from that town to Guatemala the country was infested by the factious Indians, who hovered about the roads in small parties, plundering and murdering, and showing no mercy to their victims, especially if they were foreigners. To travel ten leagues beyond Zacapa without falling in with one of these parties, he considered a matter of impossibility. The alcalde of the place, who was consulted, expressed the same opinion. With the advantage of a military escort, the attempt, he said, might be successful; but as none could be procured in that place, he advised our remaining for the present where we were.

The result of these deliberations was the suspending of our journey. After a detention of two days, a new consultation was held, in order to decide upon the next step to be taken. We were unwilling to remain much longer in Zacapa; to proceed to Guatemala was impracticable; and to retrace our steps was out of the question. In this dilemma an alternative was proposed by Don José, which was that we should proceed to Esquipulas, a town situated on the road to St. Salvador, and about sixty miles to the left of the Guatemala road. From that town the communications with the capital might possibly be open. And should

24. *Don Quixote de la Mancha*, Pt. 2, Chs. 20–21.

that not be the case, we could remain there under the hospitable roof of the curate, who was a near relative of his, and would be glad to entertain us.

As there was no reason for apprehending any danger on the road to Esquipulas, which was one lying out of the track of the insurgents, the plan of Don José was approved of and adopted. . . .

We reached the town of Chiquimula early in the afternoon, and concluded to stop there for the rest of the day. . . . As we had not proposed passing the night in this place, we had come without any letter of introduction, and, in consequence, had to apply to the alcalde for quarters in the *Cabildo*, or town-hall. This is generally the resource of travellers in Central America on arriving at a town where they have no acquaintance. . . . The alcalde very kindly offered us his own house, or he would billet us on any of the inhabitants. But we declined both these offers, and proceeded with him to the Cabildo, where a large gloomy chamber, with one table and three or four rickety chairs, was placed at our disposal.

The aspect of things here was certainly not very inviting, and thereupon Don José began to moralize, and to console himself and us with the hope of better luck in future. There was another cause for melancholy reflections in an object of a truly ominous character which I have not yet mentioned, and which met our sight the moment we entered the chamber. This was nothing less than a coffin, fortunately an empty one, for of this I satisfied myself by lifting up the lid. This coffin, a large one, covered with black cloth and silver lace, was public property, and had been used during the prevalence of the cholera in that town, not for burying the dead, but for carrying them to the grave. It was of course immediately removed into another part of the building by direction of the alcalde, who, at the same time, ordered some mattresses to be brought for our use.

Our reception by the curate, the friend and relative of Don José, was the most cordial and flattering. His house, which was situated opposite the church, and provided in front with a good portico, and in the rear with a spacious yard, was one of considerable size, but not very convenient; having only two rooms, besides the *sala*, or parlour. One of these rooms was assigned to Don José and Mr. M.; the other the good curate insisted on my occupying, though it was his own bedchamber and study. For his own accommodation, a little cot, or field-bed, was brought into the sala.

The furniture of the house was more remarkable for its classic simplicity, than for its elegance or convenience. In the principal room, the only articles composing it were a wooden bench, with a back and rests for the arms at each end, placed against the wall, and before it a massive mahogany table. This part of the household arrangement had very much the appearance of a tribunal; and when the curate sat there—which he invariably did when any one came to talk to him on business—he looked like a magistrate dispensing justice. Along the walls were distributed about a dozen chairs of no mean dimensions, and of most antiquated fashion; the seats and backs being lined with sole leather, and studded with nails, the heads of which were of polished brass, and as large as half dollars. On the side over the mahogany table there was a portrait of our Saviour, and opposite to this another portrait, representing a *nuestra Señora*.

During dinner the conversation naturally turned on the political disturbance of the country, and the state of the roads between Esquipulas and the capital. The intelligence afforded by the curate on this subject could not be more discouraging; and all hope of continuing our journey from that place was utterly relinquished. My disappointment on finding that I had come so far out of my way to no purpose, may easily be imagined. Mr. M. was seized with a fit of spleen, and talked of retracing his steps to Belize; Don José formally announced his intention of proceeding no further; so that the probability now was, that I should be left alone. Don José, however, ever fertile in expedients, suggested one, which, under the circumstances, I was fain to embrace. "You have gone," said he, "considerably out of your way; to go a little further, will only be a small addition of trouble;" and this remark he accompanied by one of his old Spanish proverbs, which corresponds to the English saying of "in for a penny, in for a pound." "The road to St. Salvador is a continuation of that by which we have arrived at this place; pursue that road, and proceed to the city of St. Salvador, which at present is the seat of Government, and where means will not be wanting for your performing, with safety, the journey to Guatemala."

In respect of the risk I might incur by adopting this advice, the curate assured me that whatever danger there might be of falling in with ordinary robbers, there was none to be apprehended from the insurgents, who, it was known, were in another part of the country. My next inquiry was in relation to the length of the journey to St. Salvador, when I learned what Don José called a little further, was upwards of a hundred miles. Having now decided on proceeding to that city, I had one point more to settle, that of persuading Mr. M. to accompany me. In this I succeeded, after a little coaxing and entreating, and just as I was helping him to the last glass of a bottle of the curate's claret which we were drinking between us.

On the 23d of May—three days after my arrival at Esquipulas—I took my departure for St. Salvador, with Mr. M., two arrieros and four mules. I was furnished by the curate with a letter to an inhabitant of the village of Ocotepeque, nine leagues distant, where it was our intention to pass the first night of this journey, and where a fresh set of mules would have to be engaged for taking us to St. Salvador. Don José had given me two letters for persons residing in the latter place.... To this gentleman, whose wit and amiable disposition had thus far enlivened our route, and whose services I foresaw we should miss, and to his hospitable relative the curate, I said, on parting, every thing that friendship and gratitude suggested.

It was a delightful morning when we left the village of Apopa for St. Salvador. A serene and cloudless sky of deepest blue was illuminated by the first rays of a refulgent sun, that rose majestically over the distant mountains; the long shadows of the trees were gradually becoming less; and the fresh dew on the grass and on the branches sparkled with the brilliancy of diamonds. The balmy softness of the atmosphere, the warbling of the birds, and the freshness of the breeze that gently breathed on us, inspired the most pleasurable emotions, and we felt happy in the mere consciousness of existence.

In our progress towards the city, we admired the beauty of the country, and the number and extent of the plantations. Several pretty farms, or country residences, with gardens and orchards, attracted my attention. The number of people was also remarkable, as we had been accustomed of late to travel many leagues at a time without meeting a human being. But it was Sunday, and the inhabitants of the neighbouring villages, in some of which there is no church, were going to the city to hear mass. They were mostly Indians. Their dress ... was extremely simple, and by no means unbecoming. That of the women was a piece of blue cotton wrapped round the waist, and reaching only a little below the knees. The upper part of the body was scantily covered by a sort of chemise, with an aperture at the top for the head, and open at the sides. This part of their dress is called *guepil,* and is elaborately, but rudely, embroidered about the neck and shoulders with coloured thread. It is not, however, considered a very indispensible article, for in the village it is often laid aside. Their head-dress was two long tresses of their own straight black hair, interlaced with a red ribbon, and wreathed round the head in the form of a turban. They wore neither shoes nor stockings. This was also the case with the men, except a few who wore a sort of sandals, called *caycos,* which they cut out of a raw hide, and fasten to their feet with thongs. The rest of the male dress was a light suit of cotton, a straw hat or a coloured kerchief on the head, and a *chamarra,* which is made of coarse cloth, and answers all the purposes of cloak, blanket, carpet, and bed. The men were slender in form, but muscular. The fine figures and graceful carriage of some of the women were remarkable. . . . Both sexes conversed in their own native language, but were not ignorant of the Spanish, for many of them saluted us, as we passed, with a *Dios los guarde,* or a *vayan con la virgen.*

On entering the suburbs of St. Salvador, the appearance of the place was that of a large straggling country town, without any semblance of a populous city. As we advanced, however, we came to some good streets, and saw some respectable houses and public buildings. At length, we reached the *plaza.* . . .

One of my first cares after arriving at St. Salvador, was to obtain information in regard to the best mode of accomplishing, in safety, my journey to Guatemala, where the President of the Republic and the diplomatic agent of the United States were both residing. With this view, I called on the Vice-President, Mr. Ibarra, who received me with much affability and politeness.[25] The apartment where I saw him was decorated at one extremity by a *dais,* or canopy, of red damask, with an arm-chair and table beneath, also covered with damask, forming altogether something like a throne. He was not sitting there, however, when I visited him, but at another table, covered with various papers and books, among which I noticed one object that seemed to me very unofficial, and rather out of place—a huge poignard, the sheath and handle of which were of silver, beautifully wrought. On my stating to him the object of my visit, he manifested the most sincere disposition to promote my views, as well on my account, as from respect to the Government of the United States. He would confer, he said,

25. Vice-president Manuel Julián Ibarra served as acting president from April to June, 1838, while Morazán was in Guatemala.

with the Secretary of State and of War on the subject, and directed me to call on that gentleman to learn his decision.

The next morning, accordingly, I waited on Don Miguel Alvarez, the Secretary alluded to. Of this gentleman a curious circumstance had been related to me, which was that his head had never been seen uncovered, for he always, and in every place, wore a handkerchief round it. On visiting him I found this to be the case, his head being covered by a piece of fine white cambric. I had some difficulty in suppressing a smile; and all I could do to keep my eyes from his head, they still wandered in that direction. This circumstance, however, was by no means injurious to his looks, for a finer and more intellectual countenance I have seldom seen, nor a brighter and more penetrating eye.

Mr. Alvarez received me with flattering marks of attention, and informed me that it had been determined to furnish me a military escort to take me to Guatemala, and that I could dispose of fifty men whenever I should think proper to undertake the journey. With this force, he said, I could proceed in perfect safety, and should have no occasion to retreat before any party of insurgents I might meet with, though twice as strong in number. This escort I was to take at a town, called *Sonsonate*, a few leagues distant from St. Salvador, but on my way from the city to that town I should be accompanied by an officer, who, for so short a distance, would be all the protection I should need.

... Before my departure, ... I resolved to attend one of the sessions of the legislative body, and having become acquainted with Don Manuel Rodriguez, a Senator, and a great admirer of the United States, I went in company with that gentleman to the Chamber of Deputies.

The sessions are held ... in a large house appropriated to that purpose. The members sit in a saloon, one half of which is separated by a balustrade, and is occupied by the public. At the opposite extremity sits the Speaker, under a canopy, with a table covered with damask before him, and a secretary at his side. The members—twenty-six in number—sit on chairs distributed along the walls, without any desks or tables before them, and look as if they were there on a visit, or had come to a party. None of them were speaking, when I entered the chamber, nor was I able at first to comprehend the nature of the proceedings. I observed that they rose one after the other, and going to the Secretary, whispered something in his ear, which the latter immediately put in writing. On my asking Mr. Rodriguez for an explanation, he told me they were electing a Secretary. This they did by giving in a whisper the name of the candidate they voted for. Of the votes thus given, a list was made in writing, by which means ballots and ballot-boxes were dispensed with.

I will not undertake to say that the soldiers of the escort were as brilliant in appearance as those of the National Guard of Paris, but neither were they so dilapidated and torn as the men with whom Falstaff refused to march through Coventry.[26] They were not encumbered with havresacks, or baggage of any kind; their firelocks, accoutrements, and chamarras, being all they had to carry. The dress, both of horse and foot, was of coarse serge, with red cuffs and collars, and straw hats. Some of them had neither shoes nor stockings; others wore only *caycos*, or sandals. The cavalry, to say the truth, were miserably mounted, but with their long lances decorated with bannerets of blue and white, they had a picturesque, if not a very military appearance.

. . . The first place we came to, after leaving Sonsonate, was an Indian village called Nahuizalco. Here I was forcibly struck by the singularity of a fact which I have already alluded to: the existence of the aborigines in all their original simplicity, and their adherence to the language and habits of their ancestors, even while living in the vicinity of large and populous towns. In Nahuizalco, the arts and usages of civilized life seemed to be utterly unknown. The greater part of the individuals of both sexes were totally uncovered from the waist upwards; the children were unencumbered by any clothes whatever. They inhabited little huts without windows, lived upon plantains and tortillas, and slept in hammocks.

A few miles further, we came to Apaneca, another Indian village, very similar to the one just described. . . .

. . . A detention of a few hours was . . . incurred, in consequence of a report that a considerable band of Carrera's people was hovering about the neighbourhood. A scout was forthwith dispatched to ascertain the fact. On his return we learned that one of the most noted leaders of the revolution had been seen in that vicinity, but with a small number of men only, and that he had betaken himself to a village in the mountains. . . .

26. J. Wilson thought less of the appearance of the guard in Omoa, Honduras, in 1825. See Ch. 1 n. 52.

After proceeding a few miles, we came to a steep rocky mountain. ... The ascent was by a narrow winding path, sufficiently abrupt and difficult. I happened to be in the advance, and was the first to reach the summit; whence I looked back upon our wild and motley *cavalgada*, horse and foot, and baggage mules, forming a long line, and toiling in a zig-zig direction up the mountain; the bannerets of the cavalry fluttering in the air, and the muskets of the infantry glittering in the sun. Of the foot soldiers, some held on by the tails of the horses, or grappled with the rocks and bushes to help themselves along, and others, to facilitate their progress, had nearly stripped themselves of their clothes, which were carried by their comrades who were mounted.

Beyond this mountain, there were others equally wild and lofty. High up, near the crest of one of them, and embosomed amid rocks and bushes, was a group of huts like a bird's nest, which the commandant pointed out to me, saying that it was the village where the rebel chief, alluded to above, had retreated. There he was, like an eagle in his eyry, which was almost inaccessible, and, doubtless, watching us with a wistful eye as we passed beneath.

. . . Wide meadows, enlivened by numerous herds of cattle and horses, were spread before us, extending in some directions as far as the eye could reach. Several pretty hamlets also occurred at intervals, with little plantations round them of maize, plantain, and sugar-cane. The road, too, was enlivened by a number of passengers going and coming, on horseback and on foot; a circumstance which in itself indicated our approach to a populous city. At length we came in full view of the city of Guatemala. The domes and spires of its lofty churches and public buildings glittered in the sun, while the white walls of the houses gleamed through the trees and foliage of its numerous gardens. The environs of the city were verdant with shady groves and cultured slopes. . . .

Just before coming to the city, I took leave of my escort. . . . The poor soldiers, who had brought me in safety to my journey's end, were not forgotten, nor the patience with which they had endured so much fatigue on my account, nor their docility and admirable subordination; and, in separating from them, I made them, in the manner that I knew would be most agreeable, a slight compensation for their services.

I entered the city through one of the principal streets, which was well paved, and provided with side-walks. The houses, though but one story high, and indeed the town in general, had a neat and respectable appearance. I was conducted to the house of the Chargé d'Affaires of the United States. This gentleman, though much surprised by my arrival, which had been quite unexpected, received me with every mark of kindness and attention. . . .

It was the 9th of June when I arrived at Guatemala; twenty-eight days since the commencement of my journey at Izabal, and about two months since my departure from Washington.

. . . A few remarks on the character and customs of the natives of Central America may not be uninteresting. It is only in the city of Guatemala, and in one or two of the larger towns, that civilization and the arts have made any considerable progress. . . . The manners and dress of the citizens of Guatemala are essentially the same as those of the corresponding classes in the mother country. The ladies, as in Spain, wear the mantilla and veil when they go to church, and appear without any covering on their heads when walking out or on a visit. They are fond of adorning their hair with flowers, and with high tortoise-shell combs, some of which are very costly and beautifully wrought. Caps are never worn; nay, they are so much disliked, that even the elderly ladies prefer an exposure of their grey locks to wearing them. If they go out in the evening, the head is protected by a shawl or handkerchief; when travelling, or on horseback, they wear a hat surmounted by a profusion of feathers. The pride and luxury of a Guatemala lady is a richly embroidered veil, a costly fan, and a valuable set of jewels. Their passion for the latter is remarkable, as also for finery of every kind. They are generally well formed and graceful, and very proud of a pretty foot. A compliment to this part of a lady's person is the surest mode of winning her smiles.

On the part of the man, their taste for dress is chiefly exhibited when they are equipt for travelling. At such times, their swords, their spurs of massive silver, their poniards with sheaths of the same metal, the trappings of their horses elaborately embroidered with silk, and their other ornaments, imply an expense of not less than a thousand dollars.

Of both sexes it may be said with justice, that they are amiable, courteous, and attentive to strangers. They are of mild disposition, and have good natural talents, an aptitude for learning, and a lively imagination. Yet in education they are exceedingly deficient. . . . Hospitality is one of their virtues, gambling one of their faults. . . . They have a peculiar, but not a disagreeable, mode of speaking, and soft mellifluous voices, with a whining accent not unlike that of the natives of Andalusia in Spain. In common conversation, they use a number of words that are foreign to the Castilian language, and are mostly derived from the Indian. Thus they use the word:—

Mecate, for *soga,* a rope;
Chilillo, " *latigo,* a whip;
Galapo, " *silla de montar,* a saddle;
Caycos, " *alpargattas,* sandals;
Milpa, " *plantio de maiz,* a corn-field;

and a number of other words which have escaped my memory. Once, on asking for a wash-bason, I used the four names given to that article in Spanish without being understood, but on saying *ponchera,* a word suggested to me by a native, my wants were attended to. Another of their peculiarities in language, is that they often speak in the third person plural, and use the pronoun *vos* instead of *ustèd,* as *que decis vos?* (what do you say?) for *que dice ustèd?* This is the old Castilian mode of speaking, which has long since been abandoned in Spain, though it is infinitely preferable to the present mode, as being much more graceful. . . .

Their amusements consist chiefly in dancing and riding on horseback, of both which they are very fond. For walking, there are many pleasant places in the suburbs and environs of the city, especially a little Indian village, called Jocotenango, which is ingrafted, as it were, on the city, and forms a curious contrast with it.[27] There are no carriages of any kind in Guatemala. The only vehicles I saw there, were two coaches that were not in use, either of which had wood enough in it to make three modern carriages, and was heavy enough to require six stout mules to draw it. Almost every house is open to visitors. In many of them a small party meet every evening, regularly and without ceremony, and pass the time in social intercourse. Formal parties are not frequent. Yet I was at one, where all the refinements of polished life seemed to be perfectly understood, and where I was agreeably surprised by the display of a tea-table, with all its accessories in the best taste.

Soon after my arrival at Guatemala, I went with the Chargé d'Af-

27. Jocotenango formed a separate *municipio* until 1879, when it became a part of Guatemala City.

faires of the United States to pay a visit to General Morazan, the President, who was not then in the city, but at his head-quarters at Villanueva, a little town about ten miles distant. On arriving there, we rode up to a house where a military guard was stationed, and which proved to be the dwelling of the General. There was a spacious yard in front, and a sentinel at the gate. We were admitted without difficulty, and, on inquiring for the President, were shown into a hall by one of the adjutants, who desired us to wait there till he announced our visit. This hall, the door of which was also guarded by a sentinel, had all the appearance of a guard-house. There was no other furniture in it but a large long table and a couple of wooden benches. It was full of officers of different ranks, who were there on duty, or waiting for orders. Their ranks could be distinguished by their epaulettes; but in their dress there was a total absence of uniformity; some wearing cocked hats with feathers, others round hats with a broad gold band round the crowns, some in blue regimentals, some in red, and many with no other uniform than a jacket with military buttons. In one thing only was there any appearance of regularity—in the long unwieldy swords and ponderous spurs with which they were all provided. In the yard were several horses, saddled and ready for service, and a number of soldiers, some loitering about, some furbishing their arms, and others gambling.

It was not long before we were admitted into the presence of the General, who received us with great courtesy. He was dressed in plain clothes, and seemed to be about forty years of age, small of stature, and rather of a dark complexion.[28] In his manner and conversation there was some appearance of constraint or reserve; yet he had a fine expression of countenance, and eyes beaming with intelligence. On taking leave of him, he told me that the military commandant at Guatemala would be directed to furnish me, on my departure, another escort to accompany me in my return to the coast.

His own talents, together with a combination of fortunate circumstances, have raised General Morazan to the distinguished station he now occupies. . . . From one success to another, he finally arrived at the Presidency. On reaching this point, he divested himself of all party feelings and political predilections. He also did not hesitate to make a temporary resignation of his civil authority, in order to direct in person the operations of the army. This policy, so far from diminishing, has rather increased his power and credit; for he is now sought and courted

28. Morazán's age in 1838 was forty-six.

by men of all opinions. He is regarded by them as their anchor of hope, or as the pilot who is to guide the ship of state in safety through the storms that assail it.[29]

The 2d of July was the day fixed for my departure. The escort promised me was furnished, and the officer commanding it made his appearance with his men at the appointed time. They were all foot soldiers, and twenty-five in number. I had declined the offer of some cavalry, having found them by experience more troublesome than useful. A young gentleman of Guatemala, a brother of the Marquis of A ***—the only titled family in the country—having occasion to make a journey to the coast, had expressed his desire of accompanying me; and this being agreed to and settled, I called for him at an early hour on the day of departure.[30] I found him busy in making his preparations; some of his servants saddling mules and loading baggage, and others setting out a table for breakfast. Several of his friends had come to accompany him for a few miles, whose horses were pawing up the ground and champing their bits in the court-yard. It was some time before we were ready to start. At length we mounted. Don Ignacio—for such was the baptismal name of my new travelling companion—bestrode a superb mule, full fifteen hands high, and in the style and fashion of his equipments exhibited a perfect model of a Central American dandy, when he is about to undertake a journey. He was armed from head to foot: his armas de agua, his rodilleras, and his cloak, were all in the best taste and of the best materials. He was attended by a servant well mounted, and by a muleteer on foot, and had altogether five mules; two for himself and servant, one to carry his baggage, another for his bedding and provisions, and a third as a sumpter mule.

We sallied forth to the number of ten or twelve persons, and attracted no little notice as we clattered over the pavement. The cavalcade proceeded at such a brisk pace, that I had some difficulty in keeping up with it; and as the mule I had under me was evidently unaccustomed to such rapid movements, and unwilling to adopt new

---

29. Montgomery's judgment seems strange in view of the disasters which overtook Morazán in 1839, but may well have accorded with the general outlook in June, 1838.

30. Juan José Aycinena, the "Marquis" of this sentence, had spent most of his life since 1829 as a Guatemalan self-exiled in the United States. See Ch. 1 n. 66 for comment concerning the title.

habits, my spurs were in constant requisition. At length, after a ride of three or four miles, we overtook the escort and the baggage mules, which had been sent on before, and the friends of Don Ignacio took their leave. Half an hour at least was consumed in the performance of this ceremony. There was such a shaking of hands, such a repetition of the words *adios* and *buen viaje*, and such interest expressed about the safety and welfare of my new friend, that one would have thought he was going to the end of the world, and might never be seen again. I was a mere spectator in the scene, being completely eclipsed by Don Ignacio, whose friends barely bestowed on me a farewell nod, as they turned their horses and galloped back to the city.

We now proceeded at a more gentle pace. The route we pursued was not the one usually taken by travellers going to Izabal, nor that by which I had arrived at Guatemala. It was a road leading through another part of the country, and which had been recommended to me as being somewhat shorter, and as affording me an opportunity of performing the latter part of my journey by water.[31] It was also considered by Don Ignacio as the preferable route. The only objection to it was that the country, in that direction, was but thinly settled, and there were fewer villages. This difficulty I submitted to the consideration of my companion before starting, but his reply was, "No importa, there is no want of haciendas on the way." But are you, I rejoined, acquainted with the proprietors of them? "No importa," said he again, "we shall be well received;" and it was definitively settled that we should proceed by the route alluded to.

. . . We came to a large river called Rio Grande. The banks were high and precipitous, the stream rapid, and apparently very deep, and I was considering how this river was to be passed—there being no bridge—when my attention was attracted by two stout cables stretched from bank to bank, about twenty feet above the water. This, I was told, was the bridge by which we were to pass. These cables lay parallel to each other, and about fifteen inches apart. Between them, and supported by them, was a double block of a corresponding width, from which was suspended a strong leather strap, like a sling. To this strap, or sling, we had to trust our lives. We took our seats in it successively, and on a signal being given, a line attached to the block was hauled upon from the opposite side of the river, when the block, with its burden, glided over the cables, till it reached the landing-place on

31. The route lay by Salamá and the Río Polochic.

that side. The soldiers indulged in many a jest, and fired off their jokes upon each other as they were hauled over the river. To me, the apparatus appeared a most rude and dangerous contrivance; and I could not but feel some uneasiness when I found myself suspended in the air by a mere strap, with a rushing stream beneath me, where, should I fall, I might either be drowned, or dashed to pieces among rocks. The baggage, saddles, and other articles, were sent over in the same way. The mules were driven into the stream, and made to swim across; but for this purpose they were led to a place considerably above the point where they were to come out on the other side; the stream being so strong, that they could not possibly have crossed it in a direct line. The shouts of the muleteers, as they forced the mules into the river, and of the men stationed on the other side to prevent their passing the landing-place, made the adjacent woods ring again; the poor animals, in the mean time, snorting and splashing, as they struggled through the water. One of the mules was near being lost, and two were severely hurt: the rest succeeded in passing without accident.

Two hours were consumed in this tedious and perilous operation. . . .

We . . . proceeded along the channel of a mountain torrent, which, though it contained but little water, was so uneven and full of loose stones, that our progress through it was painfully slow and difficult.

Emerging from this torrent, we came in view of a little plain, hedged in by rocks and thickets, and situated at the foot of a mountain. In the centre was a cluster of huts, surrounded by little plantations of maize and fruit trees. The place was a rancheria, called *el Patal*, and had altogether a most rural and picturesque appearance. The huts were only six or eight, and were inhabited by Indians.

It being now 3 o'clock—the hour at which, in that season of the year, it usually rains—and there being no probability of our finding a shelter further on for a considerable distance, it was determined to make the rancheria our resting-place for the night. I was loth to disturb the quiet of this little fairy land—this Eden in miniature—but there was no help for it, and we proceeded to take possession of the place. The best of the huts, which might more properly be called a large shed, (it being entirely open on one side,) was occupied by the officer and the escort; another was selected by Don Ignacio for himself and his servant. The former was so crowded by the soldiers, and the latter so completely destitute of any thing like comfort, that I resolved on seeking my own accommodations elsewhere.

Casting my eye around, I fixed upon a hut rather more neat and respectable in appearance than the others, and rode towards it. This hut was hemmed in by a *milpa*, or corn plantation, and by a little kitchen-garden; and I saw no means of approaching it without injuring the premises. An old Indian, with a young man, now made his appearance, whom I saluted, and addressed in the most civil manner, asking him whether that was his house, and whether he would permit me to pass the night there. The old man shrugged his shoulders, and did not, or pretended not, to understand. I repeated the question, and his answer was, *managh, managh,* which—as I afterwards learnt—means, I have none, or there is none; the poor man believing, no doubt, that I was asking him for something to eat. I then desired him, partly by signs, to show me the way to the house; but his answer was, with something like petulance in the manner of giving it, "*no hay camino,*" (there is no road.)

I now determined I would go into that hut "whether or not." Accordingly, I struck my spurs into my mule, and rode through the milpa to the door of the hut, where I tied my mule, and walked in; the old and the young Indian following me, and muttering in their native language unintelligible things. On entering the hut, I found a young woman occupied making tortillas. I sat down opposite to her, and addressed to her a few words, but to no purpose: she looked at me for a moment with an air of surprise, and then continued her work. She evidently did not understand a word of Spanish. Two little dirty naked children were sprawling at her feet; and it immediately struck me that she might be their mother. With this impression, I took one of them up, placed it on my knee, and wiping its little mouth, gave it a kiss. This act did not escape the attention of the mother—for such she proved to be—her countenance suddenly brightened up, and her full dark eyes beamed with an expression of pleasure. Pursuing my advantage, I made out to ask her whether that was her child. She seemed to understand me, and answered, *ha, ha, guahenni*—which means, yes, yes, my child. I then pointed to the other child, and asked if that, too, was her guahenni. She answered with a nod and a smile; and thereupon, I took up that one also, and caressed it as I had done the first.

The old Indian, who was the father of this young woman, and of the youth by whom he was accompanied, had stood all this time looking on in silence. The sternness of his countenance had now in a measure disappeared; and as he seemed more favourably disposed towards me, I seized that opportunity of gaining his good will by paying him a little compliment. Taking up a calabash, that happened to be near me, I poured into it a small quantity of French brandy from a little flask— once the property of my former travelling companion, who transferred it to me—and handed the beverage to the old man, with a request that he would drink it. He took the calabash, but hesitated a moment, and looked first towards his daughter, and then to his son, as if to consult them before taking a draught that peradventure might be poisoned. At length he took courage, and tossed off the brandy; then smacked his lips, and cried, "bueno!" I then poured out into the same calabash a few drops, which I drank myself. This seemed to gratify the old man excessively; I had removed all suspicions of the drink being poisoned; I had not scrupled to drink out of the same cup with him; in short, I had fairly subjugated him by an act of condescension.

Finding myself now on the best terms with the whole family, I put a few reals into the hands of the old Indian, and desired him to buy me a fowl, some eggs, or whatever he could procure.

In the mean time, the officer, who had been looking for me, made his appearance in the hut, and proposed, in case of my passing the night there, to send me a few soldiers to keep me company. This was agreed to, and my asistente and three or four others were sent accordingly. I now set the men about making a fire, that they might prepare a supper out of some eggs which mine Indian host had procured me. But how these eggs were to be cooked, was another consideration. They could not be fried, for we had neither butter nor any thing else that could serve as a substitute; nor could they be boiled, for there was no salt, and, as one of the soldiers said, "El que come un huevo sin sal, se comeria à su madre," (He that would eat an egg without salt, would eat his mother.)

Scarcely was this difficulty surmounted, when another occurred. Night was coming on apace, and we had no candles, nor any other light but that of the fire, which was insufficient to enable me to make a memorandum of the incidents which I am now recording. I represented the case to mine host, and succeeded in making him comprehend that I wanted something to make a light with; but his answer was, as before, *managh, managh*. My asistente now hinted to me, that unless I used threats, I should never succeed, as nothing was to be got from an Indian by fair means. This, however, I refused to do, and it was all the better in the end; for while these remarks were being made, the Indian had hit upon the means of complying with my wishes. Making me a sign to wait a little, he left the hut, and returned soon after with a bundle of pine knots under his arm. One of these he kindled at the fire, and seeing it emit a bright and steady flame, he held it up before me with a smile.

It now only remained to devise some means of fixing this light in such a way as to render it unnecessary for any of the men to hold it while I was writing. This new difficulty was soon disposed of by my asistente, who, casting his eyes round, and seeing a little Indian about ten years old, who had put his head in at the door of the hut, and was gazing on us with a look of wonderment, went and seized him by the collar, and planting him beside me, said, "here is a candlestick." He then put the pine knot into the child's hand, and shaking his finger at him, bade him hold himself upright, and not to budge. The little fellow, who had already learnt to yield passive obedience to the white man, exhibited on the occasion the docility peculiar to his race; and there he stood for more than half an hour, as motionless as a statue, and almost afraid to breathe, while I was bringing up my journal. I have no doubt he would have held out two hours, but there was no necessity for making the experiment. On relieving him from his task, I put a real into his hand, and made him a sign to go. He gazed for a few moments at the coin, then clutched it with his little fingers, and without uttering a word, bounded out of the hut with the agility of an antelope.

I now looked round for a place to sleep in, and, to my surprise, observed that my Indian friends—father, son, and daughter—had disappeared, and left us in exclusive possession of their house. I could not help expressing my regret at having, as it were, turned the family out of doors; but the soldiers only laughed at me, and told me not to trouble myself about them, for an Indian could sleep any-where. I resolved with myself, however, to make them some amends, the next morning, by a liberal compensation. In the mean time, I disposed myself for rest on a hurdle of cane-reeds, covering it with my leopard's skin; the soldiers, spreading out their chamarras, stretched themselves on the ground.

Telemán is situated on the banks of the Polochic, at the point where that river becomes navigable. I found it a thriving little town, with something of a commercial air. I was provided, in the house of a ladino, with very passable accommodations. It was quite apparent that the inhabitants here had had some intercourse with foreigners and strangers, as several objects of luxury or convenience were to be found in their houses, such as I had not seen since my departure from Guatemala. In the house of mine host I was agreeably surprised by the sight of a rocking chair and a tea-pot, and hailed them as indications of my being again within the precincts of civilized society.[32]

I now dismissed the escort, and made arrangements for descending the river. A canoe was engaged, accordingly, with three men to direct her course. This canoe, which had been scooped out of the trunk of a tree, measured thirty-two feet in length, and only three in breadth, and drew scarcely fifteen inches water. The after-part was covered with a roof of canes and palm leaves, as a protection against the sun and rain. Two men sat in the bows with paddles, and another in the stern, who was both helmsman and captain: the baggage was stowed away in the bottom of the boat.

In this frail and unsteady craft I embarked for Izabal.

Don Valentin, who had so kindly harboured me on my first coming to the place, welcomed me back in the most cordial manner. It was the 12th of July when I arrived there, nine days since my departure from Guatemala. There was no opportunity then for proceeding to Belize, but one presented itself on the 15th, when I embarked in a small English vessel destined for that port. . . .

On approaching the mouth of the river, my attention was attracted by a little village I had not observed in coming up; and with a mixture of surprise and pleasure, I learnt that the name of the place was Livingston. This was a compliment paid by the Central American Government to that distinguished statesman and jurist, whose criminal code had been adopted in the country, and whose character and talents were not less respected there than in the United States. The village consisted of only forty or fifty huts, but it had a thriving appearance; and some little trade was carried on there, as four or five small craft were at anchor in front of it.

Being compelled to beat up against the breeze-wind all the way, we did not arrive at Belize before the 19th. . . . My first inquiries on landing, were about my former travelling companion, Mr. M., whose

---

32. Telemán's tea pots and rocking chairs doubtless came from the British settlement of 1835–37 called New Liverpool, at about the location of today's Cahaboncito. See William J. Griffith, *Empires in the Wilderness*, pp. 138–56. Montgomery on his voyage down the Polochic mentions (his page 191) passing "a little settlement composed of foreigners, called Cajabon," one year after New Liverpool's abandonment.

house, during my stay in the place, I proposed making my home. My surprise and sorrow will easily be conceived, when I learnt that he had died only the day before. In less than three weeks from his return he had been taken ill, and in five days after was conveyed to the cemetery.

About a year after the trip of Montgomery, an ex-infantryman from England named GEORGE BYAM came to Nicaragua to live. Byam was interested in mining and hunting, not in chronicling, and when he much later wrote a book about his two-year sojourn he omitted all references to time.[33] The book on Nicaragua (published in London, 1849) was called *Wild Life in the Interior of Central America,* being written for those who love stories of adventure with big game. A year later there appeared a translation in German.[34]

Running, walking, or slouching through most of Byam's pages are the deer, the tapir, the jaguar, the cougar, the coyote, the monkey, the crocodile, and the boa which held his prime attention. But before their stories begin, Byam explains briefly how he came to reside on the isthmus (though he does not say so, in the year 1839):[35]

One of the reasons that induced me to explore the Interior of Central America, was the report I had heard of the mineral riches contained in that country, and although the report partly proceeded from persons who had not been far from the coast, yet I heard enough to make me believe that in the high mountain regions of the interior many a rich virgin mine awaited the explorer. Another reason was, the spirit of adventure inherent in almost all Englishmen; and a third was, the wish of returning home from Chili, where I was then residing, by some other route than Cape Horn. A kind friend who commanded one of her Majesty's 18 gun sloops, offered me a passage to visit Mexico, and return with him home, *via* Cape Horn and Rio Janeiro; but at that time an English gentleman, who owns a large sugar estate in Central America, arrived at Valparaiso, and offered me a passage to Realejo in his own vessel, a beautiful Yankee clipping brigantine, under United States' colours. I accepted his kind offer, and never enjoyed a sea voy-

---

33. His adventures are here roughly dated by a few remarks (pp. 17, 181, 216–21) in a later book, *Wanderings in Some of the Western Republics of America* (London, 1850), which tells of prior experiences in Chile, Peru, and Ecuador.
34. See Byam, 1850.
35. Byam, 1849, pp. 1–2, 4–10.

age more in my life; well bred and well read, Mr. B—— did the honours of his vessel in princely style....[36]

We arrived safely at Realejo after a long voyage, very short time actually at sea, but making the most of any agreeable port we stopped at; and here let me remark that, having lived four years in Chili, and that mostly in the wildest part of the province of Coquimbo, I arrived in Central America with rather peculiar advantages for prosecuting researches for minerals, or for hunting in the interior: and these advantages were the knowledge of the value of ores by sight, especially copper ones, the way of searching for them, speaking the language, a very fair use of the lasso, in which I found myself superior to most of the Indians, and a good acquaintance with the breaking and bitting of horses for the lasso. I had also brought with me an excellent Chili saddle, with lassoing girths and rings, several lassos, and dressed sheepskins, or, as they are called, pillions. I was well provided with all sorts of fire-arms, down to holster and pocket-pistols, plenty of powder, ball, shot, wadding, and copper caps, and, in short, was quite ready to take the field, after having provided horses and mules for myself and servants.

On my arrival at Realejo, I was almost immediately seized with the fever that is so prevalent on the low, muddy, pestilential shores of the western coast, and it was only the kind attention and skilful treatment of the gentleman who had brought me in his vessel that carried me through the crisis; though, one night, I overheard a conversation between him and the English vice-consul respecting the spot where I was to be buried. I shortly recovered, though very weak; and, as soon as I could sit on horseback, went up to León . . . to make the necessary preparations for a tour through the interior of the country.

I now take leave of the sort of narrative that I have given; it was only to shew that my objects in exploring Central America were partly to discover some of the rich mines I had often heard of, partly to see a country I had never seen, and to enjoy the wild sports of its immense forests, in many parts of which no Englishman had ever been, and lastly, to make my way to the Atlantic overland, and return to England after a visit to the West Indies.

My aim is not to give a connected account of two years' residence in

36. Dunlop, 1847, pp. 25–26, more openly identified the owner as Walter Bridge (or Bridges; see Stephens, 1949, 2:20); and the vessel (which Byam, 1849, p. 4, calls the "good ship A—") as the *Albert Henry*.

Central America, of which almost the whole was passed in the midst of the forest, and near the foot of the central ranges of mountains, but to give short, unconnected details of the country, inhabitants, produce, and minerals, but more especially of the wild beasts, birds, reptiles, &c., that swarm in the forests, and with whom I was much more in contact than with the half-civilised dwellers in the towns nearer the coast.

After a fortnight's residence in León, which is a large straggling town, and in which two English gentlemen were living, I made a tour in company with one of them through a great part of the interior; and, after much difficult travelling, and plenty of "roughing it," decided on a spot on which to build a couple of large huts, that might serve as head-quarters, the surrounding mountains shewing many traces of very rich copper ore. We had a piece of land cleared; and, with the help of some Indians, who lived in a village about twenty miles off, these huts were built after the manner of the country. . . .

It was situated near the boundaries of Nicaragua and Segovia; and, from being so much higher than the large wooded plains about the coast, was cooler and comparatively healthy, especially when care was taken not to get wet while warm with exercise, which almost invariably produces tertian ague, from which I suffered severely for about three months, reducing my weight from ten stone ten pounds, hard condition, to ninety-seven pounds weight Spanish, or seven stone and a half. However, directly the disease leaves a person, strength and health are rapidly regained.

There was a cool shaded stream of delicious water hardly fifty yards from the "ranchos," as these huts are called, plenty of food for the horses and mules, and the distance was about one hundred and twenty miles from León, and upwards of two hundred from Realejo.[37] My friend then returned to León, we having agreed to keep up a communication by means of mounted Indians, and I was left alone in the wilderness with a few servants, followers, and miners in embryo. . . .

Though without books, newspapers, or any mental amusement, time did not hang very heavy on my hands, except during a long continuance of rain; and, what with overlooking some mines I was teaching a few Indians to work, and a variety of field sports, I was generally glad

---

37. If these two distances were anywhere near accurate, they could be used to determine an approximate location for Byam's residence "near the boundaries of Nicaragua and Segovia." Unfortunately for such reckoning, however, El Realejo and León are nearly equidistant from any point so described.

to turn in a little after the sun set, to be up in the morning a little before he rose.

Half tame cattle we could get in abundance from a natural "corral" about nine miles distant, formed by rocks and steep hills, where a great number were kept by herdsmen in the employ of a Spaniard in León; and the forest amply supplied any extra delicacy for the table in the shape of venison, two sorts of wild turkey, partridges, &c.; and, although everything was served in true forest fashion, yet in general all hands had plentiful and wholesome meals: but this was very far from being the case on long excursions, where often, water failing, game failed likewise. Of vegetables we had none, and no bread; but we had maize, baked over the ashes into a flat cake, and now and then a substitute for cabbage, when we met with a young palm-tree (of the species that gives the palm wine).[38]

A supply of onions was forwarded from León; and, with the exception of wine or beer, the general living was far better than I have often experienced in my many travels....

These "ranchos" served me as head-quarters for two years; and, though I do not regret having thrown away such time, I certainly would not wish to pass that time over again in the same way, though I look back with pleasure to many adventures on lake and river, forest, savannah, and mountain.

There was not enough copper ore to hold Byam's attention, once he had become surfeited with the life of the forest. His trip of departure, a little more fully depicted than that of his entry, forms a quiet contrast to the very excited travel along the same route a decade after Byam's time:[39]

Having very nearly completed two years' residence in Central America, and that principally in the wildest part of the interior, I own I began to be weary of the half-savage life I had been so long leading.

A very severe wound I received on a hunting party decided me to set my face steadfastly towards the east, as soon as I should be sufficiently recovered to undertake a long journey on horseback and in canoes. I was undecided which course to pursue, but at last resolved to travel back to León; go from thence to the Pacific coast, for the purpose of making arrangements respecting funds, and, returning by

38. Reference is presumably to the coyol palm, the genus *Acrocomia*.
39. Byam, 1849, pp. 223–26, 232, 236–37, 245, 250–51.

León, proceed on to the Lake of Nicaragua, and take my chance of finding a "piragua," or large canoe, to take me to the east shore of the lake and down the river St. Juan to the Boca, or mouth of the river, on the Atlantic.

I had been lying in my rancho for a week, very much exhausted, and weak from extreme loss of blood, when, finding myself a little stronger, I determined to start for León the next morning, as, at least, I could there get some little surgical aid, of which I stood much in need, being obliged to dress my wound myself.

Having selected my steadiest horses and mules, I started the next morning, taking with me everything I meant to take home, and leaving a great many things for the Indians who came in to take leave of me: two Indians accompanied me who had been with me from the first, but the journey was more full of accidents to me than all the previous ones put together. We had hardly travelled two leagues than my horse, always used for the lasso, and a favourite, from his surefootedness, came down, for the first time, right on his nose. On the spur of the moment I disengaged the left arm that was bandaged to the side, to pull him up, and burst afresh the large artery that had been severed, and I had only time to dismount, when I had another fainting-fit. However, we managed to get to an old deserted ruin by nightfall, and the night was passed by me in much suffering.

The next morning I mounted a very quiet mule, thinking she would never start or stumble; but as we were going along a narrow trail in the forest a crash in the underwood on one side frightened her, for she no doubt took it for a wild beast, and in she bolted to the underwood on the opposite side, bruising the wound very much: many other little accidents also occurred, which, when in health, no one thinks about, but are severely felt by the suffering.

By the time we arrived at León, what with loss of blood and pain, I could scarcely keep my saddle, and was agreeably surprised to find a North American surgeon, who had taken up his residence there for a short time. He came immediately to see me, and if ever this meets his eye, I here return him most grateful acknowledgments for his kindness and liberality, for he not only attended me with the care of a brother, but absolutely refused to take the smallest remuneration for his services, and when I went to Granada he accompanied me, for fear the wound should break out afresh. However, the doctor's care, rest, and a strong constitution set me up in two or three weeks; and having gone to the coast, arranged all my affairs, and obtained two or three letters of introduction for Granada, I hired an Indian guide, took my leave of the cities and villages of the low plains, and started with my friend the doctor for Granada.

By the letters I brought with me I was enabled to make a bargain with the patron or owner of a good strong piragua, to take me down to the Boca St. Juan on the Atlantic, and if I remember right, the price was very moderate. I had a patron and ten rowers for a fortnight's voyage, to victual themselves, and I think I only paid five pounds for everything, but laid in my own provisions.

I . . . took a view of the piragua in which I was fated to live a fortnight. It was a large canoe of about forty feet in length, by about eight feet beam, with five thwarts for ten men to pull double-banked. It was hollowed out of a single magnificent tree, but the sides raised upon about two planks on each side.

The patron, or steerer, had a small compartment aft, in which he kept the provisions for his crew, his tobacco, and jar of spirits: my ramada, as it is called, occupied the part between the patron and the crew.

The ramada is a semi-circular shelter, made sometimes from leafy boughs, from whence the name; but mine was made of bent sticks covered with a tarpauling; it is a very useful shelter against the great heat and the fierce showers constantly occurring in the river St. Juan. . . .

My crew consisted of a respectable-looking patron and ten Indians, all dressed in white trowsers, white shirts, and red sashes; but after we had started and pulled up to the northern or weather shore, to avoid the heavy sea, all the rowers, but not the patron, stripped themselves perfectly naked, and remained so day and night until about a mile before our arrival at the sea-coast, when they again put on the trowsers and shirts. They had each a heavy poncho, which they put over them during the night, but never during the heavy showers that only come in the afternoon.

The last day we were on the lake we kept under-way, till midnight, when we made the entrance of the river St. Juan and cast anchor till daylight. After prayers the next morning, we unshipped the mast, and it was hidden in the forest, to be taken up on the voyage back.

The morning we arrived at the Boca we got under-way two hours before daylight, and after pulling until sun-rise, the men laid in the oars and sung their morning-hymn, after which the patron chaunted a prayer different from what I had yet heard, and which was a thanksgiving for having performed our voyage in safety. They then washed themselves and the piragua and resumed their white shirts, trowsers, and red sashes, that had been carefully stowed away since our departure. We then proceeded on our journey, and soon landed at the Boca, which consists of a few miserable huts and a shed that does duty for a custom-house.

This poor village is built on the western end of a slip of low sandy land on the left bank, about two or three hundred yards in breadth and about half a mile in length, bounded to the north and to the west by a dense jungle, with a small fresh-water stream at the edge, and on the south and east by the river and coast. Towards the eastern end stands a very curious but very comfortable dwelling, built of wood, and occupied by an old English gentleman of the name of Shepherd, who exercises great hospitality to any one in want of it, and possesses much authority among the Mosquito Indians all along the coast.[40] He was kind enough to receive me until an opportunity should occur to enable me to proceed to the West Indies. I stayed with him five days, when a man-of-war schooner packet came in, and taking my berth, I sailed for Jamaica....

THOMAS YOUNG, like George Byam, was an Englishman who resided on the Central American isthmus during the years 1839–41. Though this was a time of great tumult in isthmian affairs, Young like Byam lived on the fringes of the conflict, in such a way that his own activities were not disturbed. Young stayed always near the Caribbean shore, carrying out duties as the interested but not always enthusiastic official of a British colonization project. His sensible comments on emigration to these far-off lands were offered in his *Narrative of a Residence on the Mosquito Shore, During the Years 1839, 1840, & 1841: With an account of Truxillo, and the adjacent islands of Bonacca and Roatan*, published in London in 1842. Five years later, with a slight change in title and three pages of Miskito vocabulary added, the book was printed again.[41]

Thomas Young's *Narrative* is the middle one of three extensive per-

---

40. Squier, 1852, 1:85–89, gives a fuller portrait of Samuel Shepherd. See also Froebel, 1859, pp. 158–59.
41. See Young, 1847.

sonal accounts of the Mosquito Shore. It commences with experiences seventeen years after the last recorded by Orlando Roberts, but seventeen years earlier than most described by a later resident, Charles Napier Bell.[42] Roberts was interested in pointing out the potentialities of this shore for British commerce and influence. Bell was raised in this region when the British had actually gained the dominance Roberts was suggesting. Young in his in-between position shows some of the development of the scene, making clear that the British effort followed no well-developed guidelines, and that most of the Britishers involved were persons seeking a new life on a strange frontier where there was still room for some independence of action. Young points out his own connections with the enterprise:[43]

In the year 1839 I accepted an engagement from the British Central American Land Company, as Deputy Superintendent, to proceed, with a few others, to the Mosquito Shore, to form a Settlement at Black River, about eighty miles from the Central American Port of Trujillo, in the State of Honduras, there to establish friendly relations with the people around, so that in time trade might be opened with the Spaniards in the interior, for the introduction and disposal of such British goods as they might be willing to take in exchange.

We sailed from Gravesend in July 1839, in the brig Rose, . . . bound for Cape Gracias a Dios, there to deliver our credentials to the King of the Mosquito nation, Robert Charles Frederic, (who had been invested with the crown, on the demise of his brother George Frederic, with the concurrence of the British Government,) and from thence proceed to Black River.

. . . About one P. M., we anchored off Cape Gracias a Dios, in four and a half fathoms. The country appeared low and covered with vegetation of a rich dark green colour down to the sea beach, from which we were distant about three miles. A boat was hoisted out, and on our way to the shore, we met a strange looking native boat, called a dorey, in which were three tall and powerful looking Indians, naked, with the exception of tournous, (made from the inner bark of the ule

---

42. Bell, 1899. One other book (Squier, 1855W) provides much reliable information from the middle of the century, but is not what it purports to be, an account of one person's travel experiences.

43. Young, 1842, pp. 1–2, 11–14, 25–26, 28–29, 37–39, 41–43, 50–51, 52–53, 65–71, 90, 93–94, 98–100, 122–23, 131–33, 135–36, 138–41, 146, 148–50, 152–56, 160.

or caoutchouc tree) tied round their loins, hanging down before and behind.[44] One of them sung out, in pretty good English, "How do? me glad see you—long time you no come!" to which one of our men who had been in the country before, and who knew the Indians, replied, "Tokoy, plenty English come live with you, bring plenty every thing, too much;" on hearing which they testified the most lively satisfaction, not, however, forgetting to ask for grog. By this time another dorey, which had displayed a small flag, came alongside, two white men being seated in the stern, one a gentleman, who had resided at the Cape as a merchant for many years, and for whom some of our party had letters. He and his companion returned with us to the brig, at the same time presenting us with some ripe bananas, pine apples, and sugar-cane, which were speedily demolished. We learned from them that it had been reported the Columbians had threatened to attack the Cape, and that the residents were totally unprepared for such a visit, having no arms or ammunition, though they expected that some would shortly arrive from Belize.[45]

A fort had been commenced on the Embarcadero, close by the entrance of the Bay of Cape Gracias á Dios, and near the north channel, so as to sweep any vessel that might arrive. They had, however, only one long brass gun, a nine pounder, and a small carronade. The only materials for building the fort were wood, sand, and a little copper dross, which had been thrown out of the hold of the Rose on a former voyage. The work was progressing under the directions of an Englishman residing at the Cape, assisted by numerous Mosquito men, each contributing one, two, or three days' work, according to the king's order, which is expressed by one of his tokens, either a silver medal, formerly presented to his deceased brother George Frederic by the English, or a gold-headed stick, a sword, or something known to belong to the king. These tokens the natives never disavowed.

Much pleasure was manifested at our arrival, as we had long been anxiously looked for, and although most of our small party were going

---

44. The tree to which Young refers is *Castilloa elastica,* or the Central American wild rubber tree. His word "tournou," however, seems derived from *tunu* or *tuno,* the name of a related tree, *Castilloa fallax,* which produces nonelastic gum.

45. This "threat," which did not materialize, was based on the claim of Colombia to the Mosquito Coast as far north as Cabo Gracias a Dios, this territory having been transferred to the jurisdiction of the viceroy in Bogotá (but in name only) by Spanish King Charles IV in 1803. The Colombian claim was relinquished in 1928.

to Black River, the natives of the Cape were inspired with the idea that they were not forgotten, as they had feared they had been by their friends the English. Towards night our newly acquired friends returned to their homes, and the next morning we landed near the affair called a fort, being satisfied that we should not be molested, from the known friendship these people have towards the English. The whole face of the country appeared covered with bush of the most varied character, interspersed with tall and graceful cocoa-nut trees, and mangrove bushes, which skirted the bay, spreading their branches some distance over the water. On landing, we entered a narrow pass, and were obliged to proceed in Indian file, our view being circumscribed by the bush on each side. While traversing along, a most delicious fragrance greeted our senses, and seemed like enchantment; we found it to proceed from some lime trees in full bearing; we plucked the grateful fruit, and inhaled its odour with new life and bright hopes, handsome plants meeting our gaze at every turn, and the air was so impregnated with sweetness, that our delight could not be exceeded. At length we arrived at some clearings, on which were huts built by the natives in a very primitive manner, posts being driven into the ground, secured together, roofed and thatched, almost perpendicularly, to within five or six feet from the surface, so that all round their huts to that height was perfectly open. . . . Our approach was greeted by the loud barkings of many lean and hungry dogs, and we were obliged to use our sticks with vigour to keep them from biting our heels. Several Indians were luxuriously swinging in their hammocks made from the bark of a tree called maho, while others were squatting down by a wood-fire, smoking their short pipes. Now and then one would cry out, "Ouple tapla ourike," (Friend, give me grog.) Many women and children were attending some large iron pots, boiling the root of the cassada, and fish, and roasting plantains; they seemed to regard us with wonder and surprise.[46] Numberless pigs were running about in all directions. After passing other Indian habitations, much better arranged and built than the first we had seen, we came to the English locality, highly gratified with our interesting walk from the embarcadero, about two miles and a half, and were received by the gentleman I have before named, Mr. H——, and heartily welcomed.[47]

46. "Cassada"=cassava. For the "maho," see Ch. 1 n.51.
47. "Mr. H.—" of Cabo Gracias a Dios is nowhere really named by Young, but seems surely to have been the "H.—" of Squier, 1855W, pp. 223-72, the "Captain Haly" of Squier, *The States of Central America* (New York, 1858), p. 35, and the Stanislaus Thomas Haly of *ibid.*, p. 404.

A house being ready, we slung our hammocks, feeling happy at being relieved from the dull confinement of a small vessel, and delighted with the appearance of the natives and country.

A few days after our arrival, the king, accompanied by a number of people called soldiers and quarter-masters, came in pitpans, from his residence..., which is about seven days' travel up the Wanks river.[48]

On being presented, and delivering our credentials and gifts, he appeared highly delighted, and taking each of us by the hand in turn, said slowly and distinctly, "You are my very good friend." The king looked remarkably well, he was dressed in the uniform of a post captain in the British navy, and his deportment was very quiet and reserved, although he seemed amused when any favourite subject was started; altogether he made a most favourable impression. The king is extremely liberal, and made us a present of some young bulls. He seems much attached to the English, as do all the natives. During the life time of the late king, George Frederic, any Englishman could traverse from one end of the country to the other, without the expense of a yard of cloth, for the king's orders to all were to feed and lodge them, and provide them with horses if they were wanted. Nearly all the old chiefs who used to adopt that custom are now dead, the younger ones being more mercenary, though there are some honourable exceptions.

The inhabitants of the Cape are allowed by all to be the best looking on the shore, when not disfigured by the unsightly boolpees, of which there are three sorts, the white, blue, and scabbed; but I believe the Cape people to have less of either than any of their countrymen. To account for this species of leprosy seems to be impossible, as I have seen father and mother perfectly free from stain, and their children growing daily worse from its insidious attack; on the other hand, I have observed the parents in an aggravated stage of the disease, and their offspring perfectly free from it.[49]

The men are in general tall and athletic, with a very pleasing expression of features, but they are abominably lazy, subsisting by hunting and fishing and the produce of their plantations, which the women attend to. It is not always they can be moved from their apathy, even

---

48. "Pitpan" is from the Miskito tongue; it is a long flat-bottomed canoe.
49. The "boolpees" or *bulpis* is a skin infection endemic to the Mosquito Coast, but not a species of leprosy.

by the inducement of liquor or Osnaburg.[50] I spoke to one huge fellow, requesting he would come and work for me; his reply was, as he lazily turned in his hammock, "Me no want hook—me no want Osnabris;" consequently he refused to leave his hut, as he already had hooks and Osnaburgs. Most of the men at the Cape speak English sufficiently well to be understood, some of them speak very well, which, however, is easily accounted for, inasmuch as numbers of them go away at different times to Belize, where they sometimes stay two or three years, employed by the merchants as hunters and fishers. The women are very good looking, with large black eyes; generally well shaped, with small feet and ancles. Many of their young girls from thirteen to about eighteen, are, I may say, beautiful. Their dress is simply a tournou, which they fasten round their hips; they have also a piece of Osnaburg or print round their bodies, and hanging down as low as their knees; the legs and the body from the waist upwards being bare, except on the occasion of their festivals, when they fasten more print higher up the bosom. Round their wrists, ancles, and legs, they wear bandages made from the native cotton, and dyed blue or red; or blue, red, and white beads, strung in various ways. To describe the dress of the men is impossible, the variations are so numerous; some having nothing but a tournou, others black hats, (pieces of some gaudy ribbon being tied round them,) and checked shirts; others again, wear Osnaburg frocks and red caps; indeed, the more connection they have with the English, the more varied becomes their costume; although the intercourse with white people does not at all times tend to increase their morality.

A short time back a missionary arrived, for the purpose of giving them some idea of a future state; a house was speedily found for him, and he commenced preaching, and for a few sundays he gave some of the chiefs a glass of grog each, to entice them to hear him. At length, one sunday, a great number of the natives attended to hear the white stranger talk; on this occasion the worthy and reverend gentleman was more than usually eloquent, when one of the chiefs arose, and quietly said, "All talk—no grog—no good!" and gravely stalked away, followed by all the natives, leaving the astonished preacher to finish his discourse to two or three Englishmen present.

After I had resided a few months at the Cape, and completed all

50. "Osnaburg," from the German city of Osnabrück, is a coarse and durable cotton fabric.

necessary business there, a small schooner, the "Amity," of about sixteen tons, belonging to Mr. H——, was freighted for Black River, with such disposable goods and few remaining stores as had not already been shipped off for that place; our Superintendent, and the others of our small party, having started some time previously overland, under the guidance of the principal man in that quarter, General Lowry, to commence operations at Black River.

One of my fellow voyagers from England, Mr. W. Upton, established at the Cape, embraced the opportunity of accompanying me to see the country about the new settlement at Black River. We set sail in March, 1840, with a crew consisting of the captain and one sailor English, and three Mosquito men, but were detained several days by contrary winds, near Wanks River Mouth, not being able to round Main Cape; at length a favourable breeze sprung up, and we soon arrived off Black River Bar, but found it would be dangerous to run it, the wind blowing furiously from the north east, and we having no pilot on board; General Lowry, who sometimes acts as pilot, not being at his residence when we hove to in the night. In this extremity the captain determined to stand on and off, expecting a lull to take place, and hoping to fetch Plantain River;[51] instead of which, both wind and sea increased, and in the morning we were much to leeward. Our fresh water was nearly expended, and there appeared no probability of making Black River, for upon every tack our dull schooner lost way; we, therefore, put ourselves on short allowance, being seven in number. Towards night the wind slightly moderated, but with the same result; no chance remaining, while the wind held in the same quarter, of doing any good.

In the morning the wind increased again, and the sea running heavier, while we were suffering from intense heat with only a pint of water each per diem, our captain determined to run for some other port; and as Bonacca was distant only sixty miles, we accordingly shaped our course for that island, and on the following morning it was descried; the wind being still extremely violent, and to all appearance increasing. As much sail was carried as the schooner could possibly stagger under, and at seven P. M. just as the moon arose, we passed the first kay, and others rapidly in succession, it being the captain's intention to anchor under the lee of Half-Moon Kay. In a short time we entered the channel and thought all danger over, and we were on the point of congratulating ourselves on escaping the fury of the gale

51. Río Plátano.

now blowing outside, when the main boom broke in half, on gibing; the jib haulyards parted, and before the anchor could be got out, the poor Amity struck on a coral reef; the wind, which was blowing directly through the channel upon us, driving the sea with such force against the schooner, as to make complete breaches over her, as she was lying with her broadside exposed to its fury; a rock out of water being on her lee bow, and another on her weather quarter, so that there was no chance of relieving her. We fired signals of distress, having heard that a Scotchman lived on one of the kays, but no one came to our aid. In this emergency, our attention was directed to save the goods; I promised to reward the people well, if they exerted themselves, which they agreed to do, and immediately set to work to get the property out of the hold. Fortunately we had a small dorey with us, and before twelve o'clock five or six loads were landed on Half-Moon Kay, about one mile and a half distant; but this service was attended with great difficulty and danger, the dorey having been swamped two or three times, and all the goods capsized. The brave Mosquito men having promised that nothing should be lost, dived for them by the light of the full moon, and saved them all, but not without being sadly cut and exhausted.

The Mosquito men, William and Ben, and myself, proceeded . . . in the small dorey, and after two hours paddling, found the Scotchman, residing on Frenchman's, otherwise Sheen's Kay. He seemed delighted at our arrival, and said he had heard our guns coming from the white shoal, on the night we were on the reef, but was unable to render us any assistance, having only the use of one arm, the other being disabled by a fall from a tree. He was, therefore, prevented from either fishing or hunting, as he could not, with one hand, paddle his dorey. Sometimes the poor fellow remains for three or four months quite alone, setting his nets in the proper season for the green turtle, which he disposes of by the help of some men who remain with him for a short period, and then set sail to Trujillo, Belize, &c. His companions were then, he said, on the other side of the island felling pitch-pine trees, so as to carry a cargo to Trujillo for sale, and to hunt the wild hogs, previous to their departure, so that they might salt some of the meat for their passage to and fro, and sell the remainder, to purchase the various things required in mending his nets. The boat being large enough to carry us and the goods saved from the Amity, to Black River, he advised us to proceed on the following morning. . . .

On reaching the kay, we made a hearty supper from turtle soup, stewed grouper, and fried Johnny-cakes; I turned into my hammock, resolving to start again at day break. At sunrise I proceeded, according to the old Scotchman's directions, with my two Indians, who were well acquainted with bush travelling; but after seven hours journey, we were obliged to return, having lost our way, owing to our being misled by the numerous marks made by the pine-wood cutters; we therefore returned to the Scotchman, who hearing of our bad success, kindly offered to be our guide on the morrow. We spread a few cocoa-nut leaves outside his little hut, and after a meal on wild parsley and cocoa-nuts, hoping for better fortune the next day, myself and my two faithful companions slept as soundly as many who were reposing on beds of the softest down.

We rose with the sun, and set out with good hearts, hoping to obtain a hearty meal from the companions of the Scotchman, whom we expected to fall in with on the other side of the island. After travelling for some hours through underwood and tall trees, or cutting our way through thickets, at times climbing steep mountains, or descending them slowly and cautiously, for they were rough and steep, we arrived at the top of one of the highest, to which the guide pointed my attention, saying, it was a silver mine, which had formerly been worked by an Englishman of the name of Sheen. . . . Mac Millan (our Scotch friend) assured me, that the ore was found to be extremely good. The place certainly appears to warrant the idea of its being a mine of some sort; it being completely barren. . . .

Shortly after passing the barren mountain, we heard the welcome cry, "Searpe barrossa!" (There's the sea!) and on arriving on the sea-beach, had the mortification to find the boat had sailed, and by the fresh tracks of men and dogs on the sand, not above two or three hours.

A few days after our wreck, a small schooner, the Christopher Scott, Boaden, master, anchored off Half-Moon Kay, having been piloted in by Mac Millan. After an interview with the captain, I offered him forty dollars to land us and our goods at Black River; he promised to give me an answer in an hour; in much less time we were astonished to see the sails set, the anchor up, and the schooner sailing away; we fired guns, hoisted a flag, to no purpose—he disregarded our signals, and kept on his course. On this fresh misfortune, Mac Millan offered to lend me his only dorey, so that she might be sent to

Trujillo for assistance; being small and leaky, she was unfit to contend with such a heavy sea as there generally is between Trujillo and Bonacca, but having no other resource, Mr. William Upton, the English sailor, and two Mosquito men set sail, and in two days returned in a large Carib creer (sailing boat), belonging to, and commanded by Captain Jack, which Mr. Upton had been fortunately able to engage for forty dollars, the poor Scotchman's dorey being inside, and for the use of which he refused compensation, saying, he delighted to serve a countryman; the only articles I could induce him to take, were two pieces of pork and a little tobacco. After loading the creer with as many goods as she could possibly stow, we set sail, the captain of the unfortunate Amity staying behind to get her off the reef, with assistance he had sent for from Trujillo. Being favoured with a good wind, we in about sixteen hours reached the main land, cast anchor off Sereboyer, and breakfasted with the Carib captain, John Bull, to our great satisfaction.[52]

The Caribs behaved hospitably, bringing in cassada bread, syrup, tea-grass, and pork, and at night gave me the largest and finest hammock, and covered me with beautifully clean sheets; Captain Bull assuring me, with gravity all the time, that the house was mine and all within it, and that I might turn his wife out of doors if I liked. "I turn your wife out of doors? Are you serious?" "Si, Señor, para servir á usted," replied he, with imperturbable gravity. "Muchas gracias, Capitan Bull," I answered, finding it to be merely a Spanish compliment.

About twelve P. M. the conch shell sounded, signifying the land wind had set in. On reaching the beach I found the surf rolling in with great violence; a dorey was launched, and we got as far as the third breaker, when she filled and went over; again we attempted, and with the same fate, but in deeper water, losing a paddle and two pigs, one of which was seen to be taken by a shark. On regaining the shore, I positively refused again to contend with the fretful element, without the two Mosquito men who were on board the creer, or Captain Bull, who at this moment came up. Once more we failed, through the cowardice of the Carib who was steering, and who, on the approach of a heavy breaker, jumped overboard and swam ashore; the dorey broached to, filled, and went over. In the next attempt, under the skilful steering of Captain

52. Sereboyer was a Black Carib town about thirty miles westward from Black River, Young says on his page 69. The word "creer" seems to be from *crayer,* an old usage for a small cargo boat.

Bull, we reached our craft—the anchor was quickly up, and away we sailed, the fine land wind sending us merrily over the curling waters. When we came near the bar of Black River, Captain Jack sung out to the man who had acted so dastardly, and who was steering, "Don't look behind you;" well indeed might he say so, for the huge and impetuous waves which followed our swiftly sailing creer, seemed uplifted for our destruction; one broke on our stern quarter, nearly swamping us. "Bale! bale!" was the cry, and in a minute or two we were over the bar, and shortly had the pleasure of greeting all at the settlement of Fort Wellington, which is situated on the left bank of the lagoon, about two miles to the westward of Black River; this lagoon is about 300 yards wide.

In most undertakings for colonizing a foreign shore, the first settlers have to contend with unforeseen difficulties. It is clear that the inexperience inseparable from the exploration of a new tract, may be the cause of many misfortunes. Thus it was with us; we were the pioneers, and suffered many privations; and although the Company in London may have completed their plans with judgment, we had to witness the ravages of death at Black River, among those who came out by the Rose, in February, 1841; yet I believe every precaution had been adopted by the Company to ensure the health and comfort of the passengers.

I have before stated, that we sailed from Gravesend in the Rose, in 1839, for Cape Gracias a Dios; this vessel was to have gone from thence in ballast to Cuba, there to take in copper ore for England, and return from England again to us with further supplies, as we had not more than sufficient for six months; and she was to have continued her voyages out and home. Unfortunately our superintendent, instead of sending this vessel home by the way of Cuba, freighted her with mahogany for England. The charter party was so framed, that no day was fixed for sailing, nor any port assigned as her destination; hence she had to wait for orders at one port, and thence be despatched to another; nor did she ultimately arrive at London, until thirteen months after her departure from England. Every thing was thus thrown into disorder, the Company in London being ignorant of the proceedings of their superintendent, in whom full powers were vested, while we were in daily expectation of fresh supplies. Our superintendent was expected to have had sufficient experience, but to his experience we were little indebted, and thus, through mismanagement, we were exposed to disease and difficulties. Much of the merchandize brought out in the Rose, was, for the most part, ill adapted to an uncultivated country, or the wants of its inhabitants, and we were thrown into despondency when disappointed of supplies from England: we found all the useful goods gone in payment for labour and the provisions of the country, our own provisions having been expended. Ten acres of land had been cleared, four acres planted with cassada, which turned out the bitter sort; two large and three smaller houses had been erected for the expected emigrants, but when the Caribs and natives found we had nothing left to exchange for their labour, they refused to work. Our superintendent had obtained some supplies from Trujillo and Belize, and others would have come, if they had been ordered by him; this was neglected; and thus, instead of Fort Wellington being a settlement, and a hostelry for new comers, it was completely disorganized, and with barely the necessaries of life. In November, 1840, our superintendent received his recall, and Mr. William Upton, who had been previously located at the Cape, was appointed *pro. tem.*; but although enjoined to prepare houses for the expected visitors, we had not the means of doing so.

"If to do were as easy as to know what to do,"

we should have been prepared.[53]

In February, 1841, the brig Rose appeared off Black River, and joyfully was she welcomed; we saw relief at hand, our spirits revived, and, roused into action, we prepared for the reception of our guests, and promised ourselves much happiness, but

"All things that we ordained festival,
Turn from their office to black funeral."[54]

The brig was munificently freighted with every necessary of life, pork; beef, hams, flour, wines, spirits, ale, porter, tea, sugar, rice, &c. &c. She brought out a Mr. W. Houghton, as superintendent, and thirty-seven English and Spanish passengers. She was filled with provisions, goods, sheep, hogs, goats, dogs, turkeys, ducks, fowls, &c.; the condition of the vessel was however so bad, that one of the Company's servants sent on board from Fort Wellington, was taken ill a few hours afterwards, and refused to sleep in the berth prepared for him below;

---

53. Shakespeare, *The Merchant of Venice*, act I, scene 2, but slightly misquoted.

54. Shakespeare, *Romeo and Juliet*, act IV, scene 5.

and he and another person declared they could smell the effluvia from the brig some time before they got to her.

Disease and death seem to have been attendant on the passengers of this fated vessel, and the very elements to have joined in the work of destruction, as if the ship and its freight were doomed. The vessel was lying some distance from the shore, and before the goods and all the passengers were landed, the gathering clouds indicated a storm. The threatening north wind commenced in puffs, increasing momentarily, until its furious character placed the brig in imminent peril; its wrath increased, and she contended in vain—the raging waters tossed her to and fro, and she became unmanageable; the destiny of the ship was but too apparent—the arm of man was useless—no earthly power could contend with the mighty waters; as a cockle-shell she was cast on the shore, a plaything for the roaring surge—the waters would recede from her, and then again lash, foam, and overwhelm her; again receding, and again overwhelming—carrying her further and further in shore, until she was finally imbedded in the sand, beyond their influence. When the wrath of the storm was spent, and the wind hushed, and the waters calmed, the natives and Caribs, as well as ourselves, viewed with astonishment and regret the poor brig, thrown nearly on her beam ends within ten yards from the beach; to-day useless lumber —yesterday in all her glory; at the same time we heartily rejoiced to find that not a person was injured. The brig had the character of great strength in her build, and she well sustained it, for hardly a plank was started. As it was absolutely impossible to float her again, we got out the goods and stores, and set her on fire, to obtain the copper and other fastenings. The loss of the Rose was only the loss of money, but there she lay, while disease was triumphing over those who had escaped the destruction to which she was doomed. The cup of bitterness was not yet filled: in a few short weeks eight of the passengers were laid in their graves. Solomon says, "Boast not thyself of to-morrow, for thou knowest not what a day may bring forth."[55]

Mr. Houghton, a fine young man, died within five weeks, his death being occasioned by over anxiety, exertion, and exposure to the sun; with deep anguish did we witness his premature end, and read the beautiful funeral service over this promising young gentleman. Another followed,—another,—and another, until eight had gone to their final rest. The others fled, panic stricken, some viâ Trujillo to England, some to Roatán, &c. The typhus fever, a disorder never known in the

55. Proverbs 27 : 1.

country, attacked some of those who came by the Rose, but none others; and it is evident that the seeds of that disorder were sown in the vessel. Some of the passengers suffered from intermittent fever, brought on, in a great measure, by their own imprudence. Most of them were poor, not having the means of subsistence even for a short period, unused to the labour required in such climates, without goods wherewith to hire the natives to labour for them, and perfectly unacquainted with all they should know.

When the vessel arrived off Sereboyer, ... two of the passengers determined, in preference, to proceed along the sea-beach; taking off their shoes and stockings, they walked bare legged, exposed to the driving sand, the salt water, and the rays of the sun: on arriving at another Carib town, horses were procured for them, but so painful had their legs become, they could not ride, and were then obliged to walk the remaining distance to Fort Wellington in great suffering. They were both seized with typhus fever—in a few days one died; the other happily recovered. Amongst the others who died, were two aged people, one young woman shortly after child-birth, a young girl aged about 15 or 16, from exposure to the sun, and over exertion in attending on her friends, one child, and two infants. Many of those who came by the Rose, ought not to have left their homes, being perfectly unfitted for a foreign shore, and expecting they were to enjoy the necessaries of life without exertion on their parts.

I attributed these misfortunes to inexperience and mismanagement. If the Rose had been sent to Cuba, she might not have been sixteen months away; if so much live stock and additional passengers, seven Spaniards, had not been taken on board by Mr. Houghton, at the Grand Canaries, the vessel might have arrived clean. (Another vessel was also freighted from the Grand Canaries, with live stock, &c. for Black River, but never arrived.) If sweet cassada had been sown, bitter would not have been reaped. If attention had been paid to the Company's orders by their superintendent, plantations and houses would have been ready in proper time. If our vessel had been freighted wholly with suitable goods, much more work would have been done; and if all the Company's servants had done their duty, much distress would have been prevented.

If it be asked, what has all this to do with those who purchase this book of information respecting the country? I reply, that a record of the failure, and its causes, may be the most effectual warning to others; and it may especially serve to shew that it is useless for persons, without discrimination, judgment, perserverance, and sufficient means, to leave their homes for this country.

A short time after this occurrence, a young gentleman, Mr. B——, arrived at Black River, with two servants. He purchased, in London, some few thousands of acres, and he brought with him money and goods. After staying with us at Fort Wellington some time, he formed his opinion with judgment, made himself acquainted with all things necessary, and then took possession of his land, situated a few miles up on the eastern side of Black River. Here, in the midst of the bush, he commenced clearing, planting, and building, employing the Caribs and natives for this purpose. This young gentleman who had been brought up to one of the learned professions, adopted this life, and he assured me that he found great improvement in his health, that he was perfectly satisfied at the change, and should sit down contented. Many a pleasant day did I spend with him, and his kindness to me at various times, and on my departure from Black River, I shall ever remember with gratitude. When I left, he was still progressing in his work. This gentleman then from the gay city, places himself in the woods on the Mosquito Shore, unused to the mode of life, not driven by necessity, but led by choice; and I have, since my arrival in London, heard that he had gone far into the interior, to gain a proper knowledge of the country, and for other purposes. From this will be inferred, that capital, judgment, and discretion, are required; and that at present the Mosquito Shore is not the place for a poor man to resort to, but that any person who does so, may be assured of his personal safety.

Soon after my arrival, it was determined to proceed up the Black and Polyer Rivers to the Poyer Indians;[56] accordingly we started. . . . The autumnal rain had just commenced, and the river was much flooded; we therefore proceeded in two pitpans, each manned by six natives, for it is hard work to stem the velocity of the current at such times. As we poled up the river, our prospect was confined on each side to the thick bush and tall trees skirting the edges. . . .

At length we arrived at a spot on the western side of the river, about sixteen miles up, which, according to the statement of an old Mosquitian, had formerly been settled by the English. Landing, we attentively examined the spot, but found no traces of houses; but there had

56. The "Polyer River" is Río Paulaya. For the "Poyer Indians," see Ch. 1 n. 20.

evidently been plantations, for wherever a white man sets his foot, he leaves traces that cannot be mistaken. In one spot we found a Seville orange tree in a bearing state, the fruit however was small, in consequence of being shaded from the sun by the bush, which had overtopped it. In another place were numerous lime and lemon trees, which must, from their regularity, have been planted with care. Here another species of orange, a soursop, and some sarsaparilla; also a cacao tree, with at least fifty large pods suspending from its branches, were discovered.

The Indian Town, to my astonishment, was comprised in one large house of an oval form, about 85 feet in length and 35 feet in breadth, in which all the natives resided truly in the patriarchal style. Crickeries were erected all around close to each other, separated by two or three cabbage boards; each family having one of these compartments.[57] At one side of the house a place was divided off, about 16 feet by 10 feet, and hidden from view by green leaves, which were replenished as fast as they faded. In this place the women are kept during their confinement, and, after a few days, they are again able to attend to their multifarious duties.

On our entrance, the women were busily occupied, some pounding cassada and Indian corn together, boiling it, and making it into a beverage called oulung;[58] some preparing cassada for bread in the morning, others making tournous, others again rubbing cacao and squeezing sugar-cane; in truth the whole body of them were most busily employed, under the management of the chief's wife; the chief, who is called by the English name of officer, being absent. We were looked upon with a quiet sort of wonder, the women merely gazing for a few minutes upon the white men, of whom perhaps they had heard much, and then they resumed their pounding, boiling, and beating. The oulung is a beverage not to be despised on a warm day, by those who do not mind a particularly sour taste. After the second time of tasting it, I sought it with pleasure. Their bread too is sour, but even

57. "Crickeries" and "cabbage boards" are explained by Squier, 1855W, pp. 130 and 294, respectively, as "platforms of canes, supported on forked posts, and covered with variously-colored mats, woven of the bark of palm branches" and "partitions of the outer shells of the cabbage-palm, which, when split and pressed flat, make good substitutes for boards." Young, 1842, p. 77, says that crickeries among the Miskitos "are formed of posts four or five feet high, driven into the ground, pieces of split bamboo being laid on the top...."

58. Squier, 1855W, p. 299, describes *ulung* as made from sugarcane.

that I relished. It is made of pounded cassada into rolls, about fifteen or sixteen inches in length, and about the thickness of a man's wrist. It is then wrapped round with several layers of leaves, and slowly barbacued until done; when eaten fresh it is good, the sour taste being acquired by keeping. The house is thatched in a very neat manner with swallow-tail leaf, to about four feet from the ground, so that the rain, however violent, does not trouble them. They are noted for cleanliness.

The situation was well chosen, and a few yards from the house, down a steep pass, was a stream of water, forming innumerable cascades as it ran, leaping and dashing over the huge blocks of stone with which it abounded. Here, as we sat, our ears drank in delight at the soothing sound of the water, and we beheld with extreme gratification the verdant hills, the rich plumage of birds as they flew by, and heard the chattering monkeys filling the wood with their noise. I observed around the house numerous fowls, a few Muscovy ducks, turkeys, and pigs, and they can in general obtain game by a little exertion in hunting. The peccary, which inhabits high and dry places, often falls here before the superior dexterity and cunning of man. Warrie are not found on the Poyer mountains, so that the Indians sometimes form a party, and descend to one of the hunting passes in Black River, or such places as they are known to frequent.[59] Very few of them have guns; they merely go armed with lance and bow and arrows, and they rarely return without a noble supply of barbacued meat.

After partaking of a couple of fowls, some cassada and plantains, cocoa, and boiled cane-juice, prepared for us by these kind people, we betook ourselves to repose. Early in the morning, whilst in my hammock, an Indian woman timidly touched me, saying, "Englis," at the same time presenting me with a hot roll of bread, nicely done up in fresh leaves; another soon came to me with a bundle of oulung, and so it continued until I had three or four bundles of oulung, and nine large rolls of bread. In return, I presented them with a little tobacco, some needles and salt, and gave a clasp knife to the officer's wife. Soon after, I was agreeably surprised by several of the men arriving from the plantations loaded with sugar-cane, plantains, cacao, &c. which we very willingly received in exchange for a few hooks, needles, &c.

On inquiry, I learnt that there was another town about fifteen miles

---

59. For "warrie," see *warree,* Ch. 1 n. 15.

off, judging from the rate they travel in an hour, and in the route to the Spanish country. Before our departure, a number of Indians came from the neighbouring town, having been apprized of our arrival, bringing sarsaparilla to trade with for Osnaburg; but we not having that, or cloth of any kind, they were compelled to carry their heavy burthens back.

The Caribs who are settled on the Mosquito Shore are now numerous; one of the Mosquito kings granted portions of his land to some of their forefathers to the westward of Black River, and also at Patook; they established plantations, and lived in abundance.[60] A north wind destroyed the plantations of those settled at Patook: after which they joined their brethren westward of Black River. They are peaceable, friendly, ingenious and industrious. They are noted for their immoderate fondness for dress, wearing red bands tied round their waists, to imitate sashes, straw hats knowingly turned up, clean white shirts and frocks, long and tight trowsers, and, with an umbrella, cane or sword in their hands, they strut about, rejoicing in their fancied resemblance to some of the Buckra officers at Belize. In fact, their tout ensemble is highly gratifying.

The Carib women are fond of ornamenting their persons with coloured beads strung in various forms. When bringing the products of their plantations for sale, they appear dressed in calico bodices and some lively patterned skirts, handkerchiefs being tied round their heads, and suffered to fall negligently behind; on other occasions, when at home, they are not so particular, for there they appear almost in the costume of nature; but on the approach of a white man they flee in terror, and soon reappear equipped in all their finery.

The Caribs cannot be considered a handsome race, but they are hardy and athletic. The difference in their colour is somewhat remarkable; some being coal black, others again nearly as yellow as saffron, although as a nation they are called the Black Caribs. They are scrupulously clean, and have great aptitude for the acquirement of languages, most of the men being able to talk in Carib, Spanish and English; some even add Creole-French and Mosquito; and I have heard even the women converse in Carib, Spanish, French, &c., or Carib, English, Spanish, and so on; indeed the universality of these languages appears strange. Polygamy is general amongst them; some having as many as three or four wives, but the husband is compelled

60. For "Patook," see Ch. 1 n. 20.

to have a separate house and plantation for each, and if he makes one a present, he must make the others one of the same value: and he must also divide his time equally among them, a week with one, a week with another, and so on.

The Caribs have various feast days. Those at Christmas, and those termed Devil feasts, are the most important; the only difference being, that the one is general, while the other is confined to some particular town.

Some time previous to a Devil feast, the inhabitants of the town send messengers to summon their friends and relatives, however distant, and they surmount every obstacle to attend; coming from Belize, Stann Creek, Trujillo, &c. in their creers. This feast lasts from three days to a week, and they all contribute, by bringing their offerings of liquor. Strangers are welcomed with evident pleasure. . . . The feast commences at sunset, when the drums as well as the liquor are put into requisition, and the play and singing commence, and are kept up with all the vigour and enjoyment so characteristic of the Caribs. Glass decanters, glass tumblers, white table cloths, and English earthenware, raise a familiar sensation in an Englishman's mind. The liquor handed round in glass tumblers, English fashion, in one part, and the bottle in another. Numerous large and beautifully clean cotton hammocks are slung around for the accommodation of the old people, (who do the looking-on part,) the weary traveller, or the exhausted dancers. It is a maxim, on these events, that good drinking ought to be accompanied by good eating. They therefore take care to have a number of little tables well, and even sumptuously furnished, at which all enjoy themselves without ceremony or limitation. In one place several tables may be seen, about three feet high and two or three feet square, covered with clean white cloths, and ornamented with red or yellow fringe. On some of the cloths are placed large pieces of cassada bread, which serve as dishes and plates; others for the captains, have decanters, and every sort of crockery-ware required. On one dish is either fresh or salt pork, on others fresh or salt fish or fowl. Here you may feast youself on game of the choicest kind, such as venison, warrie, qualm; there you may satiate yourself on turtle, or tashajo; pepper-soup, in various large basins, being placed in all directions, to dip the cassada bread into, thereby to soften and improve it. . . .[61] As family

61. "Qualm"=guan, if one may judge by the associations given in Squier, 1855W, p. 212. For "tashajo," see *tassao*, Ch. 1 n. 11.

meets family they greet each other with much warmth and cordiality, and even in the midst of all their hilarity, no such thing as quarrelling takes place. Towards the morning the tables begin to look remarkably empty, nearly every thing being consumed, dishes and all, shortly however to be replenished by the provident masters of the feast, who, as soon as daylight appears, begin to put down fresh dishes and meats.

The Carib women also in great numbers join in the festivities; and it is pleasing to observe their particularly modest and quiet behaviour, so far removed as they are from civilized society. They dance and sing, the dancing being merely a movement to and fro with their hands and feet, alternately, accompanied by a peculiar intonation of voice; and I must say, I was Goth enough not to be ravished by the accompaniment.

They equip themselves on these occasions as well as their finances will permit, and the variety of hues in their dresses is remarkably pleasing. A large handkerchief of some gay colour and lively pattern is tied round the head, the ends falling on the shoulder. The body of their dress is white, reaching down the arm nearly as far as the elbow, leaving the other part bare. From the body is attached the remaining portion of their dress, reaching down to the feet, and it is always selected from some gay patterned print, having two or three flounces at the bottom; some have only one, and they therefore sew two or three pieces of red tape round the dress, at regular intervals, which relieves and sets it off. They are polite in the extreme to a stranger, kind and obliging, but above all, they must have the meed of praise for their excessive cleanliness.

The men are all jauntily equipped, and have an air of easy gaiety about them. To any stranger they are attentive; but for a white man, nothing is too good; and all are anxious, by kindness and hospitality, to make a favourable impression on him; in which they rarely fail. I am now merely speaking of them when seen at their feasts; on other occasions they have faults common to mankind.

Having some business to transact at Trujillo, I proceeded with a friend in a dorey, manned by Sambos. We set sail with a fine sea breeze, passing rapidly along the beautiful looking coast, appearing one mass of evergreen.

The city of Trujillo is built on the ascent of a hill, on the western side of a noble bay, open only to the north, and about four leagues from the Punta Castilla, across the bay. Some of the houses are shingled, and painted red, others again are white; and being built on the slope of the hill, have a pleasing appearance from the harbour. In the back ground are the lofty verdure-clad mountains, and with the numerous cocoa-nut trees which adorn the spot, form a picturesque landscape.

The place, when settled by the Spaniards, was at first considered so unhealthy, that they had almost determined to relinquish it; however it increased, and became a place of considerable importance, and the seat of government for the state of Honduras, having its convents, colleges, churches, hospital, court-house, plaza, &c. but in the reign of Charles V. the Dutch, who were then at war with Spain, took the place, and nearly destroyed it.[62] Phœnix-like it arose from its ashes, but its present appearance clearly indicates that it is fast falling to decay; the ancient remnants shew that its glory has not returned; altogether it offers the idea of a broken constitution, sinking and spiritless. Its downward course was in some measure arrested by the industry of the Caribs, who quitted Roatán to settle at this place; through them it improved, until factions and civil discords operated against it. On the various states of Central America separating from Spain, Trujillo, in common with many other towns and cities, was subjected to the miseries of civil war and its attendant horrors, rapine and murder. In the revolution which happened a few years back, a body of troops advanced on Trujillo, and in the engagements which ensued, many of the Caribs fought bravely; others fled and sought protection at Belize; and from that period, their numbers at Trujillo have greatly decreased, many emigrating and settling at Stann Creek, near Belize, and the Mosquito Shore, to avoid being called on to fight for one party one day, and for another the next. The interior of the town has now little attraction; many of the present buildings having been suffered to go to decay. The church is large, and must at one time have been a handsome building; it now looks naked and miserable; a kind of turret has been erected on one of the wings of the church, in which are two bells, to summon the inhabitants to mass and vespers, when the padre happens to be in town, and not otherwise engaged....

There are a few decent houses with jalousies and balconies, the principal part being but poor specimens of house building. The walls

62. This attack, so fondly remembered by Haefkens (see Ch. 1 n. 88), took place in 1643, a century after the reign of Charles V.

of the best houses are composed of stiff red clay, generally shingled, or white-washed outside, the roofs are either thatched, shingled, or tiled. The fort is a most wretched affair, with, I believe, only one mounted gun, and that in bad condition; several others lie scattered about, but are of little service. There may possibly be about forty soldiers, with broad sombreros, light clothing, and naked feet, their costume being regulated by their finances and taste, and as they have to clothe themselves, the diversity may be imagined. There are also four or five musicians, who play every four hours, from eight A. M. until eight P. M.; these men deserve credit, as they are self-taught. Two fifes, two kettle-drums, and big drum, compose the band.

... The personal appearance of the inhabitants is unfavourable; the Spaniards being of low stature, and appearing sallow and sickly; the Caribs, on the other hand, are tall and athletic, perfect pictures of health. The Trujillo ladies cannot be considered beautiful, and yet there is something in their contour and walk which excites admiration. The manner of wearing their handsome blue and red shawls, and their symmetrical forms are very pleasing.

On a fine moonlight evening, parties assemble to pass the time in cheerful songs to the light guitar, or dance to its delightful music, accompanied by the gay castanet. These little assemblies are pleasant, having none of that stiff formality which is met with in England, to the destruction of gaiety and mirth. The ladies walk about whenever and wherever they please, unattended by any dragons in the shape of duennas; indeed, these disagreeable appendages seem to be altogether dispensed with. In the morning they are seen wending their way to the Rio de Cristal, (Chrystal River,) for the purpose of bathing in its refreshing waters. This river, as they term it, is merely a gulley of water descending from the mountains, leaping and dashing down with violence in wet seasons, but soft and soothing in fine weather. The gentle murmurings and coolness of its waters are very grateful; in its course, it forms many pools of various depths, in which the bathers plunge. Sometimes there are several fair, no not fair, brown and black beauties in at once, and it is not unusual to see both sexes bathing at the same place. The ladies dress their beautifully long hair in two plaited tresses, which hang down to the waist.

The inhabitants are kind to strangers, but are not hospitable. There are a few French Creoles, principally, I believe, from Guadaloupe, residing in the town, from one of whom I received great kindness, during a severe sickness, in a strange place, and among a strange people. I cannot forget her sympathy, nor am I the only one who has cause to remember her with gratitude. She is attached to the English, and is unceasing in her endeavours to please them; and as she is the only person in the town that receives strangers, the English who visit Trujillo invariably stay with her, as there are no inns or hotels in this place.

After a short stay, my companion proceeded to Belize in an English barque, and I to Black River in my creer, with a crew composed of negros, who knew little of sailing a craft, in comparison with the Caribs or Mosquitians. These negros formerly belonged to San Andres, and being kept in great wretchedness, determined with some others to escape; accordingly they set sail in some small and leaky canoes, and having heard that some Englishmen were residing on the Mosquito Shore, they succeeded in reaching it, and scattered themselves in several directions where Englishmen were to be found, in search of employment. Soon after our setting sail from the Punta Castilla, the wind veered to the north east, and blew heavily. The craft having a pretty good reputation for sailing, I determined to stand out to sea towards Bonacca, so as to have a good lay at daylight. The north east wind, contrary to our expectation, continued fierce all night, and in the morning, to our astonishment, we found ourselves off the east end of Roatán, having been drifted so far to leeward by the current and headwind, partly owing to our rudder breaking, by which we were obliged to steer with a paddle. Understanding that a carpenter lived at Coxon's old kay, we proceeded there, to get the craft overhauled, as she was leaking badly.

Roatán, Ruatan, or Rattan, is . . . one beautiful mass of evergreen, from the sea-beach to the tops of the high hills; and there are many cocoa-nut gardens. A short distance from the island are numerous kays, covered with bush and cocoa-nut trees; and in several parts there is good anchorage. . . .

An instance of good fortune attended an industrious Scotchman lately. While hunting, he came upon a wide expanse of low bush, covered with large dark red berries. Cutting his way through to follow his dogs, it struck him the place had once been cleared, and picking one of the berries, he found it, to his astonishment, to be coffee, and that most of the low bush was composed of coffee trees, which had no doubt been planted by some Englishman years before. . . . Overjoyed at his good fortune, he removed from a distant kay, and settled at the nearest convenient spot, Frenchman's harbour, where he is now dwelling, surrounded by beautiful plantain walks and provision grounds. Having a large family, he finds them of the greatest service; his two eldest sons, young men, hunt, fish, and attend to the plantations, while other boys and girls are fast growing up to render him essential aid; he himself being occupied in building a small schooner for sailing to and from Belize. I was much pleased with this family, so firmly knit and bound together, and apparently so contented. On my running in to get my craft's rudder repaired a second time, he would not listen to my wish to pay him for his work. He invited me to breakfast, his sons having just brought in a fine wild hog, part of which was soon cooked, and ready for us. We sat down to a bountiful repast,—wild hog meat, peas, plantains, and coffee sweetened with boiled sugar-cane juice. . . .

On Coxon's old kay there are several white families residing, principally from the Grand Cayman's. On the island opposite the kay, are also several white and black people from the Cayman's, and their neat white houses have an interesting appearance, contrasting strongly with the houses of the inhabitants on the kay, which are dingy affairs indeed. A church is in progress of being built by the black people.

On the kay, and in various parts of Roatán, several English and Scotch families are settled, and from what I have ascertained, there seems every probability of their living in comfort and independence. A schoolmaster is now established on the kay, sent by the exertions of a few generous individuals of Belize, aided by the clergyman of that place. I was informed, that the number who attended school averaged twenty-five; amongst whom where some young people, of from fifteen to eighteen years of age. I conversed with them, and received pleasing proofs of the well working of the system, and how anxious they were for further improvement. The want of a clergyman was much complained of by the settlers, as they said they could not be married at Belize for less than ten pounds currency, which was more than they could afford; consequently, they merely lived together without entering into the marriage contract, which is often the source of much misery.

A report was raised some time ago, that a bishop was about to visit Roatán, for the purpose of marrying those who required it. The report was exceedingly gratifying, and many set about preparing themselves for the eventful occasion, but they have waited in vain.

The population of Roatán may possibly be about 200. Many more are expected to leave the impoverished soil of the Grand Cayman's Island, to settle there; so that there is reason to suppose it will soon be in a flourishing condition.

Elena is a small island at the extreme end of Roatán, where I was detained two days by the severity of the weather. On this small island, a Frenchman . . . was established, with plantations and large nets for turtling; his principal business being lime-making, by which he contrived to do well, selling his lime at Omoa, and all places around, from two and a quarter to three dollars per barrel. . . . The distance from Elena to Barbareta being only four or five miles, we paddled our craft to that place, before the sea breeze set down, but were some hours in effecting it, as we had a strong current against us, and the rain beat on the men severely, so that on our arrival at Barbareta, I determined to take refuge in the house of a Spaniard, who behaved to me and my crew in the most hospitable and exemplary manner. He appeared delighted at our arrival, and candidly said he hoped the weather would continue bad for a week longer, as that would prevent my departure. He showed me over his large and extensive plantations. . . . He had at the period of my visit four Spaniards at work, whom he hired at five dollars per month, a large expanse of ground covered with cotton trees, hundreds of papah trees, which he had planted, and the fruit of which he gave to his fowls and hogs;[63] and several fine hogs, brought when young, both from Roatán and Bonacca, those from the latter being much the largest. . . . Numbers of fowls and ducks were about his house, some large capons for the Belize market, and game cocks for the Spaniards. There were also cane patches, and with a wooden press with two rollers, he expressed the juice from his cane. A large turtle crawl was opposite his dwelling, and in it were eight turtles; and on the top he had erected a place for drying his salted fish or meat. Several turtling nets, both for hawk's-bill and green turtle, were hanging in his house. He had a good pack of dogs to hunt with, and a beautiful small schooner-rigged boat to carry his produce for sale to the various ports; without which I think he would have been many years before he could have accumulated so much about him. . . . On the whole, no place I had seen gave me such an impression of what could be accomplished by one man's perseverance, when applied to a proper object. I was astonished when Señor Ruis informed me that he had arrived on the island, about three years

63. "Papah" presumably means *papaya*.

before, with his wife and a son about eleven years of age, and with only some provisions, two or three macheets, and a gun, a few hooks and other trifles; and that he had collected all I saw in that time, plainly shewing what good tact and judgment will effect in conquering difficulties. He was, as he told me, well off. I thought at the time of the thousands of my poor countrymen struggling in vain for a decent subsistence, and who would live in independence, if similarly situated, instead of being brought to an early grave, by disappointed hopes, or the weight of a large family....

One evening, . . . Señor Ruis handed me a book, telling me he bought it in Belize. I found it to be a translation of the Bible, in Spanish, by the Bible Society; on testifying my gratification at the sight, the wife brought me down a quantity of tracts and childrens' books, all emanating from the same source, and she appeared to view them as the most precious things she had. "Ah!" said the Señor, "you English want to make all the world good; I love them for the sake of these books, and when my sons grow up, they will love them also. My countrymen are not good; they only play the guitar and dance; they call you English heretics, but I think they are greater heretics themselves." He also added, that since these works had been sent to Belize, many Spaniards were wishing for them in the interior, and that he himself knew several who had purchased some from Belize, and who liked them very much....

Between Barbareta and Bonacca, a dangerous reef of rocks extends a considerable way into the sea, between which there is only one or two small channels. . . . Our worthy Spaniard tying his little dorey to the stern of our craft, steered us till he plainly pointed out to us the channel, then bidding a thousand "Adieus," and, "Go with God," he jumped into his dorey and paddled homewards. We got safely through the narrow channel, and soon fetched Bonacca; from thence I set sail in a creer belonging to my former guide, Mac Millan, loading the large craft with cocoa nuts for our stock at Black River, and young cocoa nut trees for planting. Soon after we started, lowering clouds and spitting rain foretold what we were to expect. During the whole night and day there was one continued rain. . . . When the weather cleared up we were soon at our destination, Fort Wellington, where we now had sixteen houses, fourteen horned cattle, a number of pigs, goats, fowls, ducks, &c., many requisite stores, and a thriving plantation, in which plantains, cocos, sugar-cane, young cocoa-nut trees, Carib beans, &c. were growing luxuriantly....

At the commencement of the year, 1842, my engagement with the Company having expired, I proceeded to England, by the way of Trujillo and Belize, after receiving many pleasing proofs of kindness, in various presents made to me on my departure; the natives assembling to shake hands and wish me "I sabbe," (Good bye.) Mr. William Upton, the superintendant, and Mr. B——, accompanying me to Trujillo. A norther having ceased, we seized the opportunity of proceeding in a large creer belonging to Mr. B——. As we sailed by the coast, the appearance of the Carib towns was gratifying, shewing in pleasing colours, the progress of the Caribs towards civilization.

JOHN LLOYD STEPHENS arrived in Izabal November 3, 1839, very soon after Thomas Young had disembarked at Cabo Gracias a Dios. Stephens was a widely read author before he came to Central America, but his sojourn here was to make him famous.[64] Born in New Jersey in 1805, Stephens practised law in New York until 1834, when he followed the advice of his doctor to travel to Europe for the respite he needed to fight a throat infection. In and near Europe he traveled widely, visiting lands as far-spread as Russia, Poland, Egypt, and Arabia. A good reception accorded a series of articles about his trips encouraged Stephens to write books; his four volumes of "Incidents of Travel" published in 1837–38 brought him much attention in both North America and Great Britain. In company with Frederick Catherwood, an English artist, he next planned a new venture, a study-visit to ancient ruins of Central America and Mexico about which they had read. In August, 1839, Stephens received an appointment as diplomatic agent of the United States government to the Central American federation. His trip with Catherwood thus became a strange mixture of archeological study and politics at a time when the federation was crumbling. The two-volume report from Catherwood's brush and Stephens' pen, with the title *Incidents of Travel in Central America, Chiapas, and Yucatan,* was an immediate success on its publication in New York and London in 1841. Editions of 1842 in both cities corrected many mistakes; reprints continued until 1843 in London and 1871 in New York. Catherwood edited a one-volume edition in 1854; the same year the text appeared in German.[65] In 1939–40 the work was presented in Spanish; and in 1949 again in English, as edited and

---

64. See Victor Wolfgang Von Hagen, *Maya Explorer: John Lloyd Stephens and the Lost Cities of Central America and Yucatán.*

65. Stephens, 1854C and 1854H.

annotated by Richard L. Predmore.[66] Catherwood collaborated with Stephens on an additional and quite separate *Incidents of Travel in Yucatan* in 1843, after which each went his own difficult way, meeting again on a mutual railroad-building project in Panama in 1849–50. Both were afflicted to the ends of their lives (Catherwood died at fifty-five, Stephens at forty-seven) with the malaria which had early formed a part of their Central American experience.

Part of the charm of Stephens' Central American account stems from its close involvement with the two objects of his mission, the study of Maya ruins (which he did not know were Mayan when he wrote) and the search for a nearly nonexistent government. The rest lies in Stephens' full and frank treatment of the many other adventures he had. Aside from the political scene, Stephens offers no very comprehensive view of Central American life and civilization. Envoys Thompson and Haefkens (arriving, to be sure, in more settled times) offered real studies both of what they had seen and what they had learned from documents. Diplomat Stephens, relying on Catherwood, did the same sort of work with ancient monuments, but otherwise kept his account a personal one, made lively by his own far-going interest in so many features of the world around.

Two days away from Izabal and one from the Mico mountain, Stephens described his lodgings:[67]

> Mr. C. and I were in a rather awkward predicament for the night. The general reception-room contained three beds, made of strips of cowhide interlaced. The don occupied one; he had not much undressing to do, but what little he had, he did by pulling off his shirt. Another bed was at the foot of my hammock. I was dozing, when I opened my eyes, and saw a girl about seventeen sitting sideway upon it, smoking a cigar. She had a piece of striped cotton cloth tied around her waist, and falling below her knees; the rest of her dress was the same which Nature bestows alike upon the belle of fashionable life and the poorest girl; in other words, it was the same as that of the don's wife, with the exception of the string of beads. At first I thought it was something I had conjured up in a dream; and as I waked up perhaps I raised my head, for she gave a few quick puffs of her cigar, drew a cotton sheet over her head and shoulders, and lay down to sleep. I endeavoured to do the same.

---

66. Stephens, 1939–40 and 1949.
67. Stephens, 1842, 1:56–57.

Some nights later, after friendly receptions in Gualán, Zacapa, and Chiquimula and a harrowing experience in Camotán, the party stayed near the Honduran ruins of Copán, at the estate of a less hospitable man:[68]

After supper all prepared for sleep. The don's house had two sides, an inside and an out. The don and his family occupied the former, and we the latter; but we had not even this to ourselves. All along the wall were frames made of sticks about an inch thick, tied together with bark strings, over which the workmen spread an untanned oxhide for a bed. There were three hammocks besides ours, and I had so little room for mine that my body described an inverted parabola, with my heels as high as my head.

The ruins proved startlingly intriguing, and Catherwood (for whom more comfortable quarters were found) stayed to paint the wonders of Copán. Stephens had other business; he traveled on, via Esquipulas, to Guatemala City where he was welcomed by the British vice-consul, a Mr. Hall. Then, for about a month, he occupied the house of Charles DeWitt, former United States chargé d'affaires who in this year had committed suicide rather than return to this post of duty. While staying here, Stephens formed his impressions of the men governing the newly separate state of Guatemala:[69]

One of my first visits of ceremony was to Señor Rivera Paz, the chief of the state. I was presented by Mr. Henry Savage, who had formerly acted as United States consul at Guatimala, and was the only American resident, to whom I am under many obligations for his constant attentions. The State of Guatimala, having declared its independence of the Federal government, was at that time governed by a temporary body called a Constituent Assembly. On the last entry of Carrera into the city, in March preceding my arrival, Salazar, the chief of the state, fled, and Carrera, on horseback, knocked at the door of Señor Rivera Paz before daylight, and, by his individual pleasure, installed him as chief.[70] It was a fortunate choice for the people of Guatimala. He was about thirty-eight, gentlemanly in his appearance and manners, and, in all the trying positions in which he was

---

68. *Ibid.*, 1:94–95.
69. *Ibid.*, 1:200–203, 223–24, 247–49, 304–6, 307–8.
70. This incident actually occurred on April 13, 1839, not in March.

afterward placed, exhibited more than ordinary prudence and judgment.

I had been advised that it would be agreeable to the government of Guatimala for me to present my credentials to the chief of that state, and afterward to the chiefs of the other states, and that the states separately would treat of the matters for which I was accredited to the general government. The object of this was to preclude a recognition on my part of the power which was, or claimed to be, the general government. The suggestion was of course preposterous, but it showed the dominion of party-spirit with men who knew better. Señor Rivera Paz expressed his regret at my happening to visit the country at such an unfortunate period, and assured me of the friendly disposition of that state, and that it would do all in its power to serve me. During my visit I was introduced to several of the leading members of the administration, and I left with a favourable opinion of Rivera Paz, which was never shaken in regard to him personally.

In the evening, in company with Mr. Hall, I attended the last meeting of the Constituent Assembly. It was held in the old Hall of Congress; the room was large, hung with portraits of old Spaniards distinguished in the history of the country, and dimly lighted. The deputies sat on a platform at one end, elevated about six feet, and the president on an elevation in a large chair, two secretaries at a table beneath, and on the wall were the arms of the republic, the groundwork of which was three volcanoes, emblematic, I suppose, of the combustible state of the country. The deputies sat on each side, about thirty being present, nearly half of whom were priests, with black gowns and caps; and by the dull light the scene carried me back to the dark ages, and seemed a meeting of inquisitors.

The subject under discussion was a motion to revive the old law of tithes, which had been abolished by the Liberal party. The law was passed unanimously; but there was a discussion upon a motion to appropriate a small part of the proceeds for the support of hospitals for the poor. The priests took part in the discussion, and with liberal sentiments; a lay member, with big black whiskers, opposed it, saying that the Church stood like a light in darkness; and the Marquis Aycinena, a priest and the leading member of the party, said that "what was raised for God should be given to God alone."[71] There was an-

71. See Ch. 1 n.66 and Ch. 2 n.30 for comment on this person. Stephens earlier (1842, 1:192) referred to the title as the "ci-devant Marquisate of Aycinena."

other discussion upon the point whether the law should operate upon cattle then in being or to be born thereafter; and, finally, as to the means of enforcing it. One gentleman contended that coercive measures should not be used, and, with a fine burst of eloquence, said that reliance might be placed upon the religious feelings of the people, and that the poorest Indian would come forward and contribute his mite; but the Assembly decided that the law should be enforced by Las leyes antiguas de los Espagnoles, the old laws of the Spaniards, the severities of which had been one of the great causes of revolution in all Spanish countries. There was something horrible in this retrograde legislation. I could hardly realize that, in the nineteenth century, men of sense, and in a country through the length and breadth of which free principles were struggling for the ascendancy, would dare fasten on the people a yoke which, even in the dark ages, was too galling to be borne. The tone of debate was respectable, but calm and unimpassioned, from the entire absence of any opposition party. The Assembly purported to be a popular body, representing the voice of the people. It was a time of great excitement, and the last night of its session; and Mr. Hall and I, four men and three boys, were the only listeners.

. . . Carrera returned to the city. I was extremely desirous to know him, and made an arrangement with Mr. Pavon to call upon him the next day.[72] At ten o'clock the next morning Mr. Pavon called for me. I was advised that this formidable chief was taken by external show, and put on the diplomatic coat, with a great profusion of buttons, which had produced such an effect at Copán, and which, by-the-way, owing to the abominable state of the country, I never had an opportunity of wearing afterward, and the cost of which was a dead loss.

Carrera was living in a small house in a retired street. Sentinels were at the door, and eight or ten soldiers basking in the sun outside, part of a body-guard, who had been fitted out with red bombazet jackets and tartan plaid caps, and made a much better appearance than any of his soldiers I had before seen.[73] Along the corridor was a row of muskets, bright and in good order. We entered a small room

---

72. Stephens' personal friend "Mr. Pavon," with whom he disagreed in politics, was Manuel Francisco Pavón y Aycinena, who in the 1840's became a mainstay of Carrera's regime. Pavón's mother was a half-sister to both the second *marqués* of Aycinena and to Mariano de Aycinena.

73. "Bombazet" is a worsted cloth with smooth finish.

adjoining the sala, and saw Carrera sitting at a table counting money.

When I entered the room he was sitting at a table counting sixpenny and shilling pieces. Colonel Monte Rosa, a dark Mestitzo, in a dashing uniform, was sitting by his side, and several other persons were in the room. He was about five feet six inches in height, with straight black hair, an Indian complexion and expression, without beard, and did not seem to be more than twenty-one years old. He wore a black bombazet roundabout jacket and pantaloons. He rose as we entered, pushed the money on one side of the table, and, probably out of respect to my coat, received me with courtesy, and gave me a chair at his side. My first remark was an expression of surprise at his extreme youth; he answered that he was but twenty-three years old; certainly he was not more than twenty-five; and then, as a man conscious that he was something extraordinary, and that I knew it, without waiting for any leading questions, he continued, that he had begun (he did not say what) with thirteen men armed with old muskets, which they were obliged to fire with cigars; pointed to eight places in which he had been wounded, and said that he had three balls then in his body. At this time he could hardly be recognised as the same man who, less than two years before, had entered Guatimala with a horde of wild Indians, proclaiming death to strangers. Indeed, in no particular had he changed more than in his opinion of foreigners, a happy illustration of the effect of personal intercourse in breaking down prejudices against individuals or classes. He had become personally acquainted with several, one of whom, an English doctor, had extracted a ball from his side; and his intercourse with all had been so satisfactory, that his feelings had undergone an entire revulsion; and he said that they were the only people who never deceived him. He had done, too, what I consider extraordinary; in the intervals of his hurried life he had learned to write his name, and had thrown aside his stamp. . . . Considering Carrera a promising young man, I told him that he had a long career before him, and might do much good to his country; and he laid his hand upon his heart, and with a burst of feeling that I did not expect, said he was determined to sacrifice his life for his country. With all his faults and his crimes, none ever accused him of duplicity, or of saying what he did not mean; and, perhaps, as many self-deceiving men have done before him, he believes himself a patriot.

I considered that he was destined to exercise an important, if not a controlling influence on the affairs of Central America; and trusting that hopes of honourable and extended fame might have some effect upon his character, I told him that his name had already reached my country, and that I had seen in the newspapers an account of his last entry into Guatimala, with praises of his moderation and exertions to prevent atrocities. He expressed himself pleased that his name was known, and such mention made of him among strangers; and said he was not a robber and murderer, as he was called by his enemies. He seemed intelligent and capable of improvement, and I told him that he ought to travel into other countries, and particularly, from its contiguity, into mine. He had a very indefinite notion as to where my country was; he knew it only as El Norte, or the North; inquired about the distance and facility for getting there, and said that, when the wars were over, he would endeavour to make El Norte a visit. But he could not fix his thoughts upon anything except the wars and Morazan; in fact, he knew of nothing else. He was boyish in his manners and manner of speaking, but very grave; he never smiled, and, conscious of power, was unostentatious in the exhibition of it, though he always spoke in the first person of what he had done and what he intended to do. One of the hangers-on, evidently to pay court to him, looked for a paper bearing his signature to show me as a specimen of his handwriting, but did not find one. My interview with him was much more interesting than I had expected; so young, so humble in his origin, so destitute of early advantages, with honest impulses, perhaps, but ignorant, fanatic, sanguinary, and the slave of violent passions, wielding absolutely the physical force of the country, and that force entertaining a natural hatred to the whites. At parting he accompanied me to the door, and in the presence of his villanous soldiers made me a free offer of his services. I understood that I had the good fortune to make a favourable impression; and afterward, but, unluckily, during my absence, he called upon me in full dress and in state, which for him was an unusual thing.

. . . I passed my time in social visiting. In our own city the aristocracy is called by the diplomatic corps at Washington the aristocracy of streets. In Guatimala it is the aristocracy of houses, as certain families live in the houses built by their fathers at the foundation of the city, and they are really aristocratic old mansions. These families, by reason of certain monopolies of importation, acquired under the Spanish dominion immense wealth and rank as "merchant princes." Still they were excluded from all offices and all part in the government. At the time of the revolution one of these families was noble, with the rank of marquisate, and its head tore off the insignia of his rank, and joined the revolutionary party. Next in position to the officers of the crown, they thought that, emancipated from the yoke of Spain, they would have the government in their own hands; and so they had, but it was only for a short time. The principles of equal rights began to be understood, and they were put aside. For ten years they had been in obscurity, but accidentally they were again in power, and at the time of my visit ruled in social as well as political life. I do not wish to speak harshly of them, for they were the only people who constituted society; my intercourse was almost exclusively with them; . . . I am indebted to them for much kindness; and, besides, they are personally amiable; but I speak of them as public men. I did not sympathize with them in politics.

To me the position of the country seemed most critical, and from a cause which in all Spanish America had never operated before. At the time of the first invasion a few hundred Spaniards, by superior bravery and skill, and with more formidable arms, had conquered the whole Indian population. Naturally peaceable, and kept without arms, the conquered people had remained quiet and submissive during the three centuries of Spanish dominion. In the civil wars following the independence they had borne but a subordinate part; and down to the time of Carrera's rising they were entirely ignorant of their own physical strength. But this fearful discovery had now been made. The Indians constituted three fourths of the inhabitants of Guatimala; were the hereditary owners of the soil; for the first time since they fell under the dominion of the whites, were organized and armed under a chief of their own, who chose for the moment to sustain the Central party. I did not sympathize with that party, for I believed that in their hatred of the Liberals they were courting a third power that might destroy them both; consorting with a wild animal which might at any moment turn and rend them in pieces. I believed that they were playing upon the ignorance and prejudices of the Indians, and, through the priests, upon their religious fanaticism; amusing them with fêtes and Church ceremonies, persuading them that the Liberals aimed at a demolition of churches, destruction of the priests, and hurrying back the country into darkness; and in the general heaving of the elements there was not a man of nerve enough among them, with the influence of name and station, to rally round him the strong and honest men of the country, reorganize the shattered republic, and save them from the disgrace and danger of truckling to an ignorant uneducated Indian boy.

Such were my sentiments; of course I avoided expressing them; but because I did not denounce their opponents, some looked coldly upon me. With them political differences severed all ties. Our worst party abuse is moderate and mild compared with the terms in which they speak of each other. We seldom do more than call men ignorant, incompetent, dishonest, dishonourable, false, corrupt, subverters of the Constitution, and bought with British gold; there a political opponent is a robber, an assassin; it is praise to admit that he is not a bloodthirsty cutthroat. We complain that our ears are constantly offended and our passions roused by angry political discussions. There it would have been delightful to hear a good, honest, hot, and angry political dispute. I travelled in every state, and I never heard one; for I never met two men together who differed in political opinions.

January 1, 1840. This day, so full of home associations—snow, and red noses, and blue lips out of doors, and blazing fires and beauteous faces within—opened in Guatimala like a morning in spring. The sun seemed rejoicing in the beauty of the land it shone upon. The flowers were blooming in the courtyards, and the mountains, visible above the tops of the houses, were smiling in verdure. The bells of thirty-eight churches and convents proclaimed the coming of another year. The shops were shut as on a Sunday; there was no market in the plaza. Gentlemen well dressed, and ladies in black mantas, were crossing it to attend grand mass in the Cathedral. Mozart's music swelled through the aisles. A priest in a strange tongue proclaimed morality, religion, and love of country. The floor of the church was thronged with whites, Mestitzoes, and Indians. On a high bench opposite the pulpit sat the chief of the state, and by his side Carrera, again dressed in his rich uniform. I leaned against a pillar opposite and watched his face; and if I read him right, he had forgotten war and the stains of blood upon his hands, and his very soul was filled with fanatic enthusiasm; exactly as the priests would have him. I did verily believe that he was honest in his impulses, and would do right if he knew how. They who undertake to guide him have a fearful responsibility. The service ended, a way was cleared through the crowd. Carrera, accompanied by the priests and the chief of the state, awkward in his movements, with his eyes fixed on the ground, or with furtive glances, as if ill at ease in being an object of so much attention, walked down the aisle.

A thousand ferocious-looking soldiers were drawn up before the door. A wild burst of music greeted him, and the faces of the men glowed with devotion to their chief. A broad banner was unfurled, with stripes of black and red, a device of a death's head and legs in the centre, and on one side the words "Viva la religion!" and on the other "Paz o muerte a los Liberales!"[74] Carrera placed himself at their head, and with Rivera Paz by his side, and the fearful banner floating in the air, and wild and thrilling music, and the stillness of death around, they escorted the chief of the state to his house. How different from Newyear's Day at home!

During his residence in Guatemala City, Stephens also visited Antigua, climbed Agua volcano, and rode to Iztapa. Catherwood came in from Copán on Christmas. Stephens now decided he must go to San Salvador in search of a federal government, though everyone in Guatemala City seemed to agree that the federal government had ceased to exist. On his way to Iztapa again, this time to sail with a French Captain Le Nouvel, he took fever. A few days later, landing at Acajutla, he remained a sick man, as he did for some time thereafter:[75]

The mate and sailors took leave of me and returned to the ship. I walked along the shore and up a steep hill. It was only eight o'clock, and already excessively hot. On the bank fronting the sea were the ruins of large warehouses, occupied as receptacles for merchandise under the Spanish dominion, when all the ports of America were closed against foreign vessels. In one corner of the ruined building was a sort of guardroom, where a few soldiers were eating tortillas, and one was cleaning his musket. Another apartment was occupied by the captain of the port, who told me that the mules engaged for me had got loose, and the muleteers were looking for them. Here I had the pleasure to meet Dr. Drivon, a gentleman from the Island of St. Lucia, who had a large sugar hacienda a few leagues distant, and was at the port to superintend the disembarcation of machinery for a mill from the English brig. While waiting for the mules he conducted me to a hut where he had two Guayaquil hammocks hung, and feeling already the effect of my exertions, I took possession of one of them.

The woman of the rancho was a sort of ship's husband; and there

74. In his next paragraph, Stephens discusses the possibility that one inscription on the banner read differently.
75. Stephens, 1842, 1:320–25.

being three vessels in port, the rancho was encumbered with vegetables, fruit, eggs, fowls, and ship's stores. It was close and hot, but very soon I required all the covering I could get. I had a violent ague, followed by a fever, in comparison with which all I had suffered before was nothing. I called for water till the old woman was tired of giving it to me, and went out and left me alone. I became lightheaded, wild with pain, and wandered among the miserable huts with only the consciousness that my brain was scorching. I have an indistinct recollection of speaking English to some Indian women, begging them to get me a horse to ride to Sonsonate; of some laughing, others looking at me with pity, and others leading me out of the sun, and making me lie down under the shade of a tree. At three o'clock in the afternoon the mate came ashore again. I had changed my position, and he found me lying on my face asleep, and almost withered by the sun. He wanted to take me back on board the ship, but I begged him to procure mules and take me to Sonsonate, within the reach of medical assistance. It is hard to feel worse than I did when I mounted. I passed three hours of agony, scorched by the intense heat, and a little before dark arrived at Sonsonate, fortunate, as Dr. Drivon afterward told me, in not having suffered a stroke of the sun. Before entering the town and crossing the bridge over the Rio Grande, I met a gentleman well mounted, having a scarlet Peruvian pellon over his saddle, with whose appearance I was struck, and we exchanged low bows. This gentleman, as I afterward learned, was the government I was looking after.

I rode to the house of Captain Le Nonvel's brother, one of the largest in the place, where I had that comfort, seldom known in Central America, a room to myself, and everything else necessary.[76] For several days I remained within doors. The first afternoon I went out I called upon Don Manuel de Aguilar, formerly chief of the State of Costa Rica, but about a year before driven out by a revolution and banished for life. At his house I met Don Diego Vigil, the vice-president of the republic, the same gentleman whom I had met on the bridge, and the only existing officer of the Federal Government. From observation and experience in my own country, I had learned never to take the character of a public man from his political enemy; and I will not soil this page with the foul aspersions which men of veracity, but blinded by party prejudice, threw upon the character of Señor

76. Dunlop, 1847, p. 67, refers to Captain LeNonvel's brother as "Don Victor Lenouvel."

Vigil. He was about forty-five, six feet high, thin, and suffering from a paralytic affection, which almost deprived him of the use of both legs; in dress, conversation, and manners, eminently a gentleman. He had travelled more extensively in his own country than most of his countrymen, and knew all the objects of interest; and with a politeness which I appreciated, made no reference to my position or my official character.

His business at Sonsonate showed the wretched state of the country. He had come expressly to treat with Rascon, the head of the band which had prevented my coming from Guatimala by land. Chico Rascon, as he was familiarly called in Sonsonate, was of an old and respectable family, who had spent a large fortune in dissipation in Paris, and returning in desperate circumstances, had turned patriot. About six months before he had made a descent upon Sonsonate, killed the garrison to a man, robbed the custom-house, and retreated to his hacienda. He was then on a visit in the town, publicly, by appointment with Señor Vigil, and demanded, as the price of disbanding his troops, a colonel's commission for himself, other commissions for some of his followers, and four thousand dollars in money. Vigil assented to all except the four thousand dollars in money, but offered instead the credit of the State of San Salvador, which Rascon agreed to accept. Papers were drawn up, and that afternoon was appointed for their execution; but, while Vigil was waiting for him, Rascon and his friends, without a word of notice, mounted their horses and rode out of town. The place was thrown into great excitement, and in the evening I saw the garrison busily engaged in barricading the plaza, in apprehension of another attack.

The next day I made a formal call upon Señor Vigil. I was in a rather awkward position. When I left Guatimala in search of a government, I did not expect to meet it on the road. In that state I had heard but one side; I was just beginning to hear the other. If there was any government, I had *treed* it. Was it the real thing or was it not? In Guatimala they said it was not; here they said it was. It was a knotty question. I was in no great favour in Guatimala, and in endeavouring to play a safe game I ran the risk of being hustled by all parties. In Guatimala they had no right to ask for my credentials, and took offence because I did not present them; here, if I refused, they had a right to consider it an insult. In this predicament I opened my business with the vice-president, and told him that I was on my way to the capital, with credentials from the United States; but that, in the state of anarchy in which I found the country, was at a loss what to do; I was desirous to avoid making a false step, and anxious to know whether the Federal Government really existed, or whether the Republic was dissolved. Our interview was long and interesting, and the purport of his answer was, that the government did exist de facto and de jure; he himself was legally elected vice-president; the act of the four states in declaring themselves independent was unconstitutional and rebellious; the union could not be dissolved except by a convention of deputies from all the states; the government had the actual control in three states, one had been reduced to subjection by arms, and very soon the Federal party would have the ascendancy in the others. He was familiar with the case of South Carolina, and said that our Congress had sustained the right of the general government to coerce states into subjection, and they were in the same position.[77] I referred to the shattered condition of the government; its absolute impotence in other states; the non-existence of senate and other co-ordinate branches, or even of a secretary of state, the officer to whom my credentials were addressed; and he answered that he had in his suite an acting secretary of state, confirming what had been told me before, that the "Government" would, at a moment's notice, make any officer I wanted; but I owe it to Señor Vigil to say, that, after going over fully the whole ground of the unhappy contest, and although at that critical juncture the recognition of the Federal Government by that of the United States would have been of moment to his party, and not to recognise it was disrespectful and favoured the cause of the rebellious or independent states, he did not ask me to present my credentials. The Convention, which was expected to compose the difficulties of the Republic, was then about assembling in Honduras. The deputies from St. Salvador had gone to take their seats, and it was understood that I should await the decision of this body.[78] The result of my interview with the vice-president was much more agreeable than I expected. I am sure that I left him without the least feeling of ill-will on his part; but my great perplexity whether I had any government was not yet brought to a close.

In the mean time, while the political repairs were going on, I remained in Sonsonate recruiting.

---

77. Reference is to the South Carolina Ordinance of Nullification of 1832, put aside the following year.

78. Various plans for such conventions made in the year 1839 finally reached some fruition in one held at Chinandega, Nicaragua, in 1842.

On January 22, Stephens deserted his Sonsonate hammock for adventures in other lands. The sailing of a vessel from Acajutla to Caldera in Costa Rica gave him an opportunity for further rest, after which he planned to return to San Salvador by land. Stephens' decision to make this trip meant that he would be the first outsider since independence to describe Costa Rica in personal terms; likewise he was the first in western Nicaragua since Roberts. From Caldera, with half his strength renewed, Stephens rode through Alajuela and Heredia to San José, where he again visited a chief of state:[79]

San José is, I believe, the only city that has grown up or even improved since the independence of Central America. Under the Spanish dominion Cartago was the royal capital; but, on the breaking out of the revolution, the fervour of patriotism was so hot, that it was resolved to abolish this memorial of colonial servitude, and establish the capital at San José. . . . The buildings in San José are all republican; there is not one of any grandeur or architectural beauty; and the churches are inferior to many erected by the Spaniards in the smallest villages. Nevertheless, it exhibited a development of resources and an appearance of business unusual in this lethargic country; and there was one house in the plaza which showed that the owner had been abroad, and had returned with his mind so liberalized as to adopt the improvements of other countries, and build differently from the custom of his fathers and the taste of his neighbours.

My first visit of ceremony was to Señor Carillo, the Gefe del Estado. The State of Costa Rica enjoyed at that time a degree of prosperity unequalled by any in the disjointed confederacy. At a safe distance, without wealth enough to excite cupidity, and with a large tract of wilderness to protect it against the march of an invading army, it had escaped the tumults and wars which desolated and devastated the other states. And yet, but two years before, it had had its own revolution: a tumultuous soldiery entered the plaza, and shouting A bajo con Aguilar, viva Carillo, my friend Don Manuel was driven out by bayonets and banished from the state, and Carillo installed in his place; he appointed his father-in-law, a quiet, respectable old man, vice-chief; called the soldiery, officers, civil and military, into the plaza, and all went through the solemn farce of swearing fealty to the Constitution. The time fixed by the Constitution for holding new elections came, but they were not permitted to be held; having tried

79. Stephens, 1842, 1:358–61.

this once and failed, he does not mean to run the risk of another; and probably he will hold on till he is turned out by the same force that put him in. In the mean time, he uses prudent precautions: does not permit emigrés, nor revolutionists, nor suspected persons from other states to enter his dominions; has sealed up the press, and imprisons or banishes, under pain of death if they return, all who speak loud against the government.

He was about fifty, short and stout, plain, but careful in his dress, and with an appearance of dogged resolution in his face.[80] His house was republican enough, and had nothing to distinguish it from that of any other citizen; in one part his wife had a little store, and in the other was his office for government business. It was not larger than the counting-room of a third-rate merchant, and he had three clerks, who at the moment of my entering were engaged writing, while he, with his coat off, was looking over papers. He had heard of my coming, and welcomed me to Costa Rica. . . . He inquired particularly about Guatimala; and, though sympathizing in the policy of that state, had no good opinion of Carrera. He was uncompromising in his hostility to General Morazan and the Federal Government, and, in fact, it seemed to me that he was against any general government, and strongly impressed with the idea that Costa Rica could stand alone; doubtless believing that the state, or, which is the same thing, he himself, could disburse the revenues better than any other authority. Indeed, this is the rock on which all the politicians of Central America split: there is no such thing as national feeling. Every state would be an empire; the officers of state cannot brook superiors; a chief of the state cannot brook a president. He had not sent deputies to the Convention, and did not intend to do so; but said that Costa Rica would remain neutral until the other states had settled their difficulties. He spoke with much interest of the improvement of the roads, particularly to the ports on the Atlantic and Pacific, and expressed great satisfaction at the project of the British government, which I mentioned to him, of sending steamboats to connect the West India Islands with the American coast, which, by touching at the port of San Juan, could bring his secluded capital within eighteen or twenty days of New-York. In fact, usurper and despot as he is, Carillo works hard for the good of the state, and for twelve hundred dollars a year, with perquisites, and leave to be his own paymaster. In the mean time, all who do not interfere with him are protected. A few who cannot submit to despotism talk of

80. Carrillo's age was forty at the time of Stephens' visit.

leaving the country; but the great mass are contented, and the state prospers. As for myself, I admire him. In that country the alternative is a strong government or none at all. Throughout his state I felt a sense of personal security, which I did not enjoy in any other. For the benefit of travellers, may he live a thousand years!

Stephens' malady lingered, even as in company with European and North American friends he visited Cartago and climbed Irazú volcano. Finally in mid-February he was released from the spell, just as he began his return to San Salvador. He had originally intended going to San Juan del Norte, from there to ascend the River San Juan to Lake Nicaragua, as part of a study of the projected Nicaragua canal.[81] The illness, however, had induced him to follow a more direct route. One young lady in Liberia almost magnetized him into staying there; farther along on the way to Rivas, Nicaragua, he took time to examine ground already surveyed for the canal. In Granada, at the end of the month, he heard news of the rout of federal government forces in Honduras. From here on, Stephens did what he could to hurry along, except for an occasional close look at a volcano.

With Masaya and Managua behind him, Stephens felt uneasy in León. He decided against going to visit another chief of state, though this omission might cause him passport difficulties. At Chinandega he was apprised that he could not leave Nicaragua without the proper document. The story of his exit without permission, but with the aid of allies, from the river hamlet of Nacascolo (today Puerto Morazán) is one of his most dramatic. The Gulf of Fonseca, La Unión, San Miguel, San Vicente, and Cojutepeque now passed by rapidly, until Stephens reached an earthquake-ridden and war-imperiled city of San Salvador. Here he again contacted Diego Vigil:[82]

In the evening I called upon the vice-president. Great changes had taken place since I saw him at Sonsonate. The troops of the Federal Government had been routed in Honduras; Carrera had conquered Quezaltenango, garrisoned it with his own soldiers, destroyed its existence as a separate state, and annexed it to Guatimala. San Salvador

---

81. This intention seems plain from the remarks he made on the subject (Stephens, 1949, 1:282–83, 298–99) though they are not very specific. The editor's note (*ibid.*, 1:283) to the effect that Stephens' original intention was to visit San Juan del Sur rather than San Juan del Norte is thus mistaken as to Stephens' meaning.
82. Stephens, 1842, 2:51–55.

stood alone in support of the Federal Government. But Señor Vigil had risen with the emergency. The chief of the state, a bold-looking mulatto, and other officers of the government, were with him.[83] They knew that the Honduras troops were marching upon the city, had reason to fear they would be joined by those of Nicaragua, but they were not dismayed; on the contrary, all showed a resolution and energy I had not seen before. General Morazan, they said, was on his march against Guatimala. Tired as they were of war, the people of San Salvador, Señor Vigil said, had risen with new enthusiasm. Volunteers were flocking in from all quarters; and with a determination that was imposing, though called out by civil war, he added that they were resolved to sustain the Federation, or die under the ruins of San Salvador. It was the first time my feelings had been at all roused. In all the convulsions of the time I had seen no flash of heroism, no high love of country. Self-preservation and self-aggrandizement were the ruling passions. It was a bloody scramble for power and place; and sometimes, as I rode through the beautiful country, and saw what Providence had done for them, and how unthankful they were, I thought it would be a good riddance if they would play out the game of the Kilkenny cats. It was a higher tone than I was accustomed to, when the chief men of a single state, with an invading army at their door, and their own soldiers away, expressed the stern resolution to sustain the Federation, or die under the ruins of the capital. But they did not despair of the Republic; the Honduras troops would be repulsed at San Vicente, and General Morazan would take Guatimala. The whole subject of the revolution was discussed, and the conversation was deeply interesting to me, for I regarded it as touching matters of life and death. I could not compromise them by anything I might say, for they are all in exile, under sentence of death if they return. They did not speak in the ferocious and sanguinary spirit I afterward heard imputed to them at Guatimala, but they spoke with great bitterness of gentlemen whom I considered personal friends, who, they said, had been before spared by their lenity; and they added, in tones that could not be misunderstood, that they would not make such a mistake again.

In the midst of this confusion, where was my government? I had travelled all over the country, led on by a glimmering light shining and disappearing, and I could not conceal from myself that the crisis

83. The "chief of the state" was presumably José María Silva, acting *jefe* of San Salvador from February to April, 1840.

of my fortune was at hand. All depended upon the success of Morazan's expedition. If he failed, my occupation was gone; but in this darkest hour of the Republic I did not despair. In ten years of war Morazan had never been beaten; Carrera would not dare fight him; Guatimala would fall; the moral effect would be felt all over the country; Quezaltenango would shake off its chains; the strong minority in the other states would rise; the flag of the Republic would once more wave triumphantly, and out of chaos the government I was in search of would appear.

Nevertheless, I was not so sure of it as to wait quietly till it came to me at San Salvador. The result was very uncertain, and if it should be a protracted war, I might be cut off from Guatimala, without any opportunity of serving my country by diplomatic arts, and prevented from prosecuting other objects more interesting than the uncertain pursuit in which I was then engaged. . . .

In the excitement and alarm of the place, it was very difficult to procure mules. As to procuring them direct for Guatimala, it was impossible. No one would move on that road until the result of Morazan's expedition was known; and even to get them for Sonsonate it was necessary to wait a day. That day I intended to abstract myself from the tumult of the city and ascend the Volcano of San Salvador; but the next morning a woman came to inform us that one of our men had been taken by a pressgang of soldiers, and was in the carcel. We followed her to the place, and, being invited in by the officer to pick out our man, found ourselves surrounded by a hundred of Vigil's volunteers, of every grade in appearance and character, from the frightened servant-boy torn from his master's door to the worst of desperadoes; some asleep on the ground, some smoking stumps of cigars, some sullen, and others perfectly reckless. Two of the supreme worst did me the honour to say they liked my looks, called me captain, and asked me to take them into my company. Our man was not ambitious, and could do better than be shot at for a shilling a day; but we could not take him out without an order from the chief of the state, and went immediately to the office of the government, where I was sorry to meet Señor Vigil, as the subject of my visit and the secrets of the prison were an unfortunate comment upon his boasts of the enthusiasm of the people in taking up arms. With his usual courtesy, however, he directed the proper order to be made out, and the names of all in my service to be sent to the captains of the different pressgangs, with orders not to touch them. . . . In the afternoon intelligence was received that General Morazan's advanced guard had defeated a detachment of Carrera's troops, and that he was marching with an accession of forces upon Guatimala. A feu de joie was fired in the plaza, and all the church bells rang peals of victory.

In the evening I saw Señor Vigil again and alone. He was confident of the result. . . . He urged me to wait; he had his preparations all made, his horses ready, and, on the first notice of Morazan's entry, intended to go up to Guatimala and establish that city once more as the capital. But I was afraid of delay, and we parted to meet in Guatimala; but we never met again. A few days afterward he was flying for his life, and is now in exile, under sentence of death if he returns; the party that rules Guatimala is heaping opprobrium upon his name; but in the recollection of my hurried tour I never forget him who had the unhappy distinction of being vice-president of the Republic.

Morazán did not take Guatemala City; he was repulsed instead. When Stephens went on in mid-March to Sonsonate and Ahuachapán, he found himself riding into battle lines. The news of Morazán's failure reached him in Ahuachapán; soon after, that city was occupied by a Carrera band. Later the same day, however, the main body of Morazán's troops, in retreat from Guatemala, defeated this Carrera band. Stephens at this juncture had two brief opportunities to speak with the great leader of the federation to whose government he was accredited, but whose fortune was about to expire:[84]

General Morazan, with several officers, was standing in the corridor of the cabildo; a large fire was burning before the door, and a table stood against the wall, with a candle and chocolate-cups upon it. He was about forty-five years old, five feet ten inches high, thin, with a black mustache and week's beard, and wore a military frock-coat, buttoned up to the throat, and sword. His hat was off, and the expression of his face mild and intelligent. . . . From the best information I could acquire, and from the enthusiasm with which I had heard him spoken of by his officers, and, in fact, by every one else in his own state, I had conceived almost a feeling of admiration for General Morazan, and my interest in him was increased by his misfortunes. I was really at a loss how to address him; and while my mind was full of his ill-fated expedition, his first question was if his family had arrived in Costa Rica, or if I had heard anything of them. I did not

84. Stephens, 1842, 2:89–91, 93–95.

tell him, what I then thought, that his calamities would follow all who were connected with him, and probably that his wife and daughters would not be permitted an asylum in that state; but it spoke volumes that, at such a moment, with the wreck of his followers before him, and the memory of his murdered companions fresh in his mind, in the overthrow of all his hopes and fortunes, his heart turned to his domestic relations. He expressed his sorrow for the condition in which I saw his unhappy country; regretted that my visit was at such a most unfortunate moment; spoke of Mr. De Witt, and the relations of that country with ours, and his regret that our treaty had not been renewed, and that it could not be done now; but these things were not in my mind. Feeling that he must have more important business, I remained but a short time, and returned to the house.

In the morning, to our surprise, we found several shops open, and people in the street, who had been concealed somewhere in the neighbourhood, and returned as soon as they knew of Morazan's entry. . . . While I was taking chocolate, General Morazan called upon me. Our conversation was longer and more general. I did not ask him his plans or purposes, but neither he nor his officers exhibited despondency. Once reference was made to the occupation of Santa Ana by General Cascara, and with a spirit that reminded me of Claverhouse in "Old Mortality," he said, "we shall visit that gentleman soon." He spoke without malice or bitterness of the leaders of the Central party, and of Carrera as an ignorant and lawless Indian, from whom the party that was now using him would one day be glad to be protected. . . .

With the opinion that he entertained of Carrera and his soldiers, he of course considered it unsafe for us to go on to Guatimala. But I was exceedingly anxious to set out. . . . Carrera might arrive at any moment, in which case we might again change owners, or, at all events, be the witnesses of a sanguinary battle, for Morazan would defend the frontier town of his own state to the death.

I told General Morazan my wish and purpose, and the difficulty of procuring a guide. He said that an escort of soldiers would expose us to certain danger; even a single soldier, without his musket and cartridge-box (these being the only distinguishing marks of a soldier), might be recognised; but he would send for the alcalde, and procure us some trusty person from the town. I bade him farewell with an interest greater than I had felt for any man in the country. Little did we then know the calamities that were still in store for him; that very night most of his soldiers deserted, having been kept together only by the danger to which they were exposed while in an enemy's country. . . . Amid the fierceness of party spirit it was impossible for a stranger to form a true estimate of the character of a public man. The great outcry against General Morazan was hostility to the church and forced loans. For his hostility to the church there is the justification that it is at this day a pall upon the spirit of free institutions, degrading and debasing instead of elevating the Christian character; and for forced loans constant wars may plead. His worst enemies admit that he was exemplary in his private relations, and, what they consider no small praise, that he was not sanguinary. He is now fallen and in exile, probably forever, under sentence of death if he returns; all the truckling worshippers of a rising sun are blasting his name and memory; but I verily believe, and I know I shall bring down upon me the indignation of the whole Central party by the assertion, I verily believe they have driven from their shores the best man in Central America.

The ride from Ahuachapán via Oratorio to Guatemala City, through a tense and suspicious countryside, was not easy but was accomplished. During Stephens' absence, Catherwood had revisited Copán and had surveyed the ruins of Quiriguá, which he and Stephens had once passed unknown. Now both men wanted to visit Palenque in Chiapas, by the overland route, but were discouraged by reports that western Guatemala remained unpacified. Resolved nevertheless to go through with their plans, they sought the protection of a Carrera-signed passport, the occasion for a last visit to that man:[85]

Unable to induce any of the persons I wished to call with me upon Carrera; afraid, after such a long interval and such exciting scenes as he had been engaged in, that he might not recognise me, and feeling that it was all important not to fail in my application to him, I remembered that in my first interview he had spoken warmly of a doctor who had extracted a ball from his side. This doctor I did not know, but I called upon him, and asked him to accompany me, to which, with great civility, he immediately assented.

It was under these circumstances that I made my last visit to Carrera. He had removed into a much larger house, and his guard was more regular and formal. When I entered he was standing behind a table on one side of the room, with his wife, and Rivera Paz, and one

85. *Ibid.*, 2:136–39.

or two others. . . . His wife was a pretty, delicate-looking Mestitzo, not more than twenty. . . . The face of Rivera Paz seemed anxious. Carrera had passed through so many terrible scenes since I saw him, that I feared he had forgotten me; but he recognised me in a moment, and made room for me behind the table next to himself. His military coat lay on the table, and he wore the same roundabout jacket, his face had the same youthfulness, quickness, and intelligence, his voice and manners the same gentleness and seriousness, and he had again been wounded. I regretted to meet Rivera Paz there, for I thought it must be mortifying to him, as the head of the government, to see that his passport was not considered a protection without Carrera's endorsement; but I could not stand upon ceremony, and took advantage of Carrera's leaving the table to say to him that I was setting out on a dangerous road, and considered it indispensable to fortify myself with all the security I could get. When Carrera returned I told him my purpose; that I had waited only for his return; showed him the passport of the government, and asked him to put his stamp upon it. Carrera had no delicacy in the matter; and taking the passport out of my hand, threw it on the table, saying he would make me out a new one, and sign it himself. This was more than I expected; but in a quiet way telling me to "be seated," he sent his wife into another room for the secretary, and told him to make out a passport for the "Consul of the North." He had an indefinite idea that I was a great man in my own country, but he had a very indefinite idea as to where my country was. I was not particular about my title so that it was big enough, but the North was rather a broad range, and to prevent mistakes I gave the secretary the other passport. He took it into another room, and Carrera sat down at the table beside me. He had heard of my having met Morazan on his retreat, and inquired about him, though less anxiously than others, but he spoke more to the purpose; said that he was making preparations, and in a week he intended to march upon San Salvador with three thousand men, adding that if he had had cannon he would have driven Morazan from the plaza very soon. I asked him whether it was true that he and Morazan met personally on the heights of Calvary, and he said that they did; that it was toward the last of the battle, when the latter was retreating.[86] One of Morazan's dismounted troopers tore off his holsters; Morazan fired a pistol at him, and he struck at Morazan with his sword, and cut his saddle. Morazan,

86. El Calvario in Guatemala City was the scene of the decisive battle of March 18, 1840, the beginning of Morazán's disaster.

he said, had very handsome pistols; and it struck me that he thought if he had killed Morazan he would have got the pistols. I could not but think of the strange positions into which I was thrown: shaking hands and sitting side by side with men who were thirsting for each other's blood, well received by all, hearing what they said of each other, and in many cases their plans and purposes, as unreservedly as if I was a travelling member of both cabinets. In a few minutes the secretary called him, and he went out and brought back the passport himself, signed with his own hand, the ink still wet. It had taken him longer than it would have done to cut off a head, and he seemed more proud of it. Indeed, it was the only occasion in which I saw in him the slightest elevation of feeling. I made a comment upon the excellence of the handwriting, and with his good wishes for my safe arrival in the North and speedy return to Guatimala, I took my leave. Now I do not believe, if he knew what I say of him, that he would give me a very cordial welcome; but I believe him honest, and if he knew how, and could curb his passions, he would do more good for Central America than any other man in it.

Difficulties followed the party as it wended its way during the last three weeks of April to Sololá, Santa Cruz del Quiché, Totonicapán, Quezaltenango, Huehuetenango, Todos Santos Cuchumatán, and the border with Mexico; Stephens' description of all this great Maya territory was the first by a traveler since Gage. The tension was particularly strong about Los Altos' capital of Quezaltenango. Yet this stage of the journey held some moments of relief, when politics could be forgotten, particularly as Stephens and Catherwood examined the ruins of Tecpán, Utatlán, and Zaculeu. If on one occasion such respite from the perils of the day turned to near-hysteria, the weary band may surely be absolved of overfrivolity. The scene is Utatlán. Besides Stephens and Catherwood, there are present a guide to the ruins, a simple servant whom Stephens called Bobón, and (entering) the priest from neighboring Santa Cruz del Quiché:[87]

As we stood on the ruined fortress of Resguardo, the great plain, consecrated by the last struggle of a brave people, lay before us grand and beautiful, its bloodstains all washed out, and smiling with fertility, but perfectly desolate. Our guide leaning on his sword in the area beneath was the only person in sight. But very soon Bobon introduced

87. Stephens, 1842, 2:180–82, 187–88.

a stranger, who came stumbling along under a red silk umbrella, talking to Bobon and looking up at us. We recognised him as the cura, and descended to meet him. He laughed to see us grope our way down; by degrees his laugh became infectious, and when we met we all laughed together. All at once he stopped, looked very solemn, pulled off his neckcloth, and wiped the perspiration from his face, took out a paper of cigars, laughed, thrust them back, pulled out another, as he said, of Habaneras, and asked what was the news from Spain.

Our friend's dress was as unclerical as his manner, viz., a broad-brimmed black glazed hat, an old black coat reaching to his heels, glossy from long use, and pantaloons to match; a striped roundabout, a waistcoat, flannel shirt, and under it a cotton one, perhaps washed when he shaved last, some weeks before. He laughed at our coming to see the ruins, and said that he laughed prodigiously himself when he first saw them. He was from Old Spain; had seen the battle of Trafalgar, looking on from the heights on shore, and laughed whenever he thought of it; the French fleet was blown sky high, and the Spanish went with it; Lord Nelson was killed—all for glory—he could not help laughing. He had left Spain to get rid of wars and revolutions: here we all laughed; sailed with twenty Dominican friars; was fired upon and chased into Jamaica by a French cruiser: here we laughed again; got an English convoy to Omoa, where he arrived at the breaking out of a revolution; had been all his life in the midst of revolutions, and it was now better than ever. Here we all laughed incontinently. His own laugh was so rich and expressive that it was perfectly irresistible. In fact, we were not disposed to resist, and in half an hour we were as intimate as if acquainted for years. The world was our butt, and we laughed at it outrageously. Except the Church, there were few things which the cura did not laugh at; but politics was his favourite subject. He was in favour of Morazan, or Carrera, or el Demonio: "vamos adelante," "go ahead," was his motto; he laughed at them all. If we had parted with him then, we should always have remembered him as the laughing cura; but, on farther acquaintance, we found in him such a vein of strong sense and knowledge, and, retired as he lived, he was so intimately acquainted with the country and all the public men, as a mere looker on his views were so correct and his satire so keen, yet without malice, that we improved his title by calling him the laughing philosopher.

Under one of the buildings was an opening which the Indians called a cave, and by which they said one could reach Mexico in an hour. I crawled under, and found a pointed-arch roof formed by stones lapping over each other, but was prevented exploring it by want of light, and the padre's crying to me that it was the season of earthquakes; and he laughed more than usual at the hurry with which I came out; but all at once he stopped, and grasping his pantaloons, hopped about, crying, "a snake, a snake." The guide and Bobon hurried to his relief; and by a simple process, but with great respect, one at work on each side, were in a fair way of securing the intruder; but the padre could not stand still, and with his agitation and restlessness tore loose from their hold, and brought to light a large grasshopper. While Bobon and the guide, without a smile, restored him, and put each button in its place, we finished with a laugh outrageous to the memory of the departed inhabitants....

Chapter 3

The Economy

A MAJORITY of the travelers visiting Central America in its first two decades of independence were men interested in commerce. All three of the countries from which they came were to some degree mindful of new possibilities for trade. One would expect travelers representing such concerns to comment at large on the economy of the land. This they did, to the point where they produced entire chapters on the subject along with many memoranda engulfed in their narratives. The selections which follow are representative ones, but by no means comprehensive; they give only a hint of what may be found in the books themselves.

In 1821, as always, agriculture was Central America's first business. But at that time farming was a familiar occupation to most people around the world. It was only normal that a visitor of whatever calling would be interested in life on a large country estate to which he might be invited. Henry Dunn had such an invitation, and spent a few weeks on a farm near Santa Catarina Pinula, just before he undertook his ride to the Pacific which has already been portrayed.[1] His own description of life on a Guatemalan hacienda follows:[2]

> ... We ... arrived at the house. At this time it was inhabited only by the foreman (*mayor-domo*), and was in a decayed condition: it had been composed of three wings, with elevated corridors; but two of these were now in a ruinous state: in the third, which consisted of five

1. See above, pp. 115–16.
2. Dunn, 1829, pp. 290–95.

tolerable apartments, we took up our abode. The front corridor was hung round with the long wooden bee-hives of the country, and its situation afforded a very agreeable prospect of the surrounding hills.

The following morning we took a view of the estate, which extended about twenty miles in circumference, consisting of excellent land, in the highest state of fertility, well wooded and watered, and comprising different elevations. The house was surrounded, at some distance, and isolated on three sides from the neighbouring country, by a deep ravine; along the bed of which flowed a small river of excellent water, supplied all the year round by three springs, rising within one hundred yards of each other. The fields near were open, and partook of the character of park scenery, and in every direction furnished the most agreeable walks. Over these beautiful lands roam about eight hundred head of cattle and two hundred horses, generally of inferior quality: among them were some fine beasts, but the majority were small and bony. This property, including the house and stock, had been lately purchased for a sum equal to about six thousand pounds sterling.

We passed several hours in the grounds, and towards the close of the day had reached the summit of a high hill, which commanded a fine view of the volcanoes, and the scenery near Amatitlán. The sun was just setting with extraordinary beauty. The lake lay stretched like a mirror before us. The mountains, belted by a girdle of thick clouds, exhibited their tops shrouded in mist, which, partially obscuring the waters, hung like a gauze veil over their surface and upon the woods which covered the hills. In a short time the sun, which had been concealed while higher in the firmament, broke forth behind his mantle of clouds, tinging them with a thousand different colours: the lake glistened, as if composed of molten gold; the mountains seemed on fire; while fainter streaks illuminated the distance, as the king of day slowly sank behind the hills in indescribable splendour.

During our stay the live stock was collected on different parts of the farm, to be marked: the milder ones were driven in flocks, and the more obstinate taken by the *lazo*. The latter is a sight interesting to a stranger. On the day fixed for the taking of the wild cattle, the requisite number of persons to be employed are mounted on horses; and one end of the *lazo* (which consists of a long cord made of twisted slips of hide) is firmly bound round the tail of each horse, small branches having first been wound about it to prevent laceration. The rider then gathers the rest of the cord loosely in his hand, taking care that the extremity, which is formed into a noose, is free, and the cord unraveled. Thus prepared, he approaches the bull, who, aware of his object, generally starts off at full speed, and is as closely pursued: the animal runs and winds with surprising swiftness and celerity; but, unable to compete with the horse, is soon overtaken by his pursuer; who contrives with the greatest dexterity to throw the loose end of the lazo over his horns. The instant he finds it has taken a firm hold, he wheels round his horse, who, with the other end fastened to his tail, opposes his force to that of the bull. The animal, finding himself a prisoner, generally submits to be dragged at full speed after the man, who turns toward the pen: but if he be very powerful, or restive, the rider instantly gallops round in a circle, by which means the loose cord is quickly wound about the legs of the bull, and he is suddenly thrown to the ground. This employment often proves a dangerous one. Sometimes the bull turns and attacks his pursuer, when the greatest agility is requisite to avoid the contact: at other times the rider is thrown, by the violence of the shock which ensues when the bull, suddenly stopping, allows the lazo to be brought to its full stretch; to say nothing of the numerous falls to which both are subject, in galloping over unlevel and often rocky ground. Notwithstanding these dangers, this species of chase is the favourite amusement both of horse and man: the former is enlivened by the shouts of the spectators, and the latter urged forward by a kind of rural ambition. A spectator scarcely knows which to admire most,—the dexterity of the one, or the docility of the other.

To collect the required number was the work of three days, during which the poor creatures, as taken, were imprisoned without any thing to eat or drink, and almost suffocated by the clouds of dust they raised in their attempts to get out. On the third day, the cord was again thrown round the horns of each one, and immediately twisted about their legs; by which means one after another they were forcibly thrown to the ground, and marked with a hot iron. The mode of effecting this was as clumsy and brutal as can be imagined. The same plan was afterwards pursued with the horses, although one died upon the spot from the violence with which he was thrown to the ground. It was vain to endeavour to persuade them that by milder means they could effect their object as well: ignorant people are generally obstinate. The value of cattle is not great, and with humanity they have nothing to do. A fine cow may be purchased for a sum equal to about four pounds sterling; a sheep is worth from six to seven shillings. The value of a horse depends chiefly upon his having what is termed the *passo*,—an easy pace, something between a swift walk and a gentle trot. They may be bought from two pounds to twenty pounds; but mules are much dearer: a very ordinary one will fetch from six to eight pounds.

The other branches of rural economy are greatly neglected. Some butter and cheese is obtained, but in small quantities. Honey is more regarded. The bee-hives . . . were numerous, and contained two species of bees,—one, *manso*, or tame, which do not sting; and the other possessing the faculty in the same degree as in Europe. The former are the favourites; yet, notwithstanding their general character for mildness, we were told that at times they fight with such fury as to make it requisite to throw over the hive a cloth dipped in some sweet, which attracts their attention, and draws them from the conflict. The bees that sting, yield a species of honey thinner than the others. . . .

G. W. Montgomery, riding from Ocotepeque in Honduras to San Salvador, stopped at the estate of Joaquín San Martín, who four years earlier had served as *jefe* of the state of San Salvador. Montgomery does not mention the bees, but like Dunn he was impressed by the cattle and horses:[3]

. . . Our route . . . was not enlivened by the appearance of a single village, or even a house, till about noon, when we came to a considerable *hacienda,* or estate, called *Amayo.*

This is one of the finest estates in the country, and is the property of Don Joaquin San Martin. . . . Don Joaquin happened to be on the estate, and to our application for permission to rest under his roof for an hour or two, he replied in the most civil manner, that "his house was at our disposal." Nor was this an empty compliment, for he, at the same time, ordered dinner to be prepared for Mr. M. and me, and that care should be taken of the arrieros and the mules. This repast, which was served up on a long table, with a bench on each side, we took in a spacious hall, where, besides some furniture of a rude and primitive fashion, there were instruments of agriculture of various kinds, and saddles, bridles, swords, fowling-pieces, and hammocks.

The house was a large substantial building, with the usual court in the centre, surrounded by a corridor. In the rear of the house was a large yard, or enclosure, in which two or three hundred horses were undergoing the operation of being marked. The greater part were colts, as wild as if in a state of nature, and as nimble as deer. They were galloping and racing around the yard at a furious rate, and several men

3. Montgomery, 1839, pp. 93–94.

were employed in catching them, one after the other, which they effected by means of the *lazo,* or noose, throwing it over the neck or legs of the animal, and then pulling him to the ground, when the heated iron was applied to his quivering haunch. I afterwards had an opportunity of seeing the lazo used in the open fields, where the horse had fair play, and often led his pursuer a long chase before he was taken. A half-naked young Indian, with spurs on his bare feet, and the lazo in his hand was mounted on a swift horse, and having singled out his beast, rode into the midst of the drove to catch him. The skill he displayed in this operation, and his bold and graceful manner as a rider, while careering about the field, afforded a sight of no little interest and excitement.

The estates in this part of the country are chiefly devoted to the raising of cattle and breeding of horses, for which every facility is afforded by the vast extent of the pasture lands. In fact, we could see whole herds grazing in the plains around; and as Don Joaquin pointed to them, he expressed his fears lest some of Carrera's people, when in want of horses, should pay him a visit, and supply themselves at his expense. So cheap are horses there, that for twelve or fifteen dollars I might have selected one out of a hundred. The price of oxen is in the same proportion. That of horses seems to depend upon their training, for as soon as they have learned to pace and amble, they are estimated at five or six times the original value.

Cattle and horses, oxen and mules were raised for local purposes. A less exciting but more remunerative occupation was the procuring of cochineal for the export trade. Two districts in the state of Guatemala specialized in this industry. One of them, known to G. A. Thompson, lay in the environs of the city of Antigua which he visited:[4]

I had obtained, through the obliging interference of Mr. Bayley, an order to the steward, who inhabited the chateau of the Marquis Ayzenena, to furnish me with accommodation, of which I gladly availed myself; for, as I before said, houses were extremely scarce, and there was no such thing as an inn in the place.

. . . The steward of the Marquess's chateau had a small plot of ground inclosed with mud walls near his cottage; and, seeing him busily employed, early one morning, I joined him, to observe what he was

4. Thompson, 1829, pp. 242, 249–51.

doing. He was planting cochineal: to those who are unacquainted with the process, it may be useful to state that this operation is dissimilar from any other mode of cultivation.

The *nopal* is a plant consisting of little stem, but expanding itself into wide thick leaves, more or less prickly according to its different kind: one or two of these leaves being set as one plant, at the distance of two or three feet square from each other, are inoculated with the cochineal, which, I scarcely need say, is an insect: it is the same as if you would take the blight off an apple or other common tree and rub a small portion of it on another tree free from the contagion, when the consequence would be that the tree so inoculated would become covered with the blight: a small quantity of the insects in question is sufficient for each plant, which, in proportion as it increases its leaves, is sure to be covered with the costly parasyte. When the plant is perfectly saturated, the cochineal is scraped off with great care. The plants are not very valuable for the first year, but, from questions I put to the steward about the produce, it appeared that they might be estimated as yielding after the second year, from a dollar to a dollar and a half profit on each plant.

Not far from the cochineal, and close also to the cattle estate described by Dunn, lay land where sugarcane was grown. Honey was generally preferred as a sweetener, for the sugar was not refined. Nevertheless, the making of brown sugar cakes called *panelas* occupied the attention of many. *Panelas* actually served more than the one purpose that Dunn, who described their production, had in mind:[5]

Returning for our mules, we met with the proprietor of the trapíche, who gave us a very hospitable reception, and shewed us his mill, the great wheel of which was turned by a considerable stream descending from the mountain, and forming two small falls, one of about ten feet and the other five. At this place he employs about sixteen men, who receive, some one shilling sterling, and others nine-pence, a-day, and are occupied in the manufacture of *panelas*. The process is very simple: the cane, which grows luxuriantly in the valley, is cut, and crushed between cylindrical rollers; the juice, which flows into the vat beneath, is then boiled, and, when arrived at a sufficient degree of consistency, is poured into small hollow wooden beds, where it cools, hardens, and forms a solid cake; in which state it is sold for the manufacture of spir-

5. Dunn, 1829, pp. 303–4.

its. For these lands the proprietor paid a rent of a hundred dollars annually: he had sown the cane and built the hut and mill at a very cheap rate; and at the time we visited was able to produce six hundred and eighty pounds daily, which, reckoning two hundred and eighty days to the year, afforded a hundred and ninety thousand four hundred pounds, . . . producing, at a real and a half for each panela of five pounds weight, a sum equal to 1,428*l*. sterling. That the manufacture of these coarse loaves is more profitable, in the present circumstances of the country, than that of sugars, there can be no doubt; and this accounts for the number of these mills which are spread over the face of the country. But it is melancholy to remember, that money thus acquired is gained at the expense of the whole community;—numerous manufactories of the material cause a similar increase in spirit-shops; and by the multiplicity of these it is evident that useful agriculture is impeded, the population demoralized, and the aborigines destroyed.

Sugarcane was one of the crops brought by the Spaniards from overseas. Before the Spaniards arrived, the isthmus enjoyed a variety of fruits, which yielded only slightly to the invasion of new species from Europe. Thompson learned what many a visitor to Central America since his time has apprehended—that the tropical environment does not automatically improve the quality of foods which are more at home in the temperate zone:[6]

I gave two rials, about a shilling, for a hat full of peaches, to some Indians who were carrying them to market, and found that I had paid considerably more than their value: they were pretty well flavoured, but by no means equal to the peaches cultivated in the common gardens of England, being more like apricots than peaches both in appearance and in taste. The delicious quality of what may be termed European fruits, found in these countries, has been greatly overrated; at least it was never my lot to meet with any species of them equal in flavour to those which are brought to perfection in the old hemisphere by the effects of cultivation.

Bananas were at home in the tropics (though they were apparently first brought by the Spaniards) and were widespread by the time of independence. No one had thought yet of growing them for the export

6. Thompson, 1829, pp. 293–94.

trade, but Thomas Young noticed how popular they were with the Black Caribs of the north coast of Honduras:[7]

> ... We observed thousands of banana trees growing spontaneously, the fruit of which is so much sought after by the natives, who come from very distant parts to Black River, to gather it. Suckers in any quantity can always be obtained here, which can be put in the ground at once, and will give but little further trouble. The banana, eight months after being planted, will begin to form in bunches, and in ten or eleven months the fruit may be gathered. When the stalk is cut, some shoots are left, and they bear in a few months; by this means a banana walk may be kept up, without any other trouble than now and then dressing the roots. The ripe fruit is highly esteemed, although it is apt to disagree with Europeans, if eaten shortly before or after taking spirits. The green fruit is cut into slices by the Spaniards, and exposed to the sun, and when rubbed, forms a kind of flour, of which they are fond.

The staff of life for most Central Americans remained what it had been before the Europeans arrived—for some, cakes made of maize; for others, bread made of cassava. The enterprising Caribs, who reached this coast long after the Spaniards and shortly before independence, made cassava bread so well they were able to sell it, as Orlando Roberts noted:[8]

> ... We ran down the coast to one of the principal Kharibee settlements, about twelve miles from Black River, were received with great kindness, and readily furnished with as many fowls, and as much fruit, Kharib bread, and other provisions, as we chose to have, for which they would scarcely accept any remuneration. The method of preparing this bread, a considerable quantity of which is sent to Belize, and other places for sale, is as follows:—Having selected from their extensive plantations, some of the largest and finest cassava roots, they are carefully skinned and washed; then grated upon large tin graters, procured for that purpose from the traders; the substance is then washed in clean water, which is frequently shifted and run off, to free the cassava, which is now of a brownish colour, from a strong acid liquor, said to be poisonous; the whole mass, when sufficiently whit-

7. Young, 1842, p. 95.
8. Roberts, 1827, pp. 272–73.

ened, is put into a long bag or basket, generally made of the spathes of a particular sort of tree; this basket is placed in a perpendicular position, between two posts; and, by the application of a lever, every drop of moisture is pressed out; the farinaceous substance is then dried in the sun, and either kept for use as a substitute for flour, or made into round cakes, of eighteen or twenty inches in diameter, and about a quarter of an inch in thickness, toasted upon thin iron plates, over a clear fire of wood-ashes. When properly prepared, these cakes will keep good for months, and, when new, taste pleasantly, and are a strong nourishing food. The flour is also used in hot water as gruel, made more or less thick, seasoned with salt and Chili pepper; or, sometimes, eaten with sugar-cane syrup.

The close relationship between Central America's agriculture and the remainder of its industry, chiefly commerce, was studied rather carefully by Roberts during his two detentions in Granada. His observations, made in 1822, are colored by the fact that independence for Nicaragua at that early date was more of a Guatemalan theory than a reality. Roberts' enthusiasm was based partly, it should be remembered, on his vision of the San Juan route as a bearer of traffic from distant parts of the globe:[9]

... The situation of this city between the lakes, and its central position in respect to the Atlantic and Pacific, afford great facilities for making it the depôt for the greatest commerce in South America, or perhaps in the world. It is well built; one side of the great square is chiefly formed by the principal church; a large monastery and a convent make up the greater part of another side; the guard-house, and soldiers barracks, a third; and the principal shops in the town, front the church, and complete the square. The streets are for the most part wide, and paved with stone; and, in some places, the footpaths are raised two feet above the level of the streets, and sheltered by the balconies and projecting roofs of the houses. Many of the houses are three stories high, and, as the streets intersect each other, form squares of buildings, the longest sides of which extend from east to west. The town stands on a gently rising ground, which contributes much to its cleanliness; and the principal streets are terminated by views of the hills in the neighbourhood, or mountains in the distance. The cross streets are narrower, but the houses in general are, like those of León,

9. *Ibid.,* pp. 234–37.

large, handsome, and convenient; the apartments lofty, and better furnished than is usual in Spanish towns. Granada is said to be celebrated for its cabinet ware, the workmen possessing many beautiful kinds of wood. They are obliged, however, to work with very inferior tools,—good edge-tools being much wanted. One of the most valuable pieces of furniture in the family room is generally a crucifix, and an image of the virgin and child, in a case, richly ornamented, and illuminated at night. There is a great variety of shops, for the sale of small wares, but no indications of a full supply of any thing like valuable goods. In the principal warehouses nothing was exposed in the windows, or otherwise; every thing appeared private, and concealed, and the depositories were not thrown open as at the Havannah, Buenos Ayres, and Lima. I was given to understand that the principal trade was entirely in the hands of a few old Spaniards, natives for the most part of Catalonia and Biscay, who contrived to have the offer of every cargo that arrived at San Juan; and their transactions were managed with such secrecy, as to preclude all chance of competition:—the native Creoles seldom or never receiving any notice of an arrival, until they saw the goods going into the warehouses, which, in appearance, almost resemble prisons, but are well stocked with the most valuable productions of the country, such as indigo, cochineal, sarsaparilla, cocoa, hides, barks, &c. The greater part of the retail trade of the place is, on market and holidays, carried on by the Creoles and other natives of the country, whose shops, as I before observed, are numerous; the commodities they vend, consist of a small assortment of dry goods and earthenware:—others, the places called pulperias, resemble the hucksters shops in England; and, in these places are sold bread, cheese, agua-ardiente, pottery, glass, sugar, sweetmeats, oil, and a variety of small wares; which are also vended by people in the public square, much in the manner of our travelling Jews and pedlars. The place seems poorly supplied with medicines, and the priest generally administers to both soul and body. Close to the lake there is a pleasant promenade, much frequented in the evening by the principal inhabitants; it commands a delightful prospect of the lake, and of the hattos in the neighborhood. . . . The Strand is generally covered by daybreak with linen. I have often seen one or two hundred women and girls washing clothes in the morning, so that whether in the evening, or morning, a walk to the lake is a cheerful recreation. Near the Playa, or Embarcadero, some enterprising individuals had undertaken to build a vessel, which, from the appearance of the frame laying on the spot, I should suppose to have been intended to carry fifty or sixty tons. When she was nearly finished it was discovered that the ground had sunk, so as to cause a rise, between the slip and the lake. The ground had afterwards been levelled, and every exertion made to launch the vessel; but so ignorant were they of the use of mechanical powers, that, after several fruitless attempts, they were obliged to take the vessel to pieces.

The markets, at Granada, are abundantly supplied with beef, pork, poultry, cheese, butter, and milk from the farms in the neighbourhood, at a very reasonable rate; and with a great variety of excellent fish, and water-fowl from the lake.

The neighbouring country and forests furnish game in abundance; wheat-flour is brought from Guatemala, and the northern provinces; but the bread, used in general by the poor and middling classes, is made of Indian corn, which is also preferred by many of the gentry. The common method of preparing it is by making it into small cakes, called Tortillas;—the grain is first put into a large earthen vessel containing a strong lye of wood ashes, or lime and water, to soften it and take off the husk; it is then put upon a stone made concave for the purpose, and bruised with a small stone roller, held firmly with both hands, and rolled backwards, and forwards, until the corn is bruised to a fine paste; it is then shaped into round flat cakes, and baked on an earthen pan, or flat iron plate; the young women show great cleanliness and activity in preparing it, and, when well toasted, it will keep good for many months.

Ahuachapán in the state of San Salvador carried on a commerce less pretentious than that of Granada, but nevertheless, only four years after the coming of independence, well in touch with the non-Spanish overseas world. At least, such is the notice rendered by Thompson, another enthusiast for the possibilities of international trade:[10]

Ahuachapán is the most considerable town between Sonsonate and the capital. . . . On entering it, the road was nearly blocked up by earthenware, which they had just been taking out of the kiln, and which consisted of utensils of all shapes and sizes for domestic use,— the same constituting one of the staple articles of the manufacture of the place. We alighted at one of the best houses in the town, belonging

10. Thompson, 1829, pp. 93–94.

to a respectable man of the name of Padillo. He was much older than his wife, who, although she had, now living with her, a family of five daughters and three sons, the eldest of whom was seventeen years of age, bore the vestiges of a clever, pretty little woman. She had, doubtlessly, been very handsome, for her little daughters, whose ages were from seven to fourteen, were strikingly so, and all of them very much resembling herself. Her husband was on a visit to the family to which I had letters in Guatemala. She managed the business, for there was a shop attached to the house, in which was sold almost every thing that the community could require, with great zeal and ability. Mixed with China crapes and India Bandanas were Irish linens and Manchester cottons; and Birmingham cutlery was exposed to sale on the same counter with the coarser implements which the forges of the natives could produce.

Toward the Caribbean side of the isthmus, the transportation of goods in trade with the exterior formed an important part of the economic life of Gualán, as described by Dunn:[11]

The inhabitants of Gualán are composed of agents employed in the transmission of goods to and from Guatimala, Omoa, and Izabal; mariners, who convey them by the river Motagua, in their pitpans; and agriculturists (the Indian population), who grow wheat and maize. There are also two potteries, which employ about twenty men in the manufacture of red tiles for the floors and roofs of the houses, and a few household utensils. The market is held daily in the *plaza*; but it is very irregularly supplied.

Thompson in observations in Guatemala City was able to make some judgment on the size of the external traffic:[12]

... I looked in at the Aduana, or Custom-house, to inquire about my baggage. ... The house itself is a large square building with cellars abutting from the inner sides, for the deposit of goods and merchandize. The courtyard was occupied with bales of cochineal, indigo, hides, and other articles of traffic: there was an apparent health and activity in the trade of this little republic, which filled the mind with pleasing anticipations of its increase, or, as the French would say, its

11. Dunn, 1829, pp. 50–51.
12. Thompson, 1829, pp. 139–40.

future destiny. The long room, if I may so call it, was occupied only by six clerks, but they were "all actively employed", (as the British Boards of Commissioners in their returns to the Treasury would say,) and there might have been as many more engaged in other parts of the establishment.

On his way to the capital city earlier, the same observer had had a chance to inspect some of the local traffic:[13]

... I passed a large drove of pigs; the largest I had ever seen in point of number, but the smallest with regard to size. They were of the narrow-haunched China breed, greatly extenuated towards the loins and tail, or, as Shakespeare says, with "marvellous thin hams", particularly hog-backed and long-snouted, but they looked clean and healthy, and were destined for the market of the metropolis; in which the consumption of them is very great, as mutton is only used as a dainty, on days of festivity; the sheep being preserved on account of their wool, and the swine being thus obliged to supply their place in the shambles.

James Wilson believed that the market for woolen goods was rather slight, perhaps because his perspective was limited to the metropolis:[14]

... A German, who was here lately, sold to one merchant 190 pieces of woollens; enough, in the opinion of Señor——, to serve the place for years. Woollen cloth is only worn by the genteeler classes, and, excepting by a few, by these only on holy-day occasions. It is true, indeed, that almost every individual, above the station of a muleteer, has a cloth cloak; but these are only used when they have occasion to go out, and consequently may last for years.

Distinct ethnic groups on the isthmus, of course, followed their own ways of commerce which often involved diverse habits. With the Black Caribs, described again by Young, the outstanding trait besides that of industriousness was the prominent place in the economy accorded to women:[15]

13. *Ibid.*, p. 129.
14. Wilson, 1829, p. 133.
15. Young, 1842, pp. 123–24.

... When a Carib takes a wife, he fells a plantation, and builds a house; the wife then takes the management, and he becomes a gentleman at large till the following year, when another plantation has to be cleared. The wife attends these plantations with great care, perseverance and skill, and in the course of twelve or fifteen months has every description of bread kind in use amongst them, and as the products are entirely her own, she only keeps sufficient at home for her husband and family, and disposes of the rest to purchase clothes and other necessaries. Just before Christmas the women engage several creers, freight them with rice, beans, yams, plantains, &c. for Trujillo and Belize, and hire their husbands and others as sailors. It is the custom, when a woman cannot do all the work required in the plantation, for her to hire her husband, and pay him two dollars per week. The women travel considerable distances to their plantations, and carry their productions in a kind of wicker basket. I have known them walk from far beyond Monkey Apple Town to Fort Wellington, a distance of forty miles, to exchange their baskets of provisions for salt, calico, &c. Men accompany them on their trading excursions, but never by any chance carry the burthens, thinking it far beneath them. In the dry seasons, the women collect fire wood, which they stack in sheltered places, to be ready for the wet norths. Industry and forethought are peculiar traits of character in Carib women, consequently they easily surround themselves with necessaries and comforts.

The men can hew and plant, hunt and fish, erect a comfortable house, build a good boat, make the sails, &c.; some are capital tailors, and others good carpenters; altogether there cannot be a more useful body of men. They often go to the various mahogany works ... and hire themselves as mahogany cutters, for which, by their strength and activity, they are well fitted; they hire for five or six months, sometimes longer, for eight to twelve dollars per month, and rations. I have known some Caribs of superior manual power, and who understood the whole routine of mahogany cutting, obtain as much as fifteen and sixteen dollars per month. On the expiration of their engagement, they return to their homes laden with useful articles, and invariably well dressed. I saw a Carib belonging to Cape Town that had just returned from Belize, who sported a pair of cloth boots, a white hat, black coat, white trowsers, a fancy coloured shirt, a pair of splendid braces and an umbrella.

Mining was the occupation which seems to have intrigued more men with capital to invest than any other save agriculture and commerce. Some travelers' accounts speak excitedly of new (chiefly untried) mineral prospects, while others tend to deprecate the whole business as a kind of mirage. J. L. Stephens found droll humor rather than excitement in the operation which he came across near San Mateo, Costa Rica, as he climbed the Cerros del Aguacate:[16]

... The road had been much improved lately, but the ascent was steep, wild, and rugged. As we toiled up the ravine, we heard before us a loud noise, that sounded like distant thunder, but regular and continued, and becoming louder as we advanced; and at length we came out on a small clearing, and saw on the side of the mountain a neat frame building of two stories, with a light and graceful balcony in front; and alongside was the thundering machine which had startled us by its noise. Strangers from the other side of the Atlantic were piercing the sides of the mountain, and pounding its stones into dust to search for gold. The whole range, the very ground which our horses spurned with their hoofs, contained that treasure for which man forsakes kindred and country.

I rode up to the house and introduced myself to Don Juan Bardh, the superintendent, a German. ... It was about two o'clock, and excessively hot. The house was furnished with chairs, sofa, and books, and had in my eyes a delightful appearance; but the view without was more so. The stream which turned the immense pounding-machine had made the spot, from time immemorial, a descansadera, or resting-place for muleteers. All around were mountains, and directly in front one rose to a great height, receding, and covered to the top with trees.

Don Juan Bardh had been superintendent of the Quebrada del Ingenio for about three years. The Company which he represented was called the **Anglo Costa Rican Economical Mining Company.** It had been in operation these three years without losing anything, which was considered doing so well that it had increased its capital, and was about continuing on a larger scale. The machine, which had just been set up, was a new German patent, called a *Machine for extracting Gold by the Zillenthal Patent Self-acting Cold Amalgamation Process* (I believe that I have omitted nothing), and its great value was that it required no preliminary process, but by one continued and simple

16. Stephens, 1842, 1:345–47.

operation extracted the gold from the stone. It was an immense wheel of cast iron, by which the stone, as it came from the mountain, was pounded into powder; this passed into troughs filled with water, and from them into a reservoir containing vases, where the gold detached itself from the other particles, and combined with the quicksilver with which the vases were provided.

There were several mines under Don Juan's charge, and after dinner he accompanied me to that of Corrallio, which was the largest, and, fortunately, lay on my road. After a hot ride of half an hour, ascending through thick woods, we reached the spot.

According to the opinion of the few geologists who have visited that country, immense wealth lies buried in the mountain of Aguacate; and so far from being hidden, the proprietors say, its places are so well marked that all who search may find. The lodes or mineral veins run regularly north and south, in ranges of greenstone porphyry with strata of basaltic porphyry, and average about three feet in width. In some places side-cuts or lateral excavations are made from east to west, and in others shafts are sunk until they strike the vein. The first opening we visited was a side-cut four feet wide, and penetrating two hundred and forty feet before it struck the lode; but it was so full of water that we did not enter. Above it was another cut, and higher still a shaft was sunk. We descended the shaft by a ladder made of the trunk of a tree, with notches cut in it, until we reached the vein, and followed it with a candle as far as it was worked. It was about a yard wide, and the sides glittered—but it was not with gold; they were of quartz and feldspar, impregnated with sulphuret of iron, and gold in such small particles as to be invisible to the naked eye. The most prominent objects in these repositories of wealth were naked workmen with pickaxes, bending and sweating under heavy sacks of stones.

It was late in the afternoon when I came out of the shaft. Don Juan conducted me by a steep path up the side of the mountain, to a small table of land, on which was a large building occupied by miners. The view was magnificent: below was an immense ravine; above, perched on a point, like an eagle's nest, the house of another superintendent. . . . I waited till my mules came up, and with many thanks for his kindness, bade Don Juan farewell.

Central America for some time, however, had been using its own silver to produce its own coinage, and did not plan to give up this practice now that independence had arrived. Thompson was interested in the process:[17]

> ... I visited the Mint, and was shewn the whole establishment by the director, Don Benito Muñozo. It is a moderately sized building, and there were two presses employed in coining the new money of the republic: the greater part of the small silver currency, at this time, consisted of money called *masququina,* or pieces of ragged silver of all shapes and dimensions, varying between half the size of a sixpence and half-a-crown: it was almost impossible to know their relative values: the public, however, had no difficulty in doing so, by the assistance of some coarse and, in most cases, almost obliterated marks upon them. These pieces of tokens, for they had neither the shape nor appearance of coin, had been issued, from time immemorial, at the two provincial mints of Nicaragua and Honduras, and, in spite of the sweatings and loppings which they had evidently undergone, continued to pass, for their nominal value, with such good faith on the part of the people, that I had frequently pieces given back into my hands, as being only of the value of half reals, whilst others, of half the size, were selected as being known to represent whole ones. It is not to be wondered at, that the new coinage was eagerly sought after. Doña Vicente, my kind hostess, was particularly anxious to take a quantity down with her to Sonsonate; and I procured her some for that purpose, in exchange for golden ounces.
>
> The Mint, as at present established, is quite sufficient for the little work which it has to perform. There had been some talk of erecting a steam-engine instead of the clumsy apparatus which ... is put into action by the power of mules; but, as there is a good supply of water within two hundred yards of the place, I pointed out the cheapness and facility of employing that element in lieu of the present system and of that proposed; and, before I left the capital, I had the pleasure to find that the plan suggested had undergone some discussion in the proper quarters and was looked upon as feasible and advantageous.

One of the problems facing the new nation, making difficult the development of a viable economy, was the lack of easy access from the Atlantic side of the isthmus to the centers of population. The routes from Omoa and Izabal to Guatemala City were long and arduous with their primitive traveling conditions. That from San Juan

17. Thompson, 1829, pp. 211–13.

del Norte to Granada was really better, as Roberts said, except that an arrival in Nicaragua was of little avail in contacting settlements of the states on either side. The San Juan River route was little noticed by outsiders during these decades, but Roberts' description of the craft employed (his observations being made while he was in detention) shows that transportation on this river was really well developed:[18]

I had the liberty of laying myself at full length in the after part of the boat, the Indians being kept forward, so that no communication could take place among us. These boats are from thirty-five, to forty feet in length; the bottom, and sides, to the height of three feet, is composed of a single piece of mahogany or cedar, generally the latter, rounded similar to that of a canoe, without a keel; the stern square. Their risings consist of two planks from sixteen to eighteen inches broad; and from three and a half, to four inches thick; reaching from stem to stern, and strongly secured, as well as the bottom, by very stout timbers of the wild calabash, bally, or Santamaria wood; in other respects they are fitted up like a ship's launch, their oars are stout poles, about twelve feet in length, at the end of which is a piece of board, four feet long, and eighteen inches wide, tapered off something in the shape of an oar blade;—these oars are secured to the thowel by straps of raw hide.[19] A space of about eight feet in length at the afterpart of these bongos is planted, or decked, within about a foot or eighteen inches under the risings; and over this deck is thrown an arched awning of raw hides, much in the shape of coverings for waggons in England, completely sheltering the passengers from the sun and weather. These boats are from six to seven feet wide, draw from three to five feet water, and are pulled by from sixteen to twenty-two oars. On an average they carry about sixteen tons, and are the largest craft hitherto used on this river. The Padrone or master, and the crew, were natives of Granada *de Nicaragua*, hardy, stout, raw-boned fellows, descendants of Indians; and the boatmen wrought during the day, entirely naked.

In Guatemala City, Wilson in one of his brief notes gave an idea of the remoteness of that capital by the swiftest means of communication:[20]

18. Roberts, 1827, pp. 177–78.
19. "Thowel"=thole. The Santa Maria tree (*Calophyllum calaba*) is an evergreen. "Bally" presumably refers to the name *siruaballi* or *silver balli*, which is used for a variety of trees of the genera *Nectandra*, *Ocotea*, and *Aniba*.
20. Wilson, 1829, pp. 94–95.

June 13th.— . . . There is an individual in Guatemala, who is employed as a courier, that can go from this to Izabal and return in seven days, on foot. The latest date of letters received from England on the 10th current (by way of Belize) is March 28, thus taking seventy-five days between London and Guatemala.

Wilson touched lightly the chief problem of those who might have preferred to ride in wheeled vehicles, had there been any roads:[21]

. . . I saw a coach, a few days since, which was brought from England thirty-five years ago, and cost 2800 dollars.

Another comment from the same pen offers some comparison of prices in the Guatemalan economy:[22]

. . . Mr. —— has purchased a Spanish cloak, the cloth of which cost him equal to forty-eight shillings. In England it might be worth from seventeen to eighteen shillings. Boots cost only three dollars; but they are not nearly so good as English, either in the quality of the leather or finish.

Wilson was interested also in the cost of housing for people in the wealthier bracket of society:[23]

. . . Have heard it stated that an individual has offered 15,000lbs. of indigo in exchange for a house in this place. The house we reside in is among the most commodious that I have seen in Guatemala, and the rent of it is only £100 sterling. I understand houses in general, when rented out, do not at all pay any thing like a remunerating interest on the original cost. Individuals, however, who are able, prefer, notwithstanding, purchasing houses to renting them, as they have thus a fixed residence, and are not liable to be ejected at the will or caprice of another: instances are rare of individuals removing from one house to another.

The moderate figure for rent (per year) was matched, Wilson pointed out earlier, by a modest outlay for food. His remarks in this

21. *Ibid.,* p. 111.
22. *Ibid.,* p. 89.
23. *Ibid.,* pp. 137–38.

connection enable the reader, by pondering Wilson's words and the inferences that may be drawn from them, to grasp an idea of the scale of living of some persons who did not fare so well:[24]

... Mr.—— has purchased a Spanish cloak, the cloth of which cost —— and her aunt, a number of particulars, in regard to household expenditure in this place. They were speaking of an individual who gave his servant ten rials (five shillings) a day to procure provisions for the table, his family consisting of eight persons. This, they said, was too much. I notice that Señora —— every night after supper, gives money to the servant; and I have more than once perceived that the amount was ten rials; this, I have no doubt, is to procure provisions for the following day. And, considering that no fewer than fifteen individuals mess in the house, this is a very moderate sum indeed to procure beef, bread, rice, fish, vegetables, and fruit, and these not in scanty allowance. The table groans under abundance—at least I am almost inclined to groan when pressed, with an urgency that will scarcely admit of a refusal, to partake of what appears an endless variety of dishes.

... We learn also that the rent of the premises, which serve both for a dwelling-house and warehouse, is 500 dollars per annum. The house forms a square, having a large open space in the centre, and contains ten spacious rooms, besides kitchen, servants' apartments, stable, &c. There are also within the premises two large reservoirs for water, which are kept constantly full. The principal servant, the cook, is paid at the rate of thirty-five dollars per annum.

24. *Ibid.*, pp. 96–97.

Chapter 4

Learning

COMMENT on the intellectual world in the ten travel accounts here considered is as scarce as comment on the world of business is plentiful. One obvious reason for this is the low intellectual attainment of most persons on the isthmus at the time of independence. But it is a mistake to think that there was nothing to talk about in this realm. The fact is that the travelers themselves, with but few exceptions, were little interested in Central America's efforts along this line, and so spent little trouble investigating them. Their friends whom they mention by name from among the isthmian population are either hosts or traveling companions or politicians, almost exclusively. G. W. Montgomery, who was the best prepared of the group of writers to appreciate a native author when he found one, stayed too short a time to make many acquaintances. Of the others, the most bookish seems to have been the stringent Henry Dunn.

On his way to the capital, Dunn noticed that in the time span of six years of independence some thought had been given to the idea of instruction in Gualán, but so far no school had materialized:[1]

No provision is made for the education of the people, and the children grow up in ignorance, and oftentimes uncontrouled. Soon after the Revolution, a schoolmaster was sent from Guatimala; but as he could not get paid by the government, and the people were not disposed to support him, the doors of his establishment were soon closed.

1. Dunn, 1829, p. 50.

Farther along the same path, and twelve years later, Stephens did find a school following the Lancasterian system of training:[2]

> At Zacapa, for the first time, we saw a schoolhouse. It was a respectable-looking building, with columns in front, and against the wall hung a large card, headed,
>
> > "1st Decurion (a student who has the care of ten other students).
> > 2d Decurion.
> > MONITOR, &c.
>
> "Interior regulation for the good government of the school of first letters of this town, which ought to be observed strictly by all the boys composing it," &c.,
>
> with a long list of complicated articles, declaring the rewards and punishments. The school, for the government of which these regulations were intended, consisted of five boys, two besides the decurions and monitor. It was nearly noon, and the master, who was the clerk of the alcalde, had not yet made his appearance. The only books I saw were a Catholic prayer-book and a translation of Montesquieu's Spirit of the Laws. The boys were fine little fellows, half white; and with one of them I had a trial of sums in addition, and then of exercises in handwriting, in which he showed himself very proficient, writing in Spanish, in a hand which I could not mistake, "Give me sixpence."

In the capital, of course, there was instruction even at the time of Dunn's visit, though Dunn was not impressed by it:[3]

> ... There are two public or endowed schools for boys: one of which, belonging to the church, was established in the year 1548; and the other, which is under the direction of the municipality, about a century later. Each is endowed with an annual salary for the master, of about five hundred dollars. These situations are at present held by two ignorant old men, who conduct the schools on the ancient Spanish system. A great portion of the time is occupied in recitations, and in learning what they term the Christian Doctrine. Under such direction, the children, after years of attendance, are scarcely able to read or write decently. The united number on the books is about four hundred; but they attend very irregularly.

2. Stephens, 1842, 1:70–71.
3. Dunn, 1829, pp. 104–5.

In each of the convents girls are taught to read, as well as to sew with the greatest neatness. The boys of the higher and middle classes can generally read and write; but, among girls, the latter is a rare accomplishment. In both cases, the knowledge imparted is unaccompanied by that moral and religious instruction which alone can make it valuable.

The university evoked no greater enthusiasm from the same pen:[4]

The history of the university is not very interesting. . . . Juarros speaks of examinations in surgery, of a royal cabinet of natural history, of schools for the mathematics, and a college of physicians.[5] All these things *may* have existed, but in the present day they are unknown: the examinations have ceased, the cabinet is without specimens, and the college of physicians and the schools for mathematics are alike destitute of students and professors. . . .

In connection with the university, there are twelve professorships, and an academical senate of fifty doctors. It is needless to enumerate the chairs: they are of Latin, philosophy, theology, morals, &c. What the precise mode of imparting instruction may be, matters little: it is sufficient to know that the students generally leave the college with similar acquirements to those Gil Blas possessed when he departed from the university of Salamanca.[6]

Dunn's deprecations continued as he turned to the area of printing and books, but he also found room for a bit of admiration:[7]

To name the word Literature in connection with this part of Spanish America, seems almost ridiculous; yet a slight sketch of the labours of the printing presses of Guatimala may not be altogether uninteresting. At what period the art was first introduced, it is impossible to say; but it must have been exercised in the old city above a century ago; since a treatise on practical arithmetic, by Father Padilla, a secular priest, was printed there in the year 1732.[8] Whether any other work equally useful has issued from the same press since that period, is a problem it perhaps would be difficult to solve. Its chief occupation is to reprint

4. *Ibid.,* pp. 68–69.
5. See Ch. 1 n.59.
6. Alain René le Sage, *Histoire de Gil Blas de Santillane.*
7. Dunn, 1829, pp. 109–12.
8. The first press arrived in Guatemala in 1660.

papers from Rome; to publish the letters and charges of the Archbishop, with now and then a declamatory sermon; and to supply the good Catholics with little volumes of prayers and devotional exercises for peculiar times and seasons. Since the Revolution, however, three other presses have been established, which find employment in printing the newspapers. A number of these publications have at various times seen the light; but with the greater part it has been but to be born and die. At present they are three in number, and published weekly: one called The Gazette of the Government; another, The Gazette of the State; and the third, *El Indicador*. All these support the measures of the present administration, are equally dull and uninteresting, and have a very limited sale. No news makes its appearance in any of them until it has been generally known in the city for a month, excepting official government papers, which are exceedingly long and tedious; and with these their columns are chiefly filled. As the presses obtain little other employment, they of course are not very profitable to their owners.

The last book published, was a volume of poetical fables, by a Dr. Goyena, who styles himself a Son of Central America. These possess considerable merit, and display a degree of talent which, under proper cultivation, would have raised their author to eminence. The sale of them, however, has been scarcely sufficient to cover his expenses. . . .[9] A system of stenography has also been prepared by one of the priests; but, finding it impossible to obtain a sufficient number of subscribers to defray expenses, he has wisely abstained from printing.

The supply of books is by no means deficient, and rather exceeds the demand than otherwise. Spanish editions of heavy books—such as Universal Histories, &c.—may be found in the stores of the old merchants; and lighter works, chiefly translations from the French, and many of them very exceptionable, are to be met with in two or three different shops, opened by agents of French booksellers. Mr. Ackermann, of London, has certainly rendered a much greater service to the country, in the class of books and prints which he has endeavoured to introduce. His elementary catechisms are exceedingly valuable; and his drawings and fancy articles will probably tend to foster, if not to create, a taste for the fine arts.

---

9. Rafael García Goyena was born in Ecuador but passed most of his life in Guatemala, where he died in 1823. His *Fábulas y poesías varias* was published posthumously there in 1825, a fact which raises questions concerning Dunn's statement on expenses.

Later, a preference for the British influence over the French is again made obvious:[10]

> ... X. called, and, finding me alone, ridiculed the approaching procession (Corpus Christi) as absurd. He is evidently an infidel: having never seen religion in a simpler and purer form, he considers it altogether a system of priestcraft.—Visited his house the following day. The first book I saw was Voltaire's Philosophical Dictionary. Numbers of French books, although prohibited, have been introduced here. French novels of the worst description are to be met with in abundance: most of these are printed cheaply, with plates wretchedly coloured. Subsequently he received of me Bogue's Essay, and a copy of the New Testament, both of which he promised to read with care and attention.[11]

Dunn, try as hard as he might, was prevented by his own narrowness in matters of religion from appreciating the culture around him in all of its scope. Thompson, a more outgoing man and one more determined to see the best there was in Guatemalan society, found his visits to author José Cecilio del Valle quite exciting:[12]

> Sunday, 5th. Called again on Valle. I found him seated on a sofa extending the whole length of the end of a saloon, and conversing with three or four visitors; two of whom were Englishmen; one, Mr. John Hines, who had come out to propose a loan on the part of Messrs. Simmonds, and two Frenchmen.[13] After they had left, he showed me into a small library, so completely filled with books, in large masses, not only around the walls but on the floor, that it was with difficulty we could pick a way through the apartment. He sat himself down to a small writing table, which was also profusely stored with manuscripts and printed papers, from which he selected for me, with a zeal of earnestness and gratification heightened by the enthusiasm of his natural disposition, some documents which he had been preparing or collecting for my use. Amongst these, was a detailed statement of the branches of the revenue, preceding and subsequent to the revolution;—the bases of

10. Dunn, 1829, p. 128.
11. David Bogue (1750–1825) was a Scotch minister who helped found the London Missionary Society, the British and Foreign Bible Society, and the Religious Tract Society.
12. Thompson, 1829, pp. 208–11.
13. Regarding John Hines, see Ch. 1 n.77.

the constitution;—a plan for a factory of tobacco in Gualán—and another for the settling with foreigners the territory bordering upon the port and river of San Juan in Nicaragua. He had all the mania of authorship about him: proofs and revises and lumps of manuscript, folios and quartos and octavos, opened or interlarded with scraps of memoranda, were scattered, in profusion, over the table: it was as though he were inordinate in his requisitions at the feast of intellect. He gave me paper after paper and document after document, till I began to feel my appetite satiated at the very sight of them: they were more than I could have duly digested even had I delayed my stay in the country twice as long as I intended: I, however, took home with me as many of them as I could conveniently carry, and the rest he had the kindness to send home for me. Our being mutually engaged in researches after that sort of information to which my inquiries were particularly directed, constituted, I presume, the preliminary to that friendship which so eagerly commenced, and has since existed between this Andean Cicero and so humble a person as myself. I believe I much contributed to his feelings on this point, by presenting him with a copy of my American Dictionary, which I fortunately had with me: he expressed much satisfaction at receiving it, and no less surprise; for, although he had heard of the work, he was not aware, he said, that I was the author of it.[14]

Meager as were the pedagogical foundations of the new nation, José del Valle and men like him were saying important things in the realm of ideology, and these have been preserved in writing. Some of their reasoning took the form of history, while some made its way into essays and poems. In the fields of practical science, however, Central America had to struggle to keep up with Europe and usually lagged behind. The most obvious illustration of this fact lay in the practice of medicine. Dunn had occasion to make relevant comments during his stay on the cattle estate near Santa Catarina Pinula:[15]

During our stay in this house, one of the family was suddenly taken ill; and a messenger was immediately dispatched to Guatimala for the medical man, who arrived two days afterwards, to see his patient nearly recovered. This dilatory mode of procedure is universal. In country cases, the physician generally comes when the patient is either convalescent or buried. The individual who made his appearance on

14. See Ch. 1 n. 57.
15. Dunn, 1829, pp. 295–96. See above, pp. 229–32.

this occasion was considered the first of his profession: after the usual excuses for delay, he proceeded to unpack his little box of drugs, which contained purges, tonics, and vomits of every description; and, taking his patient's pulse, discoursed most learnedly, and at some length, upon the nature and cause of the disease, which he alternately attributed to nerves, vapours, and irritations. For this sapient essay, and sixpence worth of drugs, he received two ounces of gold. He passed the evening with us, and introduced Gall and Spurzheim's theory, of which he was a zealous disciple: new organs were discovered in new places, and localities given to the old ones, widely different from those which Dr. Gall has chosen for them.[16] But with his employers he passed for a most erudite physician, and that was sufficient. . . . Were a modest and intelligent foreigner to settle here, he would meet with little encouragement: prejudices would be strong against him; and, if he did not talk of nerves and vapours, he would get no practice.

That Europeans were not always ahead in their medical knowledge, however, appears evident in Thompson's discussion of the curative effects of guaco vines:[17]

The guaco, with its parasitical tendrils, clinging to the gigantic trees which girt the path, assures us of the presence of the most noxious serpents; for, where-ever these are found, the natives tell you that the guaco, the unfailing antidote to all their poisons, is also at hand. The root and branches of this plant, which greatly resembles the vine, divested of its foliage, are equally effective; and its power is so instantaneous and astonishing, that, had not the stories of its efficacy been repeated by persons of veracity who have tried its effect on their persons, I could hardly credit them. Some of the snakes here are so venomous that the person bitten generally dies in the course of twenty minutes: if, however, he be provided with the guaco, he bites a bit, and applies the saliva to the part: he also swallows the saliva arising from the mastication, for a few hours, and he need have no further apprehension; he is quite well.

A young man of the name of Rascon, who accompanied me to England, . . . told me that he has taken up in the palm of his hand that

16. Franz Joseph Gall (1758–1828) and Johann Caspar Spurzheim (1776–1832) were German phrenologists whose theories were very popular in Europe at the time.

17. Thompson, 1829, pp. 65–68. The name *guaco* is applied to two vines, one of them *Mikania guaco*, the other *Aristolochia maxima*, a birthwort.

dreadful little viper called the tamaulpas, the bite of which is instant death, and that the reptile became instantly inert and torpid, because he had in his hand a small piece of this wonderful plant.[18] Another person, whose servant had been bitten by the same kind of snake, was dying of a mortification which had taken place in his arm: a strong decoction of the root in brandy was poured down his throat, and also applied to the part affected: he was cured, and never afterwards felt any effect from the wound. Might not this wonderful remedy be applied to cases of hydrophobia? Not to speak of its beneficial qualities in cases of agues, dysentery, fever, and generally all those maladies which are peculiar to the human constitution in the places where it is found, I can answer for its being of a very harmless nature, for I took it by the advice and after the example of the English gentlemen, almost daily, with a view of preventing sickness, and must conclude it had the effect, never having suffered from indisposition whilst residing at Sonsonate, or other places where the climate is considered to be prejudicial to European constitutions.

18. Thompson's "tamaulpas" is presumably the *tamagás* or fer-de-lance; see Ch. 1 n. 51.

Chapter 5

Recreation and the Arts

THE REALM of the arts stands between that of learning and that of the economy in the amount of interest it stirred among the ten travelers. The more sophisticated forms of art received little attention, there being only a few of the observers who could appreciate the small activity there was. The spirit of isthmian recreation was gauged through fairly frequent attendance by the visitors at dances and the theater. James Wilson and Henry Dunn were prevented by religious scruples from very full enjoyment of such public events and frankly frowned upon most of the people's playtime habits, including the bullfight, the cockfight, the card-playing, and the gambling. Both of them nevertheless managed to take in the theater. The diplomats mixed more freely, as is generally the custom, and seemed even to enjoy themselves.

George Alexander Thompson was one of those who placed few strictures upon the customs of Central American society. Thompson did not, however, find life in the capital city itself exciting:[1]

> ... There is about half a mile out of the town, a *plaza de toros,* or theatre for bull-fights: it was now closed, as the sports always take place in the afternoon, and this being the wet season, they were here suspended, in the same manner as in Mexico, until the dry weather should set in: the boxes are covered with a slight wooden roof, sufficient to afford a shade from the sun, but very penetrable by the wet, and the lower circles being completely exposed both to one and the other, the amusement is very properly adjourned until a more convenient sea-

1. Thompson, 1829, pp. 305–6.

son: accordingly, there was no bull-fight during my residence in the capital. This and the theatre are the only two public amusements which the place affords; but the deficiency is made up by the pic-nic or gipsying parties. . . . : besides these, were occasionally little *tertullas*, or evening assemblies, enlivened with dancing and music, but rarely with any expensive collation. . . .

For real gaiety incorporating gallantry, one would repair from Guatemala City to Amatitlán at the time when the moneyed families were going there to put cares aside:[2]

During the whole of my journey, I had scarcely experienced one drop of wet; and, now, the rain poured down in such torrents, that I could hardly cross the way without being nearly drenched. There was no carriage or conveyance in the place, and, hardly, an umbrella, which was a great oversight, as the inhabitants ought to have learnt, without any almanack to tell them, to "expect much rain about this time." Indeed, the regularity and precision, with which these showers fall, when they once begin for the season, are so great, that, by the assistance of a tolerable watch, and a good horse, you may always escape them. The present tornado, unexpected as it was, seemed very little to disarrange or inconvenience the party assembled: some walked quietly through it, whilst others laughed and chatted in the passage and door-way of the house, as if prudently, though inconsiderately, waiting for its abatement: the inanimate part of creation was differently affected: the parched ground bubbled and sputtered like a drunken toper; the lanky banana crouched down and riggled like an invalid in a shower bath; and the red tiles were deserting their ranks one by one, like bad soldiers, leaving the way open to the enemy. Whilst the squall was at its height, I saw two horsemen come dashing up the street, at full speed: they stopt at the door of the cock-pit: they were each covered with a large mantle; and, without alighting, had caught up, in their arms, a damsel, a-piece, who adjusted themselves, with wonderful activity, on the pommels of the saddles: it was still raining profusely, but the mantles were thrown round the young ladies with such skill, and so completely enveloped them with their gallant knights, who darted off again, at a gallop, that I concluded they must have reached their homes in an instant, and probably without much

2. *Ibid.*, pp. 169–71. For the beginnings of this side-journey, see above, pp. 79–80.

inconvenience. The gentlemen when they had set down, returned to take up, in the same manner, till the whole of the party was thus disposed of, or had found other means of reaching their respective abodes. There was something both romantic and classical in the sight: every body has heard of the knights of old carrying off their inamoratas, and of the Romans stealing away their Sabine wives; but few can have an idea of the grace and facility with which the operation may be performed, who have not witnessed the above specimen of Guatemalian horsemanship.

Before the storm and its evocation of the strong tie between the man of society and his horse, Thompson attended an Amatitlán dance whose setting comes alive in his words:[3]

... I was asked if I should like to dance. There were nothing danced but waltzes, and I must say they were performed with great delicacy and elegance. The figures and attitudes were even more varied and multiplied than I had seen them at Mexico: there were present some of the noblest families of the place, and two or three of those of the ministry....

I had the honour of being introduced to Don José de Beteta, minister of finance: he was, here, fulfilling the part of a looker on, a character more necessary in a ball-room than the world gives them credit for; for, crowding, as they are accustomed to do, about the outer ranks of the dancers, they serve as a screen to the blunders of the awkward and diffident, and excite, by their notice, the exertions of those who dance for applause, in the ill-dissembled confidence of their pretensions:— neither pretensions nor confidence were wanting on the present occasion. The music consisted of eight guitars, played with wonderful effect: for the musicians took different parts, and seemed, occasionally, almost to forget they were playing the same tune; so strongly marked were the variations of each performer: but the effect was delightful, and the precision with which they kept their time, considering how they were travelling away from each other, very remarkable....

The scene was now all lively and exhilarating: about thirty couple, as many as the room would conveniently accommodate, were moving in graceful circles around it, impelled according to, what Newton calls,

3. Thompson, 1829, pp. 160–64. The description begins above, pp. 80–82.

though he was a philosopher, and knew nothing about waltzing, "the ratio of their centrifugal forces and the respective influence of their attractions." The door leading into the street was crowded by a motley group of the holiday company, who had sufficient curiosity to witness the proceedings of their betters, but too much modesty or diffidence to follow their example. Two or three of the front rows of this "observant class of the community" as Washington Irving has it, were squatted down in front of the door, forming a semi-circle before it; behind them were children, who could just peep over their heads; next to them, some children of a larger growth, and, behind them, standing on tiptoe, some of a larger still: the scantiness of their dress, and their exposure to the ungenial blast, as it rushed through the aperture, to equalize the temperature of the heated apartment, reminded me of a botanical show of Flemish flowers, in the month of March;—where few of them survive the exhibition; and it appeared to me that this innocent assemblage, who were caught by curiosity, would be indemnified by catching something in return, if it was only—a cold. I fell into conversation with Don Jose de Beteta: he was (for I regret to say he is since dead) a man of unimpeachable character for integrity: his abilities, though not of the first order, were respectable and adequate to the discharge of his official duties: he promised to draw up for me a report on the state of their revenue and finance, and I took the liberty of suggesting a few points with respect to the plan and contents of the proposed documents. My attention was occupied the rest of the evening by the dancers. All was over by eleven, and, in the course of half an hour after, a dead silence pervaded the whole village of Amatitlán. Just as I was dropping to sleep, I heard the sound of music, at a distance: at first, it seemed but the vibrations of harmony which the ear carries away with it from a ball, and which, like other doubtful-gotten property, is often very troublesome: it presently became more distinct, and, at last, stopped before our house, where it continued to play for an hour. It consisted of two guitars and a violin; and, by the peculiarity of some of the notes, I concluded it was executed by gentlemen-performers. This proved to be the case: they were serenading the black-eyed, amiable, little daughter of our hostess, whom I could, now, hear bustling about in her apartment, and acknowledging the compliment, which was paid to her, by a short parley held between her and her Lotharios through the iron-barred lattice of her balcony window.

If Thompson was right in judging that all the dances at Amatitlán were waltzes, matters were somewhat different thirteen years later in San Salvador when diplomat George Washington Montgomery was in attendance:[4]

> ... I went to a private ball, and had an opportunity of seeing some of the belles and fashionables of St. Salvador. The ladies were well dressed, though not exactly with that elegant simplicity which a good taste would suggest. They exhibited that passion for finery, jewels, and bright colours, so prevalent in the country. Some of them were very pretty, and of those that were not, nearly all had the advantage of being finely formed. They danced the old Spanish country-dances that are now going out of fashion in Spain, as also quadrilles and waltzes, and their performance in them was sufficiently correct and graceful.

The marimba, hallmark as it is of twentieth-century Guatemalan music and well liked throughout the isthmus, was scarcely mentioned by the travelers of these decades and nowhere accorded a position of dignity and attention.[5] In private parties in the finer Guatemalan homes, it was evidently the piano and the guitar which provided the chief entertainment in the experience of Thompson:[6]

> In the evening I went to a *tertulla* at Señor Castro's: his little daughter played and sung prettily; but her piano, which, by the bye, seemed to be greatly prized, was very old and indifferent, although it was marked, "New Patent, by Astor, 79, Cornhill."

> ... This being the octave of Corpus Christi, great feastings and revels were renewed throughout the city: I accompanied my friends to dine with a highly respectable family of the name of Gutierrez: the dinner was altogether Spanish both as to the number and quality of the dishes. The young ladies of this family were very musical; they sung and accompanied each other both with the piano and the guitar in a style equal to any I had witnessed in these countries; besides which the piano was a tolerably good one. The Padre Ramon Solis, the confessor of the family, a deputy of the congress and much appre-

---

4. Montgomery, 1839, p. 104.
5. Dunn mentioned (above, p. 110) "some lady" playing a popular air upon a "wretched" marimba, though he did not necessarily mean that all marimbas were wretched, since he spoke of a "still worse" piano.
6. Thompson, 1829, pp. 192–93, 218–19.

ciated for his talents, was also of the party, and contributed greatly to the entertainment, as he sung remarkably well, and was complete master of the guitar, accompanying himself sometimes upon that instrument and, at others, upon the piano or base-viol.

On the Mosquito Coast, Orlando Roberts found no pianos, no guitars, no bass viols, no marimbas, no violins—but there were two other instruments he noticed:[7]

I may here observe, that the English drum is the principal musical instrument of the Mosquito men, who beat it with as much dexterity, as the most practised European drummer; it came into use when the British forces were on the Mosquito Shore, and has been a great favourite ever since, every settlement having one. The only other musical instrument, which I saw, was a rude pipe or flute, rather longer than a common flute, but much thicker. It is made of the hollow bamboo,—one end is shaped like a flageolet, with hole and mouthpiece, and it has four finger-holes, the first about two thirds down the length of the instrument, the others at intervals of about half an inch; it requires considerable exertion to sound it, and produces a dull monotonous tone, with very little variation. Two of these instruments are sounded together; the performers dancing a sort of minuet, in which they advance and recede, with the most grotesque gesticulations. One of their favourite dances is a kind of representation, characteristic of an Indian courtship.

Two decades later Thomas Young found the same people making music in one other fashion, with the Jew's harp—could it have been acquired since the time of Roberts? Young also recorded and translated the words of a Miskito love song:[8]

The songs of this people are made on the inspiration of the moment, on the occasion of any particularly good or bad news; and it is at times affecting to hear a mother calling for her departed child; even the unvaried and monotonous chaunt has a charm for them, and the men will sit down and quietly listen to all the fond names which a doating mother will lavish on the child, who will, alas! never return to her. I was once much affected; for the poor woman seemed as if her whole heart and soul were centered in the child who had gone. Her surviving

7. Roberts, 1827, p. 136.   8. Young, 1842, pp. 77–78.

offspring were forgotten, in her sorrow for the lost one. The paroxysms of their grief are often so violent, that if not prevented, they would hang themselves on the first tree.

The following are the words of a song, and emanating from the wild, rude, and uncultivated heart of a savage:—

"Keker miren náne, warwar páser yamne krouekan. Coope nárer mi koolkun I doukser. Dear máne kuker cle wol proue. I sabbeáne wal moonter mopparra. Keker misére yapte winegan. Koker sombolo barnar lippun, lippun, lippunke. Koolunker punater bin biwegan. Coope nárer tánes I doukser. Coope nárer mi koolkun I doukser."

It may thus be rendered:—

"Dear girl, I am going far from thee. When shall we meet again to wander together on the sea side? I feel the sweet sea breeze blow its welcome on my cheek. I hear the distant rolling of the mournful thunder. I see the lightning flashing on the mountain's top, and illumining all things below, but thou art not near me. My heart is sad and sorrowful; farewell! dear girl, without thee I am desolate.". . .

The natives are remarkably attached to the Jews'-harp, and play extremely well upon it. They have but few tunes, and those are invariably played on particular occasions; such as leaving home, or returning to it, or on the death of any relative. At other times, when assembled together at night, one will awake, and play as he lies on his back, for the entertainment of his companions. I have often listened with very great pleasure and surprise to this little instrument, it sounds so sweetly and soothingly, and have wondered how people so utterly uncivilized, could produce such sweet tones from what may be almost considered in the light of a toy. . . .

Concerning the Caribs, Young's observation seems to have been that what they lacked in instrumentation they made up for in improvisation and energy, with the latter on occasion becoming infectious:[9]

The amusements of these people of an evening, when at work at Fort Wellington, are dancing and singing. They assemble together with their pitch-pine torches, and pass a few hours in boisterous merriment; an empty flour barrel, the head being tightly covered with a deer skin, and fastened down with pegs, serves for their bass drum; the treble is made from a piece of bamboo about two feet six inches long, covered in a similar manner; these are played with the open hands,

9. *Ibid.,* pp. 134–35.

and the result is a most extraordinary music, the oddity of which is oftentimes much increased, when accompanied by some facetious fellow on an empty box or an old kettle, on which he beats with two sticks. Soon after the music strikes up, a dancer appears, who after throwing his body into all conceivable postures, now jumping up and down grotesquely, then advancing and retreating affectedly, and then after bending himself on one side so as nearly to fall down, he kicks about with great energy, till at length he gives a whirl, a bow, and retires; another taking his place; and so it continues until they are all exhausted. Some of the Caribs dance well, at least in their way; and I have been astonished at their evolutions. It is rarely a Mosquitian dances. At their sekroes, they merely stalk in a circle, following each other, singing loudly and uncouthly....[10]

At the nightly assemblies the Sambos invariably stand aloof, silently regarding the dancers, and listening with apparent relish to the drummers, only now and then uttering a sound of pleasure, which convinces the by-standers of the interest they take in the proceedings; otherwise they might be supposed to be looking on the scene with indifference, in such repose are their features. On one occasion the Mosquito men, having nothing to call their attention away, preserved their gravity for a long time, till at length a Carib blew a reed, and said, "coosu," meaning the sound was like the cry of the curassow; the result was one unanimous burst of laughter; on a repetition of the word, another shout was raised, louder and longer than the first; their tongues were loosened, and for some time a regular Babel ensued; Spanish, English, Mosquito, Carib, Poyer, and Wankee, all jabbering together, which only ceased on the drummers recommencing.[11]

The Mosquito Coast could boast no theater. But one had not to travel far inland before dramatic representations were known and often well attended. Montgomery when he was new on the isthmus ran into his first such experience near Gualán and described it in some detail:[12]

The breakfast being disposed of, and a reasonable time having elapsed in talking and smoking, Don José made a move towards taking

10. The "sekro" or *sikro* is the Miskito festival of the dead.
11. The "Wankee" or Wanki were a subgroup of the Miskitos who lived in the vicinity of the Wanks or Coco River.
12. Montgomery, 1839, pp. 67–73. The arrival at Gualán is described above, pp. 153–54.

leave and continuing our journey. This was met by the decided disapprobation, not only of Don Juan, but of all his guests. His wife, Doña Chonita, an amiable brunette, declared we should not leave Gualán till the following morning. To do otherwise would be a want of consideration towards herself. It would also be a want of taste; since we should lose the opportunity of seeing a play that was to be performed that night in honour of Saint Isidro, whose festival occurred on the following day; and we should, moreover, be deprived of the pleasure of seeing Saint Isidro himself, arrayed in his best, upon an altar glittering with lights, and blooming with flowers.

Don José was unable or unwilling to combat the arguments of our pretty hostess, and cast a look at Mr. M. and myself, as if to consult our wishes. It was evident he was desirous of remaining. Mr. M. anticipated my concurrence, by declaring at once that he was in no hurry to depart; and as his vote gave to Don José the majority, mine was not required, and it was definitively settled that we should stay and enjoy the *fiesta*.

In the interval between breakfast and dinner, I went, in the company of one of the guests, an ecclesiastic, to take a view of the town.... My companion ... was the curate of a neighbouring town ..., and had been compelled by the political troubles of the times to abandon his flock, and take refuge in Gualán.... He seemed, however, by no means dejected by his reverses, and in the afternoon was the first to propose our setting out for the place where the fiesta in honor of Saint Isidro was to be celebrated.

About two miles out of town there was a small estate, the residence of an old Spanish officer, who had closed his military career by coming to Central America and turning farmer. He it was who had prepared the fête in question; he had caused the image of the Saint to be transferred from the church to his house, and had even composed some verses on the occasion. Don Juan and his friends having been invited, a party was formed of three ladies and nine gentlemen, including my two travelling companions and myself. We went on horseback, and took with us the *maestro de capilla* and his band. Doña Chonita rode in an English saddle on a spirited horse, which she managed with considerable skill. Her dress was not a riding habit, but a short silk gown, a hat with a profusion of black feathers, and a sort of scarf, called *rebozo*, thrown over one shoulder, and wound round the waist. The other ladies were equipped in a similar manner. The gentlemen were all mounted on good horses, or mules, gaily caparisoned, and wore light summer jackets of silk or cotton, and straw hats. Each carried a dagger, stuck in a sash of some gay coloured silk, and some had holsters and pistols....

The first object that met our view on entering the house, was the image of Saint Isidro. It was placed on a temporary altar, ornamented with bouquets of wild flowers, and wax tapers burning in plated candlesticks. The ladies, on coming into the presence of the Saint, left off talking, and tried to look devout. The gentlemen took their hats off. Very soon, however, both sexes began to whisper, then to talk loud, and then to laugh. At length, all respect for the Saint seemed to have been lost; for the gentlemen put their hats on, and some of them actually took out their segars and smoked in his face.

We were now conducted to take some refreshment at a table amply furnished with cakes, sweetmeats, orchate, lemonade, cinnamon water, and a beverage called *fresco,* an infusion of the pine-apple.[13] The house, though little better than a large hut, had a neat and holyday appearance; the walls were set off with festoons of shrubs and flowers, and the floor was strewed with leaves. A sort of barn, immediately opposite the house, had been cleared out to serve as a theatre. It was entirely open on the side that was to face the audience; the roof and sides were ornamented with branches of trees and little flags of different colours; a few boards clumsily put together answered the purpose of a stage, and a large piece of canvass that of a curtain. There was also a temporary shed of branches of the palm tree, supported by stakes, to serve, in case of need, as a shelter for the *turba multa* of the uninvited. All this, and the crowd of people flocking in from the town and the adjacent villages, reminded me of the fête described in Gil Blas, and got up in Olmedo by Thomas de la Fuente, with this difference, that there were no Latin inscriptions.[14]

Some time was consumed in arranging matters, before the play could commence. In the mean while, the audience had crowded together in front of the stage promiscuously, and in a manner not approved of by the *Patron,* (the master of the fête,) or by the curate. The latter took upon himself to remedy this confusion. He directed the maestro and his musicians, who composed the orchestra, to take position at the foot of the stage. Then separating the women from the

---

13. "Orchate" or *horchata* is the beverage sometimes called "orgeat," made of various ingredients. In its original form, it usually included a decoction of barley; more recently, in America, an emulsion of almonds.

14. *Gil Blas de Santillane,* Book 2, Chapter 9.

men, he placed the former immediately behind the orchestra, making them squat on the ground, and bidding them to keep silent. This he called the pit. Behind the women, and all round, were distributed the boys and such of the men as were of low statue. The tall fellows were directed to stand behind the short ones and the boys, or to shift for themselves as well as they could. This was the gallery. A space in front of the stage was set apart by the curate *para los señores,* (for the ladies and gentlemen.) A couple of benches were placed here, one behind the other, and this he called the front boxes. The docility and good humour with which the people submitted to the dispositions of the curate, and the respect they showed him, impressed me with a most favourable opinion of their character and feelings. The spectators sat in the open air, under the light of an old wooden chandelier bristling with tallow candles. They now began to be impatient for the play, or for something to amuse them, and the cries of *musica! musica!* though responded to by the orchestra, were soon followed by those of *la comedia! la comedia!* At length an actor steps before the curtain, and recites a prologue, the subject of which is the life and merits of St. Isidro *labrador*. The *patron* solicits our particular attention to this part 'of the performance, which he tells us is his own composition. We of course listen with admiration, and, on the conclusion of the prologue, dismiss the actor with a burst of applause. Now the curtain rises, and the play begins.

The title of this performance was *El enamorado pobre,* or the Poor Lover. The plot turns upon the rivalship of two gentlemen, who aspire to the hand of a fair lady: the one exceedingly amiable, accomplished, and handsome, but very poor; the other, destitute of every advantage, except that he is very rich. The embarrassment of the lady, before deciding in favour of either, and the arts resorted to by the lovers respectively in furtherance of their pretensions, contitute the play, which, as it is also enlivened by the witticisms of a *gracioso,* is not without some interest and merit. Of course the preference is given to the poor lover, much to the satisfaction of the audience, who applaud the lady for her good taste.

It was amusing to observe how much regard was paid by the people to the character represented, and how little to the manner of performance. The poor lover, as an actor, was decidedly inferior to the rich one; yet he was the favourite of the public, who were lavish in their praise of him, while the other, whenever he came on the stage, was received with murmurs, and ran the risk of being hissed.

It would be unfair to criticise the acting. They did their best; especially the prompter, who, if the actors committed any blunders, was certainly not to blame, for he read their parts to them loud enough for all of us to hear. He had a hard time of it, too, poor fellow, now pushing in one actor, now pulling out another, and occasionally, in a fit of impatience, thwacking his manuscript over their heads.

The play was followed by a *saynete*, or afterpiece; and when the curtain dropped, the people were so well pleased, that they gave a shout of applause, and cried out, *Brava comedia! Viva el patron!*

The only person who did not enjoy the fiesta was my English friend. The play, he said, was a bore, St. Isidro a humbug, and the people all fools. Soon after the commencement of the play, he retired into the house, and passed part of the time in taking a nap.

It was near midnight before we returned to Gualán.

James Jackson Jarves, entering the isthmus from the opposite coast, came across a theater experience in Sonsonate:[15]

On the last day of the fête, we were surprised by a benefit from the Thespian corps; though why we were thus distinguished, we were not able to divine. We were eating our breakfast, when suddenly a grand flourish of trumpets and other martial clangor caused us to start from our seats. Our landlady ran in and bade us keep a good watch over our goods and chattels. It seems she had no good opinion of the honesty of her countrymen. Scarcely were the necessary precautions taken, when the door was thrown open, and the causes of all this outcry made their appearance, and without even saying, 'by your permission, sirs,' fairly took possession of our room. . . . We were very far in the minority, and therefore came to the conclusion that discretion was the better part of valor, and smiled and welcomed them. Judging from the size of their arms, the spirits of their forefathers would have found scant room in the bodies of their diminutive descendants.

Clothed in armor *cap-á-pie*, partly tinsel and partly real, some of which bore the marks of many a hard-fought field, and for aught I know protected Alvarado and his hardy band of warriors, when, three centuries previous, they overran this province, they marshalled themselves in single file. A young girl, who would have been pretty, had her neck not been deformed by an enormous goitre, a disease almost uni-

---

15. Jarves, 1843, pp. 303–5, following a section above, pp. 129–30.

versal here, and which renders the fairest in features, the most disgusting in appearance, was tricked out as Isabella of Castile. Placing her in the centre of their group, they filed around in quick step, clashing their swords, and looking as fierce and warlike as possible. Anon, they broke out in a wild and not inharmonious pæan, interspersed with theatrical declamation. This sort of exercise warmed their blood amazingly, and quicker went their feet, as they marched and counter-marched in a variety of intricate evolutions, and louder swelled their voices. Had these feats been performed elsewhere, they would have appeared admirably, but with such a wild looking set of fellows inside, and half the cutthroat rabble of the town outside, gaping in at the doors and windows, they were not much to our satisfaction. Whether it would terminate in a forced loan on our purses, or a general rush upon our baggage, we could not determine. Our fears did them injustice. After shouting until they were hoarse, and masquerading until they were exhausted, they marched out as they came in, with a tremendous din of wind instruments and drums, and forthwith proceeded to wet their whistles for a fresh exhibition in some new quarter. This harlequin-pageant, as we were afterwards informed, was intended to commemorate the victories of Ferdinand the Catholic, over Boabdil the Moor; though to all appearances, there was at this time as much of Moorish blood as of the Castilian running in their veins, and perhaps more of the Quichen than either.[16]

In Guatemala City, despite diplomat Thompson's disparagement of some of its accouterments, the play was a frequent attraction, one which Thompson found, in his circumstances, to his liking:[17]

Sunday, 26th June. In the course of this day, after the usual services of the church, there existed much bustling and visiting. Whilst I was sitting, in the evening, reading in my apartment, the Chinese, my servant, quietly entered, and deliberately took out all the chairs, helping himself to them one by one, leaving me no other than that which I occupied: he stood patiently behind me, when, annoyed by his intrusion, I arose from my seat, and he immediately availed himself of the opportunity to seize that also. I looked out of the window, and saw two

---

16. By "Quichen" Jarves presumably meant the Quiché, chief Indian nation of Guatemala. Sonsonate's main Indian heritage was that of the Pipil, who spoke the Nahuat language of central Mexico.
17. Thompson, 1829, pp. 295–98.

Indians laden with the furniture, hastening down the street. I was so predisposed in favour of this poor fellow, on account of his blunt honesty, that I seldom interfered with any thing he did, finding that it almost always contributed to my advantage and comfort; but, being doubtful as to the validity of these points, in the present instance, I called him to me, and asked him what he meant by it? "Coliseo, Señor, el coliseo:" "The play, Sir, the play," was his answer. The family were going to the play: this was all right; for the boxes of the theatre had no benches, and it was the custom of the parties who took them, to accomodate themselves with their own chairs. My good hostess had ordered her carriage, and, about five o'clock, we all set off together, a very merry party.

We had the stage box: the curtain was not drawn up, but the house was more than half full. The orchestra was lighted with about two dozen candles, and there were nearly as many more separately affixed to the pillars which divided the lower tier of boxes. The deficiency was, however, compensated by some holes in the roof of the building, which admitted the daylight so profusely as to make the candles a work of supererogation.

The play was something about the "Glory of Independence", and abounded with allusions, which an English audience would term "claptraps." The acting was, however, equal to any I had seen at Mexico; and the audience, altogether, appeared to evince as much indifference to the pieces represented, as the best bred company in any European theatre could affect to do: I took suckets ... with the young ladies, and was rather pleased, than otherwise, with the performance.[18] We had also some glasses of champaign occasionally handed round to us, which excited, as I thought, the envy of some gentlemen in the pit, who had been smoking incessantly, and might consequently be rather thirsty.

There was a scene, not badly drawn, representing the temple of the sun: one of the actors was describing the indestructible glory of Anahuac, and had just said that its brilliance should never be dimmed, when a tremendous shower, accompanied with thunder and lightning, took place. The rain dashed down in torrents on the crazy theatre, and spouted in volumes through the crevices of the broken roof: the audience were not to be affected by words; but, acknowledging that facts were stubborn things, mustered themselves indiscriminately in patches in the pit, or jumped into the boxes to escape the effects of the tornado.

18. "Suckets"=succades or sweetmeats.

There is little encouragement given to plays at Guatemala; probably not more than was found in England previously to the time of Elizabeth.

James Wilson was blocked by his scruples from theater attendance on Sundays, but eventually found his opportunity. The performance suited his own tastes perhaps more than he expected:[19]

June 29th.—St. Peter's day; another double cross. A piece, entitled 'The Inquisition unmasked,' has been exhibited in the theatre repeatedly during our stay here. This is the only week day the theatre has been open since our arrival. Sunday is, in general, the day of performance. Went in the evening to witness the representation.

It is something very unaccountable that an exhibition, which tends so manifestly to lessen the blind respect in which the priests are held by the multitude, should have been allowed to be introduced into such a place as Guatemala; and it is truly astonishing to see how much the people relish the exhibition: good may be brought out of evil.

The drift of the piece seems to be as follows:—A priest makes dishonourable proposals to a female of a respectable family. She rejects, with disdain, his attempts to seduce her. To be revenged, he lodges information with the Inquisition that the young lady has been guilty of some dreadful crimes; and also against the father for having prohibited books in his possession, treating on botany, mathematics, &c.! The lover of the young lady is also implicated. They are all three brought before the Holy Tribunal, and found guilty on the simple allegation of the vile priest! This individual again sends for the lady privately, and offers to set them all at liberty if she will comply with his wishes, but she rejects his proposal with indignation. The father is then introduced, and the same offer is made to him, provided he will use his influence with his daughter to induce her compliance. He rejects the horrid proposal, and is then shown the rack, the blazing fire, &c., but he still remains firm. Whilst the attendants are preparing to put him to torture, a noise is heard without, which is followed by a discharge of musketry, and an instantaneous rush of soldiers into the hall of the Inquisition, shouting—Long live the Constitution—death to the Inquisition! The Inquisitors start up in the greatest alarm, and try to hide themselves from the fury of the soldiers.

The commanding officer then comes forward, and, addressing the

19. Wilson, 1829, pp. 108–10.

audience, begs they will not suppose that the representation they have just witnessed is in the least intended to lessen their esteem for their Holy Religion, or its ministers; and begs they will learn to discriminate between the true ministers of God, and those who merely assume the name to cloak their villanies. He then gives orders to demolish the engines of torture, which are obeyed with alacrity; the soldiers having knocked them to pieces with the butt ends of their musquets, the curtain drops, amid the cheers of the audience.

From what I hear, and observe, the clergy, and the more devout of the laity, do not at all relish such an exhibition. It certainly can be no very pleasing spectacle to them to see even the *cloth* treated with contempt. For no doubt it is their wish, that the people should be inspired with such reverence for them, that even if their canonicals were hung upon a barber's block they should be treated with deference. These objections go no farther, however, than whispers, and half-uttered growls; the generality of the people seem to relish the representation, and the government decidedly countenances it. The circumstance of a party of soldiers with muskets and fixed bayonets being present in the theatre, to keep order, is . . . corroborative of the truth of the latter assertion. . . .

Henry Dunn was as unenthusiastic about the theater, which he believed was soon to be abandoned, as about most other forms of Guatemalan entertainment:[20]

The stranger's first impression, that Guatimala is exceedingly dull and lifeless, will not, in all probability, be materially changed on a more intimate acquaintance—especially if he be one of that numerous class to whose very existence public amusements seem necessary —since there is not, perhaps, a city in the world where diversions of every species are more neglected.

The theatre, established about a year ago, is not much better in appearance than a country barn. In the heavy showers which frequently fall during the rainy season, the water trickles through the roof, both into the pit and boxes; and more than once umbrellas have been as usefully employed within as without the house. The scenery is wretchedly painted; and the performers, with the exception of two European comedians, are said to be inferior to the lowest village-strollers. The numbers who attended at the beginning of the year were not

20. Dunn, 1829, pp. 107–9.

sufficient to pay the expenses; and the company, having struggled some time against the losses connected with empty benches, gave public notice, in the month of July 1827, that, owing to the thin attendance of the citizens, the performances would cease; and there is now little prospect of their being renewed.

This species of amusement was originally established in the hope that it might become popular, and supersede, in great measure, the barbarous diversions of the bull-ring; but, although the pieces chosen were sufficiently licentious, and the dances somewhat indecent, with the additional temptation of the performances being on Sundays and saints' days, it was not sufficient to wean the worthy citizens from their favourite *Toros,* and the exhibitions of the latter are still well attended. These, however, only take place in the dry season, and are neither conducted in so cruel a manner as in Spain and the other parts of America, nor is the same degree of skill and courage displayed by the combatants. In the eye of the connoisseur, they are deemed far inferior to similar exhibitions in Mexico; but they still possess sufficient attractions to draw crowds of every rank, and of each sex, to witness the barbarous spectacle, and to be brutalized by its heart-hardening tendencies.

A few large card parties, a solitary ball, and one or two billiard tables, will complete the catalogue of amusements, with the exception of that infamous nest of vice and cruelty, the cock-pit; which has, however, fallen into disrepute, and is only attended by the most depraved part of the people. The most successful speculations in the department of public diversions have been those of travelling troops of equestrians and jugglers; but as they do not form any permanent source of amusement, they can hardly be considered as belonging to the city.

The neglect of observers rather than lack of achievement may be blamed for the extreme dearth of comment on Central American visual arts requiring skill of the hand. Only Dunn presents a fair appraisal of this category, which he calls the "fine arts," and even his is a very brief one:[21]

> ... In these, many of the natives excel;—a fact which may be proved by reference to the various sculptures, and copies of paintings, which have been executed by their different artists. Indeed, in the present day they can boast a miniature-painter, altogether self-taught,

21. *Ibid.,* p. 112.

who for exactness of resemblance, if not for delicacy of finish, may be placed in competition with almost any European.[22]

Engraving is executed neatly, but the artists obtain little employ.

As musical instrument makers, the Guatimalians are by no means contemptible. Two or three of the organs used in the churches, and particularly a very fine one in the cathedral, were manufactured in the city; and both in tone and outward ornament they are equal to the majority built in Europe.

Every species of fancy work, too, they produce with great delicacy. The makers of artificial flowers surpass, in the exactness of their imitations of nature, our English manufacturers; and the workers in wax —a tribe little known amongst us—succeed admirably in the production of models and specimens.

22. Presumably the reference is to Francisco Cabrera, distinguished miniaturist of Guatemala, 1780–1845.

Chapter 6

Religion

COMMENT on religious matters by the ten travelers seems nearly as extensive as that on topics of business. Religious practices, though in each case quite different from those at home, were easier for these men to understand than the activities of the intellect, where language was a problem, and those of artists from an alien background. But while economic and political considerations were important to these men's lives and were the reasons in most cases for their Central American sojourns, religion spurred their comment chiefly because of its exotic quality in their experience. The pious Protestants (Wilson and Dunn) were shocked by many traditions in an overwhelmingly Roman Catholic land, but actually described this field less adequately than some of the others who were personally less concerned. On the balance, it may be said that signs of earnestness were found by the outsiders as often as signs of negligence toward religion, and that whatever arguments there may be about the forms of earnestness involved, these arguments turn more on the matter of what constitutes true religion—Catholic, Protestant, pagan, or whatever type is named —than on the sincerity of the devotion of that time.

Orlando Roberts, except for his one trip to León, seldom had any contact with Catholicism or any other form of Christianity. Speaking of the "Mosquito men," he said:[1]

They do not seem to possess, any distinct idea, of a future state of rewards and punishments whatever others assert who may have put

1. Roberts, 1827, pp. 266–67, 270.

the question, and received a different answer. . . . They are, nevertheless, like all ignorant people, exceedingly superstitious, and believe firmly in the appearance of "duppies" or ghosts, of which they are very much afraid, attributing their appearance to some malignant design, or evil purpose. Many of the Mosquito-men dare scarcely venture out of their houses at night, without a companion, for fear of those ideal spirits. The mind of King George Frederick, was so imbued with this superstitious dread, that I have repeatedly seen him terrified to pass the threshold after sunset.

. . . Christmas is universally observed all over the Mosquito Shore, by both Indians, Samboes, and Kharibees; but for no other reason that I could ever learn, except that it was "English fashion," and happens at a time when it does not interfere with their fishing and other pursuits. They in general apply to the traders sometime beforehand to know the number of days which must elapse; and, to keep an account of these, they have recourse to the knotted cord. . . . The principal men send presents of rum, &c. to the King, which enables him to gratify fully their drunken propensities, and as they come from the most distant settlements, and none of them appear empty handed, the houses are generally crowded to the door, and there is for several days a constant scene of intoxication.

James Wilson deemed some practices which he found farther inland as not far removed from the pagan superstition of the Caribbean margins:[2]

A young gentleman, who lives close by, was present to-day while we were at dinner; I observed something tied round his neck, which appeared to be a stripe of the branch of a cocoa nut tree. I asked him in English if he had got a tailor's measure round his neck; upon the question being repeated in Spanish, the countenances of those present assumed, all at once, an uncommon air of gravity, and the lady of the house informed us, with much apparent seriousness, that it was a *blessed branch*. It is humbling to see how easily mankind is imposed upon in the matter of religion; it would appear as if nothing were too absurd to be believed, if so be it only be dignified with the name of religion. Here was a number of individuals, some of them remarkable for shrewdness and good sense in other things, who seemed firmly

2. Wilson, 1829, p. 104.

persuaded that a bit of withered twig, over which a sinful creature like themselves had muttered his *benedicion,* and fixed upon it a piece of consecrated wax, would preserve them from injury from lightning. Almost every house has branches of this stuff fastened on the outside of the windows, besides having the interior decorated with a particular sort of ornament constructed of the same material. I am given to understand that these also are considered as preservatives from the effects of lightning. Mr.——— told them he would sooner trust to an iron rod, which science had discovered and experience ascertained to be the most effectual safeguard against the destructive effects of electric fluid, than to all the *blessed branches* in Guatemala.

But while Wilson's scientific sense of propriety was offended by the blessed branches, he was more distressed over the light attitude taken by some toward various outward forms of religion:[3]

Señor——— is very regular in calling together the juvenile part of the household and the servants, at eight o'clock in the evening ('*la hora de oracion*'), to go through their devotions. It is shocking to hear the levity which goes forward on these occasions. This evening, being in the room adjoining that in which they were assembled, I had an opportunity of particularly noticing it. In praying they have a set form of words, which they all repeat at the same time. They have also responses. One repeats a particular part, and the others join in, at regular intervals, in a sort of chorus.

Several times, in the course of the evening's devotion, it appeared that the leader had commenced a wrong prayer, and sometimes it appeared as if the respondents were at fault; these blunders excited a general laugh, accompanied by remarks apparently humorous, from the increase of risibility which followed them; and so noisy did they become, that the senior male part of the family were roused from the card table to remonstrate against the impropriety of such conduct.

Henry Dunn had sharp words for the lack of religious feeling in Gualán, which he associated with a lack of good literature:[4]

There do not appear to be any books whatever in the place, excepting a few mass-books, and these are little used. The priest, a

3. *Ibid.*, pp. 90–91.
4. Dunn, 1829, pp. 49–50.

sottish being, is generally despised, and the church greatly neglected. The inhabitants appear destitute of all religious feeling. A copy of the Scriptures is probably not to be met with in Gualán; nor are they permitted to be sold or distributed without the notes of the church.

Nor, though he was careful not to express judgment on individuals, was Dunn any more impressed with the genuineness of Christianity in the capital:[5]

... It is in vain to look for many followers of the meek and lowly Jesus. The votaries both of superstition and infidelity make their voices to be heard in the streets; but true piety loves the shade, and seeks retirement. It may be that there are those who have not bowed the knee to this two-fold Baal; but if they exist, it is in the secrecy of the closet; and who they are must be left for the day of judgment to declare.

The same observer's description of the regular clergy of his time makes them out to be relics left over from the colonial regime, subsisting on the dreams of past glories:[6]

The friars, as a body, still live in hope of the re-conquest of the country by Spain, and the consequent re-establishment of their influence. I was much amused to observe the earnestness and mysterious shrug with which one of the old fathers inquired the latest news from Europe, when we visited his convent. . . . A report had been circulated in the city, that a Spanish expedition was preparing in the Havanna, and his tottering limbs seemed to derive new strength from the rumour. It was evident enough that he thought Spain the most powerful empire of the world, although policy obliged him in great measure to conceal his opinions.

Yet Dunn decried the power still held by the clergy at large, in remarks which indicate the church's influence had not died with the passing of the colony:[7]

Perhaps there is no country in the world where religious processions are so numerous, or the great mass of the people so fanatical, as in

5. *Ibid.*, p. 123.
6. *Ibid.*, pp. 117–18.
7. *Ibid.*, pp. 115–16.

Guatimala. Always distinguished for its rigid attention to the ceremonies of the Church, it now stands pre-eminent. In Buenos Ayres, Columbia, and Peru, the Revolution has in this respect effected an important change; and even in Mexico, where the power of the clergy is still great, this superstitious frenzy is materially repressed. But here, every thing remains the same as before; not a priest has been ejected, nor a friar displaced; and although their temporal influence has been somewhat lessened, their spiritual authority remains undiminished.

Wilson too wrote words in his diary on certain days to show that some of the church's ordained as well as some of its laymen were earnest and responsible Catholics for their time without ceasing to be gentlemen:[8]

Mr.———'s box of books had been detained in order that they might be examined as to the nature of their contents. He received them back yesterday, *minus* the (religious) tracts, it being judged necessary that they should undergo a more minute examination. To-day the Archbishop sent to enquire if he had them for sale, as he wished to purchase one of each kind; he also wished to be informed if he had any Bibles to dispose of. Sent an answer in the negative; but stated he was at liberty to retain one of each of the tracts; and a Spanish Bible, which he had, was also respectfully proffered....

May 28th.—One of the monks of La Merced, a most intelligent friendly looking man, has been visiting Señor ——— to-day. He got into conversation with Mr. ———: among a variety of other subjects, religion became the topic of conversation. General remarks led to particulars—prayers to saints—the right of the clergy to grant absolution—transubstantiation—and the celibacy of the priests were severally the subjects of discussion. The arguments seemed to be conducted on both sides with much temper, and they parted good friends, the monk promising to call again some day soon.

The archbishop has returned the tracts. Mr. ——— enclosed one of each, and sent them to 'His Holiness!' ...

Sabbath, May 29th.—Accompanied Señor——— to the cathedral this forenoon, but was obliged to leave before the service was concluded, as Señor ——— expected, and even requested, that we should conform with the practices of the deluded worshippers around us, in

8. Wilson, 1829, pp. 78–79.

standing up and kneeling, &c. This I could by no means comply with, and therefore left the place. Señor ——— is a most amiable and sensible man; but the Spaniards have had so little intercourse with strangers that they are unable to make sufficient allowance for difference of sentiment in the matter of religion, and they seem to expect that, even as an act of courtesy, we should comply with their forms. Mr. ——— explained that scruples of conscience, in attending to forms of which we did not know the meaning, furnished the reason for our withdrawing. This seemed to be quite satisfactory.

G. A. Thompson painted a pleasing picture of Archbishop Casaus y Torres, with whom he discussed the matter of toleration for dissenters. The two persons met early during Thompson's visit, as a result of the archbishop's initiative:[9]

In the course of the day, the Padre Castillo, one of the most influential members of the Congress, called upon me in the name of the Archbishop, the Padre Casaus, and delivered to me a polite message inviting me to take up my abode in his palace. I had with me two letters of introduction to His Grace; but, taking the proffer in the usual acceptation of the term, politely declined it. I, however, called the next day, and delivered the letters in person: I discovered that we were, mutually, acquainted with many persons at Mexico, and these were chiefly, I found, amongst the most respectable of the old Spanish families, some of whom I used to think rather dubiously of with respect to their attachment to the new systems of these governments. Not being at present acquainted with the political feelings of the Archbishop, and concluding that, under any circumstances, it would be better for me to live free and independent during my stay in the capital, I again refused the pressing offer he made me of the use of his house. This, however, I had some difficulty in effecting, as he assured me, with a good-natured expression of features, (he is a particularly handsome man about fifty,) that he was not asking me in the Spanish meaning, but in truth and sincerity, or words to this effect; and, "come", said he, opening some folding doors, which led into another suite of rooms, "I will shew you your apartments." I walked through them with him; they were handsome and commodious; but I still felt it proper to decline his kindness: though, to say the truth, I had much

9. Thompson, 1829, pp. 140–45. The padre mentioned in the first sentence was José María Castilla, an early clerical supporter of independence.

difficulty in doing so; for never did any one who offers a civility which, at the same time, he dreads will be accepted, experience greater feelings of embarrassment than I did in rejecting the sincere overtures of this kind and liberal man.

I very soon got acquainted with the history and character of Don Ramon Casaus: he is a person of engaging manners, and vigorous with respect to years and intellect. He informed me that he had thought it his duty, in the first instance, to oppose the measures of the independent party, as being subversive of the principles of the government which he was bound to uphold, and by which his authority was protected; but that, as the march of public opinion gained ground, and when he found it was absolutely the wish of the people at large to have an independent government, he was induced to relax his opposition, and, afterwards, to prevent the bloodshed which must, naturally, have taken place, pending a conflict of such a domestic nature, to give his firm and decided support to the newly established government. He was originally a friar, but is now the representative of the secular clergy, and carries, with his opinions, the influence of all the most able ecclesiastics of that denomination. It is not equally certain that all the religious corporations, as such, are so much in favour of the new order of things. I am, indeed, inclined much to doubt it; although they appear contented, speak fairly, and do not venture, by word or act, to exhibit any overt marks of opposition. With respect to the permission for Protestant worship, His Grace gave me to understand that, as far as regarded *private* worship, there could be no objection;—that the Guatemalian constitution was formed as liberally as it could possibly be, under existing circumstances: that the article relating to religion was much more general than that regarding the same subject, as enacted in the constitution of Mexico; for that, in the latter, the words are "Tit. 1. Art. 3. The religion of the Mexican nation is, and shall perpetually be, the Catholic, Apostolic and Roman: the nation protects it by wise and just laws, *and prohibits the exercise of any other whatsoever*"; whereas, in the Guatemalian constitution, the words are "Tit. 2. Art. 11. Its religion is Catholic, Apostolic and Roman, to the exclusion of the *public* exercise of any other whatsoever."

Although such are the sentiments of the first authority and, perhaps, of most of the consequential members of the hierarchy, it is to be apprehended that any thing like an alarm on the score of divine worship being carried on in a manner dissimilar from that to which the community at large have hitherto been accustomed, might produce very disagreeable effects. It must not be concealed that the people, especially the lower orders of it, are most fastidiously wedded to their forms of worship, and keep up their ceremonies with stricter observance and greater ostentation than, perhaps, the natives of any other countries in the whole of the late Spanish dominions; but they are, at the same time, of so kind and peaceable a disposition, that nothing but a direct violence to their religious feelings would be likely to excite their opposition; and, hence, amongst the numerous foreigners who had visited the capital, within the last twelve months of my arrival, (more it is supposed than had visited it within the last three centuries,) no one, as I could find, had been questioned or in any way slighted upon the grounds of having professed a faith, the tenets of which might differ from those of the established religion.

Some time after Archbishop Casaus had been exiled, complete religious toleration established by law, and most of the convents closed, G. W. Montgomery found in Ocotepeque, Honduras, a good example of the extent to which some hearts remained tuned to Catholic principles of devotion:[10]

...Mr. M.,... by a happy inspiration, pointed to a house that he had taken a fancy to, and insisted on applying there for quarters. I saw no reason for preferring that house to any other, but I complied with his wishes, and entered the house, saying, *"Ave Maria purissima!"* when a middle aged man appeared, who in a very civil manner desired me to command him. On my asking the favour of being permitted with a friend of mine to pass the night there, he made me a sign to wait, and retiring into the house, re-appeared the next moment with a woman, who, as she scanned Mr. M. and me with a glance of her dark and penetrating eyes, seemed to wait for an explanation. My request being now addressed to her, she replied, *"como no?"* (why not?) which, with the natives, is the usual and favourite mode of answering in the affirmative.

The man and woman just mentioned were brother and sister; and from the assiduity and good will with which they attended to our wants, we had every reason to congratulate ourselves on having selected their house for our abode. We were also fortunate in another respect, since on inquiring for mules to take us to St. Salvador, the brother, who was the owner of several, offered to furnish them him-

10. Montgomery, 1839, pp. 91–92.

self, and to be our guide and attendant on the road. An engagement was, accordingly, made with him, with a promise, on his part, that we should set out the following morning at an early hour. But this promise our host, Juan Rodriguez, (such was his name,) had no intention of fulfilling; for on my asking him, before retiring to rest, at what hour of the morning he would call me, he hesitated, and seemed a little puzzled. I proposed the hour of five, but this he thought too early. I then said six, and then seven, but still he seemed inclined to make it a little later. At length I brought him to an explanation. The next day, he said, was a holyday; it was the festival of the Ascension; and he could not think of going upon a journey on such a day without previously hearing mass. And as this ceremony would not take place till nine o'clock, he hoped I would defer our departure till that hour. I argued and reasoned with him, and tried to remove his scruples by adverting to the old Spanish saying, that duty is before devotion. But he retorted with another, equally good, which was:

> "Por oir misa y dar cebada,
> Nunca se perdió jornada."

And thereupon I yielded the point, and agreed not to set out till he had performed his devotions. He then told me that he had been a friar of the order of St. Francis, and that, though religious orders were now extinct in the country, it was his practice, on particular festivals, to go to church in his monkish habits, which he carefully retained, and hoped some day to resume. I no longer wondered at the scruples he had exhibited. The next morning, it was amusing to see Juan Rodriguez figuring, at first, in the garb of a friar, and then, on doffing his habits, transformed into something like a captain of banditti, with his *chamarra,* or mantle, over one shoulder, a dagger in his belt, and a rusty Toledo hanging from his side.[11]

Among laymen, too, acting under no sign of duress or compulsion, there were religious exercises not forgotten, as George Byam testified concerning his trip across Lake Nicaragua after two years in the forest:[12]

An hour before sunrise, up anchor and away; just as the sun rose the men left off pulling, and, with all heads uncovered, the patron com-

11. The Spanish city of Toledo was famous for its finely tempered swordblades.
12. Byam, 1849, pp. 238–40.

menced prayers in a half-chaunting voice, which was now and then responded to by the crew: they then sung a hymn in very fair time and tune, but in unison. . . .

After dinner, under-way again until sunset, when the patron again chaunts his prayers, and they sing together an evening hymn to the Virgin Mary. They soon after come to an anchor, taking care to keep well away from the shores and from under trees, on account of wild beasts, and, still worse, snakes dropping down from the branches. . . .

I was much struck with the pleasing simplicity of their morning and evening worship, and the more so as I had never seen the slightest sign of any worship in the woods. . . . I can truly say I joined with pleasure in their devotions, and they were pleased to see it.

A roundup of the position and activities of the church in the early republican period is provided by Thompson:[13]

. . . There is at the present time in Guatemala a cathedral, with bishops and canons. . . .

In León de Nicaragua, a cathedral, bishop, and canons.

In Comayagua, a cathedral, bishop, and canons.

In Ciudad Real, a cathedral, bishop, and canons.

And it is in agitation to erect two others; one in San Salvador, and the other in Costa Rica.

The religious communities are of the orders of Saint Francis, Saint Dominic, (very rich,) Saint Austin, Philip of Neri, Belen, (with an hospital,) Our Lady of Mercy and of the Reform, and of Saint Peter of Alcantara.[14]

These large convents of the capital have smaller ones in the other cities and towns throughout the republic; and the whole of them may contain together about 300 religious persons. Each convent has a gratuitous school for the instruction of the poor, in reading and writing, arithmetic, and the principles of religion and morality. In some districts, the religious are curates, and are much beloved by the natives,

---

13. Thompson, 1829, pp. 146–48.
14. The Congregation of the Oratory was founded by Saint Philip of Neri in Italy, 1564. The Bethlehemites, or Company of Belén, originated in Antigua, Guatemala, and were recognized as an order in 1710. Our Lady of Mercy refers to the Mercedarians, who had their beginnings in Barcelona, Spain, about 1218. Our Lady of the Reform presumably refers to the Recollects, Franciscan reformers (see Ch. 6 n. 26). The Alcantarines, a branch of the Franciscans, are the followers of Saint Peter of Alcántara in Spain (1499–1562).

whom they civilize and teach many useful arts besides those of industry and agriculture: they have sufficient influence in affairs relating to the government, and are very orderly citizens. In the capital, there are, at the most, eight convents of nuns; maintaining themselves on their own funds, and having schools for the instruction of girls: they lead a very regular life. The churches in the capital amount to thirty. They are ornamented in a most costly manner; are magnificent in their construction and munificent in maintaining great pomp and splendour in their respective religious functions: it is certain that, in the republic, the cost of religious worship is equal to twice the expenses of the government. It will be seen by the above account that the clergy are no unimportant branch of the political establishment of Guatemala.

Wilson found words of praise for the greatest religious establishment of all in the capital:[15]

... Went to the cathedral to hear mátins performed. The exterior of this building ... is admirable, but the interior is magnificent. The altar would require a connoisseur to describe it. The greater part of it seems to be silver,—the workmanship exquisite. There are two figures with wings, on each side of this altar, as large as life, and elegantly dressed. They seem intended to represent angels. The walls are covered with paintings in rich gilt frames, and all around are statues of the saints, executed in a superior style, one of them I think the largest that I have ever seen. Although the cathedral of Guatemala, as a whole, does not yield to any building I have seen, it is not so very remarkable on account of its size. Its superiority lies in design and execution.

Dunn, while criticizing at nearly every turn and indulging in some wry humor at the expense of the simple-minded, seems quite impressed by his observation of some religious customs:[16]

The superstitious and intolerant feelings of an uneducated population are lamentably visible among the lower orders. As the Archbishop passes in his carriage through the streets, the poor Indians are to be seen on either side most devoutly kneeling; and so ignorant are they of the object to which they bow, that they repeat the ceremony, not only when the empty carriage rolls by, but oftentimes when some

15. Wilson, 1829, p. 82.
16. Dunn, 1829, pp. 84–88.

other of the few clumsy vehicles kept by the wealthier inhabitants rumble along the pavement. Of this our own experience furnished an amusing, or, I ought rather to say, melancholy proof. In this instance they bent the knee quite as devoutly to a coach full of obstinate heretics, as they could have done to the pseudo-successor of St. Peter himself....

Even the better educated are slaves to the superstitions of the Church of Rome. To images of saints, and to church-doors, every passer-by takes off the hat; and at ten in the morning, when the bell tolls to announce the elevation of the Host in the cathedral, the streets and shops, parlours and kitchens, are alike filled with devout kneelers.

The etiquette connected with visiting the Archbishop partakes a little of the same character. As the visitor enters, his Grace rises to meet him, and presents his finger, on which is a valuable diamond ring called *La Esposa*, "the bride," signifying the church. This is humbly kissed by the kneeling visitant; and the ceremony is renewed every time....

Marrying and giving in marriage here, as in other countries, is distinguished by peculiar customs. When the consent of parents has been obtained, if the lover have no previous establishment he takes a house, and the parents of the lady place in it, at their own expense, a handsome bed and a plentiful supply of household linen. This having been done, the intended bridegroom, on the day previous to the celebration of the nuptials, sends to his future wife, dresses, jewels, and ornaments, in proportion to his wealth. The ceremony is generally performed before day-light on the following morning, and all attendant expenses are paid by the parents of the bride. The newly married couple then adjourn to the house of the lady's father, where they reside for fifteen or twenty days.

The other rites of the church are conducted in the same way as in other Catholic countries. Funerals are very expensive, owing not only to the number of individuals who take part in the ceremony, but also to the splendid dresses in which bodies are interred. The wealthy throw away considerable sums in the indulgence of this foolish vanity, and not infrequently expend a sum equal to fifty pounds sterling upon the interment of a new-born infant.

The most splendid funeral I witnessed in Guatimala was that of a rich Canon. The friars of the different convents, two by two, led the procession, one bearing a massy silver cross, and the others lighted wax-candles; the canons and the doctors following in their robes. After the bier walked the priests and curates, two by two; the chief of the state; the friends of the deceased; and the principal military officers. Between the house and the place of interment, a distance of about five hundred yards, were arranged, at equal distances in the street, four large tables covered with black cloth, and holding six immense wax candles in massy silver candlesticks. On each of these tables the body, extended upon a splendid bier and clothed in the richest robes, was placed: the procession formed around it, a Mass was sung, and holy water thrown upon the body by one of the doctors: after which the whole moved on to the next resting-place, where the same formalities were observed. On its arrival at the cathedral, the body was placed in the middle aisle; the members of the procession ranged themselves on either side, with their lighted tapers; crowds of spectators knelt in front, and other crowds stood in silence behind, as with one consent every voice began to sing the solemn Mass. This imposing ceremony lasted for some hours; after which the corpse was deposited in one of the vaults below the cathedral.

The lower orders generally bury in the *Santo Campo,* or consecrated ground behind the cathedral, where many simple memorials to the dead have been erected.

Montgomery spent a Sabbath day in Esquipulas, where he stayed in the home of the local priest and had an opportunity to learn directly some of the circumstances of the famous shrine:[17]

... At night I was shown into my bed-chamber, where every thing appeared to be in the same state as when occupied by the curate. In a spirit of curiosity I proceeded to examine, and note down, the various objects round me. A very pretty little crucifix of silver, suspended from the wall over the bed, was the first object that attracted my attention. Near that was a *bénitier* with holy water, and in another place a reliquary of St. Gabriel. On a table, I found a manuscript, which proved to be a Register of births, marriages, and deaths, and in a book-case that was open, the following, among other works: the Bible in latin, a breviary, Thomas à Kempis, *Institution des Curés* in French, and Taboada's Dictionary of the Spanish and French languages.[18]

17. Montgomery, 1839, pp. 85–88.
18. The title *Institution des curés* suggests a portion of a manual of canon law, such as Claude Fleury's *Institution du droit ecclésiastique de France* (Paris, 1677; republished in 2 vols., Paris, 1767); or Giovanni Devoti's *Institutionum canonicarum libri quatuor* (Rome, 1785; republished as 4 vols. in 3, Madrid,

The next morning, when the tolling of the church-bell announced the hour of divine service, we were invited by the curate to attend the ceremony of mass, which he was about to perform. We went, accordingly, notwithstanding a disposition manifested by Mr. M. to decline the invitation. The church was a large, gloomy building, combining the modern with the gothic style of architecture, and consisted of one aisle, with pilasters on the sides. The altar was surmounted by a large crucifix of wood; the floor was paved with flat bricks or tiles. The congregation was composed chiefly of women, who sat or knelt on little mats in the middle of the church. They wore mantillas over their heads, a kind of shawl, of fine white flannel or baize trimmed with white satin ribbon. Some wore the usual scarf, called *rebozo*. They were otherwise neatly dressed, but none of them had shoes or stockings. The men stood round, except a few of the better class, who were accommodated with benches, of which there was one on each side of the church. The ceremony was soon brought to a conclusion, when we returned to the house to breakfast. After this, it was proposed to pay a visit to the temple of Esquipulas, about a mile distant from the town; and mules being procured for the purpose, we started for that celebrated shrine with the curate, who, as is usual with his brethren, was admirably mounted.

The temple, or church, in question, stands by itself in the midst of a plain. It is a noble pile, and contrasts singularly with the insignificance of the town in the vicinity of which it is situated. It has a lofty and spacious dome, and at each angle a tower of considerable elevation. The architecture is sufficiently regular and chaste. As a work of art, this edifice is calculated to produce a greater impression on the beholder, from its situation in a spot where, for some hundred miles round, there is nothing of the kind bearing even a remote comparison with it. To a traveller coming in view of it on a sudden, it might look like the work of enchantment. It had to me the appearance of an Escurial in miniature. Entering the church through a lofty portal, rich with ornaments of sculpture, we took a view of the interior, which is divided into three aisles, the central one formed by two rows of heavy pillars, with their corresponding arches. On each side are various chapels, images and pictures, and the walls in many parts are covered with *ex votos*, in the shape of hands, arms, and feet, made of wax, and of-

---

1801–2; and as *Instituciones canónicas divididas en 4 libros*, Valencia, 1830). The first edition of Melchior Emmanuel Núñez de Taboada's *Dictionnaire français-espagnol et espagnol-français* appeared in Paris, 1812; the seventh, in Paris, 1833; and later editions until 1878.

fered there by devotees who have attributed to this shrine the cure of diseases they have been afflicted with. Over the principal entrance in the choir, and at the other extremity of the building, is the principal altar, in front of which, in a shrine richly carved and gilt, is an image of Christ crucified, to whom the church is consecrated. The image is about four feet high, of wood, beautifully bronzed. The ornaments about the shrine, and the image, are of gold and silver, some of them set with precious stones.

Many and wonderful are the miracles attributed to this image, the fame of which has spread far and wide in that country. Hence the number of pilgrims that come annually to offer at its feet their vows and prayers; amounting in some years to five thousand. In some cases, when the devotees have been prevented from attending personally, they have addressed their prayers in letters directed to the *Señor*, or Lord of Esquipulas. The zeal and devotion of the pilgrims is evinced by their approaching the temple on their knees, or by carrying from a considerable distance a heavy cross, or a large stone. Their reward is a bit of ribbon which has touched the image, and has stamped on it the words, *Dulce nombre de Jesus*. . . .

The curate, an amiable and sensible man, and somewhat of a scholar, was nevertheless a firm believer in the miracles attributed to the image just described. He seemed anxious to impress me with the same belief, and tried every argument that he thought calculated to remove my incredulity. At length he pressed me so hard, that I was fain to resort to a stratagem in order to escape from the toils he was spreading round me. I declared to him that if the *Señor* de Esquipulas would work a miracle in my behalf between that day and the next, and enable me to proceed to Guatemala direct and without risk, I would believe in him. The reader will be surprised to learn what follows. On getting up the next morning, and as I was leaving my chamber, the first person I met was the curate. He had been lying in wait for me; there was an arch smile on his countenance; he saluted me with the usual *buenos dias*, and expressed himself with the following words, "Did you not ask for a miracle? and did you not require that it should be a safe and direct conveyance to Guatemala? Well, sir, your conditions have been fulfilled. I have just learned the arrival in this town of a convoy of mules laden with tobacco, which, as soon as a party of soldiers appointed by the Government to escort them shall arrive, will proceed to the capital direct. Could you desire a better opportunity? will you now believe?"

I confess that the statement of the curate struck me with surprise. I affected to believe that he was jesting, but he soon compelled me to admit the truth of his assertion. On inquiring, however, into the particulars of the case, I learned that eight days at least would elapse before the arrival of the escort; that the rate of travelling of the convoy would never exceed eight or nine miles a day; that they encamped in the open fields; and that to get to Guatemala in this way, would be the business of a month. This being the case, I told the curate that it would not do, and that the miracle was no miracle after all.

The town of Esquipulas—in itself little better than a village—is remarkable, not only for the church described above, but for a fair that is held there once a year. The principal street consists of two rows of little shops, or booths, which are hired out during the fair to the merchants, or dealers, that repair thither with their goods. The concourse of people at that time is so great, that the town is inadequate to their accommodation, and they are obliged to encamp in the open fields. The number, I was assured, is seldom less than twenty thousand.

A year and a half later, Esquipulas and its priest made even a deeper impression upon J. L. Stephens:[19]

I was awaked by the sound of the matin bell, and accompanied the cura to mass. The church for everyday use was directly opposite the convent, spacious and gloomy, and the floor was paved with large square bricks or tiles. Rows of Indian women were kneeling around the altar, cleanly dressed, with white mantillas over their heads, but without shoes or stockings. A few men stood up behind or leaned against the walls.

We returned to breakfast, and afterward set out to visit the only object of interest, the great church of the pilgrimage, the Holy Place of Central America. Every year, on the fifteenth of January, pilgrims visit it, even from Peru and Mexico; the latter being a journey not exceeded in hardship by the pilgrimage to Mecca. As in the East, "it is not forbidden to trade during the pilgrimage;" and when there are no wars to make the roads unsafe, eighty thousand people have assembled among the mountains to barter and pay homage to "our Lord of Esquipulas."

... There was one street nearly a mile long, with mud houses on each side; but most of the houses were shut, being occupied only during the time of the fair. At the head of this street, on elevated ground, stood the great church. About half way to it we crossed a bridge over a small

19. Stephens, 1842, 1:168–72.

stream. . . . Ascending by a flight of massive stone steps in front of the church, we reached a noble platform a hundred and fifty feet broad, and paved with bricks a foot square. The view from this platform of the great plain and the high mountains around was magnificent; and the church, rising in solitary grandeur in a region of wildness and desolation, seemed almost the work of enchantment. The façade was rich with stucco ornaments and figures of saints larger than life; at each angle was a high tower, and over the dome a spire, rearing aloft in the air the crown of that once proud power which wrested the greatest part of America from its rightful owners, ruled it for three centuries with a rod of iron, and now has not within it a foot of land or a subject to boast of.

We entered the church by a lofty portal, rich in sculptured ornaments. Inside was a nave with two aisles, separated by rows of pilasters nine feet square, and a lofty dome, guarded by angels with expanded wings. On the walls were pictures, some drawn by artists of Guatimala, and others that had been brought from Spain; and the recesses were filled with statues, some of which were admirably well executed. The pulpit was covered with gold leaf, and the altar protected by an iron railing with a silver balustrade, ornamented with six silver pillars about two feet high, and two angels standing as guardians on the steps. In front of the altar, in a rich shrine, is an image of the Saviour on the cross, "our Lord of Esquipulas," to whom the church is consecrated, famed for its power of working miracles. Every year thousands of devotees ascend the steps of his temple on their knees, or laden with a heavy cross, who are not permitted to touch the sacred image, but go away contented in obtaining a piece of riband stamped with the words "Dulce nombre de Jesus." . . .

In the course of the day I had an opportunity of seeing what I afterward observed throughout all Central America: the life of labour and responsibility passed by the cura in an Indian village, who devotes himself faithfully to the people under his charge. Besides officiating in all the services of the church, visiting the sick, and burying the dead, my worthy host was looked up to by every Indian in the village as a counsellor, friend, and father. The door of the convent was always open, and Indians were constantly resorting to him: a man who had quarrelled with his neighbour; a wife who had been badly treated by her husband; a father whose son had been carried off as a soldier; a young girl deserted by her lover: all who were in trouble or affliction, came to him for advice and consolation, and none went away without it. And, besides this, he was principal director of all the public business of the town; the right hand of the alcalde; and had been consulted whether or not I ought to be considered a dangerous person. But the performance of these multifarious duties, and the excitement and danger of the times, were wearing away his frame. Four years before he gave up the capital, and took upon himself this curacy, and during that time he had lived a life of labour, anxiety, and peril; cut off from all the delights of social intercourse that make labour welcome, beloved by the Indians, but without any to sympathize with him in his thoughts and feelings. Once the troops of Morazan invaded the town, and for six months he lay concealed in a cave of the mountains, supported by Indians. Lately the difficulties of the country had increased, and the cloud of civil war was darker than ever. He mourned, but, as he said, he had not long to mourn; and the whole tone of his thoughts and conversation was so good and pure, that it seemed like a green spot in a sandy desert. We sat in the embrasure of a large window; within, the room was already dark. He took a pistol from the window-sill, and, looking at it, said, with a faint smile, that the cross was his protection; and then he put his thin hand in mine, and told me to feel his pulse. It was slow and feeble, and seemed as if every beat would be the last; but he said it was always so; and, rising suddenly, added that this was the hour of his private devotions, and retired to his room. I felt as if a good spirit had flitted away.

The special festivities of the church, though they did not always receive approbation, inevitably attracted the attention of a visitor who saw them firsthand. Stephens' first opportunity came as he and his companions rested in the home of one Doña Bartola in Gualán:[20]

Toward evening we again walked to the river, returned, and taught Donna Bartola how to make tea. By this time the whole town was in commotion preparatory to the great ceremony of praying to the Santa Lucia. Early in the morning, the firing of muskets, petards, and rockets had announced the arrival of this unexpected but welcome visitor, one of the holiest saints of the calendar, and, next to San Antonio, the most celebrated for the power of working miracles. Morazan's rise into power was signalized by a persecution of the clergy: his friends say that it was the purification of a corrupt body; his enemies, that it was a war against morality and religion. . . . At all events, and whatever was

20. *Ibid.*, 1:61–66.

the cause, the early part of Morazan's administration was signalized by hostility to them as a class; and, from the Archbishop of Guatimala down to the poorest friar, they were in danger; some fled, others were banished, and many were torn by rude soldiers from their convents and churches, hurried to the seaports, and shipped for Cuba and old Spain, under sentence of death if they returned. The country was left comparatively destitute; many of the churches fell to ruins; others stood, but their doors were seldom opened; and the practice and memory of their religious rites were fading away. Carrera and his Indians, with the mystic rites of Catholicism ingrafted upon the superstitions of their fathers, had acquired a strong hold upon the feelings of the people by endeavouring to bring back the exiled clergy and to restore the influence of the church. The tour of the Santa Lucia was regarded as an indication of a change of feeling and government; as a prelude to the restoration of the influence of the church and the revival of ceremonies dear to the heart of the Indian. As such, it was hailed by all the villages through which she had passed; and that night she would receive the prayers of the Christians of Gualán.

The Santa Lucia enjoyed a peculiar popularity from her miraculous power over the affections of the young; for any young man who prayed to her for a wife, or any young woman who prayed for a husband, was sure to receive the object of such prayer; and if the person praying indicated to the saint the individual wished for, the prayer would be granted, provided such individual was not already married. It was not surprising that a saint with such extraordinary powers, touching so directly the tenderest sensibilities, created a sensation in a place where the feelings, or, rather, the passions, are particularly turned to love.

Donna Bartola invited us to accompany her, and, setting out, we called upon a friend of hers; during the whole visit, a servant girl sat with her lap full of tobacco, making straw cigars for immediate use. It was the first time we had smoked with ladies, and, at first, it was rather awkward to ask one for a light; but we were so thoroughly broken in that night that we never had any delicacy afterward. The conversation turned upon the saint and her miraculous powers; and when we avowed ourselves somewhat skeptical, the servant girl, with that familiarity, though not want of respect, which exists throughout Central America, said that it was wicked to doubt; that she had prayed to the saint herself, and two months afterward she was married, and to the very man she prayed for, though at the time he had no idea of her, and, in fact, wanted another girl.

With this encouragement, locking the house, and accompanied by children and servants, we set out to pay our homage to the saint. The sound of a violin and the firing of rockets indicated the direction of her temporary domicil. She had taken up her residence in the hut of a poor Indian in the suburbs; and, for some time before reaching it, we encountered crowds of both sexes, and all ages and colours, and in every degree of dress and undress, smoking and talking, and sitting or lying on the ground in every variety of attitude. Room was made for our party, and we entered the hut.

It was about twenty feet square, thatched on the top and sides with leaves of Indian corn, and filled with a dense mass of kneeling men and women. On one side was an altar, about four feet high, covered with a clean white cotton cloth. On the top of the altar was a frame, with three elevations, like a flower-stand, and on the top of that a case, containing a large wax doll, dressed in blue silk, and ornamented with gold leaf, spangles, and artificial flowers. This was the Santa Lucia. Over her head was a canopy of red cotton cloth, on which was emblazoned a cross in gold. On the right was a sedan chair, trimmed with red cotton and gold leaf, being the travelling equipage of the saint; and near it were Indians in half-sacerdotal dress, on whose shoulders she travelled; festoons of oranges hung from the roof, and the rough posts were inwrapped with leaves of the sugar-cane. At the foot of the altar was a mat, on which girls and boys were playing; and a little fellow about six years old, habited in the picturesque costume of a straw hat, and that only, was coolly surveying the crowd.

The ceremony of praying had already begun, and the music of a drum, a violin, and a flageolet, under the direction of the Indian master of ceremonies, drowned the noise of voices. Donna Bartola, who was a widow, and the other ladies of our party, fell on their knees; and, recommending myself to their prayers, I looked on without doing anything for myself, but I studied attentively the faces of those around me. There were some of both sexes who could not strictly be called young; but they did not, on that account, pray less earnestly. In some places people would repel the imputation of being desirous to procure husband or wife; not so in Gualán: they prayed publicly for what they considered a blessing. Some of the men were so much in earnest that perspiration stood in large drops upon their faces; and none thought that praying for a husband need tinge the cheek of a modest maiden. I watched the countenance of a young Indian girl, beaming with enthusiasm and hope; and, while her eyes rested upon the image of the saint and her lips moved in prayer, I could not but imagine that her heart was full of some truant, and perhaps unworthy lover.

Outside the hut was an entirely different scene. Near by were rows of kneeling men and women, but beyond were wild groups of half-naked men and boys, setting off rockets and fireworks. As I moved through, a flash rose from under my feet, and a petard exploded so near that the powder singed me; and, turning round, I saw hurrying away my rascally muleteer. Beyond were parties of young men and women dancing by the light of blazing pine sticks. In a hut at some little distance were two haggard old women, with large caldrons over blazing fires, stirring up and serving out the contents with long wooden ladles, and looking like witches dealing out poison instead of love-potions.

At ten o'clock the prayers to the saint died away, and the crowd separated into groups and couples, and many fell into what in English would be called flirtations. A mat was spread for our party against the side of the hut, and we all lighted cigars and sat down upon it. Cups made of small gourds, and filled from the caldrons with a preparation of boiled Indian corn sweetened with various *dolces*, were passed from mouth to mouth, each one sipping and passing it on to the next; and this continued, without any interruption, for more than an hour. We remained on the ground till after midnight, and then were among the first to leave. On the whole, we concluded that praying to the Santa Lucia must lead to matrimony; and I could not but remark that, in the way of getting husbands and wives, most seemed disposed to do something for themselves, and not leave all to the grace of the saint.

In the Guatemalan capital Stephens soon experienced a commemoration more ostentatious in nature, and, for the one who described it, more romantic in tone:[21]

On the first Sunday after my arrival was celebrated the fête of La Concepcion, a fête always honoured in the observances of the Catholic Church, and this day more important from the circumstance that a probationer in the convent of La Concepcion intended to take the black veil. At break of day the church bells rang throughout the city; cannon were fired in the plaza, and rockets and fireworks set off at the corners of the streets. At nine o'clock crowds of people were hurrying to the Church of La Concepcion. Before the door, and extending across the streets, were arches decorated with evergreens and flowers.

21. *Ibid.*, 1:210–15, 222–23.

The broad steps of the church were strewed with pine leaves, and on the platform were men firing rockets. The church was one of the handsomest in Guatimala, rich with gold and silver ornaments, pictures, and figures of saints, and adorned with arches and flowers. The Padre Aycinena, the vice-president of the state, and the leading member of the Constituent Assembly, was the preacher of the day, and his high reputation attracted a large concourse of people.[22] The pulpit was at one end of the church, and the great mass of the people were anxious to hear the sermon. This left the other end comparatively vacant, and I placed myself on a step of the nearest altar, directly in front of the grating of the convent. At the close of the sermon there was a discharge of rockets and crackers from the steps of the church, the smoke of which clouded the interior, and the smell of powder was stronger than that of the burning incense. The floor was strewed with pine leaves, and covered with kneeling women, with black mantillas drawn close over the top of the head, and held together under the chin. I never saw a more beautiful spectacle than these rows of kneeling women, with faces pure and lofty in expression, lighted up by the enthusiasm of religion; and among them, fairer than most and lovely as any, was one from my own land; not more than twenty-two, married to a gentleman belonging to one of the first families of Guatimala, once an exile in the United States. In a new land and among a new people, she had embraced a new faith; and, with the enthusiasm of a youthful convert, no lady in Guatimala was more devout, more regular at mass, or more strict in all the discipline of the Catholic Church than the Sister Susannah.

After the fireworks there was a long ceremony at the altar, and then a general rush toward the other extremity of the church. The convent was directly adjoining, and in the partition wall, about six feet from the floor, was a high iron grating, and about four feet beyond it another, at which the nuns attended the services of the church. Above the iron grating was a wooden one, and from this in a few minutes issued a low strain of wild Indian music, and presently a figure in white, with a long white veil and a candle in her right hand, and both arms extended, walked slowly to within a few feet of the grating, and then as slowly retired. Presently the same low note issued from the grating below, and we saw advancing a procession of white nuns, with long white veils, each holding in her hand a long lighted candle. The music ceased, and a chant arose, so low that it required intent listening

22. Juan José Aycinena; see Ch. 1 n. 66, Ch. 2 n. 30, and Ch. 2 n. 71.

to catch the sound. Advancing two and two with this low chant to within a few feet of the grating, the sisters turned off different ways. At the end of the procession were two black nuns, leading between them the probationer, dressed in white, with a white veil and a wreath of roses round her head. The white nuns arranged themselves on each side, their chant ceased, and the voice of the probationer was heard alone, but so faint that it seemed the breathing of a spirit of air. The white nuns strewed flowers before her, and she advanced between the two black ones. Three times she stopped and kneeled, continuing the same low chant, and the last time the white nuns gathered around her, strewing flowers upon her head and in her path. Slowly they led her to the back part of the chapel, and all kneeled before the altar.

At this time a strain of music was heard at the other end of the church; a way was cleared through the crowd, and a procession advanced, consisting of the principal priests, clothed in their richest robes, and headed by the venerable provisor, an octogenarian with white hair, and tottering on the verge of the grave, as remarkable for the piety of his life as for his venerable appearance.[23] A layman bore on a rich frame a gold crown and sceptre studded with jewels. The procession advanced to a small door on the right of the grating, and the two black nuns and the probationer appeared in the doorway. Some words passed between her and the provisor, which I understood to be an examination by him whether her proposed abandonment of the world was voluntary or not. This over, the provisor removed the wreath of roses and the white veil, and put on her head the crown and in her hand the sceptre. The music sounded loud notes of triumph, and in a few moments she reappeared at the grating with the crown and sceptre, and a dress sparkling with jewels. The sisters embraced her, and again threw roses upon her. It seemed horrible to heap upon her the pomp and pleasures of the world, at the moment when she was about to bid farewell to them forever. Again she kneeled before the altar; and when she rose the jewels and precious stones, the rich ornaments with which she was decorated, were taken from her, and she returned to the bishop, who took away the crown and sceptre, and put on her head the black veil. Again she appeared before the grating; the last, the fatal step was not yet taken; the black veil was not drawn. Again the nuns pressed round, and this time they almost devoured her with kisses.

23. The vicar for Archbishop Casaus at the time of Stephens' visit, who is probably the provisor described, was seventy-year-old Antonio Larrazábal.

I knew nothing of her story. I had not heard that the ceremony was to take place till late in the evening before, and I had made up my mind that she was old and ugly; but she was not, nor was she faded and worn with sorrow, the picture of a broken heart; nor yet a young and beautiful enthusiast; she was not more than twenty-three, and had one of those good faces which, without setting men wild by their beauty, bear the impress of a nature well qualified for the performance of all duties belonging to daughter, and wife, and mother, speaking the kindliness and warmth of a woman's heart. It was pale, and she seemed conscious of the important step and the solemn vows she was taking, and to have no pangs; and yet who can read what is passing in the human breast?

She returned to the provisor who drew over her face a black veil; and music rose in bursts of rejoicing, that one who was given to the world to take a share in its burdens had withdrawn herself from it. Immediately commenced the hum of restrained voices; and working my way through the crowd, I joined a party of ladies, one of whom was my fair countrywoman. She was from a small country town in Pennsylvania, and the romance of her feelings toward convents and nuns had not yet worn off. On Carrera's first invasion she had taken refuge in the convent of La Concepcion, and spoke with enthusiasm of the purity and piety of the nuns, describing some as surpassing in all the attributes of woman. She knew particularly the one who had just taken the veil, and told me that in a few days she would appear at the grating of the convent to embrace her friends and bid them farewell, and promised to take me and procure me a share in the distribution.

During this time rockets were fired from the steps, and in the street, immediately in front, was a frame of fireworks thirty feet high, which the whole crowd waited on the steps and in the street to see set off. Everybody spoke of the absurdity of such an exhibition by daylight, but they said it was the custom. The piece was complicated in its structure, and in the centre was a large box. There was a whizzing of wheels, a great smoke, and occasionally a red flash; and as the extermities burned out, for the finale, with a smart cracking, the box flew open, and when the smoke cleared away, discovered the figure of a little black nun, at which all laughed and went away.

On Friday, in company with my fair countrywoman, I visited the convent of La Concepcion for the purpose of embracing a nun, or rather *the* nun, who had taken the black veil. The room adjoining the parlatoria of the convent was crowded, and she was standing in the doorway with the crown on her head and a doll in her hand.[24] It was the last time her friends could see her face; but this puerile exhibition of the doll detracted from the sentiment. It was an occasion that addressed itself particularly to ladies; some wondered that one so young should abandon a world to them beaming with bright and beautiful prospects; others, with whom the dreams of life had passed, looked upon her retirement as the part of wisdom. They embraced her, and retired to make room for others. Before our turn came there was an irruption of those objects of my detestation, the eternal soldiers, who, leaving their muskets at the door, forced their way through the crowd, and presenting themselves, though respectfully, for an embrace, retired. By her side was a black nun, with a veil so thick that not a lineament of her face could be seen, whom my countrywoman had known during her seclusion in the convent, and described as young, of exceeding beauty and loveliness, and around whom she threw a charm which almost awakened a spirit of romance. I would have made some sacrifice for one glimpse of her face. At length our turn came; my fair companion embraced her, and, after many farewell words, recommended me as her countryman. I never had much practice in embracing nuns; in fact, it was the first time I ever attempted such a thing; but it came as natural as if I had been brought up to it. My right arm encircled her neck, her right arm mine; I rested my head upon her shoulder, and she hers upon mine; but a friend's grandmother never received a more respectful embrace. "Stolen joys are always dearest;" there were too many looking on. The grating closed, and the face of the nun will never be seen again.

Diplomats Thompson and Montgomery described another of the celebrations which excited the inhabitants of the capital, thirteen years and a revolution against the church having transpired between the one witnessing and the other:[25]

. . . The town was all in a bustle, to celebrate the grand procession of Corpus Christi. All the houses were thrown open; garlands of ribands and flowers were streaming from the windows or suspended across the streets: at four different stations, each of them at the farthest angle from the centre of the town, were erected temporary altars,

24. "Parlatoria"=parlatory, or a conventual reception room.
25. Thompson, 1829, pp. 189–91; Montgomery, 1839, pp. 160–61.

ornamented with cut glass, looking-glasses, large silver salvers, together with other articles of gold and silver, and in short every species of wealth and finery that the inhabitants possessed. The principal families who live near the particular station, undertake, by turns, the fitting up of these altars; but it is customary for every one to contribute something towards their ornament: during the procession, in particular, these temporary altars are illuminated with a profusion of wax candles: the same are also kept burning on them for a day or two previous, and it is usual to see the young ladies of the family occupied in the office of trimming them, and in fact, taking charge of the whole arrangement.

In all the several ceremonies, both in and out of the church, the civil authorities were much employed:—church and state were intimately blended. The President was conveyed to and from the cathedral in a state carriage, drawn by four mules; two young lads of family . . . acting as postillions. In the procession, there were included all the religious orders of the place: of the order of Carmen, there were forty monks, of our Lady of Mercy thirty, Franciscans forty, Dominicans thirty, Recollects fifty, Collegians thirty; in all about 220; these were followed by 400 soldiers and fifty or sixty other persons, who also formed part of the procession.[26]

I was invited into the house of the Marquess of Ayzenena: the large rooms looking into the street were full of company; the windows were all open and the ladies were disposed in groups on the window-seats; and their mothers, many of whom were indisposed by colds, which they were thus increasing, were seated in chairs behind them. As the Host passed, the whole company knelt down, and after a minute's silence and recollection, the buzz of mirth and business again filled the apartment.

They have a great partiality for religious ceremonies and processions. That of Corpus Christi, which I witnessed during my stay there, is the grandest and the most admired. The procession was headed by a body of cavalry, composed of citizens, who were well mounted and

26. Thompson's previous listing (see Ch. 6 n. 14) does not square entirely with this one, the Carmelites (order of Carmen) being here added and the minor groups (the Augustinians and the unofficial Congregation of the Oratory and Alcantarines) subtracted. The Recollects here presumably equate with Our Lady of the Reform, and the Collegians with the Company of Belén. Juarros, 1936, 1:122–46, mentions only lay and female orders among the Carmelites, the former of which probably attracted Thompson's attention on this occasion.

dressed. Then came a number of other citizens on foot, with lighted tapers in their hands. These were followed by the authorities and the clergy; and then came the prelate, who represented the bishop, arrayed in his pontifical robes, and carrying the chalice containing the host. He walked under a canopy of silk, embroidered and fringed with gold, which was supported by four men of rank, arrayed in full uniform. The ground before him was strewed with leaves and flowers. Every head was uncovered, and every knee bent, as he passed; but this was in devotion to the host which he bore in the chalice. The prelate was followed by a coach and six horses. This was an old-fashioned state carriage, of richly carved wood, and gilt, with high massive wheels, heavy leather springs, and glass windows on each side and in front. The horses were gorgeously, though clumsily, caparisoned. Three of them were mounted by youths as postilions, and each horse was attended by a groom on foot. A guard of infantry and a military band brought up the rear; and then came the rabble—men, women, and children, of all colours. The streets along which the procession passed were covered with awnings; the houses were adorned with hangings of silk or velvet of various colours, and the windows crowded with spectators. Four altars were erected at intervals, which were illuminated with wax candles, and glittered with mirrors, artificial flowers, and a variety of ornaments of gold, and silver, and cut glass. It was altogether a most picturesque and interesting scene, in which the blending of religious and military pomp, the diversity of costumes, and the variety of novel objects that met the eye, could not fail of exciting the curiosity, and arresting the attention, of a spectator.

Quezaltenango, at Easter time in 1840, combined the ceremonial sophistication which only a larger center could provide with the unrestrained religious enthusiasm of Central America's indigenous population. Here, in John Lloyd Stephens' words, can be seen the ultimate in Central American expression of feeling for that time as reported by the observers from other worlds:[27]

> ... The cura ... was at that time engrossed with the ceremonies of the Holy Week, and in the evening we accompanied him to the church. At the door the *coup d'œil* of the interior was most striking. The church was two hundred and fifty feet in length, spacious and lofty, richly decorated with pictures and sculptured ornaments, blazing with lights,

27. Stephens, 1842, 2:209–17.

and crowded with Indians. On each side of the door was a grating, behind which stood an Indian to receive offerings. The floor was strewed with pine-leaves. On the left was the figure of a dead Christ on a bier, upon which every woman who entered threw a handful of roses, and near it stood an Indian to receive money. Opposite, behind an iron grating, was the figure of Christ bearing the cross, the eyes bandaged, and large silver chains attached to the arms and other parts of the body, and fastened to the iron bars. Here, too, stood an Indian to receive contributions. The altar was beautiful in design and decorations, consisting of two rows of Ionic columns, one above another, gilded, surmounted by a golden glory, and lighted by candles ten feet high. . . .

At about ten o'clock the crowd in the church formed into a procession, and Mr. C. and I went out and took a position at the corner of a street to see it pass. It was headed by Indians, two abreast, each carrying in his hand a long lighted wax candle; and then, borne aloft on the shoulders of four men, came the figure of Judith, with a bloody sword in one hand, and in the other the gory head of Holofernes. Next, also on the shoulders of four men, the archangel Gabriel, dressed in red silk, with large wings puffed out. The next were men in grotesque armour, made of black and silver paper, to resemble Moors, with shield and spear like ancient cavaliers; and then four little girls, dressed in white silk and gauze, and looking like little spiritualities, with men on each side bearing lighted candles. Then came a large figure of Christ bearing the cross, supported by four Indians; on each side were young Indian lads, carrying long poles horizontally, to keep the crowd from pressing upon it, and followed by a procession of townsmen. In turning the corner of the street at which we stood, a dark Mestitzo, with a scowl of fanaticism on his face, said to Mr. Catherwood, "Take off your spectacles and follow the cross." Next followed a procession of women with children in their arms, half of them asleep, fancifully dressed with silver caps and headdresses, and finally a large statue of the Virgin, in a sitting posture, magnificently attired, with Indian lads on each side, as before, supporting poles with candles. The whole was accompanied with the music of drums and violins; and, as the long train of light passed down the street, we returned to the convent.

The night was very cold, and the next morning was like one in December at home. It was the morning of Good Friday; and throughout Guatimala, in every village, preparations were making to celebrate, with the most solemn ceremonies of the Church, the resurrection of the Saviour. In Quezaltenango, at that early hour, the plaza was thronged with Indians. . . .

At nine o'clock the corregidor called for us, and we accompanied him to the opening ceremony. On one side of the nave of the church, near the grand altar, and opposite the pulpit, were high cushioned chairs for the corregidor and members of the municipality, and we had seats with them. The church was thronged with Indians, estimated at more than three thousand. Formerly, at this ceremony no women or children were admitted; but now the floor of the church was filled with Indian women on their knees, with red cords plaited in their hair, and perhaps one third of them had children on their backs, their heads and arms only visible. . . .

At the steps of the grand altar stood a large cross, apparently of solid silver, richly carved and ornamented, and over it a high arbour of pine and cypress branches. At the foot of the cross stood a figure of Mary Magdalen weeping, with her hair in a profusion of ringlets, her frock low in the neck, and altogether rather immodest. On the right was the figure of the Virgin gorgeously dressed, and in the nave of the church stood John the Baptist, placed there, as it seemed, only because they had the figure on hand. Very soon strains of wild Indian music rose from the other end of the church, and a procession advanced, headed by Indians with broad-brimmed felt hats, dark cloaks, and lighted wax candles, preceding the body of the Saviour on a bier borne by the cura and attendant padres, and followed by Indians with long wax candles. The bier advanced to the foot of the cross; ladders were placed behind against it; the gobernador, with his long black cloak and broad-brimmed felt hat, mounted on the right, and leaned over, holding in his hands a silver hammer and a long silver spike; another Indian dignitary mounted on the other side, while the priests raised the figure up in front; the face was ghastly, blood trickled down the cheeks, the arms and legs were moveable, and in the side was a gaping wound, with a stream of blood oozing from it. The back was affixed to the cross, the arms extended, spikes driven through the hands and feet, the ladders taken away, and thus the figure of Christ was nailed to the cross.

This over, we left the church, and passed two or three hours in visiting. . . .

In the afternoon we were again seated with the municipality in the church, to behold the descent from the cross. The spacious building was thronged to suffocation, and the floor was covered by a dense mass of kneeling women, with turbaned headdresses, and crying children on their backs, their imaginations excited by gazing at the bleeding figure on the cross. . . . A priest ascended the pulpit, thin and ghastly pale, who, in a voice that rang through every part of the building, preached emphatically a passion sermon. Few of the Indians understood even the language, and at times the cries of children made his words inaudible; but the thrilling tones of his voice played upon every chord in their hearts; and mothers, regardless of their infants' cries, sat motionless, their countenances fixed in high and stern enthusiasm. . . . Every moment the excitement grew stronger. The priest tore off his black cap, and leaning over the pulpit, stretched forward both his arms, and poured out a frantic apostrophe to the bleeding figure on the cross. A dreadful groan, almost curdling the blood, ran through the church. At this moment, at a signal from the cura, the Indians sprang upon the arbour of pine branches, tore it asunder, and with a noise like the crackling of a great conflagration, struggling and scuffling around the altar, broke into bits the consecrated branches to save as holy relics. Two Indians in broad-brimmed hats mounted the ladders on each side of the cross, and with embroidered cloth over their hands, and large silver pincers, drew out the spikes from the hands. The feelings of the women burst forth in tears, sobs, groans, and shrieks of lamentation, so loud and deep, that, coming upon us unexpectedly, our feelings were disturbed, and even with sane men the empire of reason tottered. Such screams of anguish I never heard called out by mortal suffering; and as the body, smeared with blood, was held aloft under the pulpit, while the priest leaned down and apostrophized it with frantic fervour, and the mass of women, wild with excitement, heaved to and fro like the surges of a troubled sea, the whole scene was so thrilling, so dreadfully mournful, that, without knowing why, tears started from our eyes. Four years before, at Jerusalem, on Mount Calvary itself, and in presence of the scoffing Mussulman, I had beheld the same representation of the descent from the cross; but the enthusiasm of Greek pilgrims in the Church of the Holy Sepulchre was nothing compared with this whirlwind of fanaticism and phrensy. By degrees the excitement died away; the cracking of the pine branches ceased, the whole arbour was broken up and distributed, and very soon commenced preparations for the grand procession.

We went out with the corregidor and officers of the municipality, and took our place in the balcony of the cabildo. The procession opened upon us in a manner so extraordinary, that, screening myself from observation below, I endeavoured to make a note of it on the spot. The leader was a man on horseback, called the centurion, wearing a helmet and cuirass of pasteboard covered with silver leaf, a black crape mask, black velvet shorts and white stockings, a red sash, and blue and red ribands on his arms, a silver-hilted sword, and a lance, with which, from time to time turning round, he beckoned and waved the procession on. Then came a led horse, having on its back an old Mexican saddle richly plated with silver. Then two men wearing long blue gowns, with round hoods covering their heads, and having only holes for the eyes, leading two mules abreast, covered with black cloth dresses enveloping their whole bodies to their feet, the long trains of which were supported by men attired like the other two. Then followed the large silver cross of the crucifixion, with a richly-ornamented silver pedestal, and ornaments dangling from each arm of the cross that looked like lanterns, supported by four men in long black dresses. Next came a procession of Indians, two abreast, wearing long black cloaks, with black felt hats, the brims six or eight inches wide, all with lighted candles in their hands, and then four Indians in the same costume, but with crowns of thorns on their heads, dragging a long low carriage or bier filled with pine-leaves, and having a naked scull laid on the top at one end.

Next, and in striking contrast with this emblem of mortality, advanced an angel in the attitude of an opera-dancer, borne on the shoulders of six men, dressed in flounced purple satin, with lace at the bottom, gauze wings, and a cloud of gauze over her head, holding in her right hand a pair of silver pincers, and in her left a small wooden cross, and having a train of white muslin ten yards long, supported by a pretty little girl fancifully dressed. Then another procession of Indians with lighted candles; then a group of devils in horrible masquerade. Then another angel, still more like an opera-dancer, dressed in azure blue satin, with rich lace wings, and clouds, and fluttering ribands, holding in her right hand a ladder, and in her left a silver hammer; her train supported as before; and we could not help seeing that she wore black velvet smallclothes. Then another angel, dressed in yellow, holding in her right hand a small wooden cross, and in the other I could not tell what.

The next in order was a beautiful little girl about ten years old, armed cap-a-pie, with breastplate and helmet of silver, also called the centurion, who moved along in a slow and graceful dance, keeping time to the music, turning round, stopping, resting on her sword, and waving on a party worthy of such a chief, being twelve beautiful children fancifully dressed, intended to represent the twelve apostles; one of them carrying in his arms a silver cock, to signify that he was the representative of St. Peter. The next was the great object of veneration, the figure of the Christ crucified, on a bier, in a full length case of plate glass, strewed with roses inside and out, and protected by a mourning canopy of black cloth, supported by men in long black gowns, with hoods covering all but the eyes. This was followed by the cura and priests in their richest robes and bareheaded, the muffled drum, and soldiers with arms reversed; the Virgin Mary, in a long black mourning dress, closed the procession. It passed on to make the tour of the city; twice we intercepted it, and then went to the Church of El Calvario. It stands on an elevation at the extreme end of a long street, and the steps were already crowded with women dressed in white from the head to the feet, with barely an oval opening for the face. It was dark when the procession made its appearance at the foot of the street, but by the blaze of innumerable lighted candles every object was exhibited with more striking wildness, and fanaticism seemed written in letters of fire on the faces of the Indians. The centurion cleared a way up the steps; the procession, with a loud chant, entered the church, and we went away.

Topical Index (1821–60)

The thirty-five books here analyzed are selected as the most revelatory travel accounts of Central America during the designated forty-year period. First there appears a listing of the books, keyed to the bibliography. A reference symbol is given for each, and the dates of the author's Central American travel:

27R	Roberts 1827	1818–Nov.? 1822
27–28H	Haefkens 1827–28 (2 vols.)	Sept. 9, 1826–1827
29D	Dunn 1829	May 1827–May? 1828
29T	Thompson 1829	May 10, 1825–July 25, 1825
29W	Wilson 1829	May 6, 1825–Aug. 24, 1825
39M	Montgomery 1839	Apr. 26, 1838–July 15, 1838
42S1–2	Stephens 1842 (2 vols.)	Nov. 3, 1839–Apr. 28? 1840
42Y	Young 1842	Oct. 1839–Jan.? 1842
43J	Jarves 1843	Jan. 24, 1838–Feb.? 1838
47D	Dunlop 1847	Apr. 4, 1844–Jan. 1, 1847
49B	Byam 1849	1839–41
50A	Arlach 1850	Sept. 25, 1845–1845?
50C	Crowe 1850	Jan. 1841–Apr. 1846
52S1–2	Squier 1852 (2 vols.)	May 1849–June 1850
53H	Heine 1853	June 18, 1851–June? 1852
54R	Reichardt 1854	Dec. 17, 1851–June? 1852
55SW	Squier 1855 (*Waikna*)	
56W	Wagner and Scherzer 1856	Apr. 28, 1853–Feb. 1854
57M2	Morelet 1857 (vol. 2)	May? 1847–Dec. 1847
57SG	Scherzer 1857 (German ed.)	Feb. 1854–May 7, 1854
57W	Wells 1857	Aug. 28? 1854–June? 1855
58T	Tempsky 1858	Apr. 21, 1854–Jan. 1855
59F	Froebel 1859	Nov. 18, 1850–Sept. 12, 1851; Oct. 3, 1855–Oct. 5, 1855; Mar. 30, 1857–1857

60T	Trollope 1860 (either ed.)	Apr. 1859–May 1859
60Wa	Walker 1860	June 16, 1855–May 1, 1857
60Wi	Wight 1860	Oct. 17, 1855–Oct. 1855
61S	Sivers 1861	1854?–1854?
61V	Valois 1861	Dec. 1848–1851?
63M	Marr 1863	Oct. 28, 1852–July? 1853
63P	Pim 1863	Nov.? 1859–Apr. 1860
66L	Leyland 1866	Jan. 1854–1856
69F	Foote 1869	Feb.? 1852–Oct.? 1859
86D	Doubleday 1886	June? 1854–Oct. 1855; Jan. 1857–Apr.? 1857
99B	Bell 1899	1841?–1857?
1909J	Jamison 1909	Dec. 1855–May? 1857

The edition chosen in each case is the fullest (in relation to Central America) published during the author's own lifetime. Peculiarities of other editions, where they exist, are mentioned in the bibliography or in the text. Squier's *Waikna,* with a fictional narrative, has no precise dates.

The schematic outline of the index is as follows:

I. People.
   A. Ethnic groups:
   B. Languages and dialects:
   C. Manners and customs:
   D. Individual persons:
II. Places.
   A. Natural characteristics:
   B. Physical description:
     1. Islands:
     2. Gulfs, bays, and lagoons:
     3. Lakes:
     4. Mountains (nonvolcanic):
     5. Rivers:
     6. Volcanoes:
   C. Cultural description.
     1. Cities and towns.
       a. Costa Rica:
       b. El Salvador:
       c. Guatemala:
       d. Honduras:
       e. Nicaragua:
     2. Departments and provinces.
       a. Costa Rica:
       b. El Salvador:
       c. Guatemala:
       d. Honduras:
       e. Nicaragua:
   D. Demography:
III. Government:
IV. Economy.
   A. Agriculture:
   B. Commerce:
   C. Other prime industries:
   D. Auxiliary activity.
     1. Communication:
     2. Transportation:
   E. Economic welfare.
V. Learning.
   A. Education:
   B. Natural science:
   C. Social science. [No entries.]
VI. Art:
VII. Religion.
   A. Catholicism:
   B. Protestantism.
   C. Freethinking.
   D. Paganism.
   E. Witchcraft.
   F. Original philosophy. [No entries.]
   G. Morality.

Subheadings, each bloc of them arranged in alphabetical order, appear wherever the schematic outline shows a colon. See the preface

TOPICAL INDEX (1821–60) 309

for comment on the special handling of ID and IIC, in contrast to all other items. In ID an attempt is made to list every chief of state, cabinet minister, general, ambassador, and bishop whom the travelers mentioned in personal terms. In IIC1, the "cities and towns" are or were clusters of population of greater than hacienda ranking; those names placed in brackets are old ones, which will not be found on recent maps. Department and province locations are given where there exist duplications of place names. In IIC2, the departments and provinces are as they exist in 1969. From a total of seventy-seven of them, only seven (three in El Salvador, two each in Guatemala and Honduras) were left untouched by the narratives of four decades.

I. PEOPLE

I.A. ETHNIC GROUPS

Americans (from the United States), 60Wa, 60Wi, 69F, 86D, 1909J
Belgians, 50A
Black Caribs, 27R, 29D, 39M, 42S1, 42Y, 50A, 50C, 55SW, 59F, 61S, 61V, 63P
Bribris [Blancos], 27R, 56W
Creoles, 27R, 27H, 29D, 57SG, 58T
Cucras, 27R
Englishmen, 27R, 29W
Germans, 54R, 56W, 63M
Guatusos, 59F
Indians (general), 28H, 29D, 39M, 42S, 47D, 49B, 50A, 50C, 52S, 57M2, 57SG, 57W, 59F, 61S, 61V, 63M, 69F
Ladinos, 27H, 29D, 50A, 50C, 57M2, 58T, 61V, 69F
Melchoras, 52S1
Miskitos, 27R, 42Y, 50C, 52S1, 55SW, 63P, 99B
Negroes, 27R, 57W, 99B
Payas, 42Y, 55SW
Quekchís, 57M2
Quichés, 58T
Ramas, 27R
Spaniards, 27R, 29D, 29T, 29W, 47D, 61V
Tauahcas, 42Y, 55SW, 99B
Tunglas, 99B
Ulvas, 27R, 55SW, 59F
Zambos, 61V

I.B. LANGUAGES AND DIALECTS

Diria dialect, 52S2
Nagrandan dialect, 52S2
Nicarao dialect, 52S2, 59F
Pipil dialect, 57SG
Quiché language, 42S2
Spanish language (Guatemala), 39M
Talamanca language, 56W
Tauira language, 55SW, 99B
Ulva language, 52S2, 59F

I.C. MANNERS AND CUSTOMS

Bathing, 29D, 29T, 42S1, 52S, 57W, 59F, 61V, 63P, 86D, 99B
Clothing, 27R, 27–28H, 29D, 29T, 29W, 39M, 42S, 42Y, 49B, 50C, 52S, 54R, 55SW, 56W, 57M2, 57W, 58T, 60T, 69F, 99B
Drinking, 27R, 29D, 29T, 42S, 42Y, 50C, 52S1, 55SW, 57M2, 57W, 58T, 60Wa, 61V, 86D, 99B, 1909J
Excursions (pleasure), 29D, 29T, 42S1, 47D, 52S2, 69F, 86D
Food, 27R, 27–28H, 29D, 29T, 39M, 42S, 42Y, 47D, 49B, 50C, 52S, 54R, 55SW, 56W, 57M2, 57SG, 57W, 59F, 61V, 63M, 63P, 86D, 99B
Gambling, 29D, 29W, 39M, 47D, 52S1, 57W, 58T
Games, 29D, 29T, 29W, 42S1, 99B
House interiors, 27R, 27H, 29D, 29T, 39M, 42S, 42Y, 43J, 47D, 50C, 52S,

53H, 54R, 55SW, 56W, 57M2, 57W, 69F, 99B
Meals, 27R, 27–28H, 29D, 29T, 39M, 42S, 42Y, 43J, 52S1, 55SW, 57M2, 57W, 59F
Sex, 27R, 29D, 29T, 42Y, 52S, 58T, 99B
Sickness, 27R, 27–28H, 29D, 29T, 29W, 39M, 42S, 42Y, 55SW, 56W, 57M2, 57SG, 57W, 59F, 60Wa, 61V, 63M, 66L, 86D, 99B
Smoking, 27R, 27H, 29D, 29T, 29W, 42S, 42Y, 47D, 50C, 52S, 57M2, 57W

I.D. INDIVIDUAL PERSONS

Aguilar, Eugenio, 47D
Alvarez, Miguel, 39M
Arce, Manuel José, 29T, 29W
Barca, Jesús, 57W
Barrios, Gerardo, 69F
Barrundia, José Francisco, 57SG
Barrundia, Juan, 29T
Beteta, José, 29T
Borland, Solon, 63P, 69F
Cabañas, José Trinidad, 47D, 52S2, 53H, 57SG, 57W, 60Wa
Cacho, José María, 57W
Calvo, Joaquín Bernardo, 56W
Carazo, Manuel José, 56W, 63M
Carranza, Bruno, 63M
Carrera, Rafael, 42S, 47D, 50A, 50C, 57M2, 61V
Carrillo, Braulio, 42S1
Carvajal, Pablo, 57W
Casaus y Torres, Ramón, 29T
Castellón, Francisco, 57W, 60Wa, 63M, 86D
Castro, José María, 56W, 63M
Chamorro, Fruto, 53H, 57SG, 59F
Chatfield, Frederick, 50C
Corral, Ponciano, 60Wa
Cruz, Vicente, 61V
Delgado, José Matías, 28H
Dimitry, Alexander, 63P
Escobar, Manuel, 57W
Escoto, Nazario, 59F, 60Wa
Ferrer, Fermín, 60Wa
French, Parker H., 60Wa, 60Wi
Fry, Birkett Davenport, 60Wa, 60Wi, 1909J
George Augustus Frederick, 63P, 99B
George Frederick, 27R
González Saravia, Miguel, 27R
Guardiola, Santos, 57SG
Guerrero, José, 86D
Guzmán, Joaquín Eufracio, 47D
Henningsen, Charles Frederick, 60Wa, 1909J
Hornsby, C. C., 60Wa, 86D, 1909J
Ibarra, Manuel Julián, 39M
Jérez, Máximo, 60Wa, 86D
Lindo, Juan, 52S2
Mayorga, Mateo, 57SG, 60Wa
Mora, Juan Rafael, 56W, 60T, 63M
Morazán, Francisco, 39M, 42S2
Muñoz, José Trinidad, 52S1, 53H, 59F, 60Wa, 86D
Oreamuno, Francisco María, 56W
Ouseley, William, 60T
Pineda, José Laureano, 54R, 59F, 63M
Pineda, Mateo de, 60Wa, 86D
Ramírez, Norberto, 52S1, 57W
Reyes, José Trinidad, 57W
Rivas, Patricio, 60Wa
Rivera Paz, Mariano, 42S
Robert Charles Frederick, 29D, 42Y
Rocha, Jesús de la, 54R, 57SG
Sacasa, Crisanto, 27R
San Martín, Joaquín, 39M
Sanders, Edward J., 60Wa, 1909J
Sandoval, José León, 52S1
Sosa, Juan Francisco, 29T
Valle, José Cecilio del, 29T
Vega, Fulgencio, 54R
Vigil, Agustín, 59F, 60Wa, 1909J
Vigil, Diego, 42S
Villacorta, Juan Vicente, 28H
Walker, William, 60Wa, 60Wi, 86D, 99B, 1909J
Wheeler, John Hill, 60Wa, 60Wi, 86D
Wyke, Charles Lennox, 63P
Zeledón, Pedro, 54R

II. PLACES

II.A. NATURAL CHARACTERISTICS

Earthquakes, 29D, 39M, 42S, 47D, 49B, 50C, 52S2, 57SG, 57W, 58T, 69F
Fauna, 27R, 27–28H, 29D, 39M, 42S, 42Y, 43J, 47D, 49B, 50A, 50C, 52S,

TOPICAL INDEX (1821–60) 311

54R, 55SW, 56W, 57M2, 57SG, 57W, 59F, 61S, 61V, 66L, 69F, 86D, 99B
Flora, 27R, 27–28H, 29D, 29T, 39M, 42Y, 49B, 50A, 50C, 54R, 55SW, 56W, 57M2, 57SG, 57W, 59F, 61S, 61V, 63M, 69F, 99B
Minerals, 27R, 29D, 29T, 42S, 47D, 49B, 52S1, 53H, 54R, 56W, 57SG, 57W, 59F, 61S
Rainfall, 27R, 29D, 29T, 29W, 42S, 42Y, 47D, 50C, 52S1, 54R, 55SW, 56W, 57M2, 57SG, 57W, 59F, 61V, 63P, 99B
Soil, 52S, 56W, 57M2, 57SG, 57W, 59F
Temperatures, 27–28H, 29D, 29W, 42Y, 47D, 50A, 52S1, 53H, 54R, 56W, 57M2, 57SG, 57W, 61V, 63M, 63P

II.B. PHYSICAL DESCRIPTION

II.B.1. ISLANDS

Barbareta, 27R, 42Y
Elena, 42Y
Granada (Isletas de), 52S, 54R, 59F
Guanaja (Bonacca), 27R, 42Y
Maíz (Islas del) [Corn Islands], 63P
Ometepe, 52S2, 59F, 60Wa, 1909J
Roatán, 27R, 42Y
San Bernardo, 63M
Tigre, 52S2, 57W, 58T, 61S
Utila, 27R
Zacate Grande, 57W
Zapatera, 52S2

II.B.2. GULFS, BAYS, AND LAGOONS

Laguna de Caratasca, 27R
Gulf of Fonseca, 42S2, 47D, 52S2, 57SG, 57W, 58T, 61S
Gulf of Nicoya, 56W
Laguna de Perlas [Pearl Cay Lagoon], 63P
Estero Real, 42S2, 52S2, 53H, 57W

II.B.3. LAKES

L. Amatitlán, 27H, 29D, 29T, 39M, 47D, 57M2
L. Apoyo [L. Salinas], 52S1, 59F
L. Atitlán, 42S2
L. Ilopango [L. Cojutepeque], 47D

L. Izabal [Golfo Dulce], 29T, 39M, 57M2
L. Managua, 27R, 42S2, 52S, 57SG, 59F, 86D
L. Masaya, 42S2, 52S2, 57SG
L. Nejapa, 52S1
L. Nicaragua, 27R, 42S1, 49B, 52S, 53H, 54R, 57SG, 59F, 60Wi, 61S, 63M, 63P, 86D
L. Petén Itzá, 57M2, 66L

II.B.4. MOUNTAINS (NONVOLCANIC)

Mico, 27H, 29D, 29T, 29W, 39M, 42S1, 43J, 57M2
[Cerro de Ule], 53H, 57W

II.B.5. RIVERS

Coco R. [Wanks R.], 55SW, 99B
Colorado R., 63P
R. Dulce, 27H, 29D, 29T, 29W, 39M, 42S1, 43J, 50A, 57M2, 61V
R. Grande de Tárcoles, 56W
[Guarumal R.], 39M, 42S2, 69F
Guayape R., 57W
María Linda R. [Michatoya R.], 57M2
[Michatoya R.], 29D, 42S1
Motagua R., 29D, 29T, 29W, 39M, 42S1, 57M2
R. Negro [Black R.], 27R, 42Y
Patuca R., 55SW
Paulaya R., 42Y
Polochic R., 39M
Prinzapolca R., 99B
San Juan R., 27R, 49B, 52S, 53H, 54R, 56W, 59F, 60T, 63M, 63P, 69F, 86D, 99B
Sarapiquí R., 56W, 60T, 63M
Tipitapa R., 42S2, 52S1, 54R, 59F
Ulúa R., 61S

II.B.6. VOLCANOES

Agua, 27H, 29D, 42S1, 47D, 61V
Concepción [Ometepe], 59F
Conchagua, 47D, 52S2
Cosigüina, 39M, 42S2, 47D, 49B, 52S2, 57SG, 57W
Fuego, 29D, 42S1, 47D
Irazú [Cartago], 42S1, 47D, 60T
Izalco, 39M, 42S1, 43J, 47D, 52S2, 57SG, 58T, 69F
Las Pilas, 52S2

Madera, 59F
Miravalles, 56W
Mombacho, 52S2, 57SG
Momotombito, 52S1
Momotombo, 86D
Pacaya, 47D
San Miguel, 47D, 57W
San Salvador, 47D, 57SG
San Vicente, 42S1
Santiago [Masaya], 42S2, 52S1, 59F, 1909J
Telica, 59F, 63M
Turrialba, 63M

II.C. CULTURAL DESCRIPTION

II.C.1. CITIES AND TOWNS

II.C.1.A. Costa Rica

Alajuela, 42S1, 47D, 56W, 63M
[Angostura], 56W, 63M
Aranjuez, 42S1
Atenas, 56W, 60T, 63M
Bagaces, 42S1, 56W
Caldera, 42S1
Cariblanco, 56W, 60T, 63M
Cartago, 42S1, 47D, 56W, 60T, 63M
El Muelle, 56W, 60T, 63M
Esparta, 42S1, 56W, 60T, 63M
Heredia, 47D, 56W, 60T
Jesús María, 42S1
La Garita, Alajuela, 42S1, 56W, 63M
La Virgen, 56W, 63M
Lepanto, 56W
Liberia [Guanacaste], 42S1, 56W
Matina, 47D, 56W
Moín, 56W
Navarro, 56W
Orosí, 56W
Pigres, 56W
Puntarenas, 42S1, 47D, 56W, 60T, 63M, 69F
San José, 42S1, 47D, 56W, 60T, 63M
San Mateo, 42S1, 56W, 60T, 63M
San Miguel, Heredia, 56W, 60T, 63M
Santa Rosa, eastern Guanacaste, 42S1
Tárcoles, 56W
Tres Ríos, 63M
Turrialba, 56W
Vara Blanca, 56W, 63M

II.C.1.B. El Salvador

Acajutla, 28H, 29T, 42S1, 43J, 47D, 69F
Ahuachapán, 28H, 29T, 39M, 42S2, 47D, 57SG
Apaneca, 28H, 29T, 39M, 42S2, 47D, 57SG
Apopa, 39M, 57SG
Ateos, 39M
Atiquizaya, 28H
[Betaca], 57SG
Chalchuapa, 47D
Chinameca, 28H, 47D, 57SG, 58T
Cojutepeque, 28H, 42S2, 47D, 57SG, 58T, 69F
Conchagua, 28H, 52S2
[El Sacario], 39M
[Guaymoca], 47D, 69F
Izalco, 28H, 39M, 42S, 47D, 57SG, 58T, 69F
Jucuapa, 28H
La Libertad, 69F
La Puerta, 57SG
La Unión, 42S2, 47D, 52S2, 57SG, 58T, 69F
[Lempa], 58T, 69F
Mercedes Umaña, 69F
Nahuizalco, 29T, 39M, 42S2
Quezaltepeque, 47D, 57SG
Salcoatitán, 29T
San Alejo, 42S2, 47D
San Antonio Silva, 47D
San Cayetano Ixtepeque, 28H
San Francisco Lempa, 57SG
San Martín, 47D
San Miguel, 28H, 42S2, 47D, 57SG, 58T, 69F
San Salvador, 28H, 39M, 42S2, 47D, 57SG, 58T, 69F
San Vicente, 28H, 47D, 57SG, 58T, 69F
Santa Ana, 28H, 47D
Santa Tecla, 57SG, 69F
Sonsonate, 28H, 29T, 39M, 42S, 43J, 47D, 57SG, 58T, 69F
Suchitoto, 57SG
Tepetitán, 28H, 47D
Usulután, 28H, 47D
Zacatecoluca, 28H

II.C.1.C. Guatemala

[Abbottsville], 50C
Agua Caliente, Guatemala, 29W
Agua Caliente, Quezaltenango, 42S2

TOPICAL INDEX (1821–60)

Almolonga, 42S2
Alotenango, 29D, 42S1
Amatitlán, 27H, 29D, 29T, 42S1, 47D, 50A, 57M2, 61V
Antigua, 27H, 29D, 29T, 42S1, 47D, 50A, 50C, 57M2, 58T, 61V
Ayutla, 58T
Barillas, Guatemala, 47D
Cabañas [Chimalapa], 27H, 29D, 29T, 29W, 42S1, 50A
Cahabón, 57M2
Cahaboncito, 39M
Camotán, 42S1
[Casas Viejas], 50A, 57M2
[Cerro Redondo], 47D
Chaac, 57M2
Chinautla, 27H, 57M2, 61V
Chiquimula, 39M, 42S1, 43J, 57M2
Ciudad Vieja, 29D, 42S, 47D, 50A, 61V
Cobán, 57M2
[Corral de Piedra], 42S2, 58T
Cuilapa [Cuajiniquilapa], 28H, 29T, 39M, 47D, 57SG
Dolores, southeastern Petén, 57M2
Dolores, western Petén, 57M2
Dueñas, 47D
El Chal, 57M2
El Obero, 29D, 42S1, 57M2
[El Pozo], 42S
El Progreso [Guastatoya], 27H, 29D, 29T, 29W, 42S1, 61V
El Puente, 50C
[El Rosario], Guatemala, 47D
Esclavos, 29T, 42S2, 47D, 57SG
Escuintla, 27H, 29D, 42S1, 47D, 57M2, 61V
Esquipulas, 39M, 42S1, 50A
Flores, 57M2, 66L
Fraijanes, 29T, 47D
Godínez, 42S2
Gualán, 27H, 29D, 29T, 29W, 39M, 42S1, 43J, 50A, 50C, 57M2, 61V
Guatemala, 27–28H, 29D, 29T, 29W, 39M, 42S, 47D, 50A, 50C, 57M2, 57SG, 58T, 61V
Huehuetenango, 42S2
Iguana, 29T, 29W, 39M, 61V
Izabal, 27H, 29D, 29T, 29W, 39M, 42S1, 43J, 50A, 50C, 57M2, 61V
Iztapa, 29D, 42S1, 47D, 57M2, 61V

Jalpatagua, 29T, 47D, 57SG
Jocotán, 42S1
[Jocotenango], 29D, 29T, 29W, 39M, 61V
Jocotillo, 42S2
Juntecholol, 57M2
La Vega, 47D
Lanquín, 57M2
[León], 42S2
Livingston, 39M, 42S1, 50A, 57M2, 61V
Los Amates, 42S2
[Los Encuentros], Izabal, 27H, 29T, 29W, 42S, 50A, 57M2
[Los Navajos], 29W
[Los Platones], 29W
[Los Verdes], 47D
Malacatán, 58T
Masagua, 29D, 42S1
Matías de Gálvez [Santo Tomás], 39M, 47D, 50A, 57M2, 59F, 61V
[Mico], 50A
Mixco, Guatemala, 42S1, 57M2, 58T, 61V
[New Liverpool], 50C
Ocós, 47D
[Omoita], 27H, 29T, 29W
Oratorio, 28H, 29T, 39M, 42S2, 47D, 57SG
Palín, Escuintla [San Cristóbal], 42S1, 47D, 57M2
Panajachel, 42S2
Parramos, 42S2
Patal, 39M, 57M2
Patzicía, 58T
Patzún, 42S2, 58T
Petapa, 29D, 39M, 47D
Poptún, 57M2
[Pozo], 50A, 57M2
Quezaltenango, 42S2, 58T
Quezaltepeque, 39M, 42S1
Quiriguá, 61V
Quiriguá Viejo, 42S2, 61V
Retalhuleu, 58T
Sacluc, 57M2
Salamá, 39M, 50C, 57M2
San Andrés, Petén, 57M2
San Andrés, Sololá, 58T
San Andrés Itzapa, 42S2
[San Antonio Aguas Calientes], 42S2
San Antonio Huista, 42S2

[San Esteban], 42S1
San Felipe, Izabal, 27H, 29D, 29T, 39M, 50A, 57M2, 61V
San Jacinto, Chiquimula, 42S1
[San José], Guatemala, 47D
San José, Jutiapa, 42S2
San José, central Petén, 57M2
San José del Golfo, 27H, 29D, 42S1
[San Juan del Obispo], 42S1
San Juan Ermita, 42S1
San Lucas, 61V
San Luis, Petén, 57M2
San Martín, 42S2
San Miguel Tucurú, 39M
[San Pablo], Zacapa, 27H, 29D, 29T, 29W, 39M, 42S1, 43J, 57M2
[San Pedro], Quiché, 42S2
San Pedro Carchá, 57M2
[San Pedro Martír], 42S1, 57M2
San Vicente Pacaya, 47D
Santa Ana, Petén, 57M2
Santa Catarina Ixtahuacán, 58T
Santa Catarina Pinula, 29D
Santa Cruz, Alta Verapaz, 57M2
Santa Cruz del Quiché, 42S2
[Santa Elena], Chiquimula, 43J
[Santa Inés Petapa], 47D
Santa María de Jesús, 27H, 29D, 42S1, 57M2, 61V
[Santa Rosalía], Escuintla, 57M2
Santa Rosalía, Zacapa, 42S1
Santiago Petatán, 42S2
Santiago Sacatepéquez, 58T
Santo Tomás Chichicastenango, 42S2
Sololá, 42S2, 58T
Sumpango, 58T
Tactic, 50C, 57M2
[Taltique], 39M
Tecpán, 42S2
Telemán, 39M
Todos Santos Cuchumatán, 42S2
Totonicapán, 42S2, 58T
Tzuncal, 57M2
Utatlán (ruins), 42S2
Villa Nueva, 27H, 29T, 39M, 47D, 57M2
Yaxché, 57M2
Yaxchilán, 57M2
Zacapa, 27H, 29T, 29W, 39M, 42S1, 43J, 50A, 57M2, 61V

Zaculeu (ruins), 42S2
Zaragoza, 58T

II.C.1.D. Honduras

Alauca, 57SG
Amapala, 52S2, 57W
Barra del Patuca [Patook], 42Y
Belén, Lempira, 57SG
Campamento, 57W
[Cape Town], 42Y
Catacamas, 57W
Cauquira, 27R
Choluteca, 53H, 57W, 86D
Cieneguita, 61S
Cofradía, Francisco Morazán, 57W
Cololaca, 57SG
Comayagua, 57SG, 61S
Comayagüela, 57W
Concepción, Olancho, 57W
Copán, 42S1
Corquín, 57SG
Coyolar, Valle, 53H
Crata, 27R
Cucuyagua, 57SG
El Real, 57W
El Retiro, 57W
El Salto, 57W
[English Town], 42Y
[Fort Wellington], 42Y
Galeras, Olancho, 57W
Gracias, 57SG
Guaimaca, 57W
Intibucá, 57SG
[Jucasapa], 57SG
Juticalpa, 57W
La Lima, southwestern Olancho, 57W
La Paz, 57SG
La Trinidad, Francisco Morazán, 57W
La Venta, southern Francisco Morazán, 57W
Las Flores, Lempira, 57SG
Lepaguare, 57W
[Little Rock], 42Y
Mamisaca, 57W
Manto, 27R, 57W
Nacaome, 52S2, 57W
[Nueva Arcadia], Francisco Morazán, 57W
Nueva Ocotepeque [Ocotepeque], 39M
[Olancho Viejo] (ruins), 57W
Olosingo, 57SG

Omoa, 27H, 29D, 29W, 59F, 61S, 66L
Pespire, 57W
[Porto Sal], 61S
Protección, Comayagua, 57SG
Puerto Cortés, 59F
Punuare, 57W
Río Abajo, Francisco Morazán, 57W
Sabanagrande, 57W
San Antonio de Oriente, 53H, 57SG
San Lorenzo, Valle, 47D
San Martín, 53H
Santa Lucía, Francisco Morazán, 57W
Santa Rosa, Copán, 57SG
Sara, 57W
Sensenti, 57SG
[Sereboyer], 42Y
Talanga, Francisco Morazán, 57W
Talgua, Lempira, 57SG
Tegucigalpa, 53H, 57SG, 57W, 61S
Telica, 57W
Trujillo, 27H, 39M, 42Y, 61S
[Tulian], 59F
Villa de San Antonio, 57SG
Yuscarán, 53H, 57SG
[Zachary Lyon], 42Y

II.C.1.E. Nicaragua

[Accawass-Maya], 99B
Acoyapa, 54R, 59F
Bluefields, 27R, 55SW, 63P, 99B
Brito, 52S2, 59F
[Brus], 55SW
Buenos Aires, 57SG, 60Wa
Cabo Gracias a Dios, 27R, 42Y, 55SW, 99B
Chichigalpa, 42S2, 52S1, 57W, 63M
Chinandega, 42S2, 47D, 52S, 53H, 54R, 57SG, 57W, 60Wa, 63M, 69F, 86D
Corinto, 52S1, 54R
Dacura [Duckwarra], 27R, 99B
Darío [Chicoya], 57SG
Dipilto, 53H, 57SG
Diría, 54R, 59F
Diriamba, 54R
Diriomo, 54R
El Castillo, 27R, 52S1, 53H, 54R, 59F, 60Wa, 60Wi, 63M, 63P, 69F, 86D
El Realejo, 42S2, 47D, 49B, 52S1, 54R, 57SG, 57W, 60Wa, 61S, 63M, 69F, 86D
El Tempisque, 52S2, 57W, 69F
El Viejo, 42S2, 47D, 52S, 57W
[English Bank], 27R
Granada, 27R, 42S1, 49B, 52S, 53H, 54R, 57SG, 59F, 60Wa, 60Wi, 61S, 63M, 63P, 69F, 86D, 1909J
[Jalteva], 52S, 59F, 63M, 86D
Jinotega, 57SG
Jinotepe, 54R, 59F
Juigalpa, 54R, 59F
La Concordia, 53H
La Leonesa, 57SG
La Paz Central [Pueblo Nuevo], 27R, 42S2, 52S1, 53H, 57SG, 59F, 63M, 69F
La Virgen [Virgin Bay], 54R, 57SG, 57W, 59F, 60Wa, 60Wi, 69F, 86D, 1909J
León, 27R, 42S2, 47D, 49B, 52S, 53H, 54R, 57SG, 57W, 59F, 60Wa, 61S, 63M, 69F, 86D
Los Cocos, 63P
Lóvago, 59F
Managua, 27R, 42S2, 52S, 53H, 54R, 57SG, 59F, 60Wa, 63M, 63P, 69F
Masaya, 27R, 42S2, 52S, 53H, 54R, 57SG, 59F, 60Wa, 63M, 63P, 69F, 86D, 1909J
Matagalpa, 57SG
Mateare, 27R, 42S2, 52S, 57SG, 59F, 63M, 69F
Moyogalpa, 59F
Nagarote, 27R, 42S2, 52S1, 53H, 57SG, 59F, 60Wa, 63M, 69F
Nandaime, 52S2, 54R, 59F, 60Wa
Nindirí, 42S2, 52S, 54R, 57SG, 59F, 63M, 63P
[Obraje], 52S2, 57SG, 57W, 60Wa, 1909J
Ochomogo, 52S2
Ocotal, Nueva Segovia, 53H, 57SG
Palacagüina, 57SG
Pedernal, 52S1, 63P
[Piakos-Maya], 99B
Playa Grande, 52S2, 57W
Posoltega, 52S1, 53H, 57W, 63M
Potosí, Rivas, 52S2, 57SG, 60Wa
Prinzapolca, 27R
Puerto Morazán [Nacascolo], 42S2, 47D

[Punta Arenas], 60Wa, 86D
Punta Gorda, 27R
[Quamwatla], 55SW, 99B
Quezalguaque, 52S1
Rivas [Nicaragua], 42S1, 52S2, 54R, 57SG, 57W, 59F, 60Wa, 86D, 99B, 1909J
Rota, 52S2
San Benito, 57SG
San Carlos, Río San Juan, 27R, 52S, 53H, 54R, 59F, 60Wi, 63P, 69F, 99B
San Jacinto, 60Wa
San Jorge, 52S2, 57SG, 59F, 60Wa, 1909J
San José, Chontales, 59F
San Juan del Norte [Greytown], 27R, 49B, 52S, 53H, 54R, 56W, 59F, 60T, 60Wa, 60Wi, 63M, 63P, 69F, 86D, 99B
San Juan del Sur, 42S1, 54R, 57W, 59F, 60Wa, 60Wi, 86D, 1909J
San Miguelito, 52S1, 54R, 63P
San Rafael del Norte, 53H, 57SG
San Rafael del Sur, 54R
San Ramón, Matagalpa, 57SG
San Ubaldo, 59F
Sandy Bay, 27R, 55SW
Sébaco, 57SG
[Subtiaba], 52S1, 57SG, 57W, 59F, 86D
Telica, 59F
Tipitapa, 52S1, 53H, 54R, 57SG, 59F, 60Wa
Tola, 60Wa, 86D
Totogalpa, 53H, 57SG
[Wawashaan], 27R

II.C.2. Departments and Provinces

II.C.2.A. *Costa Rica*

Alajuela, 42S1, 47D, 56W, 60T, 63M
Cartago, 42S1, 47D, 56W, 60T, 63M
Guanacaste, 42S1, 47D, 56W
Heredia, 42S1, 47D, 56W, 60T, 63M
Limón, 27R, 56W, 63P
Puntarenas, 42S1, 47D, 56W, 60T, 63M
San José, 42S1, 47D, 56W, 60T, 63M

II.C.2.B. *El Salvador*

Ahuachapán, 28H, 29T, 39M, 42S2, 47D, 57SG, 58T

Chalatenango, 39M, 57SG
Cuscatlán, 28H, 42S2, 47D, 57SG, 58T, 69F
La Libertad, 28H, 39M, 42S2, 47D, 57SG, 69F
La Paz, 28H
La Unión, 28H, 42S2, 47D, 52S2, 57SG, 58T, 69F
San Miguel, 28H, 42S2, 47D, 57SG, 58T, 69F
San Salvador, 28H, 39M, 42S2, 47D, 57SG, 58T, 69F
San Vicente, 28H, 42S2, 47D, 57SG, 58T, 69F
Santa Ana, 28H, 43J, 47D
Sonsonate, 28H, 29T, 39M, 42S, 43J, 47D, 57SG, 58T, 69F
Usulután, 28H, 47D, 57SG, 58T, 69F

II.C.2.C. *Guatemala*

Alta Verapaz, 39M, 50C, 57M2
Baja Verapaz, 39M, 50C, 57M2
Chimaltenango, 42S2, 58T
Chiquimula, 39M, 42S1, 43J, 57M2
El Progreso, 27H, 29D, 29T, 29W, 42S1, 50A, 50C, 57M2, 61V
Escuintla, 27H, 29D, 42S1, 47D, 57M2, 61V
Guatemala, 27-28H, 29D, 29T, 29W, 39M, 42S, 47D, 50A, 50C, 57M2, 57SG, 58T, 61V
Huehuetenango, 42S2
Izabal, 27H, 29D, 29T, 29W, 39M, 42S1, 43J, 50A, 50C, 57M2, 61V
Jutiapa, 28H, 29T, 39M, 42S2, 47D, 57SG, 58T
Petén, 57M2, 66L
Quezaltenango, 42S2, 58T
Quiché, 42S2
Retalhuleu, 58T
Sacatepéquez, 27H, 29D, 29T, 42S, 47D, 50A, 50C, 57M2, 58T, 61V
San Marcos, 58T
Santa Rosa, 28H, 29T, 39M, 42S2, 47D, 57SG, 58T
Sololá, 42S2, 58T
Totonicapán, 42S2, 58T
Zacapa, 27H, 29D, 29T, 29W, 39M, 42S1, 43J, 50A, 50C, 57M2, 61V

II.C.2.D. *Honduras*

Atlántida, 61S

TOPICAL INDEX (1821–60)   317

Choluteca, 53H, 57W, 61S, 86D
Colón, 27H, 39M, 42Y
Comayagua, 57SG
Copán, 42S1, 57SG
Cortés, 27H, 29D, 29W, 59F, 61S, 66L
El Paraíso, 53H, 57SG
Francisco Morazán, 53H, 57SG, 57W
Gracias a Dios, 27R, 42Y, 55SW
Intibucá, 57SG
Islas de la Bahía, 27R, 42Y
La Paz, 57SG
Lempira, 57SG
Ocotepeque, 39M, 57SG
Olancho, 55SW, 57W
Valle, 52S2, 53H, 57W

II.C.2.E. Nicaragua

Boaco, 59F
Carazo, 59F
Chinandega, 42S2, 47D, 49B, 52S, 53H, 57SG, 57W, 60Wa, 61S, 63M, 69F, 86D
Chontales, 54R, 59F
Estelí, 53H
Granada, 27R, 42S1, 49B, 52S, 53H, 54R, 57SG, 59F, 60Wa, 60Wi, 61S, 63M, 63P, 69F, 86D, 1909J
Jinotega, 53H, 55SW, 57SG
León, 27R, 42S2, 47D, 49B, 52S, 53H, 57SG, 57W, 59F, 60Wa, 61S, 63M, 69F, 86D
Madriz, 53H, 57SG
Managua, 27R, 42S2, 52S, 53H, 57SG, 59F, 60Wa, 63M, 63P, 69F, 86D
Masaya, 27R, 42S2, 52S, 53H, 57SG, 59F, 60Wa, 63M, 63P, 69F, 86D, 1909J
Matagalpa, 57SG
Nueva Segovia, 49B, 53H, 54R, 57SG
Río San Juan, 27R, 49B, 52S, 53H, 54R, 56W, 59F, 60T, 60Wi, 63M, 63P, 69F, 86D, 99B
Rivas, 42S1, 52S2, 57SG, 57W, 59F, 60Wa, 60Wi, 86D, 99B, 1909J
Zelaya, 27R, 42Y, 55SW, 63P, 99B

II.D. DEMOGRAPHY

Colonization projects, 50A, 50C, 54R, 56W, 59F, 61V, 63M
Population counts, 27R, 27–28H, 29D, 29T, 29W, 39M, 42S, 42Y, 47D, 50A, 52S, 54R, 56W, 57M2, 57SG, 57W, 59F, 61S, 61V
Population densities, 61S

III. GOVERNMENT

Armies, 27R, 28H, 29T, 39M, 42S, 52S2, 53H, 57M2, 57SG, 60T, 60Wa, 61V, 86D, 1909J
Boundaries, 29T, 42S, 57SG
Budgets, 29D, 29T, 47D, 56W, 57SG, 61V
Cabinets, 52S2, 54R, 57SG, 60Wa
Constitutions, 29D, 29T, 39M, 52S2, 57SG
Currencies, 29D, 42Y, 57SG, 57W
Diplomacy, 27R, 29T, 42S, 50C, 52S, 53H, 54R, 59F, 60Wa, 63P
Elections, 29T, 50C, 60Wa
Executive power, 27R, 29D, 29T, 39M, 42S, 42Y, 47D, 50A, 50C, 52S, 54R, 55SW, 56W, 57SG, 57W, 59F, 60T, 60Wa, 61V, 63M, 86D, 99B, 1909J
Forts and garrisons, 27R, 29D, 29T, 29W, 39M, 42S, 42Y, 47D, 52S, 57M2, 57W, 60Wa, 60Wi, 61V, 63M, 69F, 86D
Hospitals, 29D, 47D, 57M2, 57SG
Judiciaries, 29D, 39M, 42Y, 47D, 50C, 58T
Lawlessness, 28H, 29D, 29T, 29W, 39M, 42S, 43J, 47D, 50C, 53H, 57M2, 57SG, 58T, 59F, 60Wa, 63M, 69F, 86D
Legislatures, 29T, 29W, 39M, 41S1 52S1, 54R
Local jurisdictions, 27R, 29D, 29T, 52S1, 54R, 56W, 57SG, 57W, 58T
Mints, 29D, 29T, 39M, 52S1, 57W
Police, 28H, 29D, 47D
Political history, 28H, 29D, 29T, 39M, 42S, 47D, 50C, 52S2, 54R, 56W, 57SG, 57W, 58T, 59F, 60Wa, 61V, 63P, 86D, 1909J
Political parties, 29D, 29T, 42S, 50C, 54R, 57SG, 57W, 59F, 60Wa, 61V, 86D
Prisons, 29D
Soldiers, 29D, 39M, 42S, 43J, 47D, 49B, 50C, 52S, 57SG, 60Wa, 60Wi, 61V, 69F, 86D, 1909J

Taxes, 27R, 29D, 29T, 39M, 47D, 56W, 57SG, 57W, 60Wa, 99B
Treaties, 50C, 52S, 60Wa, 63P, 1909J
Warfare, 28H, 39M, 42S, 47D, 52S2, 53H, 57W, 59F, 60Wa, 60Wi, 63P, 86D, 1909J

IV. ECONOMY

IV.A. AGRICULTURE

Bananas, 42Y, 56W
Beans, 56W
Bees, 29D, 57W
Cacao, 47D, 52S, 54R, 56W, 57SG, 57W
Cassava, 57W
Cattle, 27R, 27–28H, 29D, 42S1, 42Y, 49B, 56W, 57W, 69F
Cochineal, 27H, 29D, 29T, 42S1, 47D, 50A, 57M2, 61V
Coffee, 42S1, 47D, 52S1, 54R, 56W
Cotton, 29D, 47D, 52S1, 54R
Fruit, 39M, 42Y, 52S1, 54R, 56W, 57W
Horses, 39M, 42Y, 57W
Indigo, 28H, 29D, 47D, 52S, 53H, 54R, 57SG
Liquidambar, 57W
Maize, 52S1, 54R, 56W
Mules, 57W
Plantains, 42Y, 54R, 57W
Potatoes, 57W
Rice, 57W
Sugarcane, 27–28H, 29D, 47D, 52S1, 54R, 56W, 57M2, 57W
Sweet potatoes, 57W
Tobacco, 29D, 47D, 52S1, 54R, 56W, 57SG, 57W
Vanilla, 27R, 55SW, 57W
Vegetables, 42Y
Wheat, 56W

IV.B. COMMERCE

Barter, 39M
Exports, 27R, 28H, 29D, 29T, 39M, 42Y, 47D, 50A, 50C, 52S1, 56W, 57SG, 57W, 61S, 61V
Fairs, 28H, 47D, 50A, 50C
Imports, 27R, 28H, 29D, 29T, 29W, 39M, 42Y, 47D, 50A, 52S1, 56W, 57M2, 57SG, 57W, 61S, 61V
Local trade, 27R, 28H, 29T, 29W, 39M, 42S1, 42Y, 47D, 50A, 50C, 52S1, 54R, 56W, 57M2, 57SG, 57W, 59F, 69F
Smuggling, 27R, 47D, 63M

IV.C. OTHER PRIME INDUSTRIES

Construction, 47D, 57M2
Fishing, 27R, 42Y, 55SW, 57M2, 57W, 99B
Hunting, 27R, 42S, 42Y, 49B, 55SW, 57M2, 57W, 66L, 86D, 99B
Lumbering, 27H, 42Y, 47D, 56W, 57SG, 57W, 61S, 66L, 99B
Manufacturing, 27–28H, 29D, 29T, 47D, 52S1, 56W, 57M2, 57W
Mining, 29D, 29T, 42S1, 47D, 49B, 52S1, 53H, 57SG, 57W, 59F, 61S
Pearling, 56W

IV.D. AUXILIARY ACTIVITY

IV.D.1. COMMUNICATION

Postal system, 29T, 29W, 42Y, 47D, 54R, 57W, 63M

IV.D.2. TRANSPORTATION

Animal transport, 27R, 27–28H, 29D, 29T, 29W, 39M, 42S, 42Y, 43J, 47D, 49B, 50C, 52S, 53H, 56W, 57M2, 57SG, 57W, 61V, 63M, 69F, 99B
Canal projects, 27R, 29T, 39M, 42S1, 47D, 52S2, 53H, 54R, 57SG, 59F, 60T, 63M, 63P
Carriages, 27H, 29D, 29T, 29W, 39M, 42S1, 50C, 69F
Carts, 27R, 47D, 50C, 52S1, 58T, 60T, 60Wa, 69F
Human transport, 42S1, 50C, 57M2, 57SG
Railway projects, 57SG, 60T, 63P
Railways, 57SG, 59F, 60T
Roads, 27R, 27–28H, 29T, 47D, 52S, 54R, 57W, 60Wa, 86D, 1909J
Shipping lines, 39M, 42S1, 57SG, 60Wa, 63M, 63P, 69F, 1909J
Water transport, 27R, 28H, 29D, 29T, 29W, 39M, 42Y, 49B, 50C, 52S, 53H, 54R, 55SW, 56W, 57M2, 57SG, 57W, 59F, 60T, 60Wa, 60Wi, 63M, 63P, 69F, 86D, 99B, 1909J

IV.E. ECONOMIC WELFARE

Economic welfare, 27R, 29D, 29T, 47D, 56W, 69F

V. LEARNING

V.A. EDUCATION

Books, 29D, 39M, 42S1, 50C
Libraries, 39M, 56W
Literacy, 27R, 29T, 39M, 42Y, 47D, 50C, 61V
Newspapers, 29D, 29W, 47D, 52S1, 57W, 60Wa, 61V, 1909J
Printing, 29D
Schools, 29D, 29W, 42S1, 47D, 50C, 52S1, 56W, 57M2, 57SG
Societies, 57M2
Universities, 29D, 29T, 39M, 47D, 50C, 52S1, 56W, 57M2, 57SG, 57W, 63M

V.B. NATURAL SCIENCE

Geology, 56W
Medicine, 27R, 29D, 29T, 39M, 42S, 42Y, 55SW, 56W, 57M2, 57SG, 57W, 63M

V.C. SOCIAL SCIENCE

[No entries]

VI. ART

Ancient monuments, 42S, 52S
Architecture, 29T, 29W, 52S1, 57M2
Dance, 27R, 27H, 42Y, 52S1, 55SW, 56W, 57W, 63M, 69F
Fiestas, 27R, 29T, 39M, 42S1, 42Y, 43J, 52S, 53H, 54R, 55SW, 57M2, 57W, 69F, 99B
Literature, 29D
Music, 27R, 27H, 29D, 29T, 29W, 39M, 42S1, 42Y, 52S, 55SW, 56W, 57M2, 57SG, 57W, 58T, 59F, 61S, 61V, 63M, 99B, 1909J
Painting, 29T, 29W, 53H, 57M2
Sculpture, 29W, 57M2
Sports, 27H, 29D, 29T, 42S1, 50C, 52S1, 54R, 56W, 57W, 69F
Story-telling, 99B

Theater, 27H, 29D, 29T, 29W, 39M, 42S1, 43J, 52S1, 56W, 59F, 63M, 69F

VII. RELIGION

VII.A. CATHOLICISM

Baptisms, 57W
Cemeteries, 42S2, 47D, 50C, 56W, 57M2
Churches, 29T, 29W, 39M, 42S, 42Y, 52S, 56W, 57M2, 57SG, 57W, 60T
Convents, 28H, 29T, 39M, 50C, 52S1
Funerals, 27H, 29D, 29W, 42S, 50C, 52S1, 57M2, 61V
Marriages, 29D, 29W, 69F
Mass, 29W, 42S1, 50C, 52S2, 57W
Pilgrimages, 29D, 39M, 42S1, 47D, 50C
Processions, 28H, 29D, 29T, 29W, 39M, 42S1, 50C, 52S, 54R, 56W, 57SG, 57W, 60T, 61V, 63M, 69F, 1909J
Regular clergy, 28H, 29D, 29T, 29W, 39M, 42S, 50C, 52S1, 59F, 61V
Secular clergy, 29D, 29T, 29W, 39M, 42S, 47D, 50C, 52S, 53H, 56W, 57M2, 57SG, 57W, 58T

VII.B. PROTESTANTISM

Protestantism, 29W, 42Y, 50C, 56W, 63P, 99B

VII.C. FREETHINKING

Freethinking, 28H, 50C

VII.D. PAGANISM

Paganism, 27R, 50C, 55SW, 58T

VII.E. WITCHCRAFT

Witchcraft, 27R, 42Y, 50C, 55SW, 99B

VII.F. ORIGINAL PHILOSOPHY

[No entries]

VII.G. MORALITY

Morality, 29D, 29W, 47D, 50C, 58T, 99B

Bibliography

AUTHORS IN TOPICAL INDEX

Arlach, H. de T. d'
1850. Souvenirs de l'Amérique Centrale. Paris.

Bell, Charles Napier
1899. Tangweera: Life and Adventures among Gentle Savages. London.

Byam, George
1849. Wild Life in the Interior of Central America. London.
1850 Wa. Wanderings in Some of the Western Republics of America. London.
1850 Wi. Wildes Leben im Innern von Central-Amerika. Translated by M. B. Lindau. Dresden.
1852. Reprint of 1850 Wi item. Dresden.

Crowe, Frederick
1850. The Gospel in Central America. London.

Doubleday, Charles William
1886. Reminiscences of the "Filibuster" War in Nicaragua. New York and London.

Dunlop, Robert Glasgow
1847. Travels in Central America. London.

Dunn, Henry
1828. Guatimala, or, the United Provinces of Central America, in 1827-8. New York.
1829. Guatimala, or, the Republic of Central America, in 1827-8. London.
1960. Guatemala, o Las Provincias Unidas de Centro América, durante 1827 a 1828. Translated by R. de León. Guatemala.

Foote, Mrs. Henry Grant
1869. Recollections of Central America and the West Coast of Africa. London.

Froebel, Carl Ferdinand Julius
1857–58. Aus Amerika: Erfahrungen, Reisen und Studien. Incomplete version of Central American portion of 1859 item, but with treatment of eastern United States added. 2 vols. Leipzig.
1859. Seven Years' Travel in Central America, Northern Mexico, and the Far West of the United States. London.

Haefkens, Jacobus
1827–28. Reize naar Guatemala. 2 vols. The Hague.
1832. Centraal Amerika, uit een geschiedkundig, aardrijkskundig en statistiek Oogpunt beschouwd. Dordrecht.

Heine, Peter Bernard Wilhelm
1853. Wanderbilder aus Central-Amerika: Skizzen eines deutschen Malers. Leipzig.
1857. Reprint of 1853 item. Leipzig.

Jamison, James Carson
1909. With Walker in Nicaragua; or, Reminiscences of an Officer of the American Phalanx. Columbia, Mo.

Jarves, James Jackson
1843. Scenes and Scenery in the Sandwich Islands, and a Trip through Central America. Boston.

Leyland, J.
1866. Adventures in the Far Interior of South Africa including a Journey to Lake Ngami and Rambles in Honduras. Liverpool and London.

Marr, Wilhelm
1863. Reise nach Central-Amerika. 2 vols. Hamburg.

Montgomery, George Washington
1839. Narrative of a Journey to Guatemala, in Central America, in 1838. New York.

Morelet, Arthur
1857. Voyage dans l'Amérique Centrale, l'ile de Cuba et le Yucatan. 2 vols. Paris.
1871. Travels in Central America. Edited by E. G. Squier and translated by Mrs. M. F. Squier. Abridged translation of Central American portion of 1857 item. New York.

Pim, Bedford Clapperton Trevelyan
1863. The Gate of the Pacific. London.

Reichardt, C. F.
1854. Nicaragua: Nach eigener Anschauung im Jahre 1852 und mit besonderer Beziehung auf die Auswanderung nach den heissen Zonen Amerika's. Braunschweig.

Roberts, Orlando W.
1827. Narrative of Voyages and Excursions on the East Coast and in the Interior of Central America. Edinburgh.

1965. Narrative of Voyages and Excursions on the East Coast and in the Interior of Central America. Gainesville: University of Florida Press.

Scherzer, Carl
1856. See Moritz Wagner.
1857 E. Travels in the Free States of Central America: Nicaragua, Honduras, and San Salvador. Considerably abridged version of 1857 G item. 2 vols. London.
1857 G. Wanderungen durch die mittel-amerikanischen Freistaaten Nicaragua, Honduras und San Salvador. Braunschweig.

Sivers, Jegór von
1861. Ueber Madeira und die Antillen nach Mittelamerika. Leipzig.

Squier, Ephraim George
1852. Nicaragua; Its People, Scenery, Monuments, and the Proposed Interoceanic Canal. 2 vols. New York and London.
1853. Travels in Central America, particularly in Nicaragua. Reprint of 1852 item. 2 vols. New York.
1854. Der centralamerikanische Staat Nicaragua. Translated by E. Hoepfner. Leipzig.
1855 W. Waikna; or, Adventures on the Mosquito Shore. New York.
1856. Adventures on the Mosquito Shore. Reprint of 1855 W item. London.
1858. The States of Central America. New York.
1860. Nicaragua; Its People, Scenery, Monuments, Resources, Condition, and Proposed Canal. Revised but shorter version of 1852 item. New York.
1891. Reprint of 1856 item. New York.
1965. Waikna; or, Adventures on the Mosquito Shore. Gainesville: University of Florida Press.

Stephens, John Lloyd
1841. Incidents of Travel in Central America, Chiapas, and Yucatan. 2 vols. New York and London.
1842. Reprint of 1841 item, with corrections. 2 vols. New York and London.
1843. Incidents of Travel in Yucatan. 2 vols. New York.
1854 C. Incidents of Travel in Central America. Chiapas, and Yucatan. Edited by F. Catherwood. London.
1854 H. Reiseerlebnisse in Centralamerika, Chiapas und Yucatan. Translated by E. Hoepfner. Leipzig.
1939–40. Incidentes de viaje en Centro América, Chiapas y Yucatán. Translated by B. Mazariegos Santizo and P. Burgess. 2 vols. Quezaltenango.
1949. Incidents of Travel in Central America, Chiapas, and Yucatan. Edited by R. L. Predmore. 2 vols. in 1. New Brunswick: Rutgers University Press.

Tempsky, Gustav Ferdinand von
1858. Mitla: A Narrative of Incidents and Personal Adventures on a Journey in Mexico, Guatemala, and Salvador in the Years 1853 to 1855. Edited by J. S. Bell. London.

Thompson, George Alexander
1812–15. The Geographical and Historical Dictionary of America and the West Indies. 5 vols. London.
1829. Narrative of an Official Visit to Guatemala from Mexico. London.

1926–27. "Narración de una visita oficial a Guatemala viniendo de México en el año 1825." *Anales de la Sociedad de Geografía e Historia*, 3:51–90, 191–229, 326–66, 429–73. Translated by R. Fernández Guardia.
1927. Narración de una visita oficial a Guatemala viniendo de México. Translated by R. Fernández Guardia. Guatemala.

Trollope, Anthony
1859. The West Indies and the Spanish Main. London.
1860. The West Indies and the Spanish Main. London.
1860. The West Indies and the Spanish Main. New York.

Valois, Alfred de
1861. Mexique, Havane et Guatemala: Notes de voyage. Paris.

Wagner, Moritz, and Carl Scherzer
1856. Die Republik Costa Rica in Central-Amerika mit besonderer Berücksichtigung der Naturverhältnisse und der Frage der deutschen Auswanderung und Colonisation. Leipzig.

Walker, William
1860. The War in Nicaragua. Mobile and New York.
1924. La guerra de Nicaragua. Translated by R. Fernández Guardia. San José, Costa Rica.

Wells, William Vincent
1857. Explorations and Adventures in Honduras. New York.

Wight, Samuel F.
1860. Adventures in California and Nicaragua, in Rhyme. Boston.

Wilson, James
1829. A Brief Memoir of the Life of James Wilson. London.

Young, Thomas
1842. Narrative of a Residence on the Mosquito Shore, During the Years 1839, 1840, & 1841. London.
1847. Narrative of a Residence on the Mosquito Shore. London.

AUTHORS FROM COLONIAL PERIOD

Alvarado, Pedro de. *An Account of the Conquest of Guatemala in 1524*. Edited by S. J. Mackie. New York: Cortés Society, 1924.
Benzoni, Giralomo. *La historia del Mondo Nuovo*. Venice, 1565 and 1572.
―――――. *History of the New World*. Edited by W. H. Smyth. London: Hakluyt Society, 1857.
Casas, Bartolomé de las. *Apologética historia de las Indias*. Tomo I of *Historiadores de Indias*. Edited by M. Serrano y Sanz. *Nueva biblioteca de autores españoles*, Tomo XIII. Madrid, 1909.
Cockburn, John. *A Journey over Land, from the Gulf of Honduras to the Great South-Sea*. London, 1735.
―――――. *The Unfortunate Englishmen*. London, 1794.

BIBLIOGRAPHY

———. "El viaje de Cockburn: de Nicoya a Chiriquí." In *Los viajes de Cockburn y Lievre por Costa Rica,* pp. 10–54. San José, 1962.
Cortés, Hernán. *Fernando Cortés: His Five Letters of Relation to the Emperor Charles V.* Edited by F. A. MacNutt. 2 vols. Cleveland: Arthur H. Clark Co., 1908.
Cowley, William Ambrosia, co-author. *Voyages and Adventures of Sir Walter Raleigh: With the Voyage of Captain Cowley.* London. 1806.
Dampier, William. *A New Voyage Round the World.* London, 1697.
———. *Dampier's Voyages.* Edited by J. Masefield. 2 vols. New York: E. P. Dutton Co., 1906.
Díaz del Castillo, Bernal. *The True History of the Conquest of Mexico.* Translated by M. Keatinge. New York: Robert M. McBride & Co., 1927.
Exquemeling, Alexandre Olivier. *De Americaensche Zee-Roovers.* Amsterdam, 1678.
———. *The Buccaneers of America.* London: George Allen & Unwin, 1951.
Fernández de Oviedo y Valdés, Gonzalo. *Historia general y natural de las Indias, islas y tierra-firme del mar océano.* Edited by J. Amador de los Rios. 4 vols. Madrid, 1851–55.
Gage, Thomas. *The English-American, His Travail by Sea and Land: or, A New Survey of the West-India's.* London, 1648.
———. *Thomas Gage's Travels in the New World.* Edited by J. E. S. Thompson. Norman: University of Oklahoma Press, 1958.
González de Avila, Gil. "Carta del Capitán Gil González de Avila a Su Majestad, dándole cuenta del descubrimiento de Nicaragua." In *Documentos para la historia de Nicaragua,* 1:89–107. Madrid, 1954–57.
Henderson, George. *An Account of the British Settlement of Honduras.* London, 1809 and 1811.
Hernández Arana, Francisco. *The Annals of the Cakchiquels.* Edited by A. Recinos and translated by D. Goetz. Norman: University of Oklahoma Press, 1953.
Raveneau de Lussan. *Journal du voyage fait a la Mer de Sud.* Paris, 1689 and 1690.
———. *Raveneau de Lussan: A Translation.* Edited by M. E. Wilbur. Cleveland: Arthur H. Clark Co., 1930.
Ringrose, Basil. *The Dangerous Voyage and Bold Attempts of Captain Bartholomew Sharp.* Part 4 of *The Buccaneers of America,* edited by W. S. Stallybrass. London: George Routledge & Sons, 1923.
Roach, John. *The Surprizing Adventures of John Roach, Mariner of Whitehaven.* Whitehaven, England, 1784.
———. *The Surprising Adventures and Sufferings of John Rhodes, a Seaman of Workington.* New York, 1798.
———. *The Powow.* Otsego, 1808.
Wafer, Lionel. *A New Voyage and Description of the Isthmus of America.* Edited by G. P. Winship. Cleveland: The Burrows Brothers Co., 1903.

OTHER ITEMS CITED

Aa, Abraham Jacob van der. *Biographisch Woordenboek der Nederlanden.* 17 vols. Haarlem, 1852–78.
Alcedo y Bexarano, Antonio de. *Diccionario geográfico-histórico de las Indias Occidentales o América.* 5 vols. Madrid, 1786–89.
Baily, John. *Central America.* London, 1850.

Cartografía de la América Central. Guatemala, 1929.

Conder, Josiah. *The Modern Traveller: A Popular Description, Geographical, Historical, and Topographical, of the Various Countries of the Globe: Mexico and Guatimala.* 2 vols. London, 1825.

Conzemius, Eduard. *Ethnographical Survey of the Miskito and Sumu Indians of Honduras and Nicaragua.* U.S. Bureau of American Ethnology Bulletin 106. Washington: Government Printing Office, 1932.

Devoti, Giovanni. *Institutionum canonicarum libri quatuor.* Rome, 1785. Republished (4 vols. in 3). Madrid, 1801–2.

──────. *Instituciones canónicas divididas en 4 libros.* Valencia, 1830.

Dictionary of American Biography. 21 vols. New York: Charles Scribner's Sons, 1928–37.

Field, Thomas W. *An Essay Towards an Indian Bibliography.* New York: Scribner, Armstrong, and Co., 1873.

Fleury, Claude. *Institution du droit ecclésiastique de France.* Paris, 1677. Republished (2 vols.). Paris, 1767.

García Goyena, Rafael. *Fábulas y poesías varias.* Guatemala, 1825.

Griffith, William J. *Empires in the Wilderness.* Chapel Hill: University of North Carolina Press, 1965.

"Guatemala." *The New Monthly Magazine and Literary Journal,* vol. 14, pt. 2 (1825), 578–93.

Hasbrouck, Alfred. "Gregor McGregor and the Colonization of Poyais, between 1820 and 1824." *The Hispanic American Historical Review* 7 (Nov., 1927): 438–59.

Hodgson, Robert. *Some Account of the Mosquito Territory.* Edinburgh, 1822.

Juarros, Domingo. *Compendio de la historia de la ciudad de Guatemala.* 2 vols. Guatemala, 1808–18. Republished (2 vols. in 1). Guatemala, 1936.

──────. *A Statistical and Commercial History of the Kingdom of Guatemala, in Spanish America.* Translated by J. Baily. London, 1823.

Lockey, Joseph B. "Diplomatic Futility." *The Hispanic American Historical Review* 10 (August, 1930): 265–94. Reprinted in *Readings in Latin American History,* edited by L. Hanke, 2:133–52. New York: Thomas Y. Crowell Co., 1966.

Luke, Harry. *Caribbean Circuit.* London: Nicholson & Watson, 1950.

Manning, William R., ed. *Diplomatic Correspondence of the United States: Inter-American Affairs, 1831–1860.* 12 vols. Washington: Carnegie Endowment for International Peace, 1932–39.

Marure, Alejandro. *Bosquejo histórico de las revoluciones de Centro-América desde 1811 hasta 1834.* 2 vols. Paris, 1913.

Núñez de Taboada, Melchior Emmanuel. *Dictionnaire français-espagnol et espagnol-français.* Paris, 1812.

Steegmuller, Francis. *The Two Lives of James Jackson Jarves.* New Haven: Yale University Press, 1951.

Steward, J. H., ed. *The Circum-Caribbean Tribes. Handbook of South American Indians,* vol. 4. U.S. Bureau of American Ethnology Bulletin 143. Washington: Government Printing Office, 1948.

Termer, Franz. "El valor histórico, geográfico y etnológico de los apuntes de John Cockburn sobre Centroamérica en el siglo XVIII." In *Los viajes de Cockburn y Lievre por Costa Rica,* pp. 55–93. San José, 1962.

Von Hagen, Victor Wolfgang. *Maya Explorer: John Lloyd Stephens and the Lost Cities of Central America and Yucatán.* Norman: University of Oklahoma Press, 1947.

Webster, Charles Kingsley, ed. *Britain and the Independence of Latin America, 1812–1830*. 2 vols. Oxford University Press, 1938.
Williams, Mary Wilhelmine. "The Ecclesiastical Policy of Francisco Morazán and the Other Central American Liberals." *The Hispanic American Historical Review* 3 (May, 1920): 119–43.
Woodward, Ralph Lee, Jr. "Economic and Social Origins of the Guatemalan Political Parties (1773–1823)." *The Hispanic American Historical Review* 45 (Nov., 1965): 544–66.

Index

(Country and colony abbreviations are as follows: B.H., British Honduras; C.R., Costa Rica; G., Guatemala; H., Honduras; N., Nicaragua; S., El Salvador.)

ACAJUTLA, S., 68, 71–72, 124, 126–29, 213–14, 217
Acapulco, Mexico, 70, 125
Accawass-Maya, N., 12*n*
Ackermann, Mr. (London publisher), 252
Aduanas, 240–41
Agua volcano, 105, 117–18, 126, 213
Aguacate mountain, 243, 244
Aguán River, 29*n*
Aguilar, Manuel, 124, 214, 217
Ahuachapán, S., 222–24, 239–40
Alajuela, C.R., 217
Alamán, Lucas, 70
Albert Henry (brigantine), 173*n*
Alcantarines, 284, 300
Alcedo y Bexarano, Antonio de, 69
Almolonga, G., 117
Alvarado, Pedro de, 2, 268
Alvarez, Miguel, 159
Amatitlán, G., 80–82, 98, 230, 258–60, 261
Amayo, S., 232–33
American people (from Spanish America), 76
American people (from the United States), 19, 26, 35
Amity (schooner), 184, 185, 187
Andalusia (Spain), 163

Andrew (uncle of George Frederick), 27
Andrew, R. J., 58
Angas, G. F., 58
Angas and Co., 58
Anglo Costa Rican Economical Mining Company, 243
Animal transport, 75–76, 93–95, 151–53
Antigua, G., 5, 6, 15, 83*n*, 98, 117, 118, 213, 233, 284*n*
Apaneca, S., 160
Apopa, S., 157
Arabia, 204
Arce, Manuel José, 14–15, 16, 78, 85, 87–90, 105*n*, 121, 123
Argentina, 36*n*
Argüello, Juan, 16
Arizona, 21*n*
Armstrong, Reverend Mr. (of Belize), 29, 31, 40*n*
Assenwass people, 11
Athens, Greece, 96
Atlantic Ocean, 47, 173, 176, 177, 218, 237
Audiencia de Guatemala, 4, 5, 13, 83*n*
Audiencia de los Confines, 4
Augustinians, 284, 300*n*

INDEX

Aury, Louis, 25, 36, 41
Aycinena, Ignacio, 165, 166, 167
Aycinena, Juan José, 79, 165, 207, 233, 296, 300
Aycinena, Mariano de, 15, 79n, 208n
Aycinena, Vicente (second *marqués* of), 79n, 208n

B——, Mr. (of Black River), 192, 204
B——o, Simon (aide to Rascon family), 74–75
Baily, John, 78, 79, 233
Bananas, 235–36
Banister (British sailor), 9–10
Barbados, 31
Barbareta (island), 54, 202–3
Barcelona, Spain, 284n
Barclay, Herring, Richardson, and Company, 79
Bardh, Juan, 243, 244
Barras (Miskito chief), 53
Barrio del Angel (Sonsonate), 74
Barrundia, José Francisco, 15
Barrundia, Juan, 15
Bartola, Doña (of Gualán), 292, 293, 294
Bathing, 129, 199
Bay Islands, 13, 17, 124
Bay of Honduras. *See* Gulf of Honduras
Bay of Mandingo, 18
Beaver (sloop of war), 58
Bees, 232
Belize, B.H., 13, 29, 33, 53, 55, 56, 58, 59, 60, 61, 66–68, 86, 87, 92, 95, 100, 101, 120, 141, 148, 151, 156, 171, 180, 183, 185, 189, 195, 196, 198, 201, 202, 203, 204, 242, 247
Bell, Charles Napier, 179
Beltranena, Mariano, 15, 85–86
Ben (Miskito sailor), 185
Benson, Mr. (of Izabal), 95
Benzoni, Girolamo: introduction, 3; good and bad Spaniards, 3–4; learning to drink chocolate, 4; unfriendliness from Indians, 4; mentioned, 11, 13
Beteta, José, 259, 260
Bethlehemites, 284, 300
Big Louis (Black Carib chief), 53, 54

Black Carib people, 29, 41, 53–54, 143, 189, 190, 192, 195–97, 198, 199, 200, 204, 236, 241–42, 263–64, 276
Black River, 21, 25, 30, 31, 32, 33, 53, 54, 179, 181, 184, 185, 186, 187n, 188, 189, 191, 192, 194, 195, 200, 203, 236
Black River Lagoon, 31–32
Blanco, Juan, 40, 41, 47
Bluefields, N., 20–21, 29, 34, 51
Bluefields Lagoon, 21
Blyatt, General (Miskito chief), 25, 26, 27
Boaden (shipmaster), 186
Bobón (aide to Stephens), 226, 227, 228
Boca del Tortuguero, 20n
Bocas del Toro, 20, 23
Bogg (Cabo Gracias a Dios merchant), 28
Bogotá, Colombia, 180n
Bogue, David, 253
Bolívar, Simón, 25n, 31n, 36n, 69n
Bonacca (island). *See* Guanaja (island)
Books, 203, 251–54
Boston, Massachusetts, 124
Boundaries, 29, 132n
Bradford (ship commander), 35
Brancman's Bluff, 29
Brazil, 54n, 64n
Bremen, Germany, 46
Brewers Lagoon, 30
Bridge, Walter, 173
Brinsmade, Peter Allan, 139n
British and Foreign Bible Society, 57, 253n
British and Foreign School Society, 57
British Central American Land Company, 179, 188, 189, 204
British Honduras, 29, 42, 58, 86
British people, 8, 13, 17, 21, 25, 32, 33, 40n, 179, 262
Brown (aide to Roberts), 34, 37, 39, 50, 52
Brown, Captain (seaman), 70, 71
Buccaneering, 6–8
Buenos Aires, Argentina, 35, 57, 69n, 279
Bull, John (Black Carib captain), 187–88

INDEX

Bullfights, 257–58, 273
Byam, George: introduced, 172; trip from Chile, 172–73; situated in the wilds, 173–75; return, wounded, to civilization, 175–77; hiring a piragua, 177; the piragua and crew, 177; on the San Juan River, 177; arrival at coast, 177–78; on devotions on Lake Nicaragua, 283–84

CABO GRACIAS A DIOS, N., 20, 23, 26, 28, 30, 34, 52, 179–84, 188, 204, 242
Cabrera, Francisco, 274
Cahaboncito, G., 171n
Cajabon, G., 171n
Cakchiquel people, 1, 2
Caldera, C.R., 217
California, 125, 136
Camotán, G., 206
Canary Islands, 191
Candido, Don (Izabal merchant), 149, 151
Canning, George, 77
Cape Honduras, 29
Cape Horn, 172
Caratasca Lagoon, 13, 29
Carib language, 195
Carib people. *See* Black Carib people
Caribbean Sea, 6, 7, 25n, 47
Carlos, Don (Miskito chief), 29
Carmelites, 300
Carrera, Rafael, 121, 122, 123, 130, 131, 132, 133, 135, 160, 206, 208–10, 211, 212–13, 218, 219, 221, 222, 223, 224–26, 227, 233, 293, 298
Carriages, 247
Carrillo, Braulio, 124, 217–19
Cartagena, Colombia, 73
Cartago, C.R., 217, 219
Casas, Bartolomé de las, 2
Casaus y Torres, Ramón, 15, 89, 280–81, 282, 293, 297n
Cascara, General (of Carrera's force), 223
Cassava, 236–37
Castilla, José María, 280
Castro, Señor (of Guatemala City), 261
Catherwood, Frederick, 204, 205, 206, 213, 224, 226, 302
Catholicism, 276–306

Cattle, 230–31
Cayman Islands, 201
Centinela (brig of war), 35–36, 37
Cerda, José Manuel de la, 86
Cerda, Manuel Antonio de la, 16
Charles IV (of Spain), 180n
Charles V (Holy Roman Emperor), 198
Chiapas, 5
Chile, 88, 141, 172, 173
China, 17, 88
Chinandega, N., 216n, 219
Chiquimula, G., 132, 133, 134–35, 136, 139, 140, 155, 206
Chiquimula department, 56
Chiriquí Lagoon, 18
Chocolate, 4
Chonita, Doña (wife of Don Juan), 265
Christopher Scott (schooner), 186
Churches, 285, 288, 301–2, 303–4
Ciudad Real, Chiapas, 284
Clementine (brigantine), 125
Clothing, 71–72, 73, 74, 157–58, 162, 183, 195
Cochineal, 233–34
Cockburn, John: introduced, 8; escape from Spanish captors, 8–9; help from a governor's lady, 9–10; solitary suffering, 10–11; mentioned, 12, 13
Coco Island, 8n
Coco River, 6, 30, 264n
Codd, Edward, 86, 87
Cojutepeque, S., 219
Colombia, 18n, 25n, 36n, 99, 180, 279
Colonization, 32–33, 188–92
Comayagua, H., 16, 284
Company of Belén, 284n
Conchagua, S., 98
Congregation of the Oratory, 284, 300n
Convention of London (1786), 86n
Convents, 5, 284–85
Copán, H., 206, 208, 213, 224
Coquimbo province, Chile, 173
Corn Islands, 36
Cornejo, José María, 15, 123
Cortés, Hernán, 2, 3
Costa Rica, 1, 3, 5, 6, 7, 8, 16, 122, 123–24, 214, 217, 218, 222, 284
Cowley, William Ambrosia, 8n
Coxon's Kay, 200, 201

332 INDEX

Creole-French language, 195
Creole people, 21, 31, 34, 73, 112–14
Cricamola River, 18, 22
Cristal River, 199
Cuba, 188, 191, 293
Cucalaya River, 29n
Cucra people, 11, 21, 29
Cuilapa, G., 105n

DACURA, N., 29
Dalby (Miskito chief), 28
Dampier, William, 7–8
Dance, 27–28, 259–61, 263–64
Darién (Panama), 1, 125
Delgado, José Matías, 15, 89, 90
Despard, Colonel (of Black River), 33
DeWitt, Charles G., 142n, 206, 223
Díaz del Castillo, Bernal, 3
Diplomacy, 85–91
Dominicans, 2, 4, 227, 284, 300
Dorrego, Manuel, 69
Drinking, 115
Drivon, Dr. (of Sonsonate), 129–30, 213, 214
Dunlop, Robert Glasgow, 126n, 130n
Dunn, Henry: introduced, 98–99; need for his book, 99–100; piety in his book, 100; departure from Belize, 100; Río Dulce beauty, 100; admission to country, 100–101; entry from Izabal, 101–2; life in Gualán, 102–4; preparation to leave Gualán, 104; pleasantness of Guastatoya, 104; arrival in the capital, 104–5; streets and squares, 105–6; homes, 106–7; one person's day, 107–12; social classes, 112–15; the people's drinking habits, 115; excursion to the country, 115–16; on toward the Pacific, 116; the scene at Iztapa, 116–17; volcano Agua, 117–18; departure for England, 118–19; Izabal and Omoa, 119–20; mentioned, 121, 126n, 257, 261n, 275; on life on a hacienda, 229–32; on the production of *panelas*, 234–35; on the economy of Gualán, 240; on education in Gualán, 249; on primary instruction in Guatemala City, 250–51; on the university, 251; on printing and books, 251–52; on the preference for French books, 253; on the practice of medicine, 254–55; on entertainment in Guatemala City, 272–73; on a miscellany of arts, 273–74; on religion in Gualán, 277–78; on religion in Guatemala City, 278; on dreams of the clergy, 278; on the power of the clergy, 278–79; on religious customs, 285–87
Dutch people, 7, 198

EARNEE, Admiral (Miskito chief), 22–23, 24, 25, 26, 27
East Indies, 88
Economic welfare, 247–48
Ecuador, 172n, 252n
Edinburgh, Scotland, 17, 57
Egypt, 204
El Calvario (Guatemala City district), 225
El Calvario (Quezaltenango church), 306
El Enamorado Pobre (play), 267–68
El Obero, G., 116n
El Progreso, G., 92n, 104n
El Realejo, N., 42, 172, 173, 174
El Salvador, 1, 2, 6, 8. See also San Salvador (state)
Elena (island), 202
Elizabeth I (of England), 271
England, 4, 5, 8, 9, 11, 17, 33, 46, 53, 60, 62, 67, 68, 87, 89, 91, 93, 109, 111, 118, 125, 132, 142, 172, 173, 188, 189, 190, 199, 204, 246, 247, 255–56, 271
English language, 26, 27, 34, 38, 41, 44, 46, 98, 124, 139, 180, 183, 195, 204, 214, 276
English people, 6, 9, 12, 20, 26–27, 28, 31, 39, 47, 54, 60, 87, 88, 116, 139, 172, 174, 181, 182, 183, 189, 192, 200, 201, 203, 264
Esmaralda (pipante), 63
Espinosa de los Monteros, Miguel, 71
Esquipulas, G., 154, 155–57, 206, 287–92
Estrella (schooner), 35, 37, 49
Europe, 3, 42, 53, 96, 99, 109, 204, 232, 254, 255n, 274, 278
European people, 31, 70, 76, 112, 113, 236, 255
Excursions (pleasure), 79–85, 115–18, 258–60

INDEX 333

Executive power, 78, 85, 87–90, 158–59, 163–65, 206–7, 208–10, 214–16, 217–21, 222–26
Exports, 19, 238
Exquemeling, Alexandre Olivier, 7

FAUNA, 54–55, 194
Federación de Centro América, 14
Ferdinand VII (of Spain), 42
Fernández de Oviedo y Valdés, Gonzalo, 2
Field, Thomas W., 12n
Fiestas, 23–28, 153–54, 196–97, 292–306
Flor-del-Mer (schooner), 35, 36, 49
Food, 103–4, 193–94
Fort Wellington, H., 188, 189, 190–92, 203, 242, 263
Forts and garrisons, 100–101
Fraijanes, G., 76
France, 4, 6, 125
Francisca, Doña, (of Gualán), 93
Franciscans, 284, 300
Francisco, Don (Spanish merchant), 148
French Creole people, 199
French language, 20n, 101, 195, 252
French people, 6
Frenchman's Harbor, 201
Fruit, 235
Fuego volcano, 126
Funerals 286–87

GAGE, Thomas: introduction, 4–5; sumptuousness in a monastery, 5; wealth from the priesthood, 5–6; cheating the sea-rovers, 6; mentioned, 7, 11, 13, 226
Gall, Franz Joseph, 255
Gallegos, José Rafael de, 124
Gálvez, Mariano, 122, 131
Gambling, 63
García Goyena, Rafael, 252
George (Miskito ruler), 28
George IV (of Great Britain), 68
George Frederick (Miskito ruler), 17n, 26, 27, 28–31, 33–34, 52, 179, 180, 182, 276
George Angas (schooner), 58
German language, 172, 204
"Glory of Independence" (play), 270
Golfo de San Blas, 18n

Golfo de Urabá, 18n
Gómez Pedraza, Manuel, 69n
González de Avila, Gil, 2
Gonzaláz Saravia, Miguel, 44, 46
Gordon, Colonel (of Black River), 32, 53
Granada, N., 16, 40, 41–45, 51, 176, 177, 219, 237–39, 246
Grand Cayman Island, 202
Gravesend, England, 179, 188
Great Britain, 11, 38, 68, 76, 86, 88, 90, 141n, 204, 218
Griswold, Susan, 96n, 98n
Guaco, 255–56
Guadeloupe, 199
Gualán, G., 62, 63, 64, 65, 92–93, 97, 102–4, 132, 135, 138, 140–41, 153–54, 206, 240, 249, 254, 264–65, 277–78, 292–95
Guanaja (island), 54, 143, 184, 187, 200, 202, 203
Guastatoya, G., 92, 104
Guatemala, 1, 2, 3, 8, 11, 15, 16, 55, 57–58, 64n, 69, 70, 77, 78, 86, 87, 88, 89, 90n, 98, 118, 122, 123, 130, 131, 158n, 206, 207, 211, 218, 219, 222, 224, 226, 233, 239, 269n, 291, 302
Guatemala City, 12, 15, 36n, 42, 55, 56, 58, 59–61, 62, 68, 74, 76, 77–79, 82n, 83n, 85–92, 98, 101, 102, 105–15, 121, 122, 130, 133, 135, 142, 143, 147, 150, 151, 154, 156, 158, 159, 161–63, 164, 165, 166, 171, 206–13, 215, 220, 221, 222, 223, 224–26, 240–41, 244–45, 246–48, 249, 250–54, 257–58, 261–62, 269–73, 278, 279–81, 284, 285–87, 289, 290, 295–301
Guatemalan people, 56, 82, 274
Guaymí language, 18n
Gulf of Darien, 18
Gulf of Florida, 87
Gulf of Fonseca, 8n, 219
Gulf of Honduras, 28, 41, 52, 53, 143, 148
Gulf of Mexico, 25n, 141
Gulf of Nicoya, 10
Gutierrez family (of Guatemala City), 261

HACIENDAS, 229–35
Haefkens, Jacobus: introduced, 96;

reminiscenses at Trujillo, 96–97; good roads and bad, 97; refugee Negroes, 97; remainder of travels, 97–98; mentioned, 99, 116n, 121, 126n, 142, 198n, 205
The Hague, Netherlands, 96
Haiti, 6
Haldane, Mr. (Edinburgh pastor), 57
Half-Moon Kay, 184, 185, 186
Hall, Mr. (British vice-consul), 206, 207, 208
Haly, Stanislaus Thomas, 181, 184
Hamburg, Germany, 46
Havana, Cuba, 11, 13, 37, 141, 143, 278
Hawaii, 124, 125, 139n, 142
Henderson, George, 13
Heredia, C.R., 217
Hernández Arana, Francisco, 1, 2, 3
Herrera, Dionisio, 16, 123
Herrera, Justo José, 123
Herrera, Próspero, 55, 56
Hervey, Lionel, 69
Hines, John, 87, 253
Hodgson, Robert, 20, 25
Honduras, 1, 2, 3, 6, 8, 11, 15, 16, 17, 56, 96, 121, 122, 123, 132, 133, 135, 137, 198, 216, 219, 220, 236, 245
Honolulu, Hawaii, 125
Horses, 232–33
Hosmore, Captain (of Black River), 32, 33
Hosmore, Mr. (son of Captain Hosmore), 32–33
Hospitality, 4, 167–70, 205–6
Houghton, W. (Fort Wellington superintendent), 189, 190, 191
House interiors, 103, 106–7, 145, 155–56
Huehuetenango, G., 226
Hunyg (Cakchiquel ruler), 1, 3

IBARRA, Manuel Julián, 158–59
Imports, 238, 240
India, 17
Indian people (of the Americas), 2, 3–4, 11, 19, 20, 21, 22, 26, 27, 28, 29, 31, 33, 34, 35, 37, 38, 39, 40, 41, 47, 50, 51, 52, 53, 54, 55, 73, 74, 80, 92, 114, 116, 117, 121, 130, 131, 133, 140, 143, 148, 153, 154, 157, 170, 173, 174, 179, 180, 186, 209, 211, 212, 214, 227, 240, 246, 276, 290, 293, 302, 303, 304, 305, 306
"The Inquisition Unmasked" (play), 60n, 271–72
Irazú volcano, 219
Irving, Washington, 142
Italian language, 3
Italy, 3, 142, 284n
Iturbide, Agustín de, 36n
Izabal, G., 55, 56, 58, 59, 61, 62n, 68, 87, 91, 94, 95–96, 97, 100, 101–2, 119, 129, 141, 148–52, 162, 166, 171, 204, 205, 240, 245, 247
Izalco volcano, 126
Iztapa, G., 116n, 117, 213

JACK, Captain (Black Carib sailor), 187, 188
Jalpatagua, G., 75n
Jamaica, 8, 11, 18, 22, 26, 28, 29, 88, 178, 227
Jarves, James Jackson: mentioned, 62n, 142; introduced, 124–25; departure from Hawaii, 125–26; in Acajutla and Sonsonate, 126–30; civil war and pills, 130–33; cross-country route, 133; a perilous journey, 133–40; at ease in Gualán, 140–41; farewell to Izabal, 141; on a theater experience, 268–69
Jesuits, 4, 129
Jocotenango, G., 163
John (brig), 67
José, Don (Spanish merchant), 150, 151, 152, 153, 154, 155, 156, 157, 264, 265
Juan, Don (of Gualán), 153–54, 265
Juarros, Domingo, 99, 251

KINGSTON, Jamaica, 17

LA CONCEPCION (Guatemala City church), 295–97, 298
La Concepcion (Guatemala City convent), 295, 296, 298–99
La Unión, S., 219
Ladino people, 114n
Laguna de Bruso, 30n
Laguna de Perlas, 21n
Lahuh Noh (Cakchiquel ruler), 1
Lake Amatitlán, 117n
Lake Izabal, 129

Lake Nicaragua, 39, 47, 49, 88, 176, 219, 283–84
Larrazábal, Antonio, 297n
Lavagnino, Francisco, 55–56, 68, 78n
Lawlessness, 130–32, 215
Lawrence, A. & A., 141
Le Nouvel, Captain (French seaman), 213
Le Nouvel, Victor, 214
Leerdam, Netherlands, 96
Leeward Islands, 53
Legislatures, 59–61, 159–60, 207–8
Leith, Scotland, 57, 67
Leo XII, Pope, 90n
León, N., 16, 34, 36n, 42, 43, 44, 45, 46–48, 49, 173, 174, 175, 176–77, 219, 237, 275, 284
Liberia, C.R., 219
Limón, C.R., 19n
Literature, 252
Little Louis (Black Carib chief), 53
Livingston, Robert R., 171
Livingston, G., 171
Local trade, 194–95, 239, 241, 242
London, England, 55, 56, 67, 68, 69n, 79n, 83n, 87n, 98, 172, 188, 192, 204, 247, 252
London Missionary Society, 253n
López de Cerrato, Alonso, 3–4
Los Altos (state), 122, 226
Los Encuentros, G., 97
Lottum, Thea van, 98
Louisiana, 20n, 122
Lowry, General (of Black River), 184
Lumbering, 242

M., Mr. (English gentleman), 149, 150, 151, 152, 155, 156, 157, 171–72, 232, 265, 268, 282, 288
McGregor, Gregor, 31, 36
M'Lean, William, 57
MacMillan (of Sheen's Kay), 186, 203
Maize, 239
Malespín, Francisco, 123
Managua, N., 45, 47, 48–50, 219
Manchester, William Montagu, fifth Duke of, 29
Manto, H., 32–33
Manufacturing, 239, 240, 274
María Linda River, 117n
Mariano, Don (of Zacapa), 154
Márquez, José Antonio, 123
Marriages, 286
Marure, Alejandro, 90n
Masaya, N., 219
Mass, 303–4
Matina, C.R., 19, 44
Matina River, 19
Mayflower (schooner), 58
Mayorga, Juan de, 88
Meals, 108, 109, 111, 145–46
Medicine, 254–56
Menéndez, Timoteo, 123
Mercedarians, 115, 284, 300
Mestizo people, 114n, 212
Mexico, 1, 3, 4–5, 14, 15, 16, 21n, 36, 45, 54n, 57, 69, 70, 74, 76, 78, 88, 99, 140, 172, 204, 226, 228, 257, 259, 269n, 270, 273, 279, 290
Mexico City, 82
Michatoya River, 116, 117n
Mico mountain, 59n, 93–94, 97, 102, 141, 205
Milan, Italy, 3
Mining, 243–44
Mints, 244–45
Miranda, Francisco, 31n
Miskito language. *See* Tauira language
Miskito people, 13, 17, 23, 25, 27, 28, 29, 34, 51, 52, 55, 178, 180, 184, 185, 187, 193n, 200, 262–63, 264, 275–76
Moctezuma II (of Mexico), 1
Molina, Marcelo, 122
Monkey Apple Town, H., 242
Montagu, William. *See* Manchester, William Montagu, fifth Duke of
Monte Rosa, Colonel (aide to Carrera), 209
Montgomery, George Washington: mentioned, 84n, 122n, 123n, 249, 299; introduced, 142; feeling for his book, 142–43; entertainment in Trujillo, 143–47; change of route, 147–48; steamboat conservatism, 148; sadnesses of Izabal, 148–51; riding mules, 151–53; fiesta in Gualán, 153–54; second change of route, 154–55; third change of route, 155–57; en route to San Salvador, 157; approach to San Salvador, 157–58; contacts with federal government, 158–59; a chamber of deputies, 159–60; a military escort,

160; primitiveness of Nahuizalco, 160; past a rebel chief, 160–61; arrival in Guatemala City, 161–62; Guatemalan life, 162–63; visit to Morazán, 163–65; departure by new route, 165–66; river crossing by cable, 166–67; an evening with Indians, 167–70; the Polochic River, 170–71; return to Belize, 171–72; on life on a horse ranch, 232–33; on an evening of dance, 261; on an evening of theater, 264–68; on the devotion of a former friar, 282–83; on religion in Esquipulas, 287–90; on a procession of Corpus Christi, 300–301
Mora Fernández, Juan, 16
Morazán, Francisco, 15, 16, 121–22, 123, 124, 131, 132, 133, 136, 158n, 164–65, 210, 218, 220, 221, 222–24, 225, 226, 227, 292, 293
Morgan, Lieut. (seaman), 71
Morier, James Justinian, 69, 77
Mosquitia, 17, 18, 19, 20, 21, 22, 40n, 53, 54, 124, 179, 180n, 182n, 192, 195, 198, 200, 262, 264, 276
Mosquito King, 18, 20, 22, 23, 25, 29, 53
Mosquito Shore. *See* Mosquitia
Motagua River, 59n, 61, 63–65, 97, 132n, 140, 141, 240
Mové people, 18n
Mulatto people, 21, 114, 117
Muñozo, Benito, 245
Murray, Captain (of Black River), 32
Mushla, 23–24
Music, 261–63

NACASCOLO, N., 219
Nahuat language, 269n
Nahuizalco, S., 160
Negro people, 11, 29, 54, 73, 114n, 117
Netherlands, 96, 98n
New Jersey, 204
New Liverpool, G., 171n
New Spain, 12
New York, 204
New York City, 19, 98, 120, 141, 142, 143, 204, 218
Newspapers, 252
Nicaragua, 1, 2, 6, 7, 8, 11, 16, 33, 36n, 44n, 121, 122, 123, 172, 174, 217, 219, 220, 237, 245, 246

North America, 204
Núñez, José, 123

OCOTEPEQUE, H., 157, 232, 282–83
O'Horan, Tomás Antonio, 86
Omoa, H., 42, 55, 56, 63, 65–66, 78n, 97, 119–20, 141, 160n, 202, 227, 240, 245
Oratorio, G., 224
O'Reilly, John, 62n, 95
Osnabrück, Germany, 183n

PACIFIC OCEAN, 6, 34, 56, 115, 116, 126, 218, 229, 237
Padilla, Father (Guatemalan priest), 251
Padillo, José de, 79, 80, 240
Paganism, 275–76
Painting, 273–74
Palenque, Chiapas, 224
Panama, 1, 2, 3, 5, 6, 8, 10, 11, 18n, 34n, 205
Panama City, 125, 126, 129
Para (Prinzapolca headman), 51
Paraguay, 21n
Paris, France, 215
Patagonia (Argentina), 21n
Patal, G., 167–70
Patook (H.), 29, 53, 195
Patuca River, 29
Paulaya River, 29n, 192
Pavón y Aycinena, Manuel Francisco, 208
Paya people, 29, 31, 32, 33, 192, 193–95, 264
Pearl Kay Lagoon, 21, 22, 29, 34, 51
Pedro (Rama chief), 51
Pennsylvania, 298
Peru, 3, 64n, 73, 88, 141, 172n, 279, 290
Petapa, G., 116
Peter of Alcántara, Saint, 284n
Philip of Neri, Saint, 284n
Philippine Islands, 4
Pipil people, 269n
Plátano River, 184
Point Burica, 11
Poland, 204
Political history, 1–2, 14–17, 121–24
Political parties, 112–13, 210–12
Polochic River, 166n, 170, 171
Portobelo, Panama, 18
Port Royal, Jamaica, 17

INDEX 337

Postal system, 246–47
Prado, Mariano, 15
Predmore, Richard L., 205
Prinzapolca, N., 21, 22–23, 25, 34, 51–52
Prisons, 11–13, 40, 42–44
Processions, 299–301, 302, 304–6
Protestantism, 203, 279
Provincias Unidas del Centro de América, 14
Puerto Cabezas, N., 29*n*
Puerto Morazán, N., 219
Punta Castilla, 198, 200
Punta Gorda River, 20, 34
Punta Mico, 20
Punta Mona, 19

QUEZALTENANGO, G., 122, 219, 221, 226, 301–6
Quiché people, 269
Quiriguá, G., 224

RACON (seaman), 53, 55
Rainfall, 62–64
Rama people, 20, 34, 51
Rascon, Chico, 215
Rascon y Cuellar, Doña Vicente, 79, 80, 84, 91, 245
Rascon y Cuellar, Eugenio, 91, 255
Rascon y Cuellar, María Jesús, 79
Raudal, G., 116
Raveneau de Lussan: introduction, 6; buccaneering life ashore, 6–7; losses of a gamer, 7; mentioned, 8, 11, 13
Recollects, 284, 300
Regular clergy, 278–79, 282–83, 284, 300
Religious Tract Society, 253*n*
Rhodes, John, 12*n*
Ribberink, A. E. M., 96*n*
Rico, Porto (shipmaster), 63
Ringrose, Basil, 8*n*
Río Coclé del Norte, 34
Río Colorado, 19–20
Rio de Janeiro, Brazil, 172
Río Dulce, 58, 100
Río Escondido, 21
Río Grande, G., 166–67
Río Grande, N., 21, 22, 29
Río Grande, S., 129, 214
Río Grande de Zacapa, 136
Río Negro, 21*n*

Rivas, N., 219
Rivera, Joaquín, 123
Rivera Paz, Mariano, 122, 206–7, 213, 224, 225
Roach, John: introduced, 11; placed in Spanish dungeon, 12; helped by a lady, 12–13
Roatán (island), 13, 53, 54–55, 190, 198, 200–202
Robert Charles Frederick (Miskito ruler), 28–29, 179
Roberts, Orlando W.: mentioned, 16*n*, 56, 143*n*, 179, 217; introduced, 17; trader from Jamacia, 17–18; residence in Panama, 18; the sarsaparilla trade, 18–19; canoe foraging, 19; Mosquito Shore plans, 19; North American competition, 19; the San Juan vicinity, 19–20; the Bluefields vicinity, 20–21; turn-around at Prinzapolca, 21; separation from other traders, 21–22; return to Prinzapolca, 22–23; mushla feast at Sandy Bay, 23–28; the government of Mosquitia, 28–31; colonization at Black River, 31–33; near execution at San Juan, 33–39; prisoner in San Carlos, 39–41; prisoner in Granada, 41–45; friendship in Managua, 45; arrival at León, 45–46; absolved of criminality, 46–47; life in León, 47–48; talk of independence, 48–49; detention in Granada, 49–50; reunion with crew, 50–51; reunion with Miskito people, 51–52; from Prinzapolca to Belize, 52–55; on the making of cassava bread, 236–37; on the commerce of Granada, 237–39; on San Juan River transportation, 245–46; on the music of the Miskitos, 262; on the religion of the Miskitos, 275–76
Robinson, General (Miskito chief), 29, 30, 53
Rodriguez, Juan, 283
Rodriguez, Manuel, 159–60
Roman River, 29
Rome, 113, 115*n*, 252
Rose (brig), 179, 180, 188, 189–90, 191
Rounce, Thomas, 9–10
Ruis, Señor (of Barbareta), 202–3
Russia, 204

ST. HELENA, G., 133
St. Lucia (island), 130n, 213
St. Vincent (island), 53, 54
Salamá, G., 166n
Salazar, José Gregorio, 130n, 206
Salt Creek, 19
San Andrés (island), 200
San Blas (Mexico), 70, 91
San Blas (Panama), 18
San Carlos, N., 34, 38, 39–41, 42, 47, 50–51
San Felipe, G., 100–101
San José, C.R., 16, 124, 217–19
San Juan, Puerto Rico, 142
San Juan del Norte, N., 20, 34–39, 43, 46, 47, 51, 178, 218, 219, 245–46, 254
San Juan del Sur, N., 219n
San Juan Obispo, G., 117
San Juan River, 20, 39, 47, 50, 176, 177–78, 219, 237, 245–46, 254
San Martín, Joaquín, 123, 232, 233
San Mateo, C.R., 243
San Miguel, S., 98, 219
San Pablo, G., 61, 92, 138, 139
San Salvador (city), 98, 105n, 121, 154, 156, 157, 158–60, 213, 217, 219–22, 232, 239, 261, 282, 284
San Salvador (state), 15, 68, 89, 90, 118, 121, 123, 124, 129, 215, 216, 225, 232
San Salvador volcano, 221
San Vicente, S., 98, 219, 220
Sandwich Islands. *See* Hawaii
Sandy Bay, 23, 29
Santa Ana, S., 98, 131, 133, 223
Santa Catarina Pinula, G., 116, 229, 254
Santa Cruz del Quiché, G., 226
Santa Elena, G., 133n
Santa María, G., 117
Santo Domingo (island), 42
Sapoti, G., 116
Savage, Charles, 78n
Savage, Henry, 206
Schools, 249–51
Scotch people, 201
Scotland, 56, 63, 67
Secular clergy, 226–27, 278–79, 289–90, 291–92
Segovia (N.), 174
Segovia River, 30n
Sereboyer, H., 187, 191

Shannon, James, 151
Shannon, Mrs. James, 151
Sheen (English miner), 186
Sheen's Kay, 185
Shepherd, Samuel, 178
Shrines, 288–89, 290–91
Silva, José María, 220n
Smith, Mr. (American trader), 19
Smoking, 108
Soldiers, 160, 161, 221
Solis, Ramon, 261
Sololá, G., 226
Sonsonate, S., 71, 72–75, 79, 98, 129–33, 159, 160, 214–17, 219, 221, 222, 239, 245, 256, 268–69
Sosa, Juan Francisco, 78
South America, 3, 6, 45, 57, 69, 237
South Carolina, 216
South Sea. *See* Pacific Ocean
Spain, 4, 5, 11, 13, 14, 86, 112, 113, 142, 147, 162, 198, 211, 227, 261, 273, 278, 284n, 291, 293
Spanish America, 147, 211
Spanish language, 3, 37, 38, 42, 68, 98, 142, 163, 168, 195, 203, 204, 264, 276
Spanish people, 1–4, 6, 7, 11, 13, 18, 20, 21, 25, 33, 34, 36, 37, 39, 40n, 41, 46, 50, 51–52, 53, 62, 63, 65, 73, 82, 100n, 102, 112, 113, 116, 145, 179, 189, 191, 198, 199, 202, 203, 207, 211, 235, 236
Sports, 257–58
Spurzheim, Johann Caspar, 255
Stann Creek, B.H., 196, 198
Stephens, John Lloyd: mentioned, 122n, 124n, 130n; introduced, 204–5; a living dream, 205; outdoors hospitality, 206; the new Guatemalan government, 206–8; call on Carrera, 208–9; character of Carrera, 209–10; an Indian revolution, 210–12; Carrera celebrates the New Year, 212–13; the federal government encountered, 213–16; Carrillo of Costa Rica, 217–19; tribulation in San Salvador, 219–22; first visit with Morazán, 222–23; second visit with Morazán, 223–24; final visit with Carrera, 224–26; the laughing philosopher, 226–27; a final laugh, 227–28; on mining in Costa Rica, 243–44; on education in Zacapa, 250; on

INDEX 339

religion in Esquipulas, 290–92; on the festivities of Santa Lucía, 292–95; on the taking of the black veil, 295–99; on Good Friday in Quezaltenango, 301–6
Sugar-cane, 234–35
Surinam, 96
Susannah, Sister (of Guatemala City), 296, 298

TAUACHA PEOPLE, 12n, 29
Tauira language, 178, 182n, 195
Tecpán, G., 226
Tegucigalpa, H., 55
Telemán, G., 170–71
Temperatures, 61–63
Texas, 21n
Theater, 264–73
Thompson, George Alexander: mentioned, 14n, 15n, 55–56, 60n, 62n, 98, 142, 205; dedication of his book, 68–69; introduced, 69–70; departure from Mexico, 70–71; arrival at Acajutla, 71; getting acquainted, 71–72; life in Sonsonate, 72–75; departure for the capital, 75; the pleasures of riding, 75–76; approach to the capital, 76–78; meeting with the president, 78–79; en route to Amatitlán, 79–80; holiday company and accommodations, 80–82; helping a traveling companion, 82–85; Arce and Valle, 85; problem of runaway slaves, 85–87; dining with the president, 87–89; leave-taking of the president, 89–91; preparation for return home, 91–92; arrival of a consul, 92; the ladies of Gualán, 92–93; last experiences in Guatemala, 93–96; on the procuring of cochineal, 233–34; on the quality of fruits, 235; on the commerce of Ahuachapán, 239–40; on Guatemalan external trade, 240–41; on Guatemalan local trade, 241; on the Guatemalan mint, 244–45; on author José del Valle, 253–54; on the curative effects of guaco, 255–56; on recreation in Guatemala City, 257–58; on recreation in Amatitlán, 258–59; on an evening of dance, 259–60; on musical instruments, 261–62; on an evening of theater, 269–71; on religious toleration, 280–82; on the organization of the church, 284–85; on a procession of Corpus Christi, 299–300
Thomson, James, 57
Todos Santos Cuchumatán, G., 226
Toledo, Spain, 283n
Toleration, 281–82
Totonicapán, G., 226
Treaty of Versailles (1783), 86
Trujillo, H., 25, 32, 37, 41, 53, 96–97, 143–48, 179, 185, 187, 189, 190, 196, 197–200, 204, 242
Tungla people, 29
Turtle Bogue, 19

ULVA PEOPLE, 11, 21, 29
United States of America, 17, 57, 78, 124, 125, 139, 141, 142, 146, 149, 151, 158, 159, 162, 172, 204, 206, 210, 215, 216, 296
Universities, 251
University of Florida Press, 17
Upton, William, 184, 187, 189, 204
Usulután, S., 98
Utatlán, G., 226–28
Utila (island), 55

VALENTIN, Don (Izabal merchant), 149, 150, 152
Valiente people, 18, 19
Valle, José Cecilio del, 14, 55, 56, 62, 85, 86, 89, 90–91, 121, 253–54
Valle de la Ermita, 12
Valparaiso, Chile, 172
Venezuela, 25n, 36n
Veragua (Panama), 18, 19
Verapaz (G.), 140
Vigil, Diego, 16, 122, 123, 214–16, 219–20, 221, 222
Villa Nueva, G., 80, 164–65
Villacorta, Juan Vicente, 15
Viré, Mr. (mining entrepreneur), 56

WAFER, Lionel, 8n
Wanki people, 264
Wanks River, 30n, 182, 184, 264n
Ward, Henry George, 69
Warfare, 2, 35–36, 219–24, 225–26
Warren, Mr. (of Black River), 32, 53
Washington, D.C., 162, 210

Water transport, 171, 177–78, 245–46
West Indies, 3, 17, 143, 173, 178, 218
Westby (British Honduran emissary), 86
Whitehaven, England, 12n
William (Miskito sailor), 185
Williams, Mary Wilhelmine, 98n
Wilson, James: introduced, 56–58; in Belize, 58; arrival in Guatemala, 58–59; at home in Guatemala City, 59; attitude toward runaway slaves, 59–60; refusal to attend theater, 60; visit to Congress, 60–61; return route, 61; departure, 61; discomforts of the return, 61–67; death in Belize, 67–68; mentioned, 86n, 87n, 98, 160n, 257, 275; on the market for woolen goods, 241; on the post to Guatemala City, 246–47; on the cost of a coach, 247; on the cost of wearing apparel, 247; on the cost of housing, 247; on the cost of living, 247–48; on an evening of theater, 271–72; on blessed branches, 276–77; on light attitudes in serious matters, 277; on differences with Catholic friends, 279–80; on a visit to the cathedral, 285
Workington, England, 12n

YAQUI PEOPLE, 1
Young, Thomas: mentioned, 124n; introduced, 178–79; departure from England, 179; arrival at Cabo Gracias a Dios, 179–82; meeting with Mosquito King, 182; Cabo Gracias a Dios customs, 182–83; shipwreck, 183–85; misfortune on Sheen's Kay, 185–86; with the Black Caribs, 186–87; arrival at Fort Wellington, 187–88; the problems of colonization, 188–92; up the Paulaya River, 192; remnants of English settlement, 192–93; Paya life, 193–95; Black Carib everyday life, 195–96; Black Carib celebrations, 196–97; departure for Trujillo, 197; life in Trujillo, 197–200; blown to Roatán, 200; the English-Scotch of Roatán, 200–202; a Spaniard on Barbareta, 202–3; departure for England, 204; on the popularity of bananas, 235–36; on the peculiarities of the Black Carib economy, 241–42; on the music of the Miskitos, 262–63; on the music of the Black Caribs, 263–64

ZACAPA, G., 61–62, 78n, 92, 102n, 135, 136–37, 154–55, 206, 250
Zaculeu, G., 226
Zafra, Doña Santa Maria, 92–93
Zambo people, 21, 23, 29, 31, 197, 264, 276
Zebadúa, Marcial, 78
Zelaya, Francisco, 123
Zepeda, José, 123